# Le Menu Gastronomique

# Le Menu Gastronomique

## An interpretation of Nouvelle Cuisine

### Jack Gillon

**Macdonald Publishers, Edinburgh**

© Jack Gillon 1981

Illustrations Alison Gow
Drawings of France Jack Gillon
Designed and Edited by Jenny Carter

Published by
Macdonald Publishers
Loanhead, Midlothian EH20 9SY

ISBN 0 904265 60 9

Printed in Scotland by
Macdonald Printers (Edinburgh) Limited
Edgefield Road, Loanhead, Midlothian EH20 9SY

*To*
*Sandria*

# Acknowledgements

I would like to thank The Observer and Hedges and Butler Ltd for their support and generosity, and Peter Green and Co. Ltd., wine merchants in Edinburgh, who have given me much good advice over the years and are to be congratulated on their enterprising list.

I am also grateful to Quentin Macfarlane, who acted as a most important catalyst when the idea of the book was first aired, and to Jenny Carter for her enthusiastic and constructive help with the design of the book; also to Doreen Orr, who not only prepared the manuscript beautifully, but also gave useful criticism and advice.

Above all, Sandria and I are indebted to our friends on both sides of the Channel for their hospitality and stimulating discussion of all things gastronomic, and particularly to M. and Mme Aymé Bernard, whose kindness ensured that our sojourn in Lyon was happy and in every respect memorable.

# *Contents*

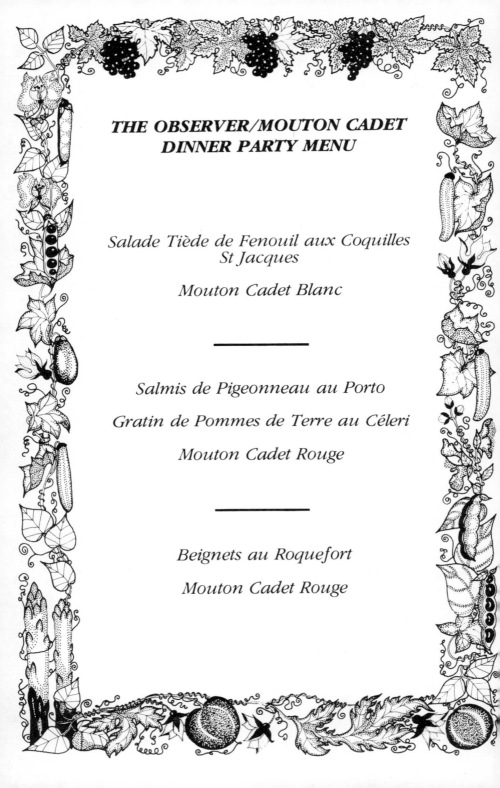

# THE OBSERVER/MOUTON CADET DINNER PARTY MENU

*Salade Tiède de Fenouil aux Coquilles St Jacques*

*Mouton Cadet Blanc*

---

*Salmis de Pigeonneau au Porto*

*Gratin de Pommes de Terre au Céleri*

*Mouton Cadet Rouge*

---

*Beignets au Roquefort*

*Mouton Cadet Rouge*

# Introduction

*Le Menu Gastronomique* is a term well known to anyone who has eaten in restaurants in France. As with much of the terminology of food and wine there is no counterpart in current English usage, and literal translations do little justice to the original. The menus in this book are based almost entirely on French cuisine, and so for the most part the dishes, even where completely of my own invention, have been given French names. This is, however, a very personal book, and my occasional forays into Italian and Spanish cookery deserve to be named appropriately, as do the occasional dishes which receive eponymous titles because of their significance for me. It is part of the fun of the Nouvelle Cuisine, to which school of French cooking this book pays homage, that dishes should be named with the same originality and personal flair with which the recipes were conceived. Many titles will therefore seem confusing to those with limited knowledge of French, but translations are given in the index of dishes at the back, and the aim of the text is not only to give methods of cooking but also to explain the concept of the dish and how to make it work. Unusual ingredients and specific techniques are explained in the glossary.

It would be presumptious of an amateur to attempt any sort of comprehensive description of the Nouvelle Cuisine, particularly now that the books by some of the leading exponents—Michel Guérard, Jean and Pierre Troisgros and Roger Vergé—are appearing in English. I leave it to them to expound at length and in detail the ways in which they have rethought traditional methods, but the movement represents not so much a dramatic change in technique as a novel philosophy of eating in the French style. It is about overcoming well entrenched conceptual barriers and defining new categories of recipes—the application of fish methods to meat cookery and vice versa, and other such ruses, being one important facet of modern originality—as much as it is about the evils of flour and the concoction of 'petites sauces'. This, like all revolutions, is a romantic movement whose intention is to liberate us from the shackles of a classical tradition which had been fossilised for many years and had lost touch with the present to such an extent that an invitation to eat in a restaurant had become something to be feared. Thanks to the new wave, whose impact is just being felt on this side of the channel at a time when there are those in France who would insist that it is already *passé*, cooking has once again become a personal and thoroughly modern art as it was in the days of Curnonsky, Escoffier and the other greats of French cuisine in the nineteenth and early twentieth centuries. Those who deride the Nouvelle Cuisine like to point out that it has all been said before, little realising that this does not obviate the need for saying it again; and if the great chefs of the past found it necessary to revise and extend the existing repertoire, how much more should we?

The menu which led to my success in the Observer—Mouton Cadet competition was rooted in the Nouvelle style, but every dish was a product of my own invention. Though deeply attached to both classical and provincial French cooking, mainly through the great standard texts of Julia Child and Elizabeth David, my own style of cooking was moving very much in this direction before we went to spend a year in Lyon. Lyon is a stronghold of one of the most distinctive of French provincial cuisines but also, paradoxically, the epicentre of the Nouvelle Cuisine as personified by Bocuse and the other ex-pupils of Fernand Point, who are scattered around the hinterland of this great gastronomic capital.

In Lyon food is the chief—often the only—subject of conversation, and learning by osmosis occurs at an extraordinary rate in such a supercharged atmosphere. To visit Les Halles and the markets of the Quais de Saône is an education in itself, and somehow looking at the array of quality produce available is one of the best sources of inspiration. But knowledge is thrown at you from every direction—television, radio, newspapers—and it is by no means a vast 'Nouvelle' propaganda machine. On one of his regular television shows Michel Guérard spent half an hour discussing the roasting of a leg of lamb and how to derive a gravy from the pan juices.

Most credit for the success of the Nouvelle Cuisine must go to Henri Gault and Christian Millau, whose support for the adventurous chefs and the gusto with which, in the columns of their annual guide and monthly magazine, they are prepared to lampoon any restaurant which is both reactionary and bad, has enabled the new philosophy to filter down from the rarified atmosphere of the great restaurants to the general public. Their success has been founded not only on their courage and consistency but also on the high entertainment value of their publications. It is good news indeed that their activities are to be extended to both Great Britain and the USA, starting with guides to London and New York.

My brief is to show how my own cooking has responded to this new challenge; but more than that I have set out to show how entirely original and unorthodox recipes can be integrated into menus for entertaining and for domestic use alone. I have tried to show how the blueprints of the recipes relate to the structure of the meal as a whole, and have therefore selected menus deliberately to illustrate the very many ways of skinning this particular cat. This is not a catalogue of recipes, though naturally I hope that my own will please others as they have pleased me in the making; it is rather a collection of signposts indicating how the modern view that freshness, delicacy and quality are all important can be grafted on to a sound traditional French and Mediterranean approach. I have tried to explain my prejudices and justify my enthusiasms, and have provided alternatives for the more outrageous or extravagant of the latter. Economy is not forgotten—this is, after all, la Nouvelle Cuisine Ecossaise—and economy of method is emphasised; but there is, of course, no substitute for quality and no possibility of success at the highest level in any sphere without the expenditure of time and energy.

It is in shopping that time and money are first spent and where the most important decisions are made. Ideas should come from the food itself rather than a preordained notion of what is appropriate for a particular occasion. If you see an especially fine vegetable, build the rest of the meal around it. Choose always what is in season—and therefore best—and always remember the impact of one dish on the next. Do not forget the importance of nutritional balance when considering the interactions of textures and flavours. Usually you will find that the correct 'artistic' solution to any menu problem is also that which is most desirable nutritionally, because our tastes are, after all, the product of nature, and in exercising them it is foolish to forget that.

Cooking, even more than eating, consists in exercising taste, and taste is a matter of making the right decision at any given time, guided only by your own analysis. Taste can only be exercised satisfactorily when technical difficulties have been mastered and the processes of cooking understood, because often the success of a dish will depend on the cook's adaptability either in terms of choice of ingredients or methods. Throughout this book I have therefore assumed that the reader has a wide basic knowledge of the techniques and terminology of cooking, but at the end of this introductory section my own approach to a range of basic techniques is summarised.

## *The Structure of the Meal*

To discuss food in terms of set menus may seem unnecessarily restrictive, but to my mind it has several advantages. It is easy to forget that the type of menu selected will have a profound effect on the meal as a social event, and I have therefore used this format to discuss specific dishes in a social context which seems appropriate. The structure of the meal determines the pattern of the occasion, and the cook must take responsibility for this in planning the menu. For instance, at a dinner party a cheese course usually seems indispensable as a point where the tempo may slacken, the wine can be discussed and more relaxed conversation allowed to develop. In this respect it often seems to me to be the true centre of the meal, and I have therefore discussed the choice of cheeses appropriate for each meal. On the other hand there are certainly occasions where this seems unnecessary, and indeed there are menus in which a cheese course would seem quite inappropriate on purely gastronomic grounds. Social occasion and gastronomic considerations must both be taken into account.

On a more practical level I have usually adhered to an orthodox four-course menu unless both cheese and dessert seemed undesirable. As a general rule fairly detailed recipes are given for all of the first and main courses; usually one of these and often both will be original. On the other hand I have made no attempt to do other than describe the sweets in the broadest terms, since for the most part they are classical and recipes can be found in more comprehensive recipe books (most can be found in *Mastering the Art of French Cooking* by Beck, Bertholle and Child). Comments on pastry are to be found later in this chapter.

The book is divided into three parts. In the first the meals are unpretentious, cheap and occasionally somewhat rustic, but in many ways it is the most important section because it deals with food appropriate to every day as well as to entertaining informally. Techniques must be practised until they are second nature, and good habits are necessary to make more ambitious cookery easy.

Part 2 deals with menus which are altogether more ambitious and a little more lavish, and I hope thoroughly interesting, but of only moderate difficulty. The dishes have been chosen in such a way as to make the final preparations—the most testing time for the cook—relatively uncomplicated.

The recipes in the third section are almost entirely original. I have tried to approach this section with a complete lack of inhibition, but fantasy must be indulged in with strict discipline, and everything has been tried and tested.

There is therefore a gradation in terms of difficulty, expense and originality from beginning to end, but of course the menus, and the recipes themselves, are merely suggestions, and I would hope that they act as a stimulus to imaginative cookery. This is a book about food rather than a cookery book. For this reason I have seldom considered it necessary to give precise lists of ingredients, far less quantities, except where exact proportions are necessary—this is, however, rare in cookery except in baking. My wish is to encourage not only enterprise but also the notion that the cook stands or falls by his or her judgment in the all-important matters of choice of menu, selection of ingredients, timing, seasoning and presentation. These are questions of taste which cannot easily be quantified, and it is all too easy to blame a recipe in which precise instructions are given when, in reality, the cook has failed to make important decisions. An open mind is at least as useful as an open book.

## *Wine and the Art of Menu Construction*

This is also a book about wine. In the days when I was happier in the cellar than in the kitchen I would choose wines to drink more or less irrespective of what was to be eaten, consumed as I was with enthusiasm for learning about wine. With experience, that enthusiasm has faded into a deeper understanding of how to enjoy wine. When the choice of wine and food is perfect (at whatever level) revelations can occur and the greatest of pleasure can be obtained. The sequence in which wines are served is no less important, and demands greater knowledge than whether the wine is red or white, sweet or dry.

Just as in choosing the menus I have tried to give examples of as many different types of approach as possible, so in deciding on the accompanying wines I have relied on an eclectic approach to show how most of the more important wines relate both to food and to each other. I have made a point of emphasising the place of dessert wines, a thoroughly British habit not at all understood in France, where the great sweet white wines are served as aperitifs or with foie gras, and champagne as the dessert wine. It is quite beyond my comprehension that anyone should ever prefer a sweet aperitif, as I find that they kill the appetite within minutes.

I have drunk all of these wines, mostly on several occasions, and most of them have come from my own cellar. Where the wines are rare or obscure—there are some, for instance, from lesser known areas of France which I discovered while living in Lyon—I have discussed possible alternatives.

Learning from experience, albeit someone else's, is easier and more satisfying than from generalisations about the merits and demerits of this or that commune, type of grape or method of vinification, though these factual details are of great interest to the serious student. It is my view that opinions are at least as interesting as facts, and the appreciation of wine, even when elevated to the level of a science, as in Michael Broadbent's *Wine*

*Tasting*, remains a very subjective matter indeed. Besides, the discussion of particular wines allows the reader the luxury of disagreeing with the author.

Whether the identity of the wines should be made known to your guests or not is a matter which depends entirely on the interest and knowledge of those present. It can certainly be embarrassing and off-putting for anyone who has no interest in wine to be confronted with an anonymous glass and asked for an assessment and identification. On the other hand 'blind' tasting is the only satisfactory way for a group of friends with a common interest to assess the quality of the wine with some measure of objectivity and at the same time train their palates.

# Notes on Practical Matters

## Some important ingredients

### Herbs

There are few menus in this book which do not call for fresh herbs. By far the most important herbs to grow are parsley, especially the flat leaf Italian kind, chives, tarragon, thyme and basil (which demands almost hot-house conditions). Of these the one which is least dispensable is tarragon. The only dried herbs for which I have any use are bay leaf and oregano. Tarragon and basil can be frozen successfully, either simply wrapped in aluminium foil or in ice cubes. Other herbs which are occasionally useful are chervil (a little fickle in our climate), the savories, mint and fennel. It is also worth mentioning the usefulness of sorrel as a herb (see Menu 3:8). I have a relative dislike of the mustiness of sage and dill and of the resinous flavour of rosemary, all of which must be employed with caution. Rosemary does, however, have the great merit of evoking the sun of Provence (see Menu 1:6).

### Seasoning

Sea-salt is now easily obtainable and there is no excuse for not using it. Black pepper has a rounder flavour than white and is always to be preferred unless it would spoil the appearance of the dish. I use enormous quantities. When adding black pepper as a final adjustment it is often worth incorporating it with a little butter, as the two seem to be synergistic. Cayenne, paprika, nutmeg and other spices should not be used indiscriminately, but rather saved for dishes where their contribution is to be noticeable.

## *Vinegar*

Vinegar is an essential agent for deglazing the sauces typical of the 'nouvelle' style. Good quality wine vinegar is essential, and it seldom matters whether you use red or white. Sherry vinegar has a voluptuous perfume which has the uncanny ability to make a vinaigrette taste as though it contained walnut oil. Herb-flavoured vinegars have only limited usefulness if your garden is adequately stocked, but raspberry-flavoured vinegar is interesting and delicious.

## *Alcohol*

If only a little wine is required in the recipe try to spare some from that which you are to drink, otherwise use the best available.

As an alternative to dry white wine I prefer fino sherry to vermouth. Sweet madeira and port are invaluable for deglazing because they caramelise easily, adding sweetness and richness of flavour to fatten a sauce, particularly when vinegar has been used as the initial deglazing agent. Spirits need not be flamed to be effective, and a tiny spot of armagnac or cognac can sometimes work wonders in a clear stock. Pastis is useful in fish cookery for its fennel-like taste.

## *Some important techniques*

As a general rule I prefer manual methods to mechanical, sieving rather than blending, whipping cream and egg whites by hand, and always making mayonnaise similarly. It is as much because I enjoy doing it and detest noisy machinery as because of the results.

## Stocks

The *fonds de cuisine,* the basis of all cookery, far from becoming obsolete, are of vital importance to the success of many of the sauces described in this book. It takes very little time and practically no effort to produce a stock which is light and aromatic. This allows you to build important flavours into your sauce right from the beginning. Long simmering is seldom necessary and can actually be deleterious; fish and poultry stocks can be made in less than an hour. Whether a stock is brown or 'white' depends on whether or not the bones/giblets and vegetables have been browned initially. When making a brown stock it is a good idea to deglaze with wine or madeira before topping up with water, and tomatoes also add colour. The most important flavouring in most types of stock is celery, which gives a particularly 'French' flavour. Onion stuck with a clove, garlic, leek, carrot and a *bouquet garni* are the other usual ingredients. Salt should never be added until the stock has been sieved, cleared if necessary, and boiled down the final volume. I am convinced that the obsession, repeated in every cookery book, with removing scum from a stock is a mistake. It is not 'dirt', but coagulated albumin and other blood proteins, and it seems to help to clear the stock if left. The only disadvantage is that you find all the debris stuck to the pot.

## Sauces

The essence of the new sauces is to use good vinegar and wine for deglazing, and to base the sauce on a small amount of highly concentrated and very good stock. Usually this can be made freshly using the bones or giblets, but the reduced stock can also be frozen in cubes. Fresh herbs often provide the final touch. Many such sauces will have enough body not to need thickening, but if a sauce needs to be 'brought together' without much thickening this can be done by swirling in chilled butter in small parcels away from the heat, or you can beat in the butter while boiling the sauce furiously. This is known as 'mounting' a sauce *(monter une sauce).* When a sauce which contains no flour is to be thickened cornflour is often adequate, but arrowroot is essential for clear sauces and is, in any case, better in consistency than cornflour. *Beurre manié*—flour kneaded with softened butter—is occasionally useful, flour or no. Vegetables, garlic or liver (in the case of fowl) can be cooked in the stock and forced through a fine sieve to thicken the sauce. Sometimes the sauce is the main point of the dish, but usually it is an essence, a perfume, to bring out the best in the meat.

## Pastry

Where pastry is important in the first or main course I have given instructions (for example, the brioche recipe in Menu 3:8). A special word is needed, however, with respect to shortcrust pastry, particularly the sweet type (pâte brisée sucrée) used for those magical French fruit tarts. Success has little to do with the exact proportions of the flour, butter, egg and sugar, but depends almost entirely on the way the dough is worked with the fingers. Speed is essential, and a marble surface helps to keep the dough cool. Make no attempt to obtain a homogeneous dough. It is a good thing if there are tiny islands of butter not fully integrated with the flour, so that the pastry has an almost flaky texture when baked. Chill the dough before rolling it, and leave it quite thick—about 1 cm. Bake it in a fairly hot oven until it is quite dark brown. It will be soft at this stage but goes crisp and biscuity on cooling. It is worth mastering, because like many another masterpiece of French cuisine it has become excessively rare in its native land. The *only* good strawberry tarts which we could find in Lyon were from Michel Guérard's *'Comptoir Gourmand',* and this was enough to convert us totally to the cause of *La Nouvelle Cuisine.*

# PART 1

## The Family Table

*St Paul de Vence, with breathtaking view of the Baie des Anges from Nice to the Cap d'Antibes.*

# Introduction

In this section the menus have been chosen for their simplicity and low cost. Such meals often provide the most surprising and memorable of gustatory experiences, because they challenge the cook to get it just right. There is no excuse for not achieving a high degree of freshness and obvious quality, because unnecessary fuss and complication are avoided, giving you time to concentrate on the taste of the food. For many of us it must have been just such tastes, encountered in all probability in an unassuming restaurant or at a family table in France or Italy, that alerted us to the joys of preparing and eating good food; yet we seldom dare to offer audaciously simple food when entertaining. This is a great pity, but if you cannot see yourself turning to the following menus for lunch or supper parties (all of the menus being eminently suitable for the former and some for the latter), I hope that at least they will stimulate a fresh look at your family fare. We find that this type of meal is particularly suitable when we have friends staying with us for some time, to fill the gaps between the more sumptuous meals described in Parts 2 and 3 in an interesting but undemanding fashion.

The wines should, of course, be chosen with the same aims of quality and freshness in mind, and there is enormous scope for variation at the cheaper end of the price range. This calls for extra care in selection, and as a general rule I would advise aiming slightly high. In other words, simple food when cooked perfectly can be lifted on to a different plane by setting it against a wine of some quality or particular interest, and occasionally such a meal can become memorable because of the relief in which a really fine wine can stand out.

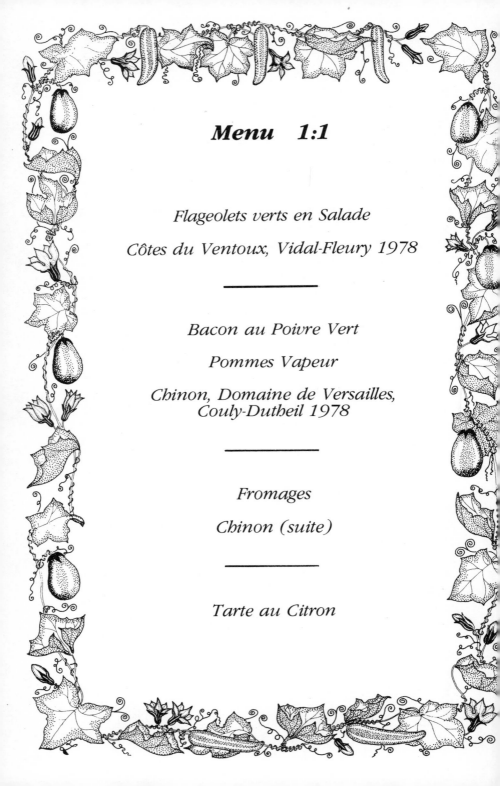

# Menu  1:1

*Flageolets verts en Salade*

*Côtes du Ventoux, Vidal-Fleury 1978*

———

*Bacon au Poivre Vert*

*Pommes Vapeur*

*Chinon, Domaine de Versailles,
Couly-Dutheil 1978*

———

*Fromages*

*Chinon (suite)*

———

*Tarte au Citron*

*Flageolets verts en Salade*  A cooked salad, which may be served hot, cold or tepid, of my favourite beans—the small green kidney beans so popular in France but often regrettably difficult to find in this country. Any kind of kidney bean can, however, be substituted. For this recipe quantities and proportions are unimportant, and can be left to the cook's judgment or whim. Better to make too much than too little, since it keeps well.

Cook the beans in a well flavoured but undersalted chicken stock (enough to cover them comfortably at the beginning) until the liquid is almost entirely absorbed. Preliminary soaking is not necessary if the beans are reasonably fresh but ensures more even cooking. The beans should remain firm.

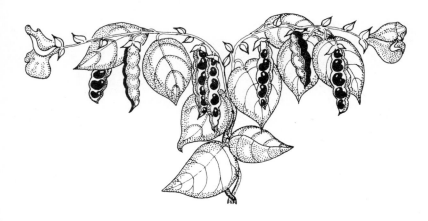

Fry chopped red pepper and onion in a heavy, fruity olive oil and add a good quantity of garlic, cut into slivers, when the peppers and onions are almost done. Add roughly diced *saucisson sec*—almost any kind of uncooked, pure pork sausage is appropriate, or salami cut into dice about 1 cubic cm—turn in the oil for a few seconds then increase the heat and stir in a tablespoonful or two of wine vinegar. Boil down until the vinegar perfume has almost disappeared, stir in the beans, adjust the seasoning and allow the flavours to marry before serving garnished with chopped Italian parsley.

*Bacon au Poivre Vert*   Considering how fond we are of bacon we ought to be thoroughly ashamed of the way we treat it in this country, and I offer this recipe as the antidote to all those half-stewed, leathery gammon steaks without which institutional and steak-house cooking would be unrecognisable.

Ask for steaks of back bacon—in Scotland I would choose a sweet-cure about 2 cms thick. Sauté the steaks moderately hard in butter for a few minutes on each side, unsalted but liberally coated with black pepper. Deglaze with a sweet sherry, madeira or marsala until the sauce is syrupy and slightly caramelised. Inject colour and fruit by adding a small quantity of redcurrant or damson jelly, then allow the sauce to amalgamate. Add drained green peppercorns to taste, reduce the heat and cook a few minutes more, turning several times. Do not overcook—the bacon must be juicy and tender. I prefer buttered new potatoes as an accompaniment, but green beans cooked equally simply would be a good choice of vegetable. In either case chopped chives would not be amiss.

The cheese board should contain light, perhaps slightly sour cheeses such as rigottes de Condrieu and under-ripe goats' cheese, with a mild soft-ripening variety (Brie, dolcelatte) for contrast. The sweet and sour theme culminates nicely with the tarte au citron, slices of lemon covered in a redcurrant glaze and baked on a shell of pâte sucrée rolled rather thinner than usual.

Either red or white wine is possible, but preferably not both. Whether you choose red, as I have done, or white, the desired qualities are the same: plenty of fruit, perhaps a touch of sweetness, and a high balancing acidity. Youth is therefore essential. I use the Côtes du Ventoux of Vidal-Fleury as a substitute for Beaujolais, which is nowadays too dear and too sweet. With the cheese the Chinon, while still obviously in the same category, will show itself to be in a different league, representing as it does a very fine vintage on the Loire. It will not be destroyed by the lemon tart, though you may prefer a glass of a sweet muscat or madeira.

*Lyon—the old and the new.*

# Menu  1:2

Melanzane Fritte all' amatriciana

Gamay du Bugey, Crussy, NV

—————

Tagliatelli Salsa di Coda alle Funghe

Gamay du Bugey (suite)

—————

Formaggi

Gamay du Bugey (fin)

—————

Gelati

Although I never hesitate to mix French and Italian dishes in one menu—as will be obvious from other sections of this book—and even to combine influences from both in the one dish, I enjoy trying to recapture the spirit and style of Italian eating by designing a meal which seems to me utterly typical. This, however, does not preclude originality, and, while neither of the first two dishes on this menu are to be found in standard texts, I hope they will be seen to be quite Italian in spirit. For an Italian dinner party I would probably choose elaborate antipasti followed by a classic such as osso bucco milanese, but for me the essence of Italy is lunch, preferably *al fresco* under a trellis of vines, and a wonderfully appetising dish of pasta. To avoid last minute work in the kitchen the aubergine fritters could be replaced by cold antipasti such as Parma ham and figs.

*Melanzane Fritte all'amatriciana*  The idea of aubergine fritters is not new, but I have never seen a recipe calling for them to be done in breadcrumbs in the Milanese style. Slice the aubergine fairly thickly, salt and allow to drain. Meanwhile prepare white breadcrumbs and as many beaten whole eggs as will be necessary. Season the eggs. Dip the aubergine slices first in the egg then in the breadcrumbs—which may be flavoured with chopped herbs and grated Parmesan cheese—and fry briskly in light Italian olive oil on each side until golden. Drain and serve as soon as possible.

The usual accompaniment to aubergine is a straight-forward tomato sauce, but the 'amatriciana' version usually reserved for bucatini or other coarse pasta is more interesting. Two Italian friends who insisted on taking over our kitchen for a day to show us how to cook real Italian food taught us this version, which gives a sauce of surprising complexity. Skin by scalding and squeeze the water and pips from 500g fresh tomatoes. Chop an onion and several cloves of garlic roughly and sweat in olive oil with a finely chopped fresh chili and some chopped streaky bacon. Stir in the tomatoes, season, and bury a bouquet garni containing parsley, bay leaf and thyme or oregano. Then stir in a large piece of the *rind* of Parmesan cheese. Cook slowly, stirring occasionally, for at least an hour. The longer it is cooked the more integrated will the flavours become. Chopped fresh basil may be added just before serving, and grated Parmesan is an essential accompaniment.

*Tagliatelli Salsa di Coda alle Funghe*  As a family we are addicted to pasta. The fresh, homemade variety is, of course, the most delicious, but in Edinburgh we are fortunate in having a thriving Italian community, which ensures that dried 'home-made' noodles of good quality are easy to obtain. We were also delighted to find on our arrival in Lyon that the Italian influence on the city's cuisine is so profound that most of the charcutiers have fresh noodles delivered daily. In Nice, where we spent part of the summer, the locals' fondness for pasta is even more evident, and in the extraordinary *vieux quartier,* as indeed in most of the surrounding towns and villages, heaps of fresh home-made ravioli, capelletti, canneloni and coloured noodles, all littered with bunches of fresh basil, beguile the eye. Making your own pasta is not as difficult or time-consuming as is generally believed, and a pasta machine, although a source of fun, is unnecessary unless you are making a large quantity. I recommend the simple recipe given by Elizabeth David in *Italian Food.*

The quality of the pasta may be important, but the glory is the sauce. It may be perfectly simple, such as olive oil with chopped fresh tomatoes and basil, or rich and intense. For a main course the latter course is usually more appropriate, and the following is my own substitute for the classic *salsa di lepre* (hare sauce). I think that oxtail is a more than adequate alternative to hare, for with long cooking the meat almost liquefies and its gelatinous quality gives a remarkably succulent sauce. One whole oxtail would easily be enough for six people. Brown the pieces of oxtail in olive oil until well coloured. Do not use flour, as this would radically alter the texture of the sauce. Deglaze with red wine and just cover the meat with a good beef stock (unsalted). Add a whole onion and several whole garlic cloves, peeled (they will dissolve in the sauce), carrot, celery and a bouquet garni of thyme, bay leaf and parsley. Cook gently, either on top of the stove or in the oven, for at least two hours, until the meat is parting from the bone. If you wish to preserve intact chunks of meat in the final sauce, remove it from the casserole and separate it from the bones (this is my own preference). Boil down the sauce to the right pitch of intensity, correct the seasoning and finish by adding the mushrooms. Ideally these should be fresh wild mushrooms such as *cèpes* (*porcini* in Italian) or *girolles,* but cultivated mushrooms—the large open ones have the best flavour—would suffice, fried in oil and simmered for a few minutes in the sauce. A better alternative is to use dried *cepes* or *girolles* or, interestingly, dried Chinese mushrooms. These will, of course, require soaking and rather longer cooking in the sauce. If you choose to mash the meat into the sauce you will find it goes further—this should be done before boiling down, since less reduction will be required. The sauce is best cooked a day ahead, but the mushrooms should be added during reheating. The noodles should simply be dressed with butter and black pepper.

Perhaps the best way to follow such a rich sauce is to nibble a sweet, crumbly corner of Parmesan, but for those with robust appetites any fine Italian cheese would be welcome. Home-made ice-cream and *cafe nero* are all that would be required to complete the illusion of being south of the Alps. A drop of Grappa would bring you back to reality.

The wine is difficult, and using French country wine may seem a bizarre choice. In Piemonte you would unhesitatingly quaff unrecordable quantities of cool, slightly *frizzante* Barbera, but the examples of this which appear in pretentious bottles for export are depressingly bitter and lacking in fruit. Nor would one of the heavyweight Italian reds be suitable, though a good young Chianti might be ideal. I am no admirer of Valpolicella or Bardolino. On the other hand the gamay grape is producing good fruity wines in many obscure corners of France, such as the Loire, the Ardeche and the Savoie, and they are often good value. The Bugey is a small VDQS region north-east of Lyon, in the foothills of the Savoie best known for its white Roussette and *méthode champenoise* Cerdon, but M. Crussy's red deservedly won a gold medal at Paris in 1979. There is no need to do other than serve the same wine throughout, but a strong white would go well with the aubergine.

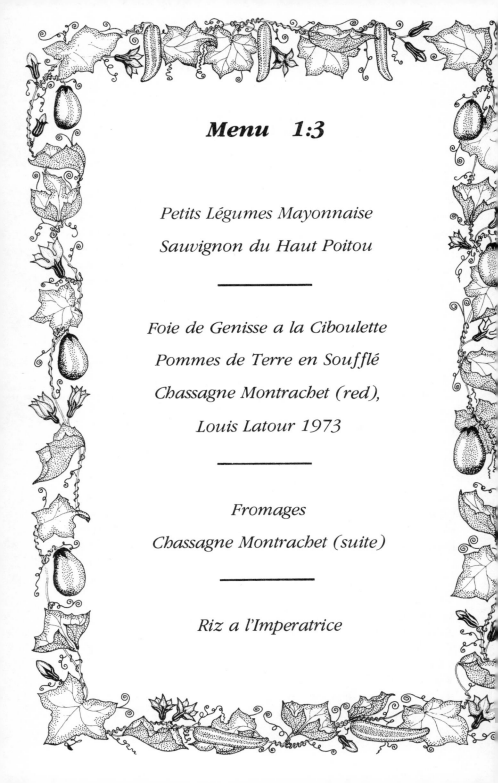

# Menu  1:3

Petits Légumes Mayonnaise

Sauvignon du Haut Poitou

———

Foie de Genisse a la Ciboulette

Pommes de Terre en Soufflé

Chassagne Montrachet (red),

Louis Latour 1973

———

Fromages

Chassagne Montrachet (suite)

———

Riz a l'Imperatrice

*Petits Légumes Mayonnaise* This deceptively simple first course has the great advantage of being almost infinitely variable, but is always appetising. It depends on the contrast between the direct, clean flavour of raw or only partially cooked vegetables—which must be of very high quality and therefore chosen according to season—with a rich, mayonnaise type of sauce. The most usual combination of vegetables would be carrots, celeriac, green beans and fresh peas, and this provides a fine combination of colours and textures. The root vegetables should be raw and the beans and peas cooked *al dente* then plunged in cold water to arrest cooking. Celeriac is commonly cut into thin batons about 10 cms long, and the carrots and beans should be cut accordingly. Celery, salsify, artichoke hearts and asparagus are possible alternatives to carrots and celeriac. The mayonnaise is best kept fairly light by substituting up to 50% groundnut or safflower seed oil for olive oil, and flavouring with lemon juice rather than vinegar. Chopped fresh herbs (parsley, chervil, chives, tarragon) add subtlety but any mayonnaise variant, including aioli and anchoiade, can be used. Olives make an attractive garnish. The vegetables may be mixed with the sauce, but a more striking effect is obtained by serving them separately, carefully arranged and coated lightly in lemon juice. The success of the dish depends on the quality and freshness of the vegetables.

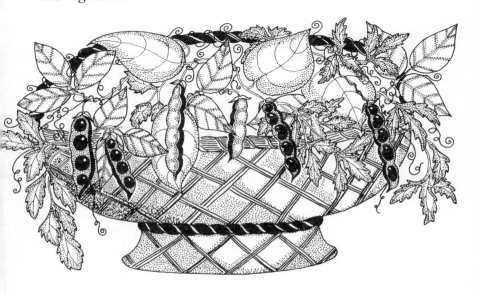

*Foie de Genisse à la Ciboulette; Pommes de Terre en Soufflé*
Calf's liver is horrendously expensive, and is in any case difficult to obtain. It is no use pretending that other types of liver are adequate substitutes, but we seem to have developed the idea in this country that liver is of no gastronomic interest. This is far from true, and if chosen and cooked well it is one of the most delicious—and cheapest—of meats. The *genisse* is a yearling heifer, and the liver, which is rich and tender, is popular in France. This is almost certainly what is sometimes sold in this country as calf's liver, and it is my first choice although lamb's liver can be excellent. Pork liver is much more fibrous and strongly flavoured, and is therefore best avoided. Have the liver cut fairly thinly—1 cm maximum. It must be cooked quickly so that the juices are sealed in and the centre of the meat remains rosy. A small amount of intensely flavoured sauce is required, but the constituents can be varied. A sweet-and-sour effect is often successful, and the classic Dubonnet and fresh orange juice reduction is delicious.

Dry the pieces of liver and dust with highly seasoned plain flour. Sauté the liver hard in a mixture of butter and oil or clarified butter until golden on both sides—no more than two minutes per side. If the pan is spacious there is no need to remove the liver before completing the sauce (indeed the flour coating helps the liaison) since this can be done very quickly. Deglaze with medium sweet sherry or madeira, adding small quantities until a rich brown glaze is obtained. While the heat is still high squeeze in about the same volume of lemon or orange juice as sherry, until the consistency is again syrupy. At this point the dish can be taken from the heat and kept warm for up to half an hour, but if it is to be kept the liver must be very rare in the first instance. Stir in a good quantity of chopped chives just before serving, having first adjusted the seasoning.

A buttery purée of potatoes would be a perfect accompaniment to this rather rich meat, but the following quasi-soufflé, with its extreme lightness of texture, is even better. For a maximum of six people, boil 1 kilo new potatoes gently in well-salted water until quite soft. Meanwhile separate the yolks from two eggs and beat the whites until stiff. Drain the potatoes and mash thoroughly with the two egg yolks, 60 g (2 oz) butter, plenty of black pepper, and enough milk, added gradually, to turn the mixture quite sloppy. Stir in a generous handful of chopped parsley, fold in the egg whites and turn into a pre-warmed soufflé dish. The dish should be lightly buttered and may be rubbed with garlic. Sprinkle freshly ground Parmesan over the top with several small knobs of butter, and place in a moderately hot oven for 10 minutes. It must not become dry and spongy but should remain light and moist with a golden crust. To prepare the dish ahead of time keep the purée warm without adding the parsley and egg whites until just before baking.

No particular cheese suggests itself, but I would tend to avoid rich, creamy varieties and choose instead a soft ripening French cheese of character, for example Pont L'Eveque or Münster, with a crumbly blue such as the under-rated Fourme d'Ambert of the Auvergne for contrast.

*Riz a l'imperatrice* is one of my favourite cold puddings, but a little goes a long way. It is a mould of rice and egg custard set with gelatine, and including candied peel and fruits. I have placed it in this menu because in concept it can be said to echo the main course, creamy starch versus intense, spicy fruit.

The sauvignon is just the grape to provide the acidity necessary to counteract the weight of a mayonnaise, and the wine from the cooperative in the Haut Poitou is justifiably the height of fashion, having nothing to lose from comparison with most Sancerre and Pouilly Fumé, but at half the price. The main course demands a light, supple red with a sweet edge, qualities typfied by burgundies from the Côte de Beaune. Louis Latour's Chassagne Montrachet, of a modest year, is not a great wine, but is not yet fully ready and will show well if decanted an hour or two in advance.

# Menu   1:4

*Oeufs en Cocotte*

*St Peray, Délas Frères 1977*

———

*Pieds de Porc Farcis*

*St Joseph, Léon Revol 1976*

———

*Fromages*

*St Joseph (suite)*

———

*Clafouti*

This meal has a rustic air and is completely without pretension. It is nowadays exceedingly difficult to find such cooking in restaurants in France, even in the most rural areas. The one sure way of encountering such food is to visit Lyon, where traditional recipes, using virtually every imaginable part of the pig, are still served in the tiny restaurants known as *bouchons*. The idea of the bouchon is that you are present almost as a paying guest in a family kitchen, and the atmosphere should be decidedly relaxed. In the past these establishments were presided over by the famous *mères* of Lyon, but alas these formidable ladies are now few in number, though their profound influence on the cuisine of the region lives on. In a bouchon you would never dream of ordering any wine other than the open beaujolais, for it is almost always delicious and fairly safe to consume in quantity. Nor would you expect the bill to lead to bankruptcy proceedings, and if you then take in a café-theatre—there will almost certainly be one within 50 yards of your bouchon—you will have experienced a thoroughly Lyonnaise evening without feeling that you have been in any way extravagant. You should not, however, plan to be too active the following morning.

*Oeufs en Cocotte* While most people start their meals in the bouchon with a Salade Beaujolaise (Menu 2:8), if I were going to choose a main course of *pieds de porc* I would probably want to have some protein in the first course. Baked eggs are delicious and extremely satisfying nutritionally. They are at their most savoury when done on a bed of fresh tomato sauce with ham and red or green peppers, but for a first course a simple cream sauce with fresh herbs is preferable. Break the eggs into buttered cocottes rubbed with garlic, season with salt and white pepper, and pour on enough double cream to just cover the yolk. Bake in a bain-marie in a moderate oven for 15–20 minutes until the white is just cooked. The yolk must remain liquid. Just before serving sprinkle with chives, tarragon or parsley and pour on a little extra cream. Serve with French bread or brown toast.

*Pieds de Porc Farci* This is a much simplified version of the classic Lyonnais dish, in which the pigs' feet would usually be pre-cooked, the small bones laboriously extracted and a stuffing based on herbs and breadcrumbs inserted. I do not find it a terrible inconvenience to have a few bones on my plate: indeed, if the surroundings and company are appropriate (and sometimes even when they are not), I take great delight in giving in to the obvious resulting temptation. Prior simmering makes the elastic skin more manageable, but can be dispensed with if you are prepared to watch carefully over the initial stages of the following process.

Choose either the trotter itself or, better, since it provides some meat and more room for the stuffing, the lowermost part of the shank. Using a small, sharp knife *(couteau d'office)* make a cavity by prising the tissues away from the bone, keeping the skin intact. Make several longitudinal incisions in the skin without cutting right through. Slice some cooked saucisson de Lyon or Paris (more commonly available here) into wedges corresponding to the length of the trotter, with a maximum diameter of about 1 cm. Insert one slice of sausage into each cavity with a sliver of garlic, a few leaves of thyme and a fresh sage leaf. Secure with a cocktail stick. Turn the trotters in oil over a modest heat, making any further incisions necessary to prevent expulsion of the sausage. When browned deglaze with wine or sherry vinegar, then gradually add brown sherry or madeira until you leave a syrupy glaze. Coat the pieds evenly with this sauce, season with salt and a generous amount of black pepper and finally add a few sprigs of thyme and three or four unpeeled cloves of garlic per trotter. Cook uncovered in a low oven for at least two hours. Watch for any sign of scorching, in which case add a little water, but allow caramelisation. When the trotters are melting and tender remove them from the sauce and crisp the skin either in a hot oven or under a low, pre-heated grill for 5–10 minutes. Complete the sauce by adding a little water and boil vigorously to dissolve the caramelised juices. Off the heat swirl in butter in small knobs until the sauce binds, and finish with a tablespoonful of Dijon mustard. You may add some double cream. The garlic cloves should be served whole with the trotters on a puddle of sauce. The best accompaniment is a mixed purée of potatoes and turnips with lots of butter and black pepper.

Sadly it is quite impossible to obtain regional Lyonnaise cheese in Britain, at least outside London. The local favourite, and justifiably, is the soft, creamy St Marcellin, made from cows' milk and with a delicate grey rind. This is rivalled by the Mont d'Or, which is similar but has an orange-coloured rind. Also popular is the Tomme de Savoie, but to taste this at its best you must go to the market in Annecy, where peasants still set up their tiny stalls, creaking under the weight of tommes of various ages. The oldest cheeses are often sold off cheaply and can be wonderful, although occasionally they can be dried out and disappointing. Any well-ripened French cheese would, however, be quite appropriate, as would the *fromage frais à la crème* so typical of Lyon, or any goats' milk cheese.

I would have the deepest admiration for anyone who could tackle a clafouti after such fare, but its inclusion seems entirely appropriate on intellectual grounds, and I can only plead for restraint in the preceding courses, particularly with the vegetable purée and cheese, so that you can enjoy this most traditional and homely of puddings. It consists of fresh cherries baked in a batter similar to that used for crêpes, in a slow oven. The cherries must be good and in my view there should be more cherry than batter. Apples are often substituted for cherries. It may be eaten hot or cold, and the remains are usually served cold at breakfast the following day.

Given my prejudice against expensive, bottled Beaujolais, I have no hesitation in turning to the Rhône for wines to accompany this menu. The Rhône vineyards are, in any case, closer to Lyon than the Beaujolais. St Peray is a tiny village on the right bank of the Rhône opposite Tain L'Hermitage, and is best known for its *méthode champenoise* sparkling white. The still white is, however, excellent, strong and dry, and resembling the white wines of St Joseph and Hermitage itself. St Joseph is still the most under-rated of the Rhône appellations, and I think that this may be attributable to the fact that it does not come from one identifiable village, but rather from a series of designated sites between Ampuis and Tournon. This red is quite typical—robust but perfumed and well-rounded. It is from a fine vintage in these parts, and will keep well.

# Menu 1:5

*Taramosaláta*

*Garvey's San Dorado fino sherry*

---

*Cassoulet de Pois Chiches
au Boudin Noir*

*Bandol, Domaine de la Tour Bon
1976*

---

*Fromages*

*Bandol (suite)*

---

This is a cosmopolitan menu, a well tried favourite hors d'oeuvre from Greece and a traditional Scottish apple pie flanking a new look at a peasant dish from the South West of France.

*Taramosaláta* There are many versions of this increasingly popular dish, and, since it is nowadays never made with the dried mullet roes on which the recipe was originally based, none can claim absolute authenticity. I dislike the common practice of using breadcrumbs for bulk, but agree that some foil for the strong and often salty flavour of smoked cod roes is essential. The most interesting version seems to me to be that given by Alan Davidson in his scholarly and indispensable book *Mediterranean Seafood.* The method could hardly be simpler: mix together ½ kilo smoked cod's roe, 350 g cream cheese, three tablespoonfuls olive oil, three tablespoonfuls finely chopped chives and, lastly, three tablespoonfuls lemon juice. Chill before serving with black olives and toasted wholemeal bread.

*Cassoulet de Pois Chiches au Boudin Noir*   On a winter's day, perhaps after a bracing walk in the hills, there are few sights to equal a steaming cauldron of cassoulet. As 'peasant' food it has no equal, combining as it does the less important pieces of duck and pig with sausages and beans. The protein and calorie values are therefore high, but the cost is low. And what a feast it can be—a genuine lucky dip.

The trouble with most cassoulet, however, is the beans. The traditional *haricots blancs* do not seem to me to be at all suitable for the length of cooking required, tending to lose texture and contributing little interest in terms of flavour. Almost any other kind of kidney bean could be substituted, but the ideal solution is to use chick peas. They are nutty in both texture and flavour, providing the ideal vehicle for a heavy and highly seasoned sauce.

Soak the chick peas overnight (500 g minimum for six). Ideally the main 'meat' should be duck either fresh or 'confit', for example the wings and legs left over after making the *caneton au poivre vert* of menu 3:2, but left-over pheasant or guinea fowl are fine substitutes and in this case use heavy olive oil instead of duck fat. One of the advantages of adding black pudding, as the title suggests, is that the fowl becomes dispensable, but let us assume that we have the appropriate left-overs.

In a large, deep iron casserole sauté the duck briskly in its fat until the skin is golden brown. Reduce the heat and add a chopped onion with several (at least six) peeled garlic cloves. Add generous chunks of bacon (or previously soaked salt port) and sausage cut in 2½-cm lengths. My favourite sausage for this purpose is the Spanish *chorizo*, which is intensely peppery and exudes a pretty red colour. It is generally available in this country. There is no harm in deglazing with a little white wine before adding an appropriate quantity of peeled, seeded and roughly chopped tomatoes, either fresh or tinned. Season generously then boil vigorously to amalgamate these ingredients before adding the chick peas and a large bouquet garni including a bay leaf, thyme, parsley and celery leaves. Mix until the meat and sauce are evenly distributed, top up with water and cook in a low oven for at least two hours. Do not allow the peas on the surface to dry out, but by the time of serving the liquid should be largely absorbed. About an hour before the anticipated serving time (which might with advantage be the following day) add a ring of black pudding and fish out the bouquet garni. Good bread of any type and a green salad are the only accompaniments required.

For the cheese board I would tend to go for firm, full flavoured cheeses such as Cantal, Gex (a lightly veined cheese appropriately from the South West), or a tomme. It would, however, be entirely in order to serve English cheeses, and this could be made to round off the meal nicely with Cox's Pippins and a handful of walnuts. If, on the other hand, you had had a particularly long walk in the hills, or it was an especially cold day, you might welcome a slice of old-fashioned apple pie with lightly whipped cream.

Taramosaláta is, like aïoli and anchoïade, so powerful in flavour that a very assertive white wine is required. Rather than a heavy, hot, southern white wine I suggest a fino sherry, and I have chosen Garvey's San Dorado because of its round and surprisingly full flavour. With the cassoulet a robust red from the South West would be a logical choice, the main contenders being Cahors, Madiran and the up-and-coming Côtes de Buzet. But to anyone who has read Marcel Pagnol's tales of tragi-comedy in the life of the peasants of Provence, any mention of chick peas will instantly evoke the sunshine and the perfumes of the Midi, and I therefore propose this fine but sturdy Bandol, one of the Midi's best red wines from the coast between Cassis and Toulon. I have, unfortunately never seen this particular wine in this country, but other wines from equally good proprietors are readily available. The Domaine de la Tour Bon is distinguished by a fine bouquet reminiscent of Pomerol, and has nothing in common with Southern Rhône wines. It is full and soft, but has body enough to sail through the flavours of the Cassoulet, and will show well with the cheese.

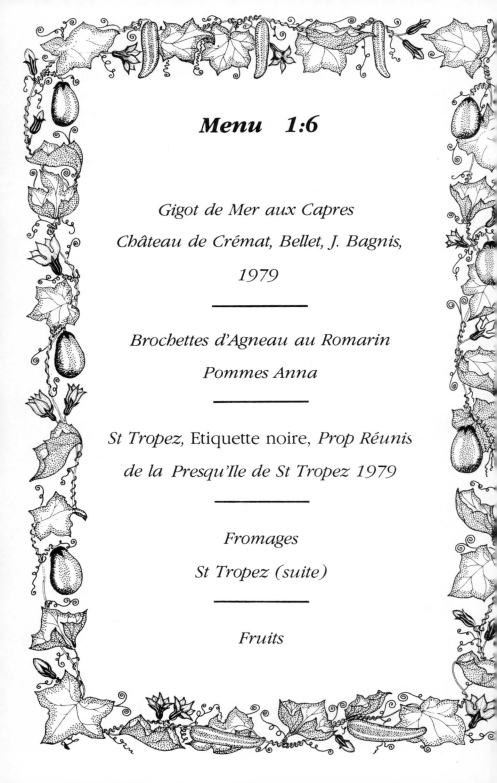

# Menu 1:6

Gigot de Mer aux Capres

Château de Crémat, Bellet, J. Bagnis,

1979

———————

Brochettes d'Agneau au Romarin

Pommes Anna

———————

St Tropez, Etiquette noire, Prop Réunis

de la Presqu'Ile de St Tropez 1979

———————

Fromages

St Tropez (suite)

———————

Fruits

With gigot followed by lamb this is at first sight perhaps a slightly puzzling menu. It is a meal to be eaten in summer, outdoors if possible. It can be prepared almost entirely in advance apart from grilling the lamb and finishing the sauce, but it will impress your guests by virtue of the subtle way in which it deals with powerful flavours. Best of all, it leaves you free to lounge around in the sun enjoying an aperitif rather than peering enviously at the assembled company from your kitchen window.

*Gigot de Mer aux Capres*   Monkfish, or angler-fish, which goes under various names in France *(lotte, baudroie)*, is not the prettiest of marine creatures until decapitated by the fishmonger. In some Cornish fishing villages the fishermen have an unappetising and fly-attracting habit of hanging the heads on the outside of the boathouses as trophies. The prepared tail is, however, very attractive to look at and handle, the creamy flesh covered by a purplish membrane which, with the cartilaginous backbone, should be removed before cooking. The French with their boundless enthusiasm for culinary metaphors occasionally refer to the whole tail as a gigot because of its shape, resembling as it does a leg of lamb. It is now easily available in this country but has been a little slow to gain in popularity and therefore has remained mercifully cheap. I was as sceptical as anyone about tales of monkfish being used as a substitute for lobster until it was pointed out to me that it is only when slightly undercooked and served cold that its flesh takes on a texture and sweetness approaching that of the unaffordable crustacean.

Allow a longitudinal half of one medium-size monkfish tail per person. Be fastidious about removing the membrane as it tends to make the fish curl during cooking. Make a small amount of fish fumet by simmering the backbones and any trimmings with a chopped onion, carrot and white of leek, seasoned with black pepper, for about 20 minutes. When the stock has acquired some flavour strain it, season the monkfish tails and poach them whole, very gently, in the stock with a dash of white wine. This should only take a few minutes, so that the fish remains almost raw in the middle. Set the fish to cool in the stock. Next prepare a light mayonnaise flavoured with lemon juice, and convert this to a *sauce mousseline* by mixing it with about the same volume of whipped cream. Stir in a tablespoonful or two of the fish fumet and a handful of washed capers, and adjust the seasoning.

To serve, slice the monkfish tails into 2-cm pieces, reconstruct the shapes in a pretty arrangement on a serving dish and pour the sauce over. Serve with toast. This dish can be made more complicated and grandiose by adding fresh mussels and/or *tomates crues concassées* (p 161), both of which add to its visual charm. Alternatively the sauce can be based on *sauce verte*— mayonnaise flavoured with a reduction of spinach, sorrel, tarragon and chevril.

*Brochettes d'Agneau au Romarin* Charcoal grilling is now immensely popular, and its difficulties, particularly in the open air, are generally underestimated, presumably because the relaxed atmosphere which accompanies barbecues encourages tolerance of poor results. The most important key to success is to overestimate both the amount of charcoal required and the length of time necessary to prepare the fire. Choice of meat is also of great importance; the fat content should be high, and the meat moist. Lamb is therefore a safe bet, particularly since it is best when cooked fairly rare. Brochettes are easy, because the pieces of meat are small and cooking times are therefore short. Large pieces of meat pose insurmountable difficulties unless pre-cooked.

If the lamb is young choose the shoulder or best end of neck, cut into cubes of about 5 cms, with a little fat attached. If you are less certain of the quality of the meat choose leg or loin. Allow also one lamb's kidney per person, split lengthwise to within 1 cm of the convex surface. Season the meat and marinate it in a 50:50 mixture of olive oil and lime or lemon juice and a generous amount of chopped rosemary for a few hours. Prepare one long skewer per person, alternating cubes of meat with mushrooms, onions and red peppers coated in olive oil and seasoned. Place the kidney in the middle of each brochette in a butterfly shape. The grilling should be done quickly, close to a hot fire, but as always you must avoid flames. Baste with the marinade while cooking.

The brochettes would be of little interest without an accompanying sauce. My wife devised this simple and quite delicious mustard sauce, which can be prepared ahead of time.

Soften an onion in butter with chopped garlic and some slivers of boiled ham. Deglaze with white wine or sherry and add a small amount of chopped, seeded fresh tomato (which need not be peeled), a bay leaf and a generous pinch of dried oregano.

*Evening the Quais de Saône, Lyon.*

Season with salt and black pepper and simmer for 20 minutes. Sieve the sauce, and if preparing it ahead of time reserve it at this point. To finish the sauce beat an egg yolk with two tablespoons double cream. Bring the sauce to just below simmering, add two tablespoonfuls to the cream and egg yolk mixture and whisk again. Then add the mixture to the sauce and stir over a gentle heat until thickened. Just before serving stir in a tablespoonful of *moutarde a l'ancienne* or *au poivre vert.* A savoury potato dish is the best accompaniment to a mustard sauce. Pommes Anna—slices of potato well seasoned and baked in a shallow dish with plenty of butter, with or without garlic—are simple and delicious.

Serve any light cheese appropriate to the weather. Brie, goats' milk and Jaarlsberg come to mind for a summer evening. To serve fresh fruit unaccompanied at the end of a meal is not necessarily an admission of defeat or laziness. Have the courage to serve only one or two fruits chosen because they are in the prime of condition, and arrange them stylishly.

The two wines chosen to accompany this menu are little known outside Provence, but the French authorities have encouraged improved methods of vinification in the region by awarding 'appellation contrôlée' status fairly generously, and standards are therefore rising very rapidly. The status of the white wines from Bellet, in the precipitous hills behind Nice, has long been acknowledged. This is a strong, dry wine with a surprisingly delicate and fresh aroma. It can be difficult to obtain outside its native region; if a substitute is necessary, one of the many excellent white Rioja would be appropriate.

The red wine made by the cooperative at St Tropez has a splendid purple colour and a warm, soft fruit flavour reminiscent of the Loire reds but with a much fuller flavour. A stylish wine, as indeed it ought to be, given the images conjured by the name, If you have not been able to bring a bottle or two back from holiday, look again to the Rioja for a suitable replacement.

# Menu 1:7

*Datiles con Jamòn*

*Harvey's 'Palo Cortado' sherry*

----

*Vitello Tonnato*

*Hermitage 'Chevalier de Sterimberg',
Jaboulet 1976*

----

*Tarte aux Abricots*

Once again a menu which illustrates how dishes from different countries can be combined with great effect. Why is it that the 'international cuisine' found in hotels and restaurants all over the world has selected the worst from each country, and then set out to make it even worse? Why can't they choose to serve a mouth-watering *vitello tonnato* rather than those abominable confections using *escalope de veau* which are to be found everywhere, especially, and most lamentably, in Italian restaurants abroad?

*Datiles con Jamòn*   From Andalucia comes the most delicious *bonne bouchée* of them all, rivalled only by the very similar Italian combination of figs and Parma ham. It consists of peeled, stoned fresh dates wrapped in a sliver of thinly cut raw ham. In Spain the snow-cured Serrano ham, which is the equal of any, would be the automatic choice. In the context of this menu it has to be admitted that nothing can be said against Parma ham and figs, but the latter are even more difficult to obtain here than fresh dates. Also in favour of the Spanish version is the fact that they can be eaten easily with fingers or cocktail sticks as an accompaniment to a fine aperitif. This Spanish habit of serving dainty savouries, or *tapas*, before proceeding to table is well worth acquiring and is particularly pleasant—and useful from the cook's point of view—at an informal lunch.

*Vitello Tonnato*   This is undoubtedly one of the great meat dishes of the world, and one of the least well known. The long cooking and marination of the meat in broth and finally in the sauce itself leads to a remarkable blend of flavours so that it becomes a dish apart—neither meat nor fish, but both at once. It is not difficult, but can be made into a most elegant and impressive presentation. It can be made even more easily by making the sauce in a blender, but I have a strong disinclination to use the blender if I can avoid it, partly because of the noise and mess, and partly because I object to the over-smooth and often slightly frothy sauce which can result.

Choose a boneless, rolled veal roast of about 1.5 kg for 6–8 people. Shoulder would be a reasonable choice but is unlikely to be easily obtainable in this country, so you may have to use the more expensive leg or fillet. Bury a few anchovy filets and slivers of garlic deep in the flesh by making incisions along the grain with a small, sharp knife. Blanch the meat by boiling it in water for a minute or two, then rinse it in cold water.

In a heavy iron pot cover the meat with good chicken stock (undersalted), a glass of dry white wine, and chopped onion, carrots and celery. Add a bouquet garni containing bay leaf, thyme and parsley, a dozen or so black peppercorns and a few peeled garlic cloves. Bring to the boil then simmer covered until the meat is very tender (about 1½–2 hours). Remove about 1½ cups of the stock and boil it down until the flavour is concentrated but not too salty, then reserve this—you should have about ½ cup—for later use. Allow the meat to cool in the remainder of the stock.

The tuna fish sauce is a mayonnaise variant. Chop the contents of a four ounce tin of tuna fish in olive oil with four anchovy fillets which have soaked in water for 10 minutes and force the mixture through a fine sieve to make a purée. Beat an egg yolk in a pre-warmed bowl until it is frothy, then add the above purée with the juice of half of a lemon. Beat about a cup of good olive oil into this mixture as if making a mayonnaise, until the sauce is very thick. Next thin the sauce to a creamy consistency by stirring in the reduced, cooled stock. You may add some double cream if a smoother consistency seems desirable. Finally stir in two to three tablespoonfuls of washed capers and adjust the seasoning.

When the veal is cool remove the string and trim away any unsightly fat—the stock should, of course, be reserved for future use. Slice the veal thinly and sprinkle lightly with salt. Spread a thin layer of sauce on the serving dish and then arrange the veal slices neatly. Cover the meat with the remainder of the sauce, cover the dish and refrigerate for a few hours, or, better, overnight. Take the veal out of the refrigerator for at least an hour before serving. Garnish with lemon quarters and black olives and serve with a salad of grated carrot, and a good wholemeal bread or *grissini* (Italian bread sticks which can be bought in packets in any good delicatessen).

Less elaborate versions of this dish can be delicious; for instance, rolled turkey breast can be substituted for veal, or left over roast pork can be dressed in a similar sauce. Tuna fish-flavoured mayonnaise is also good with hard boiled eggs as an entrée or light luncheon dish.

I would not serve cheese in this meal, but would progress straight away to a pastry dessert such as a classic French open tart with a crème pâtissière filling, covered for instance with fresh apricot halves braised in white wine and sugar to make a syrup which can be reduced with a little apricot jam to make a glaze. Toasted almonds may be sprinkled on top.

The flavour of dates with raw ham is intense, sweet and at the same time salty, and does not flatter a white table wine. Choose instead a sherry with plenty of character, such as Harvey's Palo Cortado, and serve it chilled. If this seems unduly extravagant, a Sercial or Verdelho madeira with its strong, burnt taste would be better than an ordinary amontillado sherry.

Any fine white wine could be served with the veal, as long as it is quite dry, full in body, and possesses fairly high acidity. White burgundy would be an almost automatic first choice, but use this instead as an opportunity to serve a powerful, heady wine from one of the lesser known areas. I have yet to taste a white Italian wine which could do justice to this wonderful dish, so I would tend to go instead for a white Rhône. The Hermitage 'Chevalier de Sterimberg' of Paul Jaboulet is not typical of its appellation, being lighter in colour and fresher on the palate than the usual rather weighty and sometimes almost tannic, straw-coloured whites from l'Hermitage. This is because Jaboulet is using new methods of vinification, and while this does not give wines which will age gracefully in the old style—the 1976 is now (1981) passing its peak—the wine retains an impressive fullness of flavour combined with a marvellous flowery perfume and a good, crisp finish. It is almost impossible to identify 'blind' but to me bears a strong resemblance to Savennières, and that is no bad thing. It could prove very interesting to open a *demi-sec* Vouvray or Coteaux du Layon with the apricot tart, for the sake of comparison.

# PART 2

## *Food for Friends*

# Introduction

In this section an air of sophistication will be evident when the menus, or rather individual dishes, are compared with those of Part 1. I emphasise that this comment applies only to individual dishes because the theoretical basis of the menus remains unchanged. In general, therefore, I have tried to avoid having more than one dish which requires lengthy or last minute attention, and have kept complicated or difficult techniques to a minimum. By using more refined—and therefore often more expensive—ingredients in an imaginative way, I have tried to indicate how finesse and style can be achieved without tears. These are not intended to be menus for important occasions, although you may well consider individual dishes suitable for 'lifting' into a grander environment.

I suggest instead that you aim to produce meals like this for just a few friends who are interested in gastronomy, because they are more likely to appreciate the true quality of such food, served as it will be without any pretence or extravagance, and you will notice, as cook and host, two great advantages from this kind of approach. The first is that you will find time to talk to your guests without last minute panic, and the second is that the cooking itself is, by and large, fairly undemanding, and you will therefore be able to prepare and serve a meal which you know will be both interesting and good without fear of failure. This is important for your own enjoyment of the occasion, and that, after all, is the only valid reason for doing it, and you may even feel confident enough to have your friends wander into the kitchen with their aperitifs while you finish the preparations. Encourage this (if your kitchen is big enough) because it will interest those of your friends who are so inclined, while also giving those less interested in gastronomy a sense of involvement in the evening's entertainment, combined with an insight into your reasons for trying to cook well, and into the pleasure you derive from applying the methods which you have mastered. I suspect that many people who enjoy eating but who become defensive when confronted with exceptionally good food and wine are simply puzzled by it all, wondering whether some mystery or special training is involved, or whether a freakish amount of effort and study are required. There is also the question of motivation, and your guests who venture, no doubt with some trepidation, into your kitchen should instantly appreciate that the essence of your cooking is not the shedding of blood, sweat and tears to impress people at any cost, but the thoughtful pleasure you obtain from doing simple things skilfully, efficiently and imaginatively.

In many ways, therefore, this is the style of cooking which gives the most pleasure to the greatest number of people. It should also please the person choosing the wine, for here anything is possible and fantasy is desirable. In Part 1 it would be absurd to make too much fuss about the wine, while in Part 3 you will naturally want to dust off your most carefully guarded treasures. Here you can choose top quality wine from any part of the globe and at whatever price suits you, and the context provided by the meal should encourage enthusiastic discussion of your choice. Blind tasting, as mentioned in the introduction, is most appropriate to this type of meal, and can often start at the aperitif stage with a glass of white wine, still or sparkling, served with *tapas* (see Menu 1:7) or other savouries. At the end of the evening even those guests for whom deprivation of gin and tonic or whisky caused deep resentment may thank you as they tuck into your best cognac with a clear head.

# Menu 2:1

*Beignets au Roquefort*

*Chateau Jolys, Jurançon, NV*

---

*Salmon Steaks au Poivre*

*Pointes d'Asperges au Beurre*

*Clos de la Coulée de Serrant,*
*Savennières, Mme Joly, 1973*

---

*Roquefort*

*Clos de la Coulée de Serrant (suite)*

---

*Diplomate*

*Quarts de Chaume,*
*Domaine des Baumards 1971*

It would not be unreasonable to claim that this menu embodies all the cardinal principles of the Nouvelle Cuisine, yet there are no green peppercorns and not a drop of sherry vinegar. It is a very great pity that chefs all over France have paid lip service to Nouvelle methods by indiscriminately throwing these two excellent ingredients around to the extent that the predictable wave of reaction has latched on to them as 'clichés' which are typical of what is implied to be a boring and stereotyped approach. Where these recipes are new is mainly in the composition of the sauces, and this is achieved by the simple device, found also in other menus in this and Part 3, of applying what I can only describe as inter-category adaptations. That is to say that new, and very striking, effects can be gained by applying meat methods to fish, sweet methods to vegetables, and so on.

The first course should be seen not as pastry stuffed with vegetables in a cheese sauce, which would instantly invite a heavy béchamel concoction, but as a salad seasoned with Roquefort and wrapped in delicate pastry. Similarly the inevitable, albeit, when successful, delectable, notion of serving salmon steaks in a rich creamy sauce is avoided by concentrating on 'steak' rather than 'salmon', and once this intellectual divide has been bridged the best of all fish can be seen in a marvellous new light. The meal is devoid of heaviness though abundant in complex, at times pungent, flavours and high seasoning; solace, like sunshine after a thunderstorm, appearing in the tactful form of the famous political pudding.

*Beignets au Roquefort* A bitter-sweet salad with crunchy walnuts and redolent of the sealed-in aroma of melting Roquefort, delicately encapsulated in crisp, wafer-thin pastry. Simple enough in theory, and in practice far from difficult, the only main problem is likely to be that of availability of ingredients. You may wish to try other salad vegetables with a different blue cheese and a more conventional pastry shell, but if you are familiar with the extraordinary flavour of Roquefort you will rightly realise that it is best to avoid such a 'second best' approach and instead rethink the whole dish.

For 12 turnovers of about 8 cms x 5 cms, two of which will be enough per person, chop four large Belgian chicories or *endives* roughly, having first wiped them carefully. Turn them briskly in light olive oil or any tasteless vegetable oil (groundnut or safflower) until they begin to soften—a matter of seconds. Deglaze first with port or madeira, then the juice of a lemon, season well and allow to cool in the refrigerator. Next prepare the pastry shells. The ideal pastry for this purpose is the Middle Eastern *fila,* but this is difficult to make (Claudia Roden gives instructions in *A Book of Middle Eastern Food*) and is usually obtainable from delicatessens. Alternatively you may use pre-packed spring roll pastry from Chinese delicatessens. Cut the pastry to the desired shape and size and brush the inside lightly with oil. To the cooled salad add roughly chopped walnuts and Roquefort, mix equal portions and place on the pastry cut-outs, leaving enough room to fold the pastry comfortably and secure the envelopes by tucking in the free end. Deep-fry the turnovers in hot oil for a few minutes until golden brown, by which time the cheese should just be on the point of melting. Serve hot, garnished with watercress. The advantage of deep-frying these heavenly little parcels rather than baking them is that every last atom of aroma is captured until a knife breaks through the pastry.

*Salmon Steaks au Poivre* It may seem curious to take a recipe for beef steaks, the most difficult of all foods to make 'interesting', and apply it to salmon, surely one of the easiest, for which so many grand recipes abound, but I can only protest that the recipe seems to me far more appropriate for salmon than beef which, if it is of the highest quality, can only be ruined by any interference other than the application of heat.

Allow a 2.5 cm-thick middle salmon steak per person, and divide each into two *'aiguillettes'* (literally 'little needles') by removing the central backbone, and remove the skin. Salt the fish lightly and rub with coarsely ground peppercorns, mainly white but also some black for its rounder flavour. In France you would no doubt use the trendy *poivre rose* to match the colour of the salmon. Set the steaks in the refrigerator for one hour. Meanwhile prepare a fish fumet with the trimmings by simmering in half water, half white wine with carrot, onion and fresh leaf fennel, aiming for a final volume of about a cupful for six steaks.

Sauté the steaks briefly in butter without searing; in this respect the treatment must be different from that for beef. When barely cooked the salmon can be removed and kept warm in a low oven in a tightly sealed parcel of aluminium foil. Soften a handful of finely chopped shallots in the butter until golden, then deglaze with armagnac or cognac and the juice of a lemon. The remarks in the introduction notwithstanding, sherry vinegar is a good alternative to the lemon juice but should precede the brandy. Reduce to a golden essence, add the fish glaze and allow the sauce to amalgamate for a few minutes. If sweetness or colour are lacking, add a teaspoonful of tomato purée. (The recipe may be halted at this point, the salmon steaks having been allowed to cool in foil, to be reheated at the last minute in the sauce). At the last moment bring the sauce to the boil then swirl in two ounces of good butter in small parcels until the sauce binds and glistens. Add a handful of chopped fresh fennel leaves, arrange the salmon elegantly either on a warm platter or on individual plates, and decorate with the sauce, which should not be over-abundant. By far the most appropriate vegetable accompaniment is asparagus tips, fortunately in season at the same time as salmon, boiled until *al dente* and turned in butter.

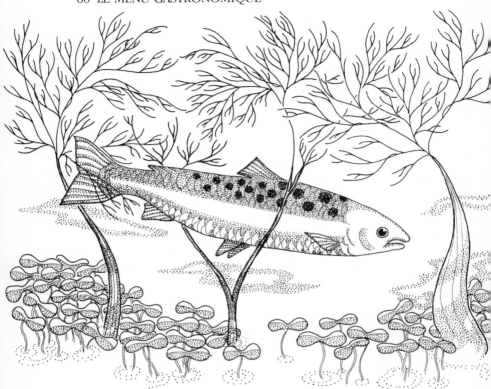

Normally I object to cheese after a main course of fish, but here there is no difficulty, and although any fine cheese could be served, an attractive symmetry can be achieved by presenting Roquefort, whose interests will be served by the fine white wine chosen for the fish. It is not a cheese to set against your finest claret. The best vehicle for such cheese is undoubtedly the Bath Oliver.

*Diplomate,* or *Pudding de Cabinet,* is a classic but not too complicated dessert combining the creaminess of egg custard with spicy, rum- or kirsh-soaked candied fruits and seedless raisins. It may be prepared a day in advance. The *crème anglaise* is poured into a mould lined with liqueur-impregnated sponge fingers, alternating with layers of the dried fruits, and is then slowly baked in a *bain-marie* until set. It must not reach simmering point or the custard will curdle.

A considerable challenge is provided by an all white wine meal, for the wines must be both interesting and assertive enough to stay the course. The problem is that very few white wines blossom in the glass in the way that the best reds ought. The succession of wines must therefore be of interest just as the individual wines must rise to the challenge, and I have chosen to introduce the two fine Loire wines with an uncommon wine, the only connection between them being the name 'Joly' and the shape of the bottle.

The dry white Château Jolys from Jurançon is, nonetheless, a fine wine with ample body and a lemony flavour which stands up well to the Roquefort pastries. It is, however, a little straightforward, and this will bring out the tremendous quality and complexity of the Savennières. Madame Joly's Coulée de Serrant is an extraordinary wine which is difficult to compare with any of the better known great white wines because of its very individual but in no way idiosyncratic style. It will delight and intrigue the most discerning of guests, and should not lose the battle against peppercorns and Roquefort. The 1973 is perhaps nearing the end of its lifetime, having faded appreciably between 1976 and 1979, but fortunately the Loire enjoyed several good vintages in the late 1970's and supplies should not be difficult to find.

Savennières is a thoroughly unassuming village on the right bank of the Loire downstream from Angers, and the casual visitor would be hard pressed to guess that it was the home of the great wine. On the opposite bank of the Loire, beginning at Rochefort, there stretches a small area more obviously dominated by the vine, as testified by roadside advertising and signs indicating *visites des caves*. This is the narrow little valley of the Layon, a tributory of the Loire which erodes deeply into a plateau to provide ideal conditions for making an intense, fragrant, sweet white wine which lives forever. The grape is the Chenin Blanc which is used for the dry Savennières, but here the sheltered valley encourages the *pourriture noble* which shrivels and concentrates the grapes to an extraordinary degree of sweetness. The domaine des Baumards consistently produces very fine wines from Savennières and the Côteaux du Layon, and this 1971 Quarts de Chaumes is just reaching maturity.

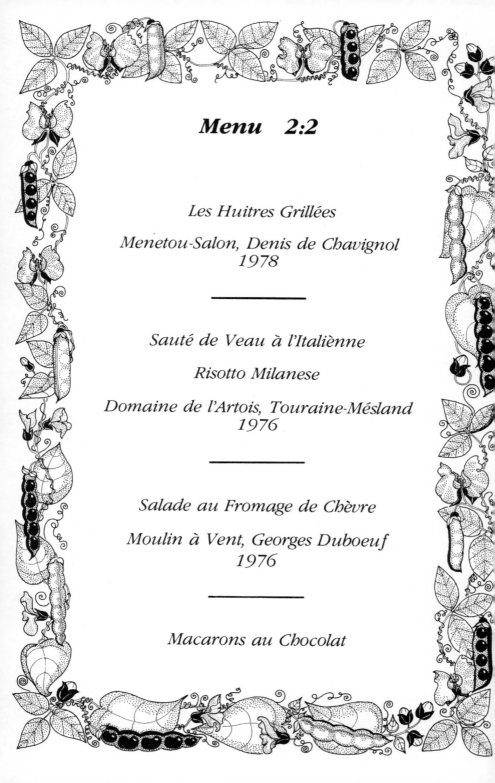

# Menu   2:2

*Les Huitres Grillées*

*Menetou-Salon, Denis de Chavignol*
*1978*

---

*Sauté de Veau à l'Italiènne*

*Risotto Milanese*

*Domaine de l'Artois, Touraine-Mésland*
*1976*

---

*Salade au Fromage de Chèvre*

*Moulin à Vent, Georges Duboeuf*
*1976*

---

*Macarons au Chocolat*

If the previous menu seemed streamlined and thoroughly modern, here is something quite homely, but in its way transformed by the inclusion of grilled oysters. These remain ludicrously expensive and difficult to find, but happily those which are farmed on the West Coast of Scotland have a very fine flavour. The taste of oysters when prepared in this way is so intense that a little goes a long way, and you might find that four per person, accompanied by good wholemeal bread and butter, will be adequate. In any case the main course is rich and filling, and this is therefore a meal which can be seen as having an arch shape, since the salad and then macaroons represent a decrescendo necessitated by the weight of the risotto.

*Les Huitres Grillées*   Fond though I am of the sea and its smells I am not keen on raw oysters without complication. By grilling them in this way with an aromatic crust of herbs and breadcrumbs nothing of the flavour is lost, and they seem to gain in complexity what they lose in assertiveness. At a pinch you could substitute large mussels for oysters, but they would have to be opened by steaming in white wine or cider and a little of the juice spooned carefully into each on the half-shell. It would, however, undoubtedly repay the effort. In France, Italy or Spain, for instance on holiday, the same method can be applied to various large clams, though some of these tend to go rather tough when cooked, and the grilling therefore has to be finely judged.

Crumple a sheet of aluminium foil and pack it loosely on your grill pan. If several panfuls are to be done it is best to prepare them all in advance on spare racks, removing each to a warm oven as the oysters are done. Open the oysters carefully, remove flakes of shell and loosen the flesh from the deeper half of the shell, then set each carefully in the foil so that it will be stable enough for none of the juice to be lost. Squeeze a little lemon juice into each oyster and season with black pepper. Next prepare the 'farce' by chopping shallot, garlic and parsley finely, and mix them with a small quantity of white breadcrumbs and grated parmesan. The breadcrumbs should be barely discernible in the final dish. Place a small knob of butter on each and grill the oysters very quickly under a fierce heat until bubbling. Serve as soon as possible with lemon quarters and French bread or, as indicated above, wholemeal bread and butter.

*Sauté de Veau à l'Italienne*   I have chosen a French name for this dish because the end result, though conceived as a quick and light substitute for *osso bucco milanese* and deliberately employing a method derived from that for the risotto milanese below, strikes me as being more French than Italian. Stewing veal is easily obtained and is quite adequate, but noisettes cut from the fillet would be even better. On the other hand you can go 'down-market' and substitute diced pork for a more ordinary occasion, perhaps changing the tone slightly by adding chopped green peppers to the initial sauté.

Prepare a good veal or chicken stock, unsalted but strongly flavoured with celery, carrot, black peppercorns and a *bouquet garni* of thyme, parsley, bay leaf and tarragon. Dry the cubes of meat thoroughly and brown them quickly in olive oil. Add chopped shallots and a stick or two of chopped celery, reduce the heat and fry gently until golden, then add a good quantity of shredded garlic. Season quickly with a little salt and plenty of black pepper, raise the heat and deglaze with fino sherry. As soon as a syrup has formed add a little stock, then, when the sauce boils again, add chopped fresh tomato which has been previously peeled by scalding and seeded. Boil this hard to reduce and amalgamate the sauce, then gradually add the rest of the stock, stirring frequently, until the meat is tender. The heat should be kept fairly high and this therefore requires vigilance, but a little caramelisation is desirable to bring out the flavour. Altogether this takes about 25 minutes, and at this point the dish can be set aside and either kept warm for a short time or cooled and reheated later. At the last minute add a mixture of chopped parsley, tarragon, garlic and lemon peel to simulate the *gremolata* usually served with osso bucco.

*Risotto Milanese*   This is not a dish for slimmers or those with a bad family history of coronary artery disease, for it has to be rich and buttery to be successful. It is often underrated because it is seldom prepared properly, and you should not even attempt it unless you have the true Arborio rice from Piemonte. No other rice has the correct crunchy texture and glutinous quality necessary for the sauce. As for the veal an excellent veal or chicken stock is required, and you can therefore kill two birds with one stone.

Turn the rice, without having washed it, in a good quantity of butter over a low heat with a chopped shallot or two until the rice is impregnated. Add a few shreds of garlic and deglaze with fino sherry. You will then have a thick, glutinous mass which will tend to stick to the pan, and you should therefore choose a heavy, non-stick pot with a rounded bottom. A wooden fork is then used to stir the rice while you gradually add the stock over a moderate heat until the rice is just cooked. This takes about 20 minutes, the stirring and addition of stock being carried out every three or four minutes. When the rice is just cooked but remains distinctly *al dente* add a strong infusion of saffron, and just before serving mix in a good quantity of extra butter, plenty of freshly grated Parmesan and a handful of chopped Italian flat-leaf parsley.

Instead of a formal cheese board, serve a refreshing salad incorporating a variety of salad greens such as young spinach and sorrel, rocket and dandelions with fresh herbs (Italian parsley, chives, summer savory and basil). Mix this with chopped goat's cheese and *tomates crues concassées*. The latter are simply roughly chopped, seasoned tomatoes which have first been peeled by scalding and divested of seeds and pith before being added to an otherwise finished dish. The assembled salad is then turned in a light vinaigrette seasoned with salt and lots of black pepper.

To round off this meal I suggest a taste of chocolate, and the ideal dessert would be home-made dark chocolate ice cream with macaroons, but you may simply choose to serve chocolate-coated macaroons which you have made yourself, accompanied by strong coffee.

I bought the first two wines listed here in Michel Guérard's *'Comptoir Gourmand'* in Lyon, intrigued by their unfamiliar names. Each bore the legend *'Selectioné par M Guérard'*, and I had to concur with his judgment that for little-known wines these are extraordinarily good.

Menetou-Salon is an almost extinct appellation near Sancerre and Pouilly Fumé, and its white wine, made like these from the Sauvignon, is indistinguishable from its more celebrated neighbours. In fact, close inspection of the label reveals that this wine is made by one of the better-known Sancerre growers. Highly perfumed, but full of fruit suggesting currants and with high balancing acidity, this is just the wine for the oysters, and if you can find it you will pay much less than for the traditional, and so often disappointing, Chablis.

The Touraine-Mésland is less unusual in that the gamay grape is being cultivated increasingly in the middle Loire. Here the wine produced from it seems softer and fatter than Beaujolais, the very easily recognisable gamay smell being masked in a very ripe aroma suggesting damp undergrowth, an entirely healthy bouquet which suggests extreme ripeness. My original tasting note comments on a similarity to the smell of Burgundy, and this is also true of the very fine Moulin à Vent of Georges Duboeuf, so I think this comparison would be fascinating. 1976 was of course a fine year in both the Loire and the Beaujolais, and both of these wines have had time to develop their Burgundian attributes to the full. I think that the Domaine de l'Artois would show well, but that the Beaujolais would appear the more stylish wine, and would be perfect with the *salade au fromage de chèvre.*

*Gigondas, Vauchise.*

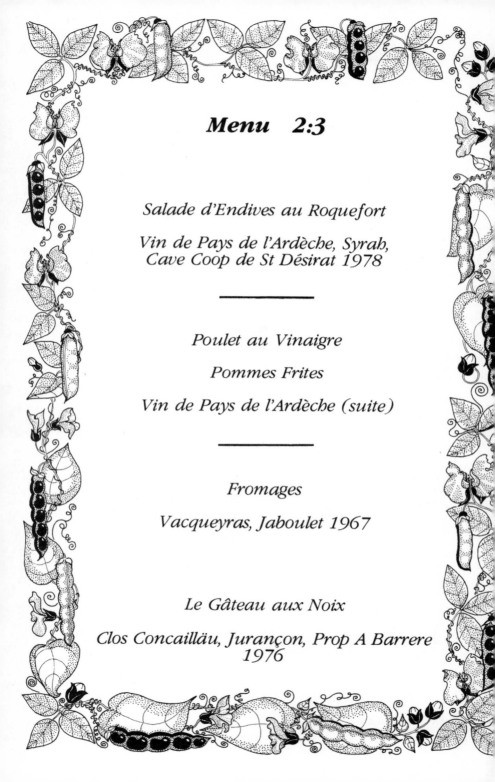

# Menu 2:3

*Salade d'Endives au Roquefort*

*Vin de Pays de l'Ardèche, Syrah,*
*Cave Coop de St Désirat 1978*

―――――――――

*Poulet au Vinaigre*

*Pommes Frites*

*Vin de Pays de l'Ardèche (suite)*

―――――――――

*Fromages*

*Vacqueyras, Jaboulet 1967*

*Le Gâteau aux Noix*

*Clos Concailläu, Jurançon, Prop A Barrere*
*1976*

If the preceding menu could justifiably be judged to have an arch
shape, this must be considered a straight line, for the four
courses have more or less equal weight—in spite of the chips.
This is French cooking at its simplest and incomparable best.

*Salade d'Endives au Roquefort*   At almost every dinner party to
which we were invited while living in Lyon a large chunk of
Roquefort dominated the cheeseboard. To what extent the
obligation to provide what is seen in France as by far the best
cheese in the world represents understandable chauvinism, or
to what extent it reflects the depressingly liturgical and
unadventurous approach to their own food which is prevalent in
modern France, and which must have been sensed by the
originators of the Nouvelle Cuisine, I cannot be sure. All I can say
is that it is not my favourite cheese, and many a time I would
rather have seen a ripe Epoisses or a melting Boursault, or
indeed a St Marcellin and a few local goat's milk cheeses in the
prime of condition. It is, though, undeniable that Roquefort
stands apart by virtue of its salty, pungent and highly individual
flavour. At its best, which is seldom, it is very good to eat on its
own, but usually I think it offers most when its particular taste
and stridency are offset in some way, as in the following salad or
the not too dissimilar *beignets au Roquefort* of Menu 2:1.

The bitter but slightly squishy characteristics of chicory
*(endives)* contrast well with the cheese as long as texture is
replaced, and for this purpose I would use both a crunchy salad
green such as curly endive or, better, red batavia, and walnuts.
Fresh herbs, particularly chives, add refinement.

Wipe the chicory and remove any damaged leaves. Chop
roughly in rounds and stir-fry in light olive oil until just
beginning to soften. Deglaze with a good quantity of flavoured
wine vinegar (tarragon, chives or raspberry), then season well
with black pepper but no salt and cool quickly in the refrigerator.
Meanwhile wash, dry and tear up the other salad ingredients and
mix with crumbled Roquefort and roughly chopped walnuts.
Toss at the last minute with the chicory and its dressing, and
season with salt.

*Poulet au Vinaigre* Formerly known as *Poulet sauté à la Lyonnaise,* this is the most common recipe for chicken which one encounters in the restaurants of Lyon. I hesitate to give recipes for chicken, since chicken recognisable on account of its taste has not been available in this country for twenty years, but this recipe, and that for *médaillons de volaille* (Menu 2:7) would not be disastrous with either of the two types of chicken available to us in this country—the frankly tasteless and the pseudo-kipper. Grilling and roasting bring out the fishy flavour of the British battery chicken, and must regrettably be avoided. If you live near London you might be tempted to dig deep and serve a *Poulet de Bresse* from Harrod's on a very special occasion. Even in France, however, the Bresse chickens are twice as expensive as other excellent types, and are normally reserved for grand recipes including truffles. There may at last be light at the end of the tunnel and we may not have to cross the Channel to rediscover that wonderful flavour so evocative of childhood, for recently we have discovered quite superb chickens lurking innocently and quite untrumpeted on the shelves of a large chain-store.

A sauté of chicken is essentially a simple affair, but the recipe for *poulet à la lyonnaise* given in *Larousse Gastronomique* is altogether too simple to be of much interest. On the other hand Michel Guérard, in his *Cuisine Gourmande,* gives an elaborate version in which he uses a mixture of white wine, mustard, Armagnac and tomato purée in place of stock, adding this to the deglazed pan juices with whole unpeeled garlic cloves cooked with the chicken and squeezed through the sieve. This approach is interesting, but in my experience somehow unsatisfactory and laboured. I have nothing but praise, however, for his suggestion that *tomates crues concassées* should be added to the finished sauce, and would only add that a handful of chopped basil mixed with the tomatoes is a celestial alternative to parsley or chervil. Here is my own version.

Use the wings and legs of the chicken, seasoned generously with salt and black pepper. Brown the pieces of chicken in butter over a moderate heat until they are well and evenly coloured. Pour off the brown butter, reduce the heat, add a little extra butter, cover the pan and cook gently, without letting the chicken stick, until it is cooked but remains juicy (about 20 minutes). Add chopped shallot and a clove or two of garlic cut into lengthwise slivers. When these are soft raise the heat and deglaze with good red wine vinegar (about one dessertspoonful per person), scraping up all the caramelised juices until they dissolve. Cover the pan and let the vinegar reduce to an essence. Remove the chicken and keep it warm in a covered dish. To make the sauce add a cupful or two (depending on the quantity of chicken) of a rich brown chicken stock strongly flavoured with tarragon and containing a judicious drop of Armagnac. Boil the sauce down until the intensity of flavour and seasoning are correct, then swirl in chilled butter in small parcels, off the heat, until the sauce thickens. Finally add a tablespoonful of Dijon mustard and the chopped *tomates crues concassées* (see glossary) with their accompanying herbs, and garnish the pieces of chicken with this rich brown sauce.

*Pommes Frites*  A consultant colleague claims that 95% of the population suffer from a well-known lower intestinal ailment, and the other 5% are liars. In the case of chips I would say that 5% of the gastronomic fraternity love chips and the other 95% know what they are missing, but can't admit it to themselves. Excepting, of course, the Belgians, who know what they like and are most unfairly, and hypocritically, derided by the French for their unabashed devotion to the perfect chip. Every cookbook should carry a recipe for chips. I say that with feeling because we spent many years eating the soggy results of our experimentation with different fats, different potatoes, different pots and different temperatures, until we discovered the correct method, which renders failure practically impossible. For ordinary sized chips the fat should only be moderately hot, and the initial cooking should last under 10 minutes. Next the vital step—carefully remove the by now soft chips and drain them, and allow them to cool to room temperature. They can be cooked to this point several hours in advance. To complete the cooking plunge the chips into almost smoking fat for a few minutes only, until they are crisp and golden. It is with great difficulty that I have restricted myself to one chip-containing menu in this book.

Here is the perfect opportunity to serve a selection of the more powerful French cheeses. Combine one of the washed-rind soft-ripening varieties such as Chaume, Pont l'Evèque or Münster, exuding as they do all the odours of the farmyard, with a full-flavoured blue from the Causses, the Auvergne or Bresse. Rigottes de Condrieu would provide a refreshing contrast.

*Le gâteau aux noix,* also known as *Le St André,* is a rich sponge cake made with whole eggs and incorporating a large quantity of freshly ground walnuts, and these impart to the cake an interestingly 'meaty' texture as well as their fine flavour. The nuttiness makes this cake very suitable for a fruity garnish and I particularly like an orange flavour. It horrifies some people, but I find the cake delicious when soaked in fresh orange juice with just a hint of Grand Marnier, and topped with whipped cream. Orange butter icing is also delicious but the result is rather heavy.

The Cave Cooperative at the beautifully named St Désirat de Champagne near Anonnay in the Ardèche is pursuing an interesting policy of producing single grape varietal wines with quality in mind. The gamay has proved a little disappointing but the 1978 Syrah is a strong, deeply coloured wine with good fruit and a typical Syrah flavour. Annonay lies quite close to the North Rhône vineyards, and the success of the Syrah grape is therefore not surprising. This is the grape which gives backbone and a very recognisable perfume to the Rhône wines and often benefits from judicious blending, but the growers at St Désirat are to be complimented for their enterprise. The 1978 will last a good many years, but is supple enough to accompany the first two courses while supplying the necessary robustness of flavour.

The 1967 Vacqueyras of Paul Jaboulet Aîné is a good partner for the strong French cheeses, which are inimical to all but the sturdiest of red wines, and shows what a fine Syrah can achieve in the hands of an expert *viticulteur,* albeit in a blend. Normally Vacqueyras, one of the Côtes du Rhône Villages from the area east of Orange and close to Gigondas, is reckoned to be at its best when between five and ten years old, but this wine is far better than its fairly humble *appellation* suggests, and testifies to the great skill of the house of Jaboulet, universally accepted as one of the best *négociant-viticulteurs* of the Rhône. It is just ready now, powerful and complex.

Sweet white wine is catching on again in France, to the great relief of all those who feared that the great pudding wines might disappear altogether, so labour-intensive are they in their production. In France, however, they are served as aperitifs, as an accompaniment to *foie gras,* or with cheese, particularly Roquefort. You may be interested to try these experiments, though I can think of nothing better to kill the appetite than a rich Sauternes; but when all is said and done the place for a pudding wine is with the pudding. Some thought should be given to the choice of sweet wine to go with any particular pudding, and here I have chosen a fresh, moderately to very sweet Jurançon with a distinct hint of orange on the nose.

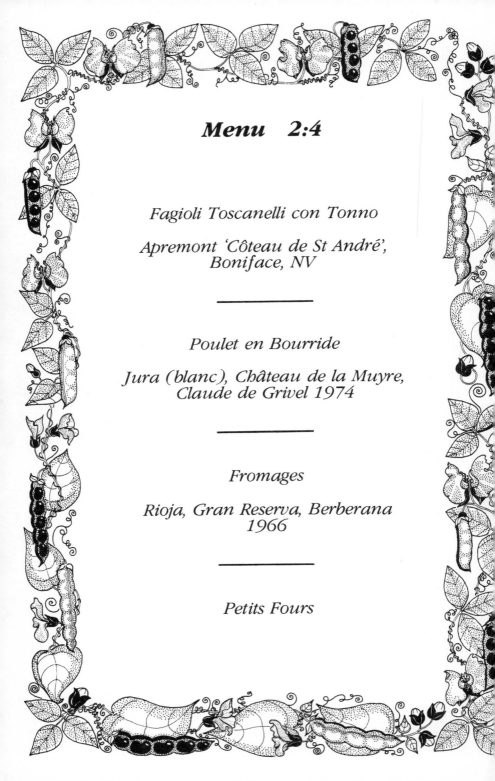

# Menu 2:4

*Fagioli Toscanelli con Tonno*

*Apremont 'Côteau de St André',*
*Boniface, NV*

---

*Poulet en Bourride*

*Jura (blanc), Château de la Muyre,*
*Claude de Grivel 1974*

---

*Fromages*

*Rioja, Gran Reserva, Berberana*
*1966*

---

*Petits Fours*

If you are less than fond of garlic this menu, which once again links France and Italy, is not for you. The classic bean salad from Tuscany provides a suitably rustic introduction to an adaptation for chicken of the rightly famous *bourride* from the Midi. The *bourride* is a dish of fish, usually a good white fish such as turbot, brill or monkfish (although I have been served a delicious version containing mackerel and boiled potatoes), in a rich sauce thickened with aïoli, a strongly garlic-flavoured mayonnaise. This is extraordinarily filling, so whatever way you choose to end the meal you should bear this in mind so as to avoid turning the meal into a digestive assault course.

*Fagioli Toscanelli con Tonno*  The natives of Florence are sometimes called the 'bean-eaters' by other Italians, and not without reason. As well as serving beans as the traditional, and very satisfactory accompaniment to the renowned Florentine grilled beef, they have devised this most effective salad of haricot beans and tuna fish, which is best kept simple, particularly in the present context, but can be adapted successfully by, for instance, varying the type of bean or using a mayonnaise-type suace or even an anchoïade. White haricot beans are the usual choice, cooked until tender in either water or stock, then drained and, when cool, mixed with tinned tuna fish in olive oil, roughly broken up. The salad is dressed with a vinaigrette in which lemon juice is substituted for vinegar, and a fruity olive oil should be used. The inclusion of fresh herbs is essential, parsley and chives being adequate, but the ideal choice for beans is summer savory. A small amount of finely chopped raw garlic would help prepare the palate for the rigours of the *bourride*.

*Poulet en Bourride*  Chicken is remarkable in its ability to retain its own character in the face of virtually any type of sauce or method of cooking and, of course, the better the chicken the more true this is. If you can find a genuine boiling fowl which is not simply a geriatric, fishmeal-fed battery product, this dish will be all the better because of the added strength of flavour to be found in the flesh. In this case you would boil the chicken in water with a little wine and all the vegetable and herb ingredients necessary for a good stock, before finishing the sauce as suggested below, but I have assumed that most readers will be using roasting chicken and will choose to follow this quick method, which is essentially a sauté.

Joint the chicken, season the pieces with salt and pepper, and brown in a small quantity of olive oil without allowing the flesh to stick to the base of the pan. Deglaze with dry white wine or vermouth and cover the chicken with a good, undersalted, white chicken stock. Add at least four whole, unpeeled cloves of garlic per person and a *bouquet garni* of thyme, bay leaf and parsley. Simmer gently until the chicken is tender (about ½ hour).

Meanwhile prepare a thick mayonnaise with olive oil but do not salt it. Instead of basing the sauce on raw crushed garlic I prefer to tame the flavour by cooking the whole cloves with the chicken, as above; then when the chicken is ready, pressing the whole cloves through a fine sieve. The garlic purée is then stirred into the mayonnaise. Remove the pieces of chicken and keep warm on the serving platter. Boil the stock down to as small a volume as possible to intensify the flavour, the limiting factor being the degree of saltiness. Aim for about one cupful per pint of mayonnaise, a quantity which should serve six to eight people. Strain the hot stock and pour it when just off the boil into the mayonnaise, stirring vigorously. The sauce should have a beautiful creamy consistency and a complex, savoury aroma. Pour it over the chicken garnished with chopped parsley. I, feel however, that the usual Provençal garnish of croutons rubbed with garlic detracts from the finesse of the dish. Serve either with plain boiled potatoes or a green vegetable such as broccoli. Vast quantities of good French bread are essential for mopping up the sauce.

Although a rich pudding is inadvisable after such a main course, a cheese course is certainly desirable. It would be diplomatic to match Italian and French cheeses, perhaps even to invite comparison between Gorgonzola and Bleu de Bresse, Taleggio and Reblochon. End with no more than a mouthful of sweet, or serve homemade *petits fours* with coffee. These can range from sugar-coated almonds or simple macaroons to tiny tarts bearing, for instance, one strawberry. Coconut and dark bitter chocolate should also be represented on any display of *petits fours.*

One of the great delights of living in the centre of France is the accessibility of the Savoie and all its produce for the table. The wines of the region are much better than is often supposed, and are not overshadowed by the quality of the cheese, raw ham and freshwater fish. The two best whites are Seyssel (Menu 3:2) and Apremont. This example of the latter is bottled *'sur lie'*, directly off the lees without racking, a practice which gives tremendous freshness and occasionally slight *pétillance* allied, in the most successful instances, with a huge volume of bouquet and a good balance of fruit and acidity. The effect is wonderfully reviving. These are not wines to keep, and they seldom bear a vintage date, indicating that they should be drunk within the year. Sadly this seems to inhibit British wine merchants from importing these most drinkable wines.

The Jura lies not far to the north of the Savoie, an altogether less imposing landscape which, paradoxically, produces much more 'serious' white wines than the Savoie. These can attain a state very similar to fino sherry, and this is the style of Château Chalon, the most famous wine of the region. Others, however, are made, like white burgundy, from the pinot chardonnay and at their best can match the finest of white burgundy—no small feat, and one which is not widely acknowledged. This Château de la Muyre is just such a wine, magnificently constituted with a long, complex flavour indistinguishable from Meursault.

Only a generous red wine could accompany the cheese after such fare, and it would have to be of very high quality. Your guests will have been hopelessly wrong in trying to identify the previous two wines, so give them a chance by setting this entirely fair puzzle. It is fair because this is utterly typical Rioja, not, as sometimes happens with older wines, mistakable for red burgundy. It is a very fine wine with a suaveness and directness of flavour which should allow identification even in these highly extenuating circumstances. Like all fine Rioja it is vastly underpriced in spite of the recent upsurge of interest in Spanish wines.

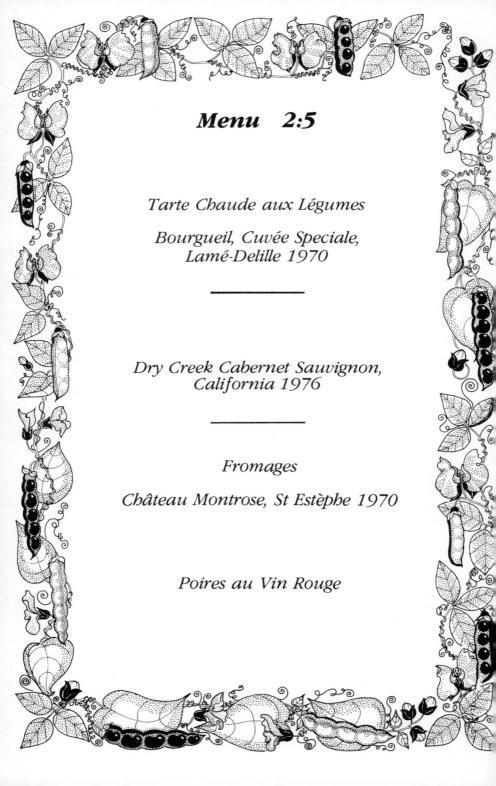

# Menu 2:5

*Tarte Chaude aux Légumes*

*Bourgueil, Cuvée Speciale,
Lamé-Delille 1970*

---

*Dry Creek Cabernet Sauvignon,
California 1976*

---

*Fromages*

*Château Montrose, St Estèphe 1970*

*Poires au Vin Rouge*

Vegetable pie, roast game with turnips and pears in red wine—there is nothing new under the sun. But we can shuffle the cards a little even if we cannot add to their numbers. The following treatment of these very traditional foodstuffs is not necessarily any better than the old fashioned methods, but I hope there is room in the world for both ways of seeing. And seeing in a very important part of this meal, for each course is intended to be visually striking as well as offering a new look in purely gustatory terms at the simplest of country fare.

At first sight this may seem a more ambitious menu than most in this section, at least from the technical point of view, and possibly also from the gastronomic, but nothing is difficult and all that is required is a carefully thought out plan of action, for much may be done in advance. Organisation and timing are essential to good cooking but, as in the matter of measuring quantities, my own approach is quite empirical. A clear general idea of what is needed, and a complete inability to be flustered, will serve you better than a minute-by-minute timetable. The pastry shell and its contents can be prepared an hour or two in advance; the final assembly takes little time and can be done during the preparation of the rabbit. You must, on the other hand, resist the temptation to peel the vegetables for the main course well in advance and leave them soaking in water, for this leeches out their flavour (taste the water if you are sceptical). The stock for the rabbit and the pears in red wine can be prepared up to a day in advance.

This is a light meal which should create an impression of elegance. Although the courses may each appear insubstantial the flavours are concentrated and each dish should be appreciated without hurry. As an experiment in trying to focus attention on the food, I suggest that you do not serve bread until the cheese appears. The wines are, needless to say, selected for a combination of elegance and concentration of flavour.

*Tarte Chaude aux Légumes*    The *trompe-l'oeil* effect of this dish is certainly a source of great fun, but the combination of textures is also interesting and the flavour of the young vegetables is nicely emphasised. The aim is to produce a tart which resembles in appearance and texture a French open fruit tart (e.g. *tarte aux fraises*), where the fruit segments, glistening with a light film of glaze, nestle on a bed of *crème pâtissière,* the whole contained in an almost sculpted shortcrust pastry case. As well as being a visual pun this could serve as an *amuse-gueule* if you were to make tiny tarts containing one vegetable segment each, to be eaten with the aperitif. In the best French restaurants the chef takes some trouble over these little titbits, for they alert the palate and create the correct frame of mind for appreciating a fine and leisurely meal.

For six people bake a 250-cm (10-inch) pastry shell, blind, using a shortcrust pastry *(pâte brisée)* made entirely with butter and containing a generous pinch of granulated sugar (see Introduction, page    ). The pastry should be rolled out thick, to about 1 cm. This shell can be prepared the day before.

The *'crème pâtissière'* takes the form of a *sabayon* made with the white part of leeks, and this can be made several hours ahead. It is exactly similar to the *sauce sabayon* to be served with *suprêmes de phaisan en brioche* (Menu 3:8) except that here I overcome my antipathy towards the blender, a frothy, even-textured sauce being required, and the sorrel is omitted since a pale creamy colour is desirable. Soften the chopped white parts of two or three leeks with a chopped shallot or two in an ounce of butter, in a heavy iron casserole, stirring occasionally. Add a small glass of fino sherry and a cupful of white chicken stock, season and cook gently for 15 minutes. Blend this mixture with two tablespoonfuls of double cream, and transfer the sauce to a clean pan. Beat two egg yolks with a little cold water until frothy, and add them gradually to the sauce, which should be just off the boil. Beat constantly over a low heat until the mixture thickens but be very careful not to allow it to boil. The vegetables can also be cooked in advance. Carrots, mandatory for their colour, turnips (which can be sliced to imitate French apple and pear tarts), asparagus and salsify are the best vegetables to choose. They should be peeled and shaped attractively, then cooked briskly in a little salted water with butter and a teaspoonful of sugar until the vegetables are just tender and a glaze begins to form. Deglaze with tarragon vinegar, then brown sherry or madeira, and continue adding the sherry little by little over a high heat until an adequate amount of sauce remains when all the alcohol has been boiled off. If you are using asparagus it should be boiled in salted water alone, and added to the sauce when it has been completed. Season with black pepper and allow to cool.

The tart is best served hot. Spread a thick layer of *sabayon* on the pastry shell and arrange the vegetables attractively on top, pouring on any remaining glaze. Heat through quickly in a hot oven, taking care not to allow the sabayon to reach boiling point.

*Baron de Lapereau Printannier*  This is really a misnomer, because although the *baron,* that is, the saddle and hind legs in a piece, looks splendid on a platter dressed with its sparkling brown sauce and surrounded by whole spring vegetables, it is impossible to carve, and so I suggest using only the *rable,* or fillet, removed from the bone. One fillet serves one person. You will therefore require three rabbits for six people, but this is not wasteful because the remaining pieces can be used for a *lapin à la moutarde* or *rillons de lapereau à la moutarde* (Menu 3:7).

For many years I have been trying to find an alternative method of cooking rabbit so as to bring out the tender succulence of the flesh without resort to stewing it. Roasting and grilling, however, simply do not work because the flesh, though moist, is devoid of fat. One answer was provided by Signor Rocca, patron of the Hotel Giardino Felicin in Monforte d'Alba, a loquacious, charming but incorrigibly bossy man known to all as Giorgio. In his hotel, which is a gastronomic wonderland in the heart of the delightful Barolo country, what Giorgio says goes (and if he says you go for a picnic to the Alps today, heaven help you if you resist). One of Giorgio's pastimes is the rearing of domestic rabbits in hutches under the dining room, which, when these have had enough lettuce to render them impossibly fat and sleek, mysteriously disappear from their hutches only to emerge on platters in the celestial upper floor, after a longish time in the purgatory of the oven. The white flesh of these creatures is cooked until black and caramelised by, I think, roasting in a moderate oven with constant bastings of Barolo. The result is marvellous but I confess that I have not been able to reproduce the method successfully, though the results have been far from unpleasant. Fortunately good wild rabbit is cheap and plentiful enough to allow experimentation, and finally I came to the following solution, which, as the name suggests, bears a passing resemblance to *Navarin printannier*.

Prepare the rabbit fillets and coat with freshly ground black pepper. Do not salt them. Make a rich stock by first browning the bones from the saddle with the flesh from the flanks in a little butter, with chopped onion and carrot. Deglaze with a generous glass of red wine, cover with water and add an onion stuck with a clove, chopped celery, a few juniper berries and black peppercorns, and a handful of unpeeled garlic cloves. Simmer for about two hours, by which time the stock will be almost clear. Strain the liquid and reserve it—this can be done in advance.

Carefully peel spring turnips and carrots leaving on each a small tuft of green shoots. Cook them to a glaze in water, salt, sugar and butter as for the *tarte chaude aux légumes*. Deglaze with red wine and add a little stock to form a small amount of sauce. Adjust the seasoning. Now brown the fillets carefully in butter in a heavy sauté pan, then transfer them to individual *papillotes* of aluminium foil. Pour a little of the sauce from the vegetables on each and add a sprig of fresh thyme before sealing the envelopes tightly. Place in a moderate oven for 10–15 minutes. They can be kept warm in a low oven with the door ajar for up to 30 minutes, but the initial cooking time should be shortened correspondingly.

Meanwhile pour the stock into the pot in which the vegetables had been cooked (these having been removed), and bring to simmering point to dissolve the caramelised juices. Deglaze the sauté pan with red wine, a little wine or sherry vinegar, and add the stock gradually until the concentration and seasoning are just right (the sauce can be prepared ahead up to this point).

Just before serving turn the vegetables in the sauce, to which the liquid from the fillets has been added, and thicken lightly with arrowroot to give the sauce a beautiful sheen. Arrange the vegetables around the edges of a warmed platter and cover the base with the sauce. Slice the fillets lengthways on the bias and arrange in fan shapes in the centre of the platter. Decorate with thyme flowers or chives.

To persist with the theme of elegant simplicity try serving a single soft ripening cheese, such as a large piece of ripe Brie, or a whole Camembert, Langres or St André. A selection of biscuits is preferable to bread, oatcakes being particularly suitable for this type of cheese.

The pudding, pears poached in red wine, is, of course, a classic which echoes the first course—the arch structure again. This is a dessert which appeals to the chefs in the Nouvelle Cuisine school, made modern by the entirely plausible addition of black pepper. More important is the quality of the pears, which must be firm, juicy and perfumed, the quality of the red wine and the judiciousness of the quantities of sugar, cinnamon and lemon peel. Aim for a light syrupy consistency, remembering that the sauce thickens as it cools. The most effective way to serve pears is whole, peeled and cored but with the stalk attached, the base flattened to allow them to stand upright on a plate. Pour the sauce round and over the pears.

These wines may seem very disparate, but there is a thread of logic. It is surprising how often the red Loire wines, when aged, are taken for clarets of a light year, but of course they are made from the *cabernet franc,* also used to some extent in Bordeaux. The suppleness and lack of weight of this well-aged and very fine Bourgueil complement the vegetable tart refreshingly and with style.

The other two wines are more obviously related, and have the right combination of vigour and class to set beside the food. Both are in their infancy but are remarkably enjoyable to drink at this stage if decanted two or three hours ahead. The Californian Cabernet Sauvignon will impress by its concentration and 'Frenchness' of style, while the Montrose is quite simply superb, claret at its best with an intense perfume of chocolate, vanilla and cedar (which will doubtless change with age) and an almost creamy texture.

Instead of serving wine with the pears provide each guest with a tiny glass of *eau de vie de poire* before coffee.

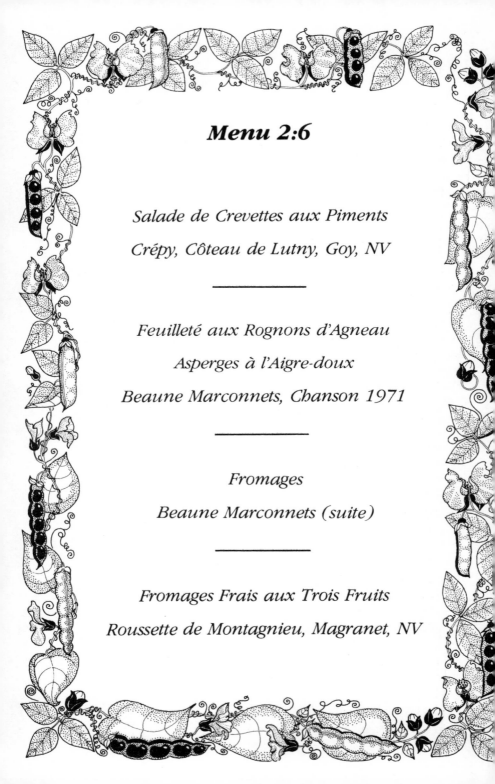

# Menu 2:6

Salade de Crevettes aux Piments

Crépy, Côteau de Lutny, Goy, NV

———————

Feuilleté aux Rognons d'Agneau

Asperges à l'Aigre-doux

Beaune Marconnets, Chanson 1971

———————

Fromages

Beaune Marconnets (suite)

———————

Fromages Frais aux Trois Fruits

Roussette de Montagnieu, Magranet, NV

I suppose every cook has his or her favourite way of overcoming the perennial problem as to what to cook on any given occasion. For those awkward moments when you have little time to plan in advance there are one or two items which are always handy to have around, and this menu illustrates the kind of way in which they can be used. In the freezer I always like to have fish or shellfish, offal such as sweetbreads or kidneys, and puff pastry, which for most purposes is perfectly acceptable in its commercial form. Peppers, avocados and aubergines are all susceptible to conjuring tricks, the magic ingredient in many cases being raw or boiled ham. It is particularly worth having these raw ingredients to hand when you have friends staying for some length of time, and you can have immense fun working out how best to use them.

*Salade de Crevettes aux Piments*   I readily admit that I was nervous about this combination when I first conceived it. The prospect of the contrasts in colour and texture pleased me and encouraged boldness. In the end I was surprised by the subtle way in which the flavours interact to give definition to each other. Every ingredient must be of the very highest quality.

Try to obtain all three colours of pepper—red, green and the brilliant yellow which is sweetest of all. Place a slice of raw ham on each plate (the salad would be impossible to serve neatly from a large platter) and on it arrange the peppers sliced into rounds, overlapping them and varying the colours. Use least of the green variety and most of the yellow to avoid emphasising the more aggressive and slightly bitter taste of the less ripe green pepper. Intersperse the peppers with peeled prawns (lobster, monkfish and salmon are good substitutes) and a few strips of ham. The dressing is all important, since the successful combination of the flavours depends on it. Use a mayonnaise as a vehicle for a particular unifying flavour and thin to a creamy consistency with cream, single or double as necessary but not whipped. The first time I made this salad I used for the mayonnaise olive oil in which peppers had been gently fried for a previous *antipasto*. This was highly successful, but Dijon mustard or a pinch of curry powder can be equally interesting. The acidity should be in the form of lemon or lime juice rather than vinegar. Garnish with citrus slices and whole prawns.

*Feuilleté aux Rognons d'Agneau*   The feuilleté, really no more than an old fashioned vol-au-vent, is one of the favourite art forms of the Nouvelle Cuisine. It has several merits: it looks grand, it makes a little meat go a long way and is perfect as a means of providing a filling accompaniment to a rich sauce. The current fashion is for a single large pastry shell, usually oblong in shape, but you may justifiably serve any shape or size you choose. The meat (or fish, vegetable or mushroom) in the filling must be tender and succulent, and, as I have hinted above, my own favoured standby is offal. It seems to me quite the best way of serving kidneys, and also braised or sauté sweetbreads, for the flaky pastry provides a textural contrast with the meat which can be further accentuated by the vegetable accompaniment.

The reason why feuilletés are popular with Nouvelle Cuisine chefs, however, is that they are ideal for the *petites sauces* of intense concentration but little bulk which can be contrived according to the whim of the chef. Mustard sauce is, of course, classical as an accompaniment for kidneys, and this version is similar to that given with *brochettes d'agneau* in Menu 1:6. While the puff pastry is being baked, sauté the carefully cleaned, whole lamb kidneys gently in butter until they are well coloured and resistant to the touch (about five minutes). They should remain very definitely pink inside. Remove them and keep warm without slicing them. Soften a chopped shallot or two in the sauté pan with a little chopped ham and a few shreds of garlic. Reduce with sherry vinegar when the shallot is golden, then with madeira and allow to caramelise slightly. Expand the sauce with a well flavoured stock of veal or chicken and chopped, seeded fresh tomatoes. Simmer for 20 minutes, strain and thicken with cream and egg yolks, then add a good handful of mixed fresh herbs (parsley, chives, chervil, tarragon). Turn the kidneys in the sauce then slice them thickly before arranging them in the pastry shell.

*Asperges à l'Aigre-doux*   As a foil for the richness of the feuilleté, and also to inject a note of colour, a well chosen spring vegetable is essential. If asparagus is either out of the question or out of season I can suggest no better alternative than whole young carrots, which can be treated in exactly the same way. Boil the vegetables until they just begin to soften, drain them and cool by holding under running cold water. This can be done well in advance. Finish their cooking in butter with a generous amount of black pepper, deglaze with sherry vinegar then, over a fairly high heat, add sweet sherry or madeira in small amounts until you have the correct amount of sauce—just enough to coat the vegetables.

A cheese board sits perhaps a little uncomfortably in this menu, and I would happily leave it out, particularly at lunch or if dinner has started late. Any cheese served should be mild and firm in texture—English, Swiss, maybe even Scottish.

The best thing about the popularity of cheesecake in this country is the easy availability of fresh cream cheese. It can be used to great effect in savoury dishes, but is a marvellous alternative to ice cream when mixed with an equal volume of double cream and a little caster sugar (in which it is worth keeping a vanilla pod), and chilled. Strawberries or raspberries are excellent with this, but in the month of June this little salad is delightful. Marinate wild or alpine strawberries (*fraises des bois*) in lemon juice and vanilla sugar, then just before serving mix in equal amounts of chopped apricots and cherries.

A white wine of great quality is not appropriate for the highly flavoured salad, so choose instead any wine of high acidity and large bouquet. Crépy is the Savoie white which most closely approaches the style of the Swiss wines from the other bank of Lac Léman. The Côteau de Lutny of M Goy has a slight sparkle which is most appetising.

The main course is patently difficult company for red wine. The Côte de Beaune provides the desired combination of suppleness, finesse and slight sweetness to come through the complex sauces without being distorted as a dry wine, for instance Bordeaux, would be. The Beaune Marconnets of Chanson Père et Fils is a little light in colour for the fine year of 1971, even for a Beaune, but it has a good, concentrated pinot flavour and shows plenty of class.

The wine which I have chosen for the dessert is something of an oddity, being made from the roussette grape which, in the Savoie and the neighbouring Bugey (which carries VDQS appellation), usually produces a dry wine. I can only assume that when I bought this Montagnieu it had some bottle age—difficult to tell when no vintage date is given, as is common practice in this region. At any rate the wine had a distinct sweetness which made it indistinguishable from a Côteaux du Layon but without the intense sweetness of Quarts de Chaume or Bonnezaux. Vouvray would be a good alternative.

# Menu   2:7

Moules Camargaises

Sancerre, Clos des Roches,
Vacheron 1979

---

Médaillons de Volaille Fines Herbes

Champignons à la Crème de Ciboulette

Château Carbonnieux,

---

Rigottes de Condrieu

Sancerre, Lelièvre 1978

---

To end this section of the book on a very seasonal note here are
two menus, the first of which is as obviously designed for warm
summer days as the second is for winter. It is not my fault that in
this country you can no longer tell the difference between the
two seasons. Things are not what they were even in France,
where people go around muttering *'il n'y a plus de saisons'* every
time a cloud passes from April onwards. In fact the seasons are
much better defined on the Continent than in this country,
where we remain the rheumatic, bronchitic prisoners of the sea.
We can always pretend, and try to produce meals which are as
good as holidays.

*Moules Camargaises*  It is curious how many people have no
qualms about mussels while remaining very wary of other
shellfish, snails and frogs' legs. I think it must be that their
gorgeous colours and tremendously evocative smell of the sea
make them irresistible, and in this recipe the colour contrasts
are emphasised by a bright red tomato sauce and brilliant green
chopped basil.

Make a fresh tomato sauce by melting a chopped onion in
olive oil with plenty of garlic. Add a little white wine then peeled,
seeded tomatoes of good colour. Season, add a sliver of lemon
peel, and cook gently for 20 minutes. Meanwhile open the
scrubbed mussels by steaming in a large pot with a glass of white
wine. The heat must be high and the mussels cooked no longer
than it takes to open them all. Shake the pot vigorously a few
times during the few minutes this process takes. Pour the liquid
obtained into a cup to allow any sand to settle. Arrange the
mussels on the half-shell in the serving dish and keep warm.
Over a fairly high heat incorporate the mussel juices into the
sauce until there is no excess liquid. Adjust the seasoning then
blend or sieve the sauce. Add a generous amount of chopped
basil and pour it over the mussels. Plenty of sauce is needed, but
it must not be watery or insipid in flavour. If basil is not available
substitute parsley and a good dessertspoonful of *pesto alla
Genovese*, of which a fairly satisfactory version is easily obtained

in jars from Italian delicatessens. A slightly more refined version can be made by using butter rather than oil and blending with cream, but to my mind it is less good and the sauce has a disturbing habit of tasting rather like canned tomato soup.

*Médaillons de Volaille Fines Herbes*   Chicken Kiev is one of the most delectable of foods, but it is a little tricky to prepare and very difficult to cook in any quantity without an enormous pan for deep frying. The following method makes the final preparation much easier to handle, and loses none of the succulence of the chicken breasts. Guinea fowl can be substituted for chicken with great effect if you are unhappy about the quality of chicken available.

Remove the whole chicken breasts (one per person) from the bone and discard the skin. Cut the breasts into 'medallions' about 2.5 cms thick, then marinate for two or three hours in milk in which you have previously made a hot infusion of fresh tarragon and allowed to cool. Dry the pieces, dust them with flour seasoned with salt, black pepper and chopped tarragon, dip them in beaten egg then good breadcrumbs not too finely ground. Fry the pieces quickly, about three or four minutes each side, in clarified butter. Serve on individual plates surrounded by the following sauce, or your own alternative. Do not pour the sauce over the chicken or the crisp breadcrumbs will be no longer so. A simple green vegetable or buttered peas is all that is needed by way of accompaniment.

*Champignons à la Crème de Ciboulette*   This rich little sauce is easy to make and is suitable for many meat dishes. It is not meant to be served copiously. For the *médaillons de volaille* the most suitable mushrooms would be *chanterelles (girolles)* or *morilles,* while *cèpes* would be good with beef or game. Sadly we shall usually have to settle for button mushrooms *(champignons de Paris),* but these are adequate. Choose mushrooms which are closed to avoid blackening the sauce.

Fry the mushrooms briskly in butter until they are golden brown, then remove them from the pan. Deglaze with tarragon vinegar and a touch of white wine or vermouth, and add a small amount of chicken stock and a shaving of lemon peel. Simmer for a minute or two to assemble the flavours, adjust the seasoning then add a good quantity of double cream. Boil down to the correct consistency then mix in a teaspoonful of *moutarde a l'ancienne*. Improve the colour with tomato purée if necessary, and add a large quantity of chopped chives. Pour around the meat, the mushrooms strewn on top.

Summer in France is the time for goats' cheeses, but it is also the perfect time to eat the *Rigottes de Condrieu,* a small, almost fresh cows' milk cheese from the Rhône valley. They have a bright orange rind which is no more than a covering of dust, and a distinctly sour taste accompanied by a perfume of soft fruits. Packed individually in cellophane, they are occasionally seen in this country.

It is all too easy to resist choosing a sorbet when a choice of dessert is offered, so simple and uncomplicated do they seem. That is their charm, and they should be made from fruits which are very acidic with an assertive flavour. Lemon and blackcurrant are best, and I have chosen the latter because it might be an amusing way to end a meal where two Sancerres have been served. Wines made from the sauvignon grape often have a distinct bouquet of blackcurrant *leaves,* and the taste of the fruit itself will probably seem surprisingly different.

It is extremely unorthodox to frame a fine, mature wine with two young wines only tenuously related, but as will by now be clear this type of structure intrigues me. There is little to choose between the two Sancerres, although I think the 1978 of Gerard Lelièvre takes the palm by virtue of its immense flowery nose and slightly fuller flavour. The Graves, though not one of the region's élite, was a beautiful wine when I last tasted it in 1976. It was rich and honeyed, almost sweet, the semillon grape beginning to show through the sauvignon, and I am certain that it will have kept splendidly. Some bottle age is necessary in a Graves when set beside Sancerre, because in youth it can seem stony and austere, lacking the blousy qualities which make the Sauvignons of the upper Loire so popular.

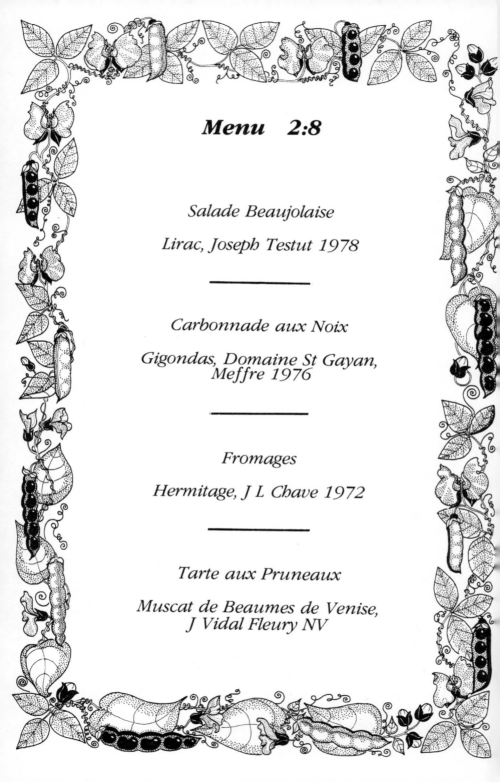

# Menu 2:8

Salade Beaujolaise

Lirac, Joseph Testut 1978

———

Carbonnade aux Noix

Gigondas, Domaine St Gayan,
Meffre 1976

———

Fromages

Hermitage, J L Chave 1972

———

Tarte aux Pruneaux

Muscat de Beaumes de Venise,
J Vidal Fleury NV

I give this menu partly as an excuse for a tasting of the most robust of Rhône wines, the only claim which I can make to originality being the *tarte aux pruneaux*. This exercise is obviously best kept for a winter's evening, but it would be very welcome on the bitterly cold June evening in Edinburgh on which I am writing these words. Strangely enough I can see scores of swallows from my window, but I must assume that they are flying around to keep warm rather than anything else.

I also happen to like this hearty sort of food, and wish that more people would adopt this style of cooking for unambitious dinner parties. It is easy on the digestive system, and it seems to me more logical when costs have to be contained to combine such a menu with assertive and interesting wines, which need not be expensive, rather than partnering more elaborate food with second-rate and frequently insipid wines from famous areas.

*Salade Beaujolaise*    This salad goes under various names, but in Lyon, where I believe it has its origins, it is currently called *beaujolaise*. I suspect that this name may suit the proprietors of the *bouchons,* who like to make much of the Beaujolais connection, and not without reason, because the best Beaujolais I have drunk has been served in open carafes in bouchons. These must be the only restaurants in the world where the quality of the house wine matters, competition for custom being fierce and word of mouth the best form of advertising.

Essentially this is a green salad garnished with bacon, hard boiled eggs, walnuts and croutons. Chop streaky bacon roughly into cubes *(lardons),* and fry these in a good quantity of olive oil. When the bacon is cooked pour in wine vinegar to taste and allow it to evaporate almost completely. You may then add a little walnut oil *(huile des noix),* which should be used with discretion as it has a very pronounced flavour which can be overwhelming.

You may use any good crisp lettuce, but batavia is best. Spinach or rocket add interest, and fresh herbs can also be added. Mix the greens with chopped hard-boiled eggs and top quality walnut halves, preferably fresh rather than kiln-dried. The walnuts from Grenoble are regarded as the best in France. Dress the salad with the tepid bacon and its vinegar-flavoured oil and add hot croutons fried in oil or bacon fat. In Lyon you would probably be served *pain de campagne,* or possibly even rye bread *(pain de seigle),* both of which are gaining in popularity as true *pain viennois* becomes more difficult to find even in Lyon, for so long the heart of French bread-making.

*Carbonnade aux Noix*   I can think of no objection to walnuts followed by more walnuts, but here, even if you are the most dedicated of walnut eaters, you would be hard pressed to recognise them if you had never encountered the pickled variety before. These are harvested in July when the shell is green and soft, and the nut barely formed. If you have ever handled them at this stage in their development you will know of their propensity for staining the fingers black, and it comes as no surprise that when pickled whole in vinegar they turn jet black (see *Good Things* by Jane Grigson for details of how to pickle walnuts yourself). They are good as pickles, but also make a wonderful addition to beef stew. My own preference is to use them in a *carbonnade à la flammande* already gloriously blackened with Guinness.

Brown the beef in a little oil or dripping, then add chopped shallot and carrot, and deglaze with a bottle or two of Guinness. Top up as necessary with beef stock. Add a good bouquet garni including celery leaves, a whole onion or two and the contents of a jar of pickled walnuts, drained but not washed. Cook the stew gently for a long time, being careful both now and when serving to disturb it as little as possible for fear of breaking the walnuts. Adjust the seasoning before serving and thicken the stew if you wish with either *beurre manié,* or cornflour. As an accompanying vegetable serve glazed turnips, carrots or salsify. If you choose to serve potatoes the best option is to bake them in their skins and serve with parsley and chive butter. Suet dumplings with fresh herbs are even better as a source of calories.

This would be a good opportunity to serve well matured English cheeses, but the Hermitage will stand up well to strong French cheeses. I would choose a Tomme de Savoie if possible, and might choose to contrast it with the sweet, nutty flavour of Emmental or Jaarlsberg. These are cheeses which can be eaten in quantity, even nibbled on their own, allowing a good look at the wine and facilitating a comparison of all three reds if you have cunningly held back a little of the first two.

That there are nuts in the *tarte aux pruneaux,* almonds in this case, may come as less than a surprise. Prunes are under-rated, as I think this method demonstrates. The biggest and best come from California and are available everywhere. The almonds must be good and fresh.

Soak the prunes overnight in white wine, choosing if possible a medium sweet middle-Loire wine such as Vouvray, with a few peeled almonds. The next day poach the prunes in the wine with enough vanilla sugar to make a light syrup when the cooking is complete. Remove the prunes, and finish the glaze after first decanting it if there is much debris. A little redcurrant jelly helps both colour and texture, but avoid reducing the glaze to the point where it will become a sticky caramel as it cools.

Bake a 1-cm thick shell of pâte-sucrée until the edges just begin to brown, and allow it to cool—this can be done the day before. Halve the prunes as neatly as possible, removing the stones, and arrange them in a cartwheel fashion on the pastry base. Sprinkle toasted flaked almonds between the 'spokes', dress with the glaze and finish baking in a hot oven. Serve cold, *without cream.*

There are two regions of France which are entirely self-sufficient in wine, in that they produce top quality wine of every type (there is no shortage of regions self sufficient in quantity). These two areas are the Loire where, however, the reds might be considered to fall short of the very highest quality, and the Rhône, which goes one better by offering a variety of different types of red wine, any of which on its day and in the appropriate context, can rival the other great red wines of the world. The opportunity of structuring a meal so that all the wines from such a region can be tasted is worth taking, both because it is logically satisfying and also because it provides a feel for the wines of the region which is difficult to obtain simply by trying individual wines. The best way to get to know them is, of course, to visit the vineyards, but the present exercise is quite educational, showing not only what different grape combinations can produce within the same region but also the influence of bottle age.

You can never compare wines fairly when they are served in sequence with different foods, even if they are from the same grape and made in the same year, so, unless major concessions are made in terms of the menu—for example by serving several wines with a single course or cold buffet—the general rule must be that the wines should provide a logical and interesting sequence and should be appropriate to the food.

The absence of a sparkling wine from the menu is perhaps a glaring omission in view of my comments above. The Rhône does, however, produce a very excellent *méthode champenoise* wine at St Peray, a small village next door to Cornas on the right bank of the river just west of Tournon. In this wine a strong, distinctive flavour is combined with great finesse and a reliable mousse. It would not readily be mistaken for champagne, but its quality is obvious. M Pierre Darona made a fine example in 1978 which would make an ideal aperitif.

The problem, if it is one, with Rhône reds is their enormous scale and alcohol content. At least eight people would therefore be required to dispose of one bottle of each of the wines suggested. Lirac and Gigondas can reasonably be compared, lying fairly close together and employing similar varieties of grape. Of the two the Lirac is usually softer and fruitier, often a little sweet and going towards Chateauneuf du Pape in style, while the wines from Gigondas often seem thicker. The latter can be unpleasant in youth but both of these wines come on rapidly, and seldom improve beyond ten years. M Testut's Lirac is a beautifully made wine from the great 1978 vintage, already

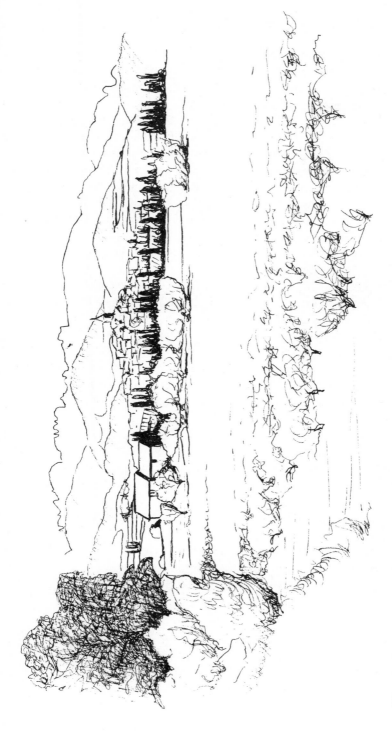

*Vineyards near Vacqueyras, Vaucluse, with Dentelles de Montmirail in the distance.*

round and drinkable but capable of greater things in a few years. The 1976 Gigondas from the Domaine St Gayan is, however, fully mature now and very fine with an almost delicate, refined bouquet unusual for the region.

It is difficult to write about Hermitage without quoting Professor Sainsbury's description of it as 'the manliest of wines', for the simple reason that it is so apt. This is an heroic example, which when young was thoroughly undrinkable. It was black in colour and sooty in flavour, leaving a rather acrid aftertaste. The tannin is now slipping away to show a wine of power and great quality, which will keep for many a year. These are therefore massive red wines, but the subtler, and in my opinion finer, reds from Côte Rôtie and Cornas (see Menu 3:7) could be studied in the same way.

On one of my frequent visits to the offices of Vidal-Fleury at Ampuis, during our sojourn in Lyon, I made a point of discussing their excellent Muscat de Beaumes de Venise, which I found delightful but which also seemed to me to be rather obviously fortified with alcohol in spite of the appellation *vin doux naturel*. I was assured, with a certain amount of tut-tutting and eyebrow-raising, that the fortification of such wine was out of the question, but I have since learned from Learmonth and Master's fine book on the wines of the Rhône that it is usual to arrest fermentation with pure alcohol. When the wine is very young this is easily detectable. I can only assume that since in this case Vidal-Fleury are simply *negociants* acting for a *viticulteur* in Beaumes de Venise they are a little unfamiliar with the vinification methods. This does not, however, prevent them from choosing a good one, less heavy than some with a beautifully fragrant muscat perfume. The concentration and fruit are ideal for the *tarte aux pruneaux*, but if you cannot finish the bottle at one sitting do not despair, for it keeps for a week or two in the refrigerator if you replace the cork. Could any wine be more sweetly named?

# PART 3

## The Special Occasion

# Introduction

We have never been much given to feasting in these islands, at least not for several centuries. Even Christmas Day is seen as mortification of the flesh as much as an excuse for a genuine gastronomic treat. The fault may lie with our austere Protestant tradition, particularly in Scotland where the weather also makes it likely that any form of outdoor festivity will turn into an ordeal. Nor must we forget that village life is almost extinct even in rural areas, and as we have lost touch with the land the instinct to celebrate its goodness to us seems to have died. The difference in attitude in France and the Latin countries is striking for the visitor unaccustomed to such an approach to life in the community. Christmas, New Year's Day, Easter and 14 July (Bastille Day) are all major events in the French calendar, celebrated *en famille* in the grand manner, and other special days, religious and secular alike, are liable to similar treatment. First a visit to *Les Halles* or the local *traiteur* to procure the oysters, smoked salmon, beef fillet or pheasant, then the silver and glassware are polished and the fun begins in the kitchen while father rummages in the cellar. On 14 July every village in France then has a fireworks display and a free dance in the village square, and on a balmy evening there is the chance to have coffee and liqueurs in your favourite café.

This kind of public display, particularly as an expression of religious or political fervour, is not to everyone's taste, but I am sure that the desire to find an occasional excuse for self-indulgence is healthy. Surely a visit from friends or family is all the encouragement the enthusiastic cook needs to spread his or her wings. For many the menus of the first two sections may have to suffice, whether for lack of time, money or expertise, and I hope my point is proved that it is possible to regale your friends with such food and wine without shame. But if these strictures do not apply I hope that the approach outlined in this last section will encourage you to develop your own uninhibited *cuisine gourmande*. Failures are bound to occur, and must be carefully analysed, but are less likely if you adhere to the principles of quality of ingredients, simplicity and boldness of approach and the avoidance of complication for its own sake.

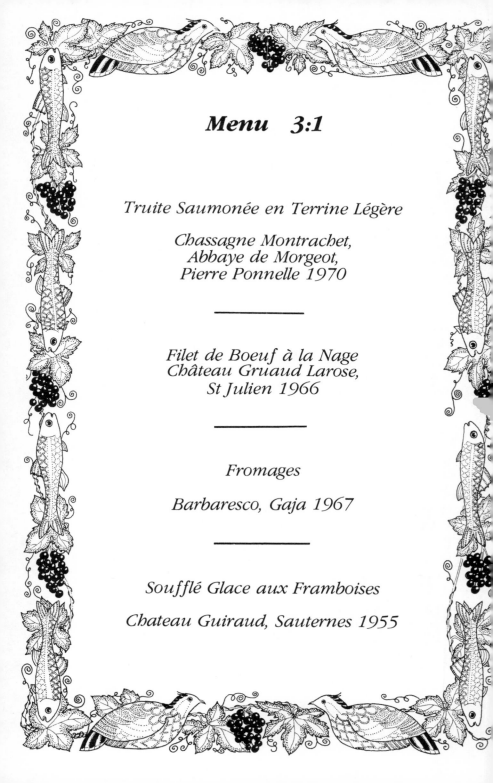

# Menu 3:1

*Truite Saumonée en Terrine Légère*

*Chassagne Montrachet,*
*Abbaye de Morgeot,*
*Pierre Ponnelle 1970*

---

*Filet de Boeuf à la Nage*
*Château Gruaud Larose,*
*St Julien 1966*

---

*Fromages*

*Barbaresco, Gaja 1967*

---

*Soufflé Glace aux Framboises*

*Chateau Guiraud, Sauternes 1955*

The principal ingredients and overall structure of this first *menu gourmand* create an impression of a grand, one might almost say classical, style. The quality of the raw materials is brought out, however, by somewhat unorthodox means. There is a good deal of work involved, but it is possible, even desirable, to do most of this well in advance. There is very little element of risk apart from the careful attention needed to cook the beef perfectly, and these dishes are very pleasing for the cook, particularly since there are a great many options open in both first and main courses for alternative flavourings and accompaniments. Though grand in appearance the meal is much lighter and easier to digest than one might anticipate.

To strike, if I may, an unashamedly parochial note, let me suggest this menu as a celebration of the incomparable Scots larder, and as my own contribution to our national cuisine. It may serve no useful purpose to labour the point that though our little country is blessed with an unlimited supply of the best fish, beef and game in the world we have acquired an entirely justified notoriety for one of the world's most lamentable of cuisines. That this was not always so—it would be astonishing if it were, given the deep tradition of friendship between Scotland and France—is illustrated beautifully by F Marian McNeill in *The Scots Kitchen,* a most readable and entertaining book. A renaissance is long overdue, but the signs of change are evident in Edinburgh, where the increasing interest of the populace in the quality of foodstuffs has led to a remarkable improvement in the basic food shops such as fishmongers and butchers as well as in the delicatessens. There is as yet regrettably little evidence that this mood of optimism and interest has been caught by the restaurateurs.

*Truite Saumonée en Terrine Légère*  The discrepancy in price between salmon and sea trout will forever remain a mystery to me, for if anything the smaller fish is the better of the two. Either would do just as well for this dish, which is really a cross betweeen an aspic, a mould and a terrine, all of which have their particular drawbacks. The aspic retains the texture and flavour of the fish but few people enjoy eating the jelly, and the textures always strike me as slightly unpleasant. Moulds or timbales of fish are apt to be bland, while pâtés and terrines of fish suffer from a heaviness of texture and flavour quite inappropriate to the streamlined elegance of the fish. The solution is simple—flakes of salmon trout set in a rich cream sauce based on a lightly jellied fish stock and flavoured with herbs and cucumber.

Make a clear, strong fish stock with bones of sole or turbot, onion, carrot, leek, fennel, lemon peel and peppercorns. Strain the stock. For six people you will need about one pint of stock and 1½ lbs (750 g) fish. Remove the fillets of fish from the bone, leaving the skin attached, season them and plunge them into the boiling stock. Remove the pan from the heat and set to cool in the refrigerator. This will give you an idea of how much natural jelly is in the stock as well as allowing the fish to absorb the flavours with no danger of over cooking. When cool remove the fish after gently warming the stock if it has set, skin it and break the flesh into large flakes. Add double cream to the stock until it forms a rich, heavy sauce, adjust the seasoning and add a little gelatine melted in hot water. No precise advice can be given about the quantity required, but you are very unlikely to need more than 2 or 3 teaspoonfuls of powdered gelatine per pint of sauce. Test the quantity by putting a little on a saucer and chilling it. When the sauce is almost cool but not set add the fish and herbs (tarragon or fennel) and mix gently. Oil the insides of individual soufflé dishes lightly, place a decorative cucumber ring or sprig of tarragon in the base of each and fill with the mixture. Cool in the refrigerator overnight and serve turned out onto individual plates. Surround each *timbale* with a crescent of sauce or salad. The flesh of peeled, seeded tomatoes, roughly chopped, lightly seasoned with salt, pepper and fresh basil, mixed with diced cucumber and a little lemon juice, is both visually stunning and provides a refreshing contrast.

*Filet de Boeuf à la Nage*   I have declared elsewhere that good beef requires only the application of heat, any other interference tending to detract from it. This is a challenge that few serious cooks could resist, and I myself have been wrestling with the problem for a long time, because beef so often seems appropriate to an occasion but the prospect of roasting it simply seems boring, while the only other viable idea, Beef Wellington, is over-elaborate and seldom convincing. Too much can go wrong—soggy textures, muddy flavours. It was with considerable trepidation, however, that I decided on the following method of half-poaching, half-roasting the meat. It does solve another problem arising with *boeuf à la mode* (braised in red wine), where the exquisite sauce is often let down by the boiled beef. Using the following method the beef is not like either roast or boiled beef, but the whole dish is light, aromatic and given to a highly refined accompaniment. It may at least be a relief to the reader that the beef is not served with custard, nor is it covered with snow: *'à la nage'* just means 'swimming'.

Success lies in the basic sauce, which is like that of *boeuf à la mode*. Marrow bones, pork knuckle and trotters are browned thoroughly with onions, carrots and celery (most important), and a bottle of red wine poured over. Cover with water, add whole garlic cloves, an onion stuck with a clove, peppercorns and a bouquet garni. Cook gently for three hours, strain and reserve overnight. Degrease thoroughly before further use. Remove all fat from a whole beef fillet, coat it lightly with olive oil and lots of black pepper. Brown the meat thoroughly and fiercely. Meanwhile bring the stock to a fast rolling boil in a deep pan just wide enough to take the beef. Poach the beef in the stock for 15 minutes, remove the beef and set it to dry at room temperature. It will continue to cook gently. The stock must not have been salted up to this point or the beef would now weep juices. Now salt the stock and keep it warm.

In a separate pan parboil the vegetable accompaniment— small white turnips, artichoke hearts, carrots, salsify, asparagus in your chosen combination. Deglaze the beef sauté pan with tarragon vinegar and make a caramelised sauce with Malmsey madeira, then expand it with a little of the stock. Add the parboiled vegetables and allow them to exude a little liquid into this thick, sweet sauce. Turn the by now tepid beef in this sauce to coat it thoroughly, then finish cooking for 10 minutes in a hot oven. Add the stock to the sauté pan, or vice-versa if necessary, adjust the seasoning and thicken with arrowroot. The sauce is deliberately voluminous, and should be clear, dark brown and shiny. Covering the serving platter with sauce, arrange the vegetables neatly round the periphery, including whole garlic cloves rescued from the stock-pot. Finally carve the beef, season the slices and place it in the centre of the platter. The accompaniments can be served either on the same dish or separately. No better complement could be imagined than individual brioches stuffed with a suitable meat and/or mushrooms. I have used pigeon breasts turned in butter with preserved *cèpes,* finished in a thick cream sauce based on the beef stock, the pigeon meat and mushrooms (both of which must remain almost raw) roughly chopped. A truffled sauce would also be good. Alternatively you may use home made ravioli stuffed with a truffled forcemeat and poached in the sauce.

I am not so partisan as to suggest that Scotland's cheeses are fit company for her beef and salmon. Any fine cheese will, however, be feasible, and the Barbaresco might like to find itself partnered by a ripe, creamy Gorgonzola.

The Scottish climate is not entirely inhospitable to fruit trees, but is in certain areas more suited to soft fruits. The raspberries and strawberries from the plain of Strathmore known as the Carse of Gowrie are the equal of any. This strip of alluvial soil on the north bank of the Tay between Perth and Dundee is so covered with raspberry canes that at first glance they could be taken for vineyards. The area is also favoured by an abundance of game, including the wild duck and geese which rest here on their migratory paths.

The soufflé glacé is something of a forgotten dessert, but the chef of the Auberge de Savoie in Annecy has perfected the art. It is a dense, custard-based mousse, frozen and served in slices with lightly whipped cream to which you may add crumbled, home-made praliné.

The sea-trout is flattering to white wines, and you may therefore choose from a wide range, but a fine white burgundy is most appropriate. 1970 was a rather uneven year for whites, but the best have aged with elegance, and Pierre Ponnelle's Abbaye de Morgeot is very fine.

A classic cabernet sauvignon is unbeatable with the beef. Chateau Gruaud Larose, particularly in that fine year 1966, is a round, generous claret with a full, sensuous but refined perfume. It has been subject to disparaging remarks by wine writers, nobably Edmund Penning-Rowsell, on account of its full, rich, style, and this seems to me quite unfair. These are qualities that claret often lacks, and I have no hesitation in rating this the best 1966 I have drunk.

For the cheese, particularly if it is strong, a change of grape would be welcome. A fine Rhône, perhaps, or why not surprise your friends with one of Italy's best reds. Gaja's Barbaresco is complex and silky, a wine of great finesse and 'breed'.

The sweet wine has, therefore, to stand up to these very formidable precedents, and an old, honeyed Sauternes will sit nicely with the raspberries. I bought this 1955 Château Guiraud in unlabelled bottles without capsules from a merchant in Edinburgh whose assurances that the wine was genuine were good enough for me. It is luscious, not in the least faded, and could be nothing other than a *Premier Cru* from Sauternes.

# Menu  3:2

Langoustines Beausoleil

Seyssel, Clos de la Taconnière,
Georges Mollex, NV

—————

Caneton au Poivre Vert

Pommes de Terre à la Sarladaise

Bonnes Mares, Jaboulet Vercherre
1969

—————

Fromages

Viña Pomal, Reserva Especial 1953

—————

Oeufs à la Neige

At first sight you may reasonably wonder if this meal might turn out to be rather 'pale' and perhaps lacking in definition. That this is not so is because the duck is cooked in a way unfamiliar to us in this country, and is accompanied by a rich, savoury dish of potatoes. The creaminess of the first course and dessert, the one reflecting the other, are therefore quite appropriate, but it is best to avoid serving over generous helpings of either of these.

*Langoustines Beausoleil* The name of this quite straightforward seafood salad is a complete invention occasioned by the way I arranged it on individual plates the first time I served it. I propose it as an illustration of how to rethink a 'standard' dish, in this case avocado with prawns. There is nothing wrong with the usual way of serving this—the prawns in sauce mayonnaise or marie rose heaped on the half avocado—but it can be served in a more elegant fashion and made more sumptuous by substituting *langoustines* (scampi), lobster or salmon for prawns. This is important in Great Britain, where large, juicy prawns are seldom available, and if they are have usually been cooked. Raw ham or smoked salmon make an interesting contribution by rounding out the otherwise sharp and, in the case of the avocado sometimes slightly bitter, flavours.

The basis of the dish is a tomato flavoured sauce mousseline. Make a purée of fresh tomatoes by chopping the flesh roughly then reducing it over a moderate heat with a dash of sherry vinegar and, if liquid is needed, a drop of fino sherry. Strain the purée through a fine sieve, season it generously with salt, black pepper and a pinch of cayenne, and allow it to cool. Mix this into a well seasoned mayonnaise containing lemon juice, and add rather less than an equal volume of lightly whipped cream. Marinate the langoustine tails in lemon juice with white pepper. Halve and peel the avocados (in that order), then cut transversely into crescents. Sprinkle with lemon juice to prevent discolouration, then wrap each in a thin slice of *jambon cru* or smoked salmon. Make a pool of sauce on each plate, then arrange the shellfish and crescents of avocado alternately around the edge so that they break from the free edge of the circle like the rays of the sun. Serve with toasted brown bread.

*Caneton au Poivre Vert* The notion that duck has to be smothered in a sweet sauce with fruit, with or without cream, is so deeply ingrained that it almost comes as a shock to realise that it can be a thoroughly savoury meat to be accompanied by an essentially brown sauce. It is true, however, that the success of this method, which could hardly be left out of any book paying more than lip service to the Nouvelle Cuisine, depends to a great extent on the type and quality of the duckling. Wild duck is best, for this is really a roasting method most applicable to game birds. The best version of this *classique nouvelle,* (if I can be allowed to use such a term), which I have encountered was the *canard sauvage au poivre vert* at Fernand Bise's lovely restaurant 'Le Cottage' in Talloires, that most enchanting spot on the shores of Lake Annecy. More commonly, the *canard de Barbarie* is employed in France. It is better for this purpose than our typical Norfolk duck, having darker flesh and rather less subcutaneous fat. The *caneton Rouennais* is even better, partly because these birds are not usually bled, and this with their naturally dark flesh makes them quite similar to wild duck. The trouble with British ducks is the absence of blood from the muscle. Generally, therefore, I reserve this recipe for the winter months when wild mallard and teal are plentiful.

Remove the legs from the ducks and reserve them for the *cassoulet de pois chiches* of Menu 1:5, or for making your own *confit de canard.* Next remove the breast section on the bone by disjointing from the carcase at the shoulder with a sharp knife, then cutting along the edge of the ribcage using kitchen scissors. You will be left with the backbone and ribcage with wings attached, and the giblets. Make a brown stock by first frying the pieces of carcase till they are golden brown, reducing with sherry then simmering for about an hour with an onion stuck with a clove, carrot, celery, garlic and black peppercorns. Strain the stock and reduce it by half.

If using wild duck smear softened butter over the skin of the breasts and coat with freshly ground black pepper and a little salt. If using a domestic duck all that is needed is a light film of oil, as the duck will have ample subcutaneous fat. Roast the breasts skin uppermost in a very hot oven for 15–20 minutes depending on size. Towards the end of this cooking time you may paint the skin with honey and more freshly ground pepper.

When they are done—that is, the skin is golden but when pricked the juices are quite bloody—cover loosely with aluminium foil, reduce the oven to very slow, and leave the breasts to rest like this, the oven door ajar, for 10 to 15 minutes. The flesh will by then have become a beautiful even pink and some juices will have appeared in the roasting pan. Put the breasts to keep warm, degrease the roasting pan and deglaze with sherry vinegar and brown sherry or madeira, then add the duck stock and a tablespoonful or two of green peppercorns, without first draining them. Simmer for a few minutes while carving the breasts from the bone. Slice the flesh diagonally into

long thin *aiguilletes* and arrange these on the plate in a fan-shape. Finish the sauce by incorporating cold butter into it in little parcels. This is called 'mounting' *(monter)* a sauce with butter and it can be done in two ways. The easiest way is to beat the sauce constantly as it boils vigorously, adding the butter gradually. Alternatively you can add the butter off the heat, swirling the pan gently in a circular motion. The aim of this is not to thicken the sauce—that could be done with arrowroot if desired—but to make a smooth, rich emulsion. It will not hold for any length of time and therefore should be poured over the meat straight away.

*Pommes de terre à la Saladaise* Sarlat-le-Caneda is a little market town in the heart of the Dordogne, whence come duck, goose and truffles. It is very easy to form the impression that truffles are vastly over-rated, because they can easily become 'lost' in an already complex sauce, and the truffles themselves are relatively tasteless when cooked. To get the best out of them marry their complex, intriguing perfume to a simple but excellent basic ingredient (meat, fish or vegetable) and cook them in such a way that the flavour is imprisoned. Colette liked truffles roasted whole in the embers of a wood fire, and I'm sure so would I. You will see that it is not silly or wasteful to use truffles in a potato dish. Quite the reverse.

Choose firm, waxy potatoes and slice them about 3 mm thick. Press a garlic clove into softened butter and smear this round the inside of a large fireproof gratin dish. Arrange the potato slices in layers, seasoning each layer generously with salt and black pepper, adding slices of truffle from time to time (one medium truffle is plenty for a dish large enough for eight to ten people). Pour a good quantity of duck or goose fat over the potatoes, season the top layer and cook in a medium oven for about 1½ hours. It is well worth reserving duck fat from a previous occasion for this purpose, but if you are cooking domestic duck you can roast the duck breasts on a rack over the potatoes so that the fat drips onto them, their first hour's cooking having been accomplished with a little butter. Then transfer the duck breasts to rest in a separate pan to collect the juices for the sauce. It is difficult to decide whether the truffle juices should be added to the sauce or to the potatoes near the end of their cooking. I suggest you go for broke and do the latter, because I have never known anything reveal the truffle flavour so well as this *gratin Perigourdin.*

Winter cheeses are called for here. Roquefort would be perfect but its effect on the wine is iniquitous. Stilton or any other not too strong blue, a tomme, Cantal or Comté. Walnuts would be appropriate, and oatcakes or Bath Oliver biscuits.

*Oeufs à la neige* suggests a mountain of snow-white meringues coated with egg custard *(crème anglaise),* while *oeufs à la nage* brings to mind the image of meringues swimming in a sea of custard. Either version is acceptable, though I prefer the latter. Spoonfuls of stiffly beaten egg whites are poached in milk with vanilla sugar, and the milk in them used to make a rich egg custard. Serve cold.

Of the various white wines from the Savoie described in this volume this Seyssel is by far the best. The Mollex family seem to own two vineyards which produce indistinguishable wine—the Clos de la Taconnière, which is easily obtainable in the beautiful food shops of Annecy, and the Clos de la Péclette, which features on the wine list of nearly every restaurant in the region. Within a few weeks in 1980 we paid 20 francs for a bottle in the *Restaurant Garcin,* 30 francs in the (one Michelin star) *Auberge de Savoie,* both in Annecy, and 40 francs in *Le Cottage* at Talloires. In each case the wine was underpriced, so very beautiful it is, but the prices provide an interestingly accurate indication of the quality of the restaurants. I have no words to describe this wine without invoking crystal clear mountain streams and Alpine perfumes, but it is worth noting that it is a *big* wine, full of flavour, complex and long on the palate.

The main course seems to me to be made for as fine a burgundy as you can find. For some strange reason—perhaps by association with the poor wines made in Bordeaux that year—the magnificent 1969's remain undervalued. The wines of Chambolle Musigny are to me the most likeable of burgundies, and the Bonnes Mares vineyard is my favourite. This 1969 from Jaboulet Vercherre is rich but stylish, deep, long and dry at the finish. The colour is that unmistakeable burgundy garnet, best appreciated in the glass of the person sitting opposite you at the table, for somehow it seems to catch and reflect the light as it goes through the wine in a diagonal away from the eye.

The wines of the Rioja are tremendously popular at the moment by virtue of what Gault et Millau designate their *rapport qualité-prix.* They are, however, being drunk too young. The strong, oaky nose, which is not in itself unattractive but is quite unsubtle, fills out with age into a voluminous and very 'French' perfume. If I say that this Viña Pomal special reserve is the equal of any first growth claret I have drunk, and better than most, it will be a better service to it than trying to describe it in words. Quite simply a great wine.

No wine with the custard? Probably not, though here, if anywhere, is the place for the medium sweet wines, such as those of the middle Loire, which are otherwise difficult to accommodate in any meal, or a chenin blanc from California, for instance the 1979 Almaden.

# Menu  3:3

Crévettes au Petit Suisse

Le Meursault de Ropiteau 1976

———

Friture de Phaisan

Petits Choux aux Foies

Château Figeac, St Emilion 1964

———

Fromages

Château La Mission Haut Brion,
Graves 1962

———

Bavarois aux Oranges

Château Coutet, Barsac 1950

At this point the menus have reached a level of complexity which renders introduction or apology superfluous. It is safe to assume that anyone wishing to cook in this way has a love of the kitchen and enough technical competence not to be daunted by the seeming grandeur of the dishes, and will be rewarded by the discovery—true in all disciplines—that things are often simpler than they might seem at first sight.

*Crévettes au Petit Suisse*  To whet the appetite for the richness of the main course here is a truly 'nouvelle' salad which is in itself satisfying as well as appetising. Think carefully about the proportions of the main ingredients, for it is most important not to 'lose' the prawns in the greenery. The salad should be based on good, crisp lettuce or any mixture of suitable leaves (try Chinese cabbage), garnished with good, large prawns (or *langoustines*) and chopped avocado as a desirable but optional extra. Make the dressing by mixing Petit Suisse (the number obviously depending on the number of people: about one per four people is enough) with single cream and a little lemon juice until a light, liquid consistency is obtained. It must not be too thick or the salad will not be satisfactorily coated, and if further thinning is necessary it would be best to use a little stock made from the prawn shells. Adjust the seasoning and finish with prepared Dijon mustard, adding it gradually until the correct degree of piquancy is present, and add tomato purée for sweetness and colour if it seems indicated. Chopped fresh tarragon and chives may be added either to the dressing or to the salad, which must be mixed thoroughly at the last minute. Serve with *grissini*.

*Friture de Phaisan; Petits Choux aux Foies*  Pheasant is the most difficult of fowl to roast. The line which divides a moist, perfectly cooked breast from a dry disaster is a fine one indeed. The problem cannot be solved, as in the case of pigeon, partridge or even grouse, by cooking the meat rare, for it must be cooked through. Such delectable and expensive flesh is too good to risk, and in fact it can be treated in the same ways as chicken breasts with sometimes astounding results. The legs can be used to give great character to a simple dish such as the *cassoulet aux pois chiches* (Menu 1:5). This approach offers much more scope for imaginative cooking than resorting to a casserole braise.

The title *'friture de phaisan'* is deliberately vague, because you may choose to copy the recipe for deep-fried *medaillons de volaille* (Menu 2:7) or, as I myself prefer, cook it exactly like chicken Kiev, that is to say the breasts removed whole to include the first wing joint, skinned, stuffed with chilled herb and garlic butter, coated in egg and breadcrumbs and deep fried for 10–15 minutes. Do not be nervous about this seemingly short cooking time—the fat must be very hot so that the flesh cooks to the point where the butter in the middle has just melted.

If pheasant is prepared in this simple way an extravagant accompaniment is in order. A crisp, fresh vegetable is essential, but so is a rich sauce, and so you may stuff little puffs of choux pastry (chosen instead of puff or brioche for its lack of substance) with a vegetable, mushrooms or, as I suggest, chicken livers in a rich, spicy sauce.

Soften a chopped shallot or two in butter until golden, then add the seasoned livers with shredded garlic and a good quantity of lemon juice. Poach the livers quickly over a fairly high heat, adding dry white wine from time to time just to keep the mixture moist, turning the livers carefully without breaking them. They should be just cooked but still pink inside as the sauce becomes an essence—this takes but a few minutes. Expand the sauce with double cream, adjust the seasoning and add chopped chives. Stuff the *petits choux* carefully and heat through quickly in a hot oven. It will be plain that the livers and the pastry may be cooked well in advance, assembled and reheated at the last minute, but be sure not to overcook the livers in the first place. Incidentally, if the cream is omitted the livers can be served as an effective accompaniment to a *salade beaujolaise* (Menu 2:8).

The cheese course in a meal of this nature is an essential resting place to allow the pace to slacken and the conversation to expand. Attention falls naturally on the wine, and the only requirements of the cheese board are that the cheeses should be fine, but as far as possible friendly to wine; the very best of French cheeses are therefore appropriate to all of these concluding menus, served with oatcakes and Bath Olivers if good French bread is not available. My own favourite cheeses are Epoisses, Langres and the best of all goat cheeses—Sainte Maure—a cheese which transcends the seemingly limited appeal of ordinary goats' milk cheeses when genuinely 'fermier' and fully mature. The extraordinary Vacherin Mont d'Or also deserves mention, although it is a cheese with such a penetrating flavour that I would never serve it with red wine, choosing instead a lively, strong white such as Côte de Jura blanc. The true Vacherin is Swiss, although similar versions bearing the same name are made in the Savoie. It is a fat, creamy cheese surrounded by pine or cherry bark which permits it to ripen to an almost liquid consistency after only about six weeks. It is a winter cheese which, it is said, should be eaten with a spoon.

Fools, syllabubs and mousses are always popular, so it is surprising how seldom one encounters the most sublime pudding of this genre—*crème bavarois*. Based on a fruit flavoured custard mixed with whipped cream and egg whites, and set with a little gelatine, the result is a light but extraordinarily rich and fruity dessert. Orange and apricot are the best fruits to choose, and you may serve it with pouring cream and toasted almond flakes.

There is something about the hints of cheese and mustard in the salad dressing which seems to demand white burgundy, or at any rate the roundness and fruit of the *pinot chardonnay* grape. Yet it is not the ideal partner for a fine old white burgundy, requiring a measure of acidity. The house of Ropiteau has for some time been marketing a generic Meursault of outstanding quality (notably in 1969). This 1976 is vivacious, concentrated and very stylish. We have not seen the best of it yet, but for the moment it will do perfectly for our purposes.

A rich, round St Emilion with finesse could not be bettered with the pheasant. Mention of the 1964 Château Figeac fills me with nostalgia, for like one or two other wines in this book it came into my cellar from the closing-down sale of that most philanthropic of wine merchants, Joules of Stone, when they were taken over by a large brewery consortium. Their bottlings of claret were impeccable in spite of the lack of confidence generated by the labels and capsules. I opened my last bottle of this Figeac in France in April 1980. It seemed overjoyed to have been taken home to meet its fate, and my tasting note simply says 'poignantly good'.

The 1964's are generally still in good condition, but the variation in quality is as marked as it ever was. A much more even year was 1962, my own favourite if only because it was widely available at reasonable prices in the early 70's when I became interested in wine. In those days people were consuming the 62's frantically in the conviction that they (the wines) would be over the hill by 1975. Not so, because the best of them had a balance and natural sweetness which has seen them gracefully enter the 80's, all except those which had a little too much acidity. La Mission Haut Brion was one of the biggest wines of the vintage which, even as late as 1980 did not seem totally ready, even in half bottles. The warmth of flavour is quite typical of the red Graves wines, which generally did well in 1962 (Château Pape Clement is another for which I have very fond memories).

Do not be tempted to think that the orange flavour of the *bavarois* makes it unsuitable as a backgroud to a fine sweet wine, because it is rich enough and the flavour attenuated enough to go perfectly with the most silken and elegant of the sweet Bordeaux. Chateau Coutet is, in youth, slighter than most wines whose natural sweetness derives from the *pourriture noble,* but in the best years it has a balance and elegance of style which permit it to last almost indefinitely. We came across this marvellous 1950 on the wine list of the Grand Hôtel de Bordeaux in Tours, a good but rather staid hotel-restaurant in front of the station, in whose cellars one would not expect to find such treasures. If there is none in your own cellar the 1971 is just about ready and the 1975, though far too young at present, will soon become magnificent.

*Château Petrus, Pomerol.*

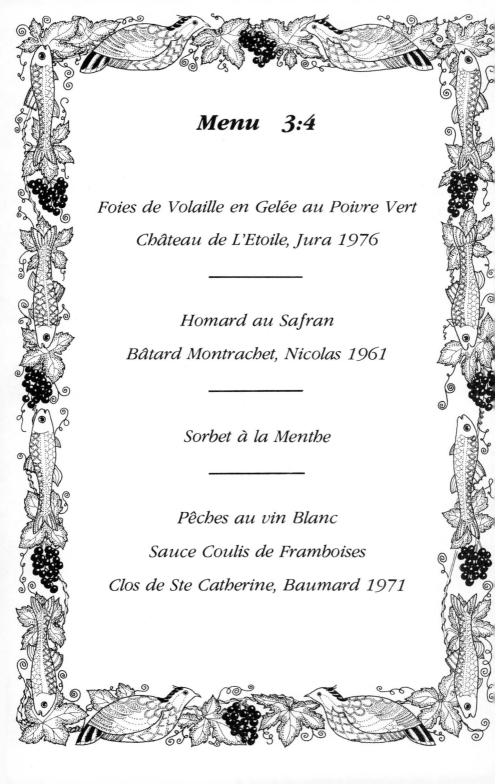

# Menu   3:4

Foies de Volaille en Gelée au Poivre Vert

Château de L'Etoile, Jura 1976

———————

Homard au Safran

Bâtard Montrachet, Nicolas 1961

———————

Sorbet à la Menthe

———————

Pêches au vin Blanc

Sauce Coulis de Framboises

Clos de Ste Catherine, Baumard 1971

The introductory comments to Menu 3:3 notwithstanding, there is no denying that this menu needs something by way of an apology—more, perhaps, than I can afford, since I must confess that though I have no reservations about the individual dishes the courage to put them together has so far been lacking. At best this may be a glimpse of the Nouvelle Cuisine in 1984, at worst a joke reminiscent of the absurd Italian Futurist cooking of the pre-war years; but I think it would be fun.

The theme is not difficult to discern. Each course, with the sorbet excepted, consists of a very lightly cooked delicacy set in an intense, shining sauce (jellied in the case of the first course).

*Foies de Volaille en Gelée au Poivre Vert*    Fresh duck and goose livers, whether fat or otherwise, are not generally available to us in this country, and even in France are prohibitively expensive. We could, however, make much greater use of chicken livers than the ubiquitous *pâté de foie de volaille,* which is to my mind the worst possible way to present them. In a subtle sauce they make an excellent filling for a feuilleté or other pastry (see Menu 3:3), or cooked whole they make an interesting addition to mixed salads. For an alternative to pâté here is an adaptation of Michel Guérard's *Foie gras frais en gelée de poivre.*

Clean and dry the livers, which should be of the best quality available, being careful to keep them intact but cutting away any green spots (this is bile from the gallbladder and has a pronounced bitter taste, but is quite harmless. The green colour does not indicate that the livers are spoiled.) Season them well with salt and black pepper. In a sauté pan bring a little water or stock and a knob of butter to the boil, reduce the heat, add the livers and cook at simmering point, covering the pan. Turn the livers once during cooking. They should remain pink in the inside, requiring only a minute or so on each side. Drain them and allow them to cool.

The jelly is a very simple sweet-and-sour sauce set with gelatine. In a saucepan dissolve three teaspoonfuls of powdered gelatine in about ½ pint (500 ml) cold water by bringing it slowly to the boil. In a second pan dissolve a tablespoonful of sugar in four tablespoonfuls of wine vinegar (scale up the quantities as necessary) and simmer until this sauce caramelises to a rich brown colour. Pour this syrup into the dissolved gelatine and add a teaspoonful of Armagnac or Cognac. Set the pan in a basin of crushed ice and stir it until the jelly begins to 'take'. At this point mix in a good quantity of washed green peppercorns.

Arrange the livers in the form in which they are to be presented. An irregular form, whether on a platter or on individual plates, offers pleasing artistic possibilities, but if you prefer the whole dish can be set in a terrine or soufflé dish and unmoulded later (this is necessary if it is to be held for a day or two). If 'sculpting' you simply arrange the livers as you wish then pour the almost-set jelly over and around them. Serve with toast and garnished with leaves of cress or matchsticks of raw carrot and spring onion.

*Homard au Safran*   Assuming that the point of departure is a cooked lobster (allowing one of medium size for two people), this recipe is just as simple as the previous one. *Langoustines,* prawns and crayfish can all be used in the same way. Split the lobster and crack the claws. Remove the meat and reserve it, and extract the coral, which is not required for this dish and can therefore be served on canapés with the aperitif (for which purpose champagne if possible).

Make a light, fresh but well flavoured stock from the shell, including in the *bouillon* a little white wine, onion, celery or leek, fennel, carrot, garlic, lemon peel and crushed white peppercorns but no salt. Half an hour's simmering is enough. Do not remove scum, because, as explained in the introduction, I am convinced that it helps to clarify the stock, and occasional stirring is also beneficial. Strain the stock into a tall receptable which will allow it to be decanted off its sediment, and set it aside to settle and cool. With any luck you will find that the stock is almost clear, but if it is cloudy you will have to clear it with beaten egg white, starting from cold and gradually heating to just below simmering point, then pass the stock through muslin and reduce it by boiling to about half its initial volume. It will almost certainly not require salt, but the flavour may need to be intensified by the judicious addition of sherry, madeira or armagnac and lemon juice. Make a separate infusion of saffron and decant this into the sauce, which should now have a deep orange colour and an intense aroma. Thicken with arrowroot until the sauce coats the back of a spoon, then add the flesh of the lobster and heat gently for a minute or so. Garnish with chives and a little warm, seasoned tomato flesh with chopped basil.

There are interesting alternatives for both the sauce and the accompaniments. The saffron may be replaced by shreds of stem ginger preserved in syrup, and this is wonderful when served with a *riz pilau* containing toasted almonds or sautéed cashew nuts, and home made chutney or Michel Guerard's *confiture d'oignons à la grenadine* to replace the tomato. With the saffron sauce a fresh vegetable is preferable to rice, for example asparagus tips, artichoke hearts or fresh peas with a little mint. If you are using prawns or *langoustines* a 'cassoulet' of great originality could be made by mixing the finished dish, tomato included, with previously cooked haricot blancs and a leavening of lemon juice and fresh herbs. This would be best as a first course, and could be served cold or tepid.

The only conceivable cheese appropriate to this meal would be *fromage frais à la creme,* or Petit Suisse, but it would almost certainly be unwelcome, whereas a tangy, not sweet sorbet would be sensational, particularly on a hot summer's day. To counteract the richness of the meals served (and expected) in the best restaurants many French chefs are offering these 'savoury' sorbets between courses. Mint is an especially good flavouring for this purpose—the *nouveau trou Normand.*

A sorbet consists of a sugar syrup with a fruit or other flavouring, fast-frozen while being continually stirred.

For six to eight people, dissolve 100 g sugar in 500 mls water and bring to the boil. Chop a handful of mint leaves and infuse with half of the syrup for fifteen minutes. Strain the infusion back into the syrup and add a small glass of crême de menthe. Freeze in a plastic bowl, stirring in from the sides as crystals form, until a dense, almost solid consistency is reached. Freeze for at least a few hours, and remove from the freezer about fifteen minutes before use.

The dessert needs little description but there is no harm in emphasising that the aim is to bring out the natural perfumes of the fruit—not to mask them. If the peaches are slightly underripe (better from the point of view of texture) peel them by scalding, halve them and poach for a very short time in a small quantity of white wine with sugar and lemon juice. If the peaches are ripe turn them, peeled, in the syrup for seconds only, and allow them to cool. Make a purée of carefully washed and dried raspberries in the blender with sugar and lemon juice then pass the purée through a fine sieve. Serve cold.

Many experimental combinations suggest themselves with this menu, for instance sweet wine, possibly German, with the chicken livers, red (Beaujolais or Beaune) with the shellfish, but it is equally suitable for an orthodox sequence of fine whites.

There are two distinct styles of wine made at Château L'Etoile, and this is problematic since they are not distinguished by the label (incidentally, I am not referring to the 'vin jaune' versus the normal white). Within a few months in 1980 I tasted one wine which was indistinguishable from very fine white burgundy and another, bearing the same label and vintage date (1976) which was much more reminiscent of a montilla or light fino sherry. The answer to this problem is to serve it, as here, with a dish for which either is appropriate. I would guess that the difference between the two wines had nothing to do with storage, but that the first was indeed made from the pinot chardonnay which is planted to a limited extent in the Jura.

The lobster demands a full wine with no more than a trace of sweetness. Nothing could surpass a top-class white burgundy of one of the many fine vintages of 1960's. The 1961 Bâtard Montrachet from Nicolas is quite splendid. Should you choose to finish the sauce with ginger a younger wine, 1976 for example, would be less in danger of being swamped.

The Clos de Sainte Catherine is a vineyard in the Côteaux de Layon owned by the Baumard family. Reluctant though I am to give away what must be a secret (the wine remains underpriced) I can think of no wine more obviously designed for this dessert. It is a delicate but exquisitely sweet wine which stays young almost forever.

*Côte Rôtie—the vineyards of Vidal Fleury and de Boisseyt on the Côte Blonde. Peach trees in the foreground.*

# Menu  3:5

*Timbales au Gruyère*

*Château de Riquewihr,*
*Riesling Vendange Tardive,*
*Alsace 1971*

———

*Pintadeau au Petit Suisse*

*Petits Pois aux Champignons*

*Château Leoville Lascases, St Julien 1960*

———

*Salade aux Noix*

*Château Mouton Baron Philippe,*
*Pauillac 1961*

———

*Soufflé au Citron*

*Wachenheimer Luginsland Riesling Spätlese,*
*Dr Bürklin-Wolf 1971*

There are many ways of introducing a note of originality into a meal without recourse to all-out modernism. Here is a menu which owes little to 'nouvelle' methods, although it does embrace the principle of avoiding weighty, flour-based sauces, but it is sufficiently different in structure from most orthodox menus to be at once interesting and, in a sense, classical. The first and last courses are close enough in concept to suggest a symmetry which can be reflected in the choice of wine. I have chosen to frame two fine clarets with two rieslings which in themselves provide an illuminating comparison.

*Timbales au Gruyère*  The great advantage of serving timbales or ramekins as a first course is that they allow you to present a hot, interesting dish without tiresome last-minute preparations. This is in contrast to most hot fish dishes, which really must be cooked and sauced just before serving. Timbales are full of possibilities both in terms of the basic ingredient and the 'petite sauce' which accompanies them. They are also very attractive in appearance, and I would always aim to have them on the table in individual portions before inviting the guests into the dining room.

This is one of the very simplest of timbale recipes but one of the most satisfying by virtue of its direct, savoury taste which ensures that they are appetising where more elaborate versions can be destructive to the appetite. For six timbales bring ½ litre (1 pint) milk to the boil, season with salt, white pepper and nutmeg, and in it melt 100 g (4 oz) grated Gruyère. Beat two whole eggs and three egg yolks until frothy and pour the hot milk on to this mixture very gradually, beating to form a custard. Coat the inside of the ramekins with a film of butter or tasteless oil and fill each to the brim with the custard mixture. Bake in a bain-marie in a moderate oven until the custard is set (about 30 minutes). Serve surrounded by the sauce and crowned with a sprinkling of chopped chives or parsley. Many different types of sauce suggest themselves. In summer a fresh tomato sauce, sieved, highly seasoned and flavoured with basil or oregano, in winter a brown, meaty gravy made with the guinea-fowl giblets. At all events heavy, creamy sauces are best avoided, although a fish sauce, even sauce Nantua, would be interesting.

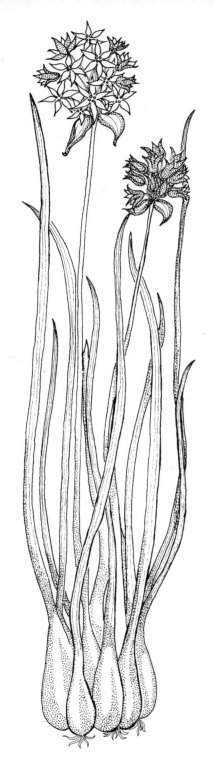

*Pintadeau au Petit Suisse*
Since battery methods for rearing guinea-fowl were introduced they have become enormously popular in France, and appear frequently on restaurant menus both because they are cheap and ostensibly more interesting than chicken and because they fall easily into four portions per bird. Quality has inevitably suffered, though not to the same extent as in the case of battery chickens because the birds are not usually fed on fish meal. The effect of all this is to have encouraged the view that the guinea-fowl is a superior chicken, whereas it is a kind of domestic pheasant, at its best, and scarcely distinguishable from its close relation, when half-wild. When living in Dundee, where the world's finest game is far from scarce, we were lucky enough to hear of an enlightened farmer who had a small number of just such fowl. Indeed they had to be shot, so wild were they, and they were at least as big as any pheasant—and better than any such that I have ever tasted. Normally they are slightly smaller than pheasant and this makes them easier to roast successfully in spite of sharing the tendency to dry out in cooking, since they can be cooked more quickly.

This recipe can be applied equally to pheasant, and indeed to chicken. The stuffing, based on Petit Suisse, is not a stuffing at all in that it is not for eating, its purpose being to moisten and flavour the flesh from within, and by melting during cooking to provide the basis for a complex sauce.

For each bird (you will need two for six to eight people) mix two Petits Suisses with a little softened butter, a chopped shallot, a little chopped ham or bacon, some fresh tarragon, a squeeze of lemon juice and generous seasoning with salt and black pepper. If possible add the liver, chopped, and pack this stuffing into the cavity. Rub the skin all over with softened butter and coat with black pepper, and roast in a hot oven for 25–30 minutes, until the juices are still just showing pink. Reduce the oven to cool, leave the door ajar and allow the bird to rest for 15 to 20 minutes. Collect the pan juices, keeping the guinea-fowl warm in the cool oven, remove as much grease as possible and finish the sauce with port, double cream and chopped fresh tarragon or parsley. If much coagulated cheese is present the sauce may be passed through a fine sieve. It may be garnished with *tomates crues concassées*.

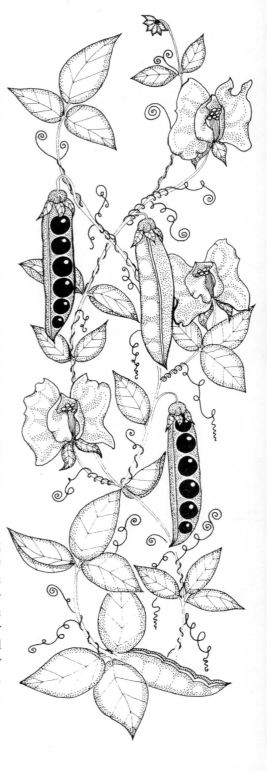

*Petits Pois aux Champignons* We British are right to cook tender young peas for the shortest possible time before serving them with butter and fresh herbs (such as mint), and the French are wrong to scoff at our custom. But, as Sir Roger de Coverley was wont to remark when called upon to arbitrate in industrial disputes on his estates (would that he were here today to take charge of anglo-french relations), much may be said on both sides, for remarkably few people in these isles realise how delicious and satisfying a dish of braised peas can be. The French, the Italians and the Spaniards all adore them, frozen peas are perfectly suited for this treatment, and there are no worries about timing—so why do they never appear on restaurant menus?

The French way of braising peas in butter with lettuce hearts is wonderful, but mushrooms—especially the more exotic *morelles* and *chanterelles*—go particularly well with guinea-fowl. Sauté the mushrooms very briskly in a mixture of oil and butter until they are well browned, reduce the heat and add a chopped onion with some extra butter, and cook gently for a few minutes. Boil the peas, whether fresh or frozen, in salted water for a few minutes, drain them and add them to the mushrooms, mixing them well together with extra butter and a little stock made from the giblets. Braise, covered, in the lower part of the oven for at least 30 minutes. Finish with a little double cream, lemon juice and chopped parsley.

Since cheese has been used in both of the preceding courses a mixed salad would be preferable to a straightforward cheese board, and would provide textural contrast to the rest of the meal. Base the salad on an unusual green such as endive, include a generous amount of walnuts and a cheese of character—feta, goat, Stilton or Roquefort. Use a little walnut oil in the not-too-vinegary dressing. Good French bread is essential.

In my view mousses and other such desserts are served more often than they ought to be for the simple reason that they are easy and can be made well in advance. They are not usually appropriate for important dinners, being both limited in interest and bad for wine. Soufflés, on the other hand, repay the trouble of making them and the risky matter of putting them in the oven at just the right moment. Here, too, the impact of the anti-flour movement is being felt, and lighter soufflés based on a purée of fruit rather than a floury custard are being found to be perfectly satisfactory if enough care is taken in whipping the egg whites. A pinch of salt added at the beginning is helpful, and it is worth avoiding beating the whites too stiff. Lemon soufflé, served straight from the oven, may be accompanied by the apricot glaze suggested in Menu 3:8.

When planning this menu my initial design was to play a trick by serving the German riesling with the first course and the Alsatian with the dessert, a previous experience of a well-aged German wine with the cheese timbales having proved rewarding. However, a preliminary tasting revealed the German wine to be much the sweeter of the two, though they are very similar in flavour, bouquet and concentration.

I am not over-fond of the riesling grape. It seems to produce wines too close to the flavour of the grape, frequently lacking in complexity and length and therefore a little monotonous on the palate. This is true even of these very fine examples, but they are far from dull and provide considerable interest in this for them unusual setting.

The inclusion of the 1960 Château Leoville Lascases is an undisguised act of self-indulgence. It is my favourite château, and in this 'off' year (see Menu 3:8 for discussion of lesser vintages) it produced a wine which continued to improve in an extraordinary fashion throughout the 70's. In 1980, when, on New Year's Eve, I drew the cork from my last remaining bottle my sadness was relieved only by the beauty of the wine.

A claret of unusual, gentle beauty can only be followed by one of its more muscular siblings. After the Lascases the '61 Mouton Baron Philippe will seem very assertive, but in face of the strong cheese content and inevitable vinegar in the salad it will not appear coarse. Even at 20 years these 1961's need to be opened several hours in advance, whereas no more than half an hour would do for the Lascases.

# Menu 3:6

Bisque de Crustaces

*Meursault Charmes, Louis Jadot 1969*

———

Ris de Veau Aimée

*Beaune Grèves, Pierre Ponnell 1959*

———

Feuilleté aux Poires

*Château Rieussec, Sauternes 1961*

Of all the menus in this volume this is my favourite, the one which most stimulates a salivatory glow of anticipation. The reason is not simply that this is the style of eating which will leave me exhilarated and satisfied but not in the least over-full; it also has great personal significance for me, the sweetbreads being the dish which I cooked when my wife brought my daughter, Aimée, home from hospital to change our lives in the most delightful way.

*Bisque de Crustaces*  When I hear others talking about how they love soups and make them frequently I always feel guilty and a little ashamed, because I have never enjoyed soup and still seldom do, even though I admire the best examples (*soupe au pistou,* for instance) and realise that they are both economical and nutritious. Fish soups, however, are different. Fun to prepare and capable of great subtlety and refinement, these are my favourite fish dishes. They also complement wine in a way that no other soup can. Many different styles of fish soup are possible, the choice depending on the occasion and the rest of the menu as well as the fish and vegetables available. I have no preference among the four basic types: rough chowder or broth; dense, Mediterranean bouillabaisse with pounded shells, croutons and rouille; delicate, creamy soup of freshwater fish; or a rich, heady bisque of shellfish.

For a bisque you may start with either raw or pre-cooked shellfish (lobster, prawns, langoustines, or crab: the crab is in no way inferior). I have little to add to the excellent method given by Jane Grigson in *Fish Cookery.* If the fish is raw, cook it gently in butter and oil until coloured. Remove the flesh and return the shells to the pan (start from this point if using cooked fish). Add a little chopped onion and garlic, diced carrot and celery or leek, and stew gently until the onion is golden. Add a handful of pudding rice, allow it to absorb some of the butter, then deglaze with brandy or pastis (flaming is unnecessary). Add a glass of dry white wine and top up with water or fish stock. Stir in a few black peppercorns, some lemon peel and a sprig of fennel, and a few tomatoes, seeded but not peeled, if a pink colour is preferred. Simmer for about an hour, remove the largest pieces of shell, then strain the soup through a fine sieve, pressing well down on the debris to force through as much of the vegetable and rice purée as possible. Adjust the seasoning, stir in any coral you may have reserved, and the chopped meat, and thicken generously with double cream. Sprinkle a little chopped parsley on the surface before serving with toast or good wholemeal bread.

*Ris de Veau Aimée* Sweetbreads are still regarded with considerable suspicion in the British Isles, probably because even when people learn that they represent either pancreas or thymus they are none the wiser. When we served lamb sweetbreads to my mother-in-law she ate them dutifully then remarked that she had never thought she could eat 'these', but would not enlarge on what she thought they might be. It puzzles me greatly how the two organs have come to be thought interchangeable, having neither anatomical nor functional similarities. The pancreas, the long, rather rectangular and firmer type, is a digestive organ lying in the abdomen, while the thymus, or throat sweetbread, lies in front of the heart and is a most important part of the immune system, particularly in the young animal where it is quite large. The confusion seems to me even more remarkable in view of the fact that the thymus is infinitely superior as food. Allow one entire veal sweetbread per person. The following method can also be applied to lamb sweetbreads which are more often available, but the soaking and blanching can be omitted, and you must allow several per person.

Soak the sweetbreads in acidulated water for a few hours then blanch them for five minutes in boiling water. Allow them to cool then remove as much of the surrounding membrane as possible without allowing them to fall apart. Dust them with seasoned flour and sauté them briskly in clarified butter. Within a few minutes they will be a beautiful golden brown colour. Flame with calvados or brandy, then add small amounts of sweet Madeira, marsala or sherry over a high heat, allowing each addition to evaporate and caramelise slightly, until you have a rich brown sauce. Add a few slivers of lemon peel and some lemon juice early in this process. Season again with black pepper then transfer the sweetbreads with their sauce to a covered, pre-warmed dish and put them in a cool oven to rest for a maximum of 20 minutes. If they exude much juice the sauce may have to be boiled again before it is poured over the individual sweetbreads, which may be garnished with matchsticks of spring onion and carrot.

Almost any vegetable can accompany this dish but starch—potatoes or rice—is unthinkable. I suggest Chinese cabbage stir-fried in butter with raw ham and spring onion, or *petits pois à la française* (braised in butter with lettuce hearts).

There is no particular reason not to have cheese, but I think I would prefer to omit it unless a single fine cheese such as an Epoisses is available.

The sweet can afford to be fairly substantial, indeed it is the perfect occasion for *pâtisserie*. Pears cooked first in red wine with cinnamon and cloves until almost caramelised go well in a large feuilléte spread first with a light layer of crème patissière or frangipane. But any beautiful tart or pastry will be suitable.

The bisque demands the finest, 'biggest' and most voluptuous of white burgundy, and I have chosen this 1969 Meursault Charmes of Louis Jadot for just these qualities. It is frankly sweet. When serving it with salmon I was once asked, only half jokingly, why I was serving Barsac.

White burgundy would also be a good choice with the sweetbreads, or a fine riesling from Alsace or Germany (but not if preceded by white burgundy). As is usually the case with these intense, sweet sauces the most suitable red wine to choose is from the best vineyards of the Côte de Beaune. The 1959 Beaune Grèves of Pierre Ponnell illustrates how this seemingly lightweight wine can age beautifully in fine years by virtue of its balance of sweetness and acidity. If cheese is to be served the opportunity exists for showing a Côte de Nuits of equivalent age and quality, a Vosne-Romanée or Chambolle Musigny, or Calvet's superb 1959 Clos de Vougeot.

Pâtisserie is the perfect setting for fine dessert wine, and with puff pastry and caramelised pears an old Sauternes is the wine of choice. Recent vintages of Rieussec have disappointed me, although the 1975 is said to be wonderful, but this 1961 was luscious to a fault.

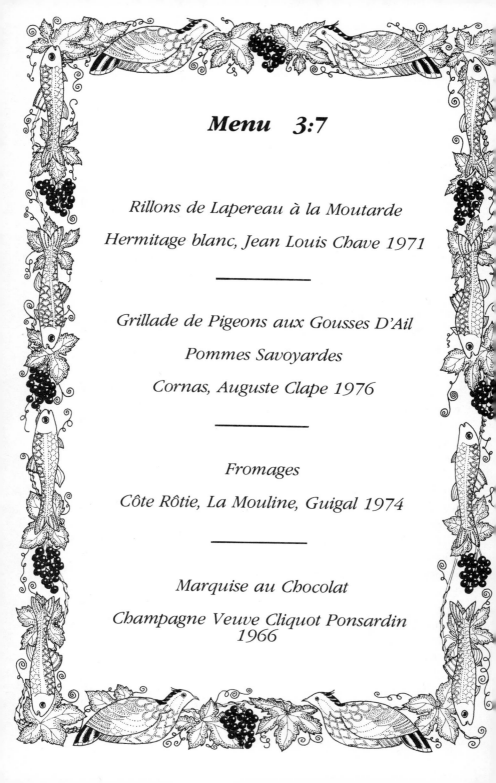

# Menu  3:7

Rillons de Lapereau à la Moutarde

Hermitage blanc, Jean Louis Chave 1971

———

Grillade de Pigeons aux Gousses D'Ail

Pommes Savoyardes

Cornas, Auguste Clape 1976

———

Fromages

Côte Rôtie, La Mouline, Guigal 1974

———

Marquise au Chocolat

Champagne Veuve Cliquot Ponsardin
1966

That game of various sorts figures so prominently in these closing pages reflects both my own enthusiasm for cooking and eating it, and the impact that 'nouvelle' methods have had on our hitherto limited repertoire. Once convinced that game cookery requires lightness of touch rather than endless marination and cooking in gallons of port (not that traditional recipes are to be despised), the way is clear for imaginative and refined recipes. Rabbit and pigeon are cheap, and as well as being generally inexpensive this menu has the considerable merit of allowing a good deal of advance preparation.

*Rillons de Lapereau à la Moutarde*   Rabbit in mustard sauce is one of the best of traditional game recipes, particularly if the rabbit is young. It is also well known that rabbit flesh can be used in rillettes or rillons, although its lack of fat demands that it be used in conjunction with fat pork. In this recipe the two methods are combined to provide a rich, subtle first course which also looks splendid. It should be made at least one day in advance, but should be served at room temperature to ensure that the 'sauce' is not too solid. Compare this recipe with the *truite saumonée en terrine légère* of Menu 3:1.

One whole young rabbit should suffice for six ramekins. Joint the rabbit and season with salt and black pepper. Chop four rashers of streaky bacon crosswise into thin strips and sweat these gently in a generous amount of butter. Add the rabbit and turn it in the butter over a gentle heat until it is well impregnated, but do not allow it to colour. Mix in some roughly chopped onion, celery and carrot, and a sliced clove or two of garlic. Moisten with a glass of dry white wine and cover with unsalted game stock. Cook the rabbit until it is quite tender (about ¾ to 1 hour), remove it from the stock and allow it to cool. Strain the stock and boil it down to about half its original volume with ¼ pint of double cream and a dash of cognac. Add one heaped teaspoonful of powdered gelatine dissolved in a little warm stock. Adjust the seasoning, including a generous dash of grated nutmeg, and stir in two tablespoonfuls of *moutarde à l'ancienne*.

As the sauce cools shred the rabbit flesh using a fork to pull the fibres apart, then fry the rabbit liver quickly in butter, chop it into small cubes and add to the flesh. Mix all the meat with the sauce, which should be heavy, full-flavoured and fairly salty. Pour into lightly oiled ramekins and chill overnight in the refrigerator. Remove them from the fridge at least two hours before unmoulding them, and serve with either watercress or grated carrots and black olives.

*Grillade de Pigeons aux Gousses d'Ail*  The idea of cooking pigeons very briefly so that the flesh remains rare seems to alarm most people who are accustomed to the orthodox view that its meat is so tough that it requires long cooking until it acquires the consistency of the dessert in this menu. Devoid though I am of missionary zeal, (preferring, like a true Scot, to keep quiet about things which others mistakenly disparage), I would be happy if more pigeons, which are abundant and cheap in Great Britain, were cooked like tournedos or kidneys, because the flesh is juicy, tender and delicious. They should not be hung, and are best when the flesh is the colour of steak and the skin light fawn rather than grey/black. Autumn is the best season when they have been gleaning in the cornfields, and a layer of subcutaneous fat indicates a bird of outstanding quality, the equal of any partridge or pheasant. This is the quality of pigeon required for grilling. Allow one per person.

Beginning with a longitudinal cut along the backbone (or underside), bone the pigeons keeping the skin intact, and disjointing wings and legs as you work on each side towards the breastbone, which may be retained by snipping the wishbone and cutting along the ribcage with kitchen scissors, but I prefer to remove the flesh from the breastbone while keeping the overlying skin intact. This is quite a challenge and is in itself considerable fun. Make a good stock from the carcases, including celery, carrot, an onion stuck with a clove, a handful of black peppercorns, and a *bouquet garni* of bay leaf and thyme but no salt. Cook about four unpeeled cloves of garlic per person in the stock for about $1\frac{1}{2}$ hours. Strain the stock, allow the sediment to settle, decant it clear and boil down to less than half its volume with a small glass of armagnac. The flavour should be that of a magnificent game consommé. Thicken with arrowroot dissolved in a little port and reserve while cooking the pigeons.

Season the insides of the pigeons and inside each place a slab of tarragon butter if you have removed the breastbone.

Reconstitute their shape by skewering along the free edge of the skin, rub the skin with softened butter and season with salt and black pepper. Grill under a moderate heat for a few minutes only on each side, then allow them to rest for 10 minutes under the switched-off grill before serving.

Finish the sauce by adding the garlic cloves, which have been fried gently in a little butter until browned, and a handful of chopped chives. There is no need to be nervous about the garlic, which will have lost its pungency and taken on a sweet, nutty flavour. The flesh is extracted by pressing on one end of the clove with a knife. Arrange the pigeons, skewers removed, on a pool of sauce surrounded by garlic cloves. A gratin of potatoes, of which the savoyarde version using cream and gruyère is a good example, provides the perfect accompaniment.

This of all menus provides the setting for a sumptious selection of the best French cheeses including goats' and the strongest soft-ripening varieties. The powerful flavours of the main course would tend to subdue the cheeses and even blue such as Roquefort would be unlikely to overwhelm the Côte Rôtie under these circumstances.

Chocolate and game have an affinity one for the other, and this is worth bearing in mind while building a menu. The *marquise au chocolat,* sometimes also known as *le pavé au chocolat* since it is usually served as a slab cut from the chilled mould, surrounded by a rich sauce (Michel Guérard suggests a coffee-flavoured crème anglaise), is a mixture of dense chocolate sauce with beaten egg yolks and whipped cream, set in a mould lined with sponge fingers. The 'cream' may be studded with candied orange peel.

My enthusiasm for the wines of the Rhône has already been amply expressed (see Menu 2:8). On this occasion the food seems to be made for the wines of the North Rhône, the best of which are increasingly being acknowledged to be among the world's best. Jean Louis Chave's 1971 Hermitage blanc is the most 'tannic' white wine I have ever come across, firm, almost austere, but with great depth of character which will only be revealed with the passage of time.

The two reds are equal in stature, and either would run a first growth claret from a good year very close indeed. Auguste Clape's Cornas is consistently magnificent, a rich, deep-coloured wine which comes on remarkably early. The 1976, tasted in France in 1980, is already delicious, but the 1978, which will almost certainly be one of the greatest of red wines, is still very raw indeed. The flavour of this Cornas is much closer to that of Côte Rôtie than to Hermitage (to which it is more closely related geographically), and both have a distinct resemblance to claret, though with an intensity which claret often lacks and all too seldom replaces with racy elegance. With great age the best Côte Rôtie becomes light and feminine, with a gentle, soft-fruit nose, but in relative youth Guigal's *première cuvée* is full and rich. *La Mouline* is a single vineyard on the Côte Blonde, from which slope the wine is said to be more stylish and elegant than that from the Côte Brune. Guigal was trained by the oldest company of viticulteurs in Ampuis, the *maison* J Vidal-Fleury who also make a very fine wine which takes many years to show at its best. It is generally accepted that *La Mouline* is the best from the Côte, and although the 1974 vintage was far from great, this wine is a revelation for those who remain sceptical about the Rhône.

Chocolate is not kind to wine, and in any case a heavy, sweet wine would not be desirable after such heavyweight reds. It is the French custom to serve champagne with dessert, a practice which I normally abhor. With age, however, some champagnes develop a distinctly chocolate-like bouquet. The 1966 Veuve Cliquot did not hold its mousse well in half bottles, but this is not too disastrous when it is to be partnered with chocolate pudding.

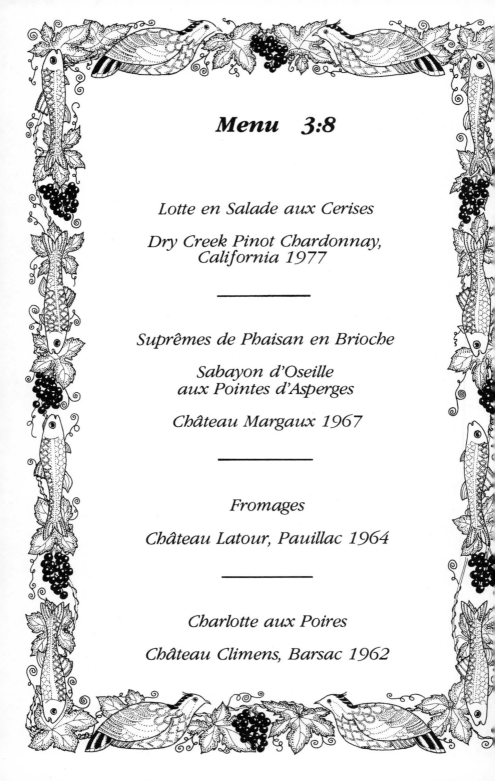

# Menu 3:8

*Lotte en Salade aux Cerises*

*Dry Creek Pinot Chardonnay,
California 1977*

———

*Suprêmes de Phaisan en Brioche*

*Sabayon d'Oseille
aux Pointes d'Asperges*

*Château Margaux 1967*

———

*Fromages*

*Château Latour, Pauillac 1964*

———

*Charlotte aux Poires*

*Château Climens, Barsac 1962*

If my purpose has been made clear the blueprint for this menu will be easily discerned. The difference between success and failure in gastronomy is the same as that between erotic art and pornography: to avoid the latter (if such is your purpose) the essential is to treat the meat with respect—even love. Dress it so that it is enticing, perfumed and beautiful to look at, but aim to reveal its true self. Originality is not in itself a virtue, but invention must be based on knowledge, skill, patient thought and the exercise of a discriminating palate. And a little courage.

*Lotte en Salade aux Cerises*   The essence of both first and main courses is the contrast of sweet and sour, but it must be under very strict control. The salad is quite simple, and any shellfish could be used but monkfish poached gently in a little white wine with seasoning will not make you wish for lobster if it is cooked perfectly—that is, quite considerably underdone. The basic salad ingredient should be red batavia in small shreds with variety in the form of young spinach, sorrel and rocket. The interest comes from the admixture of mushrooms, preferably an unusual variety such as *chanterelles,* cooked *à la greque* then mixed in their turn with pickled morello cherries to form an elaborate dressing.

The method for pickling the cherries is simple and is given by Elizabeth David in *French Provincial Cooking.* Wash a pound of morello cherries (tinned if necessary, but first drained) and pack them into preserving jars to three-quarters full. Boil ⅔ pint (300 ml) of white wine vinegar with 6 oz (150 g) of granulated sugar and a few cloves. When this is cold pour it over the cherries and secure the tops of the jars. Leave for a month if possible. Useful as a pickle in their own right, they can be used in sweet-and-sour sauces of various sorts. Not the least of their attraction is the pretty pink colour they impart to a sauce or salad dressing.

Arrange the salad carefully on individual plates, the monkfish cut into sizeable discs. Scatter freshly chopped parsley as a final garnish.

*Suprêmes de Phaisan en Brioches*   No further discussion of the cooking of pheasant is necessary following my comment in Menu 3:3. Here is another way of encapsulating all its subtleties without damaging the texture. It may be unashamedly 'nouvelle', but there are also echoes of a distant past—game pie with a sweet-and-sour sauce—very medieval. _Plus ça change_ . . . change is more often apparent than real.

A brioche which has been denied its second and final rises is undoubtedly the best type of pastry to choose for any sort of sauced meat, for instance _filet de boeuf en croûte_. It does not deserve its daunting reputation, because it is neither difficult nor particularly time consuming, though it is undeniably messy and, at first, somewhat alarming. Dissolve 0.6 oz dry yeast in ¼ cup of warm water, add a tablespoonful of sugar and set this mixture in a warm place for 10 minutes. Sieve ½ lb (500 g) flour with ½ tablespoonful salt on to a suitable surface, preferably marble. Make a well in the centre and into it break two eggs. Next add the yeast and mix the whole together until the dough begins to hold together (this is the stickiest and most worrying of processes—work as quickly as possible with the tips of the fingers). Let the dough rest for two minutes then knead with the heel of the hand until it becomes elastic. Work in 3 oz (75 g) chilled butter rather gradually in small parcels. When the dough is formed place it in a bowl several times too large, cover it with a towel and leave it in a warm place (70°F, 21°C) until it has doubled in volume. Deflate the dough, knead it thoroughly then refrigerate until it is needed. Remove it from the refrigerator one hour before rolling. Roll it quite thin.

Remove the pheasant breasts from the bone, leaving behind the wing joint and remove the skin. Fry them gently in butter for a few minutes, making no attempt to cook them through. Remove the pheasant, deglaze with wine vinegar then add madeira (Malmsey) until a caramelised sauce has formed. Add a little concentrated game stock until taste and volume are correct and thicken slightly with arrowroot if necessary—the sauce should just coat the back of a spoon. Further complexity can be introduced in the form of preserved fruit—apricots in madeira or the pickled cherries of the first course—mushrooms (ideally _cèpes_), or truffles. Coat the suprêmes with the sauce and allow them to cool covered.

After rolling the pastry and cutting it into sizes appropriate for a _'papillote'_ for each pheasant breast, slice the latter thickly then reconstitute their shapes on the pastry with slices of fruit or truffle interspersed, coat with the sauce (there should be very little) and seal the 'pasties', piercing a hole to let gases escape. Brush with beaten egg and bake in a high oven for five minutes then reduce the heat to moderate until they are evenly golden and the sauce just begins to escape. Wait no longer before serving with a sauced vegetable such as the following.

*Sabayon d'Oseille aux Pointes d'Asperges*   The *sauce sabayon* is a frothy, mousse-like sauce of great richness. It is usually made in the blender but I prefer to leave it rather coarse and variegated. Chop leek, onion and garlic (mostly leek) and cook in butter for about 15 munutes until they are soft. Add ½ glass of port, reduce, then add double cream, salt, pepper and nutmeg. Cook for a further 15 munutes (it can be cooked ahead of time up to this point). Chop a good quantity of sorrel and add it at this stage, cooking it for a few minutes until the sorrel reduces. Beat two egg yolks in two tablespoonfuls of cold water until they are frothy. Reheat the vegetables to just below boiling point then, away from the heat, incorporate the yolks gradually, whipping gently until the mixture becomes quite thick. Pour the sauce around (but not over) the pastries on individual plates, and decorate with asparagus tips turned in butter.

Magnificent though the claret is its health must not be endangered by the more aggressive cheeses, so avoid Roquefort, Munster, Vacherin, Pont l'Eveque and all but the most delicate of blue cheeses.

For an important occasion a fine charlotte is an unsurpassable dessert. Splendid to look at, sublime in texture and full of fruit, nothing shows a fine dessert wine to greater advantage. It is 'only' a *crème anglaise* set with gelatine and whipped cream, and moulded within a palissade of sponge fingers, the fruit being embedded in the custard in layers to enhance the visual impact when it is served in slices. Pour a little clear sauce—a *coulis* of soft fruits or a glaze made with apricot jam, white wine and lemon peel—around each slice.

The 1977 Pinot Chardonnay from the Dry Creek vineyards in Sonoma County is more than equal to the extraordinary demands made on it here. Not only is it required to act as curtain-raiser to the best of Bordeaux, but it must also withstand the mixed bitterness and acidity of the cherries, set as they are against the sweetness of the fish. There is no bitterness in the wine, but it has great generosity of flavour, just enough residual sugar and a distinctive lemony acidity commonly seen in the best white burgundy, especially young Puligny, from which it is to me indistinguishable. The standing of the best Californian wines is no longer in dispute even in France, where the shock waves from their performance in Gault et Millau's 'Olympiade des Vins' in 1979 have not yet settled, reinforced as they were by the announcement the following year that Baron Philippe de Rothschild and Robert Mondavi were to join forces.

Bordeaux vintages are too often judged far too early, or at least the wrong criteria are applied to certain types of wine. In 1960, 62 and, I am beginning to think on the basis of very recent experience, 1969, light, in youth thin and astringent, but essentially healthy and stylish wines were made, which, when enough time had elapsed (at least 10 or 12 years) became gentle, 'feminine' and eminently drinkable wines such as are not made anywhere else. In other years, the critics are too keen to sing the praises of wines which are initially appealing but in the long run fall apart from lack of backbone—or tannin. 1967 and 1964 were both of this latter type of vintage, but these two first growths are atypical. The Margaux was not attractive in youth, lacking flesh and suffering by comparison with the fatter and sweeter wines of the year, but it is now a delight, the perfume and flavour developing miraculously from year to year.

The 1964 Château Latour is different—for long acknowledged the best of a very mixed bunch. It is a large, voluptuous and indubitably great wine, and nothing in all the world is better than great claret.

Of the many challenges to Château d'Y quem's supremacy in the matter of great sweet wine, none runs it closer than Château Climens. Its richness requires time to emerge, and the 1962 is now at its peak, long, intense and beautifully balanced.

# List of Principal Dishes

## First courses or starters

**Menu**

*Beignets au Roquefort*  2:1
Spring rolls with Roquefort and endives

*Bisque de Crustacés*  3:6
Shellfish bisque

*Crevettes au Petit Suisse*  3:3
Prawn salad with Petit Suisse and mustard sauce

*Datiles con Jamon*  1:7
Fresh dates wrapped in raw ham

*Fagioli toscanelli con tonno*  2:4
Tuscan salad of haricot beans with tuna

*Flageolets verts en salade*  1:1
Green kidney bean salad with sausage and sweet pepper

*Foies de volailles en gelée au poivre vert*  3:4
Chicken livers in aspic with green peppercorns

*Gigot de mer aux capres*  1:6
Cold monkfish with capers, sauce mousseline

*Les Huitres grillées*  2:2
Oysters grilled with herbs and breadcrumbs

*Langoustines beausoleil*  3:2
Salad of scampi with avocado and raw ham

*Lotte en salade aux cerises*  3:8
Mixed salad of monkfish, mushrooms
and pickled cherries

*Melanzane fritte all'amatriciana*  1:2
Breadcrumbed aubergine fritters with *amatriciana* sauce

*Moules camargaises*  2:7
Mussels with tomato and basil sauce

*Oeufs en cocotte*  1:4
Baked eggs with cream and chives

*Petits légumes mayonnaise*  1:3
Mixed raw vegetables with lemon mayonnaise

*Rillons de lapereau à la moutarde*  3:7
Ramekins of rabbit set in cream and mustard

*Salade beaujolaise*  2:8
Mixed green salad with eggs, bacon and walnuts

*Salade de Crevettes aux Piments*  2:6
Sweet pepper salad with prawns and raw ham

*Salade d'endives au Roquefort*  2:3
Salad of chicory with Roquefort and walnuts

*Taramosalata*  1:5
Pâté of smoked cods' roes

*Tarte chaude aux légumes*  2:5
Hot vegetable tart with sabayon sauce

*Timbales au Gruyère*  3:5
Ramekins of egg custard with Gruyère

*Truite saumonée en terrine légère*  3:1
Ramekins of salmon trout in jellied cream sauce

## *Main courses*                    *Menu*

*Bacon au poivre vert*  1:1
Bacon steaks with green peppercorns

*Baron de laperau printannier*  2:5
Saddle of rabbit with spring vegetables

*Brochettes d'agneau au romarin*  1:6
Lamb kebabs with rosemary, mustard sauce

*Caneton au poivre vert*  3:2
Roast duck breast with green peppercorn sauce

*Carbonnade aux noix*  2:8
Beef stew with beer and pickled walnuts

*Cassoulet de pois chiches au boudin noir*  1:5
Chick pea cassoulet with black pudding

*Feuilleté aux rognons d'agneau*  2:6
Lamb kidneys with mustard sauce in puff pastry

*Filet de boeuf à la nage*  3:1
Beef fillet in clear sauce with spring vegetables

*Foie de genisse à la ciboulette*    *1:3*
Young beef liver in sweet and sour sauce with chives

*Friture de phaisan*    *3:3*
Pheasant breast fried in breadcrumbs with mushroom
   and chive sauce

*Grillade de Pigeon aux gousses d'ail*    *3:7*
Grilled pigeon with herb butter and clear sauce
   with garlic cloves

*Homard au safran*    *3:4*
Lobster with clear saffron sauce

*Medaillons de volaille fines herbes*    *2:7*
Nuggets of chicken breast fried in breadcrumbs
   with tarragon

*Pieds de porc farcis*    *1:4*
Pig's trotters roasted with sausage stuffing

*Pintadeau au Petit Suisse*    *3:5*
Roast guinea fowl with Petit Suisse and ham stuffing

*Poulet au vinaigre*    *2:3*
Sauté of chicken with vinegar sauce

*Poulet en bourride*    *2:4*
Chicken in Provencal garlic sauce

*Ris de veau Aimée*    *3:6*
Veal sweetbreads in Madeira

*Salmon steaks au poivre*    *2:1*
Sautéed salmon steaks in rich pepper sauce

*Sauté de veau a l'italienne*    *2:2*
Veal stew in Italian tomato and herb sauce

*Suprêmes de phaisan en brioche; sabayon d'oseille*
   *aux pointes d'asperges*    *3:8*
Breast of pheasant with sweet and sour sauce in
   brioches; asparagus tips with sabayon of sorrel

*Tagliatelli salsa di coda*    *1:2*
Fine noodles with oxtail sauce

*Vitello tonnato*    *1:7*
Cold braised veal with tuna and capers

# Desserts

*Note:* As a general rule, full recipes are not given for desserts, the exceptions being *sorbet à la menthe* (not treated as a dessert) and *tarte aux pruneaux*. For the most part these are classic recipes which can be found in comprehensive French cookery books such as *Mastering the Art of French Cooking* by Beck, Bertholle and Child. English translations seem inappropriate.

## *Menu*

| | |
|---|---|
| *Bavarois aux oranges* | 3:3 |
| *Charlotte aux poires* | 3:8 |
| *Clafouti* | 1:4 |
| *Diplomate* | 2:1 |
| *Feuilleté aux poires* | 3:6 |
| *Fromages frais aux trois fruits* | 2:6 |
| *Fruits* | 1:6 |
| *Le Gâteau aux Noix* | 2:3 |
| *Gelati* | 1:2 |
| *Macarons au chocolat* | 2:2 |
| *Marquise au chocolat* | 3:7 |
| *Oeufs à la Neige* | 3:2 |
| *Pêches au vin blanc, sauce coulis de framboises* | 3:4 |
| *Petits fours* | 2:4 |
| *Poires au vin rouge* | 2:5 |
| *Riz a l'imperatrice* | 1:3 |
| *Soufflé au citron* | 3:5 |
| *Soufflé glacé aux framboises* | 3:1 |
| *Sorbet à la menthe* | 3:4 |
| *Sorbet cassis* | 2:7 |
| *Tarte au citron* | 1:1 |
| *Tarte aux abricots* | 1:7 |
| *Tarte aux pommes* | 1:5 |
| *Tarte aux pruneaux* | 2:8 |

# Index of Wines

| | |
|---|---|
| Bonnes Mares | 3:2 |
| Chassagne Montrachet | 1:3, 3:1 |
| Meursault | 3:3, 3:6 |
| Cabernet Sauvignon (California) | 2:5 |
| California | 2:5, 3:8 |
| Carbonnieux (Château) | 2:7 |
| Champagne | 3:7 |
| Chassagne Montrachet | |
| red | 1:3 |
| white | 3:1 |
| Château | |
| Carbonnieux (Graves) | 2:7 |
| Climens (Barsac) | 3:8 |
| de Crémat (Bellet) | 1:6 |
| Coutet (Barsac) | 3:3 |
| de l'Etoile (Jura) | 3:4 |
| Figeac (St Emilion) | 3:3 |
| Gruaud Larose (St Julien) | 3:1 |
| Guiraud (Sauternes) | 3:1 |
| Jolys (Jurançon) | 2:1 |
| Latour (Pauillac) | 3:8 |
| Leoville Lascases (St Julien) | 3:5 |
| Margaux (Margaux) | 3:8 |
| Le Mission Haut Brion (Graves) | 3:3 |
| Montrose (St Estephe) | 2:5 |
| Mouton Baron Philippe (Pauillac) | 3:5 |
| de la Muyre (Jura) | 2:4 |
| de Riquewihr (Alsace) | 3:5 |
| Rieussec (Sauternes) | 3:6 |
| Chinon | 1:1 |
| Climens (Château) | 3:8 |
| Clos Concaillau (Jurançon) | 2:3 |
| Clos de la Coulée de Serrant (Savennières) | 2:1 |
| Clos des Roches (Sancerre) | 2:7 |
| Clos de Ste Catherine (Côteaux du Layon) | 3:4 |
| Clos de la Taconnière (Seyssel) | 3:2 |
| Cornas | 3:7 |
| Côteaux du Layon | 2:1, 3:4 |
| Côte Rôtie | 3:7 |
| Côtes du Ventoux | 1:1 |

Coulée de Serrant (Clos de la) (Savennières)        2:1
Coutet (Château)                                    3:3
Crépy (Savoie)                                      2:6

Domaine de l'Artois (Touraine-Mésland)              2:2
Domaine des Baumards
   Clos de St Catherine                         3:4
   Quarts de Chaume                             2:1
Domaine St Gayan (Gigondas)                         2:8
Domaine de la Tour Bon (Bandol)                     1:5
Domaine de Versailles (Chinon)                      1:1
Dry Creek (California)                         2:5, 3:8

Figeac (Château)                                    3:3

Gamay
   Beaujolais                                   2:2
   du Bugey                                     1:2
   Touraine-Mésland                             2:2
Gigondas                                            2:8
Graves
   Ch Carbonnieux                               2:7
   Ch La Mission Haut Brion                     3:3

Haut Poitou, Sauvignon du                           1:3
Hermitage
   white                                   1:7, 3:7
   red                                          2:8

Jura
   Ch de l'Etoile                               3:4
   Ch de la Muyre                               2:4
Jurançon
   Clos Concaillau                              2:3
   Ch Jolys                                     2:1

Latour (Château)                                    3:8
Leoville Lascases (Château)                         3:5
Lirac                                               2:8
Loire
   Bourgueil                                    2:5

Riesling                                          3:5
Rioja
    Berberana Gran Reserva                         2:4
    Viña Pomal                                     3:2
Roussette de Montagnieu                            2:6

St Emilion                                         3:3
St Estephe                                         2:5
St Joseph                                          1:4
St Julien                                    3:1, 3:5
St Peray                                           1:4
St Tropez                                          1:6

Sancerre                                           2:7
San Dorado                                         1:5
Savennières                                        2:1
Seyssel                                            3:2
Sherry                                       1:5, 1:7
Sauternes
    Ch Guiraud                                     3:1
    Ch Rieussec                                    3:6
Sauvignon
    du Haut Poitou                                 1:3
    Menetou Salon                                  2:2
    Sancerre                                       2:7
Savoie
    Apremont                                       2:4
    Crépy                                          2:6
    Seyssel                                        3:2

Touraine-Mésland                                   2:2

Vacqueyras                                         2:3
Vin de Pays (de l'Ardèche)                         2:3
Viña Pomal                                         3:2
Vendange Tardive                                   3:5
Veuve Cliquot Ponsardin                            3:7

Wachenheimer Luginsland                            3:5

# Glossary

*Aïoli*  A garlic-flavoured mayonnaise, the glory of Provençal cuisine; can be served as a garnish for cold fish, meat or vegetables, or added to a sauce to give character. The essential ingredient in *bourride* (Menu 2:4). It is made by pounding peeled garlic cloves in a mortar to a paste (allow two per person), then mixing these thoroughly with beaten egg yolks (two for six people). Then beat in good Provençal olive oil (500–750 ml, ½–¾ pint) until the sauce is very solid. Season and thin slightly with lemon juice before use.

*Al dente*  Untranslatable Italian phrase to describe the exact degree of cooking necessary for pasta and vegetables, implying that they should remain distinctly resistant when bitten.

*Amuse-gueule*  Literally 'tease the palate', savoury titbits of the chef's invention to be eaten with the aperitif (see *tapas*).

*Anchoïade*  Pungent anchovy paste made by pounding anchovy fillets with raw, peeled garlic, then thinning with a little olive oil and lemon juice. Useful as a snack, spread on croutons and heated in the oven, or as an addition to rustic salads of beans, lentils or chick peas.

*Appellation controlée*  The highest approved category of French wines, which must reach a designated alcoholic strength, and which are also subject to tasting controls by government inspectors.

*Beurre manié*  Softened butter mixed, by hand, with a roughly equal proportion of plain flour, used to thicken stews such as *boeuf bourguignon* and *coq au vin*. Small amounts are swirled into the sauce until it thickens and shines.

*Bouquet garni*  A mixture of herbs (usually bay leaf, parsley or chervil, thyme) tied in a bunch and added to stocks, stews and braises.

*Confit* Duck or goose preserved by being cooked thoroughly in its own fat and sealed in jars until needed, for example for a *cassoulet.*

*Crème anglaise* Real egg custard, served with fruit desserts or used as the basis for ice creams and *Bavarois.* Beat 75 g granulated vanilla-flavoured sugar into five egg yolks until the mixture becomes pale. While continuing to beat, add 375 ml ($\frac{3}{4}$ pint) boiling milk in a thin stream. Stir the mixture in a heavy saucepan over a moderate heat until the custard thickens. Remove immediately from the heat before the eggs scramble, and beat for a minute to help the custard to cool.

*Crème patissière* The thick custard used in French fruit tarts. Made exactly like crème anglaise except that twice as much sugar is used and 100 g plain flour beaten in before adding the milk. There is no danger of the eggs scrambling.

*Deglazing* The addition of a small quantity of alcohol or vinegar to the pan after *sautéeing* meat, in order to dissolve the pan juices and coagulated particles before completing the sauce, while the pan is still very hot—the alcohol must be boiled off completely.

*Farce, farci* French for stuffing and stuffed, respectively.

*Flageolets verts* Dried green kidney beans sold pre-packed, imported, in delicatessens. There is no English name.

*Fumet* Term used for a light fish stock usually made with bones of the fish whose fillets are being cooked, with added herbs and seasonings.

*Mayonnaise* Classic sauce made by beating egg yolks (two for six people) in a warm bowl, then slowly beating in olive oil (about 500 ml, $\frac{1}{2}$ pint) until a thick sauce forms. Usually seasoned with salt and lemon juice.

*Méthode champenoise* The extremely labour-intensive method of making natural sparkling wine, originated in Champagne. An indication that sparkling wine is made in the traditional fashion and is of high quality.

*Papillote* Little envelopes or parcels of paper, foil or pastry within which meat, fish, vegetables or fruit may be cooked in the oven, sealing in moisture and flavour.

*Pesto alla Genovese* A highly perfumed paste made by pounding fresh basil leaves, pine kernels and grated Parmesan cheese with a little olive oil. Used to heighten the flavour of tomato sauces or soups such as *minestrone,* or as a dressing for pasta. Can be bought ready-prepared in jars.

*Poivre vert* Green, or unripened, peppercorns preserved in brine and sold in jars. Now widely available.

*Sauté* Literally to make meat jump in a little fat over a fierce heat, to cook the exterior and seal in the juices as a preliminary step.

*Tapas* Delightful savouries, often fish or shellfish, served with aperitifs in Spain. Usually more substantial than the *amuse-gueule* served in France.

*Tomates crues concassées* Raw tomatoes peeled by scalding with boiling water, the pips removed by cupping half the tomato in the palm of the hand and squeezing gently, and chopped roughly. Served, seasoned with salt, pepper and sometimes herbs and garlic, as a garnish for rich sauces.

*Vinaigrette* Classic French salad dressing, consisting of three parts olive oil to one part vinegar (the proportions are a matter of taste), seasoned with salt and pepper.

*VDQS* (Vin delimité de qualité superieure) The second highest category of French wine, below Appellation Controlée in status but still subject to strict controls of quality and strength.

# Bibliography

Simone Beck, Louisette Bertholle and Julia Child, *Mastering the Art of French Cooking*, London, 1966.

Robert J. Courtine (ed.), *Larousse des Fromages,* Paris, 1973.

Elizabeth David, *French Provincial Cooking*, London.

Elizabeth David, *Italian Food,* London, 1963

Alan Davidson, *Mediterranean Seafood,* London, 1972.

Jane Grigson, *Fish Cookery,* London, 1975.

Jane Grigson, *Good Things,* London, 1973.

Michel Guérard, *La Cuisine Gourmande,* Paris, 1978.

Hugh Johnson, *The World Atlas of Wine,* London, 1971.

John Livingston-Learmonth and Melvyn Master, *The Wines of the Rhône,* London, 1978.

Edmund Penning-Rowsell, *The Wines of Bordeaux,* London, 1973.

Claudia Roden, *A book of Middle Eastern Food,* London, 1968.

# Index

## Index of dishes, under main ingredients

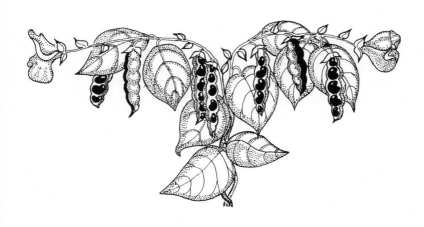

WHAT READERS AND CRITICS SAY ABOUT
ALICE SEBOLD'S

# THE
# LOVELY
# BONES

"Mesmerizing. . . . Sebold deals with almost unthinkable subjects with humor and intelligence and a kind of mysterious grace. . . . *The Lovely Bones* takes the stuff of neighborhood tragedy—the unexplained disappearance of a child, the shattered family alone with its grief—and turns it into literature."
— Katherine Bouton, *New York Times Book Review*

"Sebold teaches us much about living and dying, holding on and letting go, as messy and imperfect and beautiful as the processes can be—and has created a novel that is painfully fine and accomplished, one which readers will have their own difficulties relinquishing, long after the last page is turned."
— Paula L. Woods, *Los Angeles Times*

"Don't start *The Lovely Bones* unless you can finish it. The book begins with more horror than you could imagine, but closes with more beauty than you could hope for. . . . Alice Sebold has done something miraculous here."
— Ron Charles, *Christian Science Monitor*

"Savagely beautiful. . . . A strange and compelling novel."
— Monica Wood, *San Francisco Chronicle*

"A keenly observed portrait of familial love and how it endures and changes over time. . . . A deeply affecting meditation on the ways in which terrible pain and loss can be redeemed — slowly, grudgingly, and in fragments — through love and acceptance. . . . Ms. Sebold's achievements: her ability to capture both the ordinary and the extraordinary, the banal and the horrific, in lyrical, unsentimental prose; her instinctive understanding of the mathematics of love between parents and children; her gift for making palpable the dreams, regrets and unstilled hopes of one girl and one family."        — Michiko Kakutani, *New York Times*


"Sebold takes an enormous risk in her wonderfully strange debut novel. . . . Sebold slips easily from the ordinary pleasures of a suburban childhood to moments of eerie beauty. . . . A stunning achievement."        — *The New Yorker*


"Here is a writer who honors fiction's primary gift — the infinity of possibilities — by following her imagination to wondrous and terrifying places."        — Karen Sandstrom, *Cleveland Plain Dealer*


"Susie Salmon is one of the more captivating creations of recent fiction. Sebold has crafted a gripping tale of tragedy and grief. . . . Part detective story, part family drama, part meditation on what lies beyond, *The Lovely Bones* is a page-turner in the most literary sense. . . . Nothing short of a revelation."        — Elaina Richardson, *O*

ALSO BY ALICE SEBOLD

*Lucky*

# THE

# LOVELY

# BONES

*a novel*

*Alice Sebold*

**BACK BAY BOOKS**

LITTLE, BROWN AND COMPANY

NEW YORK BOSTON

Back Bay Books / Little, Brown and Company
Time Warner Book Group
1271 Avenue of the Americas, New York, NY 10020
Visit our Web site at www.twbookmark.com

Originally published in hardcover by Little, Brown and Company, July 2002
First Back Bay trade paperback edition, April 2004

The characters and events in this book are fictitious.
Any similarity to real persons, living or dead,
is coincidental and not intended by the author.

David Mehegan's article on Alice Sebold and *The Lovely Bones,* which is reprinted in
the reading group guide at the back of this book, first appeared in the *Boston Globe*
on February 25, 2003. Copyright © 2003 by Globe Newspaper Co. (MA).
Reprinted with permission.

Library of Congress Cataloging-in-Publication Data

Sebold, Alice.
  The lovely bones / Alice Sebold.—1st ed.
    p. cm.
  ISBN 0-316-66634-3 (hc) / 0-316-16881-5 (pb)
    1. Murder victims' families—Fiction.  2. Teenage girls—Crimes against—Fiction.
I. Title.
PS3619.E26 L68 2002
813'.6—dc21                                                    2001050622

20 19 18 17 16 15 14 13 12

Q-MART

Book design by Jo Anne Metsch

Printed in the United States of America

*Always, Glen*

# THE

## LOVELY

## BONES

Inside the snow globe on my father's desk, there was a penguin wearing a red-and-white-striped scarf. When I was little my father would pull me into his lap and reach for the snow globe. He would turn it over, letting all the snow collect on the top, then quickly invert it. The two of us watched the snow fall gently around the penguin. The penguin was alone in there, I thought, and I worried for him. When I told my father this, he said, "Don't worry, Susie; he has a nice life. He's trapped in a perfect world."

## ONE

My name was Salmon, like the fish; first name, Susie. I was fourteen when I was murdered on December 6, 1973. In newspaper photos of missing girls from the seventies, most looked like me: white girls with mousy brown hair. This was before kids of all races and genders started appearing on milk cartons or in the daily mail. It was still back when people believed things like that didn't happen.

In my junior high yearbook I had a quote from a Spanish poet my sister had turned me on to, Juan Ramón Jiménez. It went like this: "If they give you ruled paper, write the other way." I chose it both because it expressed my contempt for my structured surroundings à la the classroom and because, not being some dopey quote from a rock group, I thought it marked me as literary. I was a member of the Chess Club and Chem Club and burned everything I tried to make in Mrs. Delminico's home ec class. My favorite teacher was Mr. Botte, who taught biology and liked to animate the frogs and crawfish we had to dissect by making them dance in their waxed pans.

I wasn't killed by Mr. Botte, by the way. Don't think every person you're going to meet in here is suspect. That's the problem. You never know. Mr. Botte came to my memorial (as, may I add, did almost the entire junior high school — I was never so popular) and cried quite a bit. He had a sick kid. We all knew this, so when he laughed at his own jokes, which were rusty way before I had him, we laughed too, forcing it sometimes just to make him happy. His daughter died a year and a half after I did. She had leukemia, but I never saw her in my heaven.

My murderer was a man from our neighborhood. My mother liked his border flowers, and my father talked to him once about fertilizer. My murderer believed in old-fashioned things like eggshells and coffee grounds, which he said his own mother had used. My father came home smiling, making jokes about how the man's garden might be beautiful but it would stink to high heaven once a heat wave hit.

But on December 6, 1973, it was snowing, and I took a shortcut through the cornfield back from the junior high. It was dark out because the days were shorter in winter, and I remember how the broken cornstalks made my walk more difficult. The snow was falling lightly, like a flurry of small hands, and I was breathing through my nose until it was running so much that I had to open my mouth. Six feet from where Mr. Harvey stood, I stuck my tongue out to taste a snowflake.

"Don't let me startle you," Mr. Harvey said.

Of course, in a cornfield, in the dark, I was startled. After I was dead I thought about how there had been the light scent of cologne in the air but that I had not been paying attention, or thought it was coming from one of the houses up ahead.

"Mr. Harvey," I said.

"You're the older Salmon girl, right?"

"Yes."

"How are your folks?"

Although the eldest in my family and good at acing a science quiz, I had never felt comfortable with adults.

"Fine," I said. I was cold, but the natural authority of his age, and the added fact that he was a neighbor and had talked to my father about fertilizer, rooted me to the spot.

"I've built something back here," he said. "Would you like to see?"

"I'm sort of cold, Mr. Harvey," I said, "and my mom likes me home before dark."

"It's after dark, Susie," he said.

I wish now that I had known this was weird. I had never told him my name. I guess I thought my father had told him one of the embarrassing anecdotes he saw merely as loving testaments to his children. My father was the kind of dad who kept a nude photo of you when you were three in the downstairs bathroom, the one that guests would use. He did this to my little sister, Lindsey, thank God. At least I was spared that indignity. But he liked to tell a story about how, once Lindsey was born, I was so jealous that one day while he was on the phone in the other room, I moved down the couch—he could see me from where he stood—and tried to pee on top of Lindsey in her carrier. This story humiliated me every time he told it, to the pastor of our church, to our neighbor Mrs. Stead, who was a therapist and whose take on it he wanted to hear, and to everyone who ever said "Susie has a lot of spunk!"

"Spunk!" my father would say. "Let me tell you about spunk," and he would launch immediately into his Susie-peed-on-Lindsey story.

But as it turned out, my father had not mentioned us to Mr. Harvey or told him the Susie-peed-on-Lindsey story.

Mr. Harvey would later say these words to my mother when he

ran into her on the street: "I heard about the horrible, horrible tragedy. What was your daughter's name, again?"

"Susie," my mother said, bracing up under the weight of it, a weight that she naively hoped might lighten someday, not knowing that it would only go on to hurt in new and varied ways for the rest of her life.

Mr. Harvey told her the usual: "I hope they get the bastard. I'm sorry for your loss."

I was in my heaven by that time, fitting my limbs together, and couldn't believe his audacity. "The man has no shame," I said to Franny, my intake counselor. "Exactly," she said, and made her point as simply as that. There wasn't a lot of bullshit in my heaven.

Mr. Harvey said it would only take a minute, so I followed him a little farther into the cornfield, where fewer stalks were broken off because no one used it as a shortcut to the junior high. My mom had told my baby brother, Buckley, that the corn in the field was inedible when he asked why no one from the neighborhood ate it. "The corn is for horses, not humans," she said. "Not dogs?" Buckley asked. "No," my mother answered. "Not dinosaurs?" Buckley asked. And it went like that.

"I've made a little hiding place," said Mr. Harvey.

He stopped and turned to me.

"I don't see anything," I said. I was aware that Mr. Harvey was looking at me strangely. I'd had older men look at me that way since I'd lost my baby fat, but they usually didn't lose their marbles over me when I was wearing my royal blue parka and yellow elephant bell-bottoms. His glasses were small and round with gold frames, and his eyes looked out over them and at me.

"You should be more observant, Susie," he said.

I felt like observing my way out of there, but I didn't. Why didn't I? Franny said these questions were fruitless: "You didn't and that's that. Don't mull it over. It does no good. You're dead and you have to accept it."

"Try again," Mr. Harvey said, and he squatted down and knocked against the ground.

"What's that?" I asked.

My ears were freezing. I wouldn't wear the multicolored cap with the pompom and jingle bells that my mother had made me one Christmas. I had shoved it in the pocket of my parka instead.

I remember that I went over and stomped on the ground near him. It felt harder even than frozen earth, which was pretty hard.

"It's wood," Mr. Harvey said. "It keeps the entrance from collapsing. Other than that it's all made out of earth."

"What is it?" I asked. I was no longer cold or weirded out by the look he had given me. I was like I was in science class: I was curious.

"Come and see."

It was awkward to get into, that much he admitted once we were both inside the hole. But I was so amazed by how he had made a chimney that would draw smoke out if he ever chose to build a fire that the awkwardness of getting in and out of the hole wasn't even on my mind. You could add to that that escape wasn't a concept I had any real experience with. The worst I'd had to escape was Artie, a strange-looking kid at school whose father was a mortician. He liked to pretend he was carrying a needle full of embalming fluid around with him. On his notebooks he would draw needles spilling dark drips.

"This is neato!" I said to Mr. Harvey. He could have been the hunchback of Notre Dame, whom we had read about in French class. I didn't care. I completely reverted. I was my brother Buckley on our day-trip to the Museum of Natural History in New York, where he'd fallen in love with the huge skeletons on display. I hadn't used the word *neato* in public since elementary school.

"Like taking candy from a baby," Franny said.

\* \* \*

I can still see the hole like it was yesterday, and it was. Life is a perpetual yesterday for us. It was the size of a small room, the mud room in our house, say, where we kept our boots and slickers and where Mom had managed to fit a washer and dryer, one on top of the other. I could almost stand up in it, but Mr. Harvey had to stoop. He'd created a bench along the sides of it by the way he'd dug it out. He immediately sat down.

"Look around," he said.

I stared at it in amazement, the dug-out shelf above him where he had placed matches, a row of batteries, and a battery-powered fluorescent lamp that cast the only light in the room—an eerie light that would make his features hard to see when he was on top of me.

There was a mirror on the shelf, and a razor and shaving cream. I thought that was odd. Wouldn't he do that at home? But I guess I figured that a man who had a perfectly good split-level and then built an underground room only half a mile away had to be kind of loo-loo. My father had a nice way of describing people like him: "The man's a character, that's all."

So I guess I was thinking that Mr. Harvey was a character, and I liked the room, and it was warm, and I wanted to know how he had built it, what the mechanics of the thing were and where he'd learned to do something like that.

But by the time the Gilberts' dog found my elbow three days later and brought it home with a telling corn husk attached to it, Mr. Harvey had closed it up. I was in transit during this. I didn't get to see him sweat it out, remove the wood reinforcement, bag any evidence along with my body parts, except that elbow. By the time I popped up with enough wherewithal to look down at the goings-on on Earth, I was more concerned with my family than anything else.

My mother sat on a hard chair by the front door with her mouth open. Her pale face paler than I had ever seen it. Her blue eyes staring. My father was driven into motion. He wanted to know details and to comb the cornfield along with the cops. I still thank God for a small detective named Len Fenerman. He assigned two uniforms to take my dad into town and have him point out all the places I'd hung out with my friends. The uniforms kept my dad busy in one mall for the whole first day. No one had told Lindsey, who was thirteen and would have been old enough, or Buckley, who was four and would, to be honest, never fully understand.

Mr. Harvey asked me if I would like a refreshment. That was how he put it. I said I had to go home.

"Be polite and have a Coke," he said. "I'm sure the other kids would."

"What other kids?"

"I built this for the kids in the neighborhood. I thought it could be some sort of clubhouse."

I don't think I believed this even then. I thought he was lying, but I thought it was a pitiful lie. I imagined he was lonely. We had read about men like him in health class. Men who never married and ate frozen meals every night and were so afraid of rejection that they didn't even own pets. I felt sorry for him.

"Okay," I said, "I'll have a Coke."

In a little while he said, "Aren't you warm, Susie? Why don't you take off your parka."

I did.

After this he said, "You're very pretty, Susie."

"Thanks," I said, even though he gave me what my friend Clarissa and I had dubbed the skeevies.

"Do you have a boyfriend?"

"No, Mr. Harvey," I said. I swallowed the rest of my Coke, which was a lot, and said, "I got to go, Mr. Harvey. This is a cool place, but I have to go."

He stood up and did his hunchback number by the six dug-in

steps that led to the world. "I don't know why you think you're leaving."

I talked so that I would not have to take in this knowledge: Mr. Harvey was no character. He made me feel skeevy and icky now that he was blocking the door.

"Mr. Harvey, I really have to get home."

"Take off your clothes."

"What?"

"Take your clothes off," Mr. Harvey said. "I want to check that you're still a virgin."

"I am, Mr. Harvey," I said.

"I want to make sure. Your parents will thank me."

"My parents?"

"They only want good girls," he said.

"Mr. Harvey," I said, "please let me leave."

"You aren't leaving, Susie. You're mine now."

Fitness was not a big thing back then; *aerobics* was barely a word. Girls were supposed to be soft, and only the girls we suspected were butch could climb the ropes at school.

I fought hard. I fought as hard as I could not to let Mr. Harvey hurt me, but my hard-as-I-could was not hard enough, not even close, and I was soon lying down on the ground, in the ground, with him on top of me panting and sweating, having lost his glasses in the struggle.

I was so alive then. I thought it was *the worst thing in the world* to be lying flat on my back with a sweating man on top of me. To be trapped inside the earth and have no one know where I was.

I thought of my mother.

My mother would be checking the dial of the clock on her oven. It was a new oven and she loved that it had a clock on it. "I can time things to the minute," she told her own mother, a mother who couldn't care less about ovens.

She would be worried, but more angry than worried, at my

lateness. As my father pulled into the garage, she would rush about, fixing him a cocktail, a dry sherry, and put on an exasperated face: "You know junior high," she would say. "Maybe it's Spring Fling." "Abigail," my father would say, "how can it be Spring Fling when it's snowing?" Having failed with this, my mother might rush Buckley into the room and say, "Play with your father," while she ducked into the kitchen and took a nip of sherry for herself.

Mr. Harvey started to press his lips against mine. They were blubbery and wet and I wanted to scream but I was too afraid and too exhausted from the fight. I had been kissed once by someone I liked. His name was Ray and he was Indian. He had an accent and was dark. I wasn't supposed to like him. Clarissa called his large eyes, with their half-closed lids, "freak-a-delic," but he was nice and smart and helped me cheat on my algebra exam while pretending he hadn't. He kissed me by my locker the day before we turned in our photos for the yearbook. When the yearbook came out at the end of the summer, I saw that under his picture he had answered the standard "My heart belongs to" with "Susie Salmon." I guess he had had plans. I remember that his lips were chapped.

"Don't, Mr. Harvey," I managed, and I kept saying that one word a lot. *Don't.* And I said *please* a lot too. Franny told me that almost everyone begged "please" before dying.

"I want you, Susie," he said.

"Please," I said. "Don't," I said. Sometimes I combined them. "Please don't" or "Don't please." It was like insisting that a key works when it doesn't or yelling "I've got it, I've got it, I've got it" as a softball goes sailing over you into the stands.

"Please don't."

But he grew tired of hearing me plead. He reached into the pocket of my parka and balled up the hat my mother had made me, smashing it into my mouth. The only sound I made after that was the weak tinkling of bells.

As he kissed his wet lips down my face and neck and then began to shove his hands up under my shirt, I wept. I began to leave my body; I began to inhabit the air and the silence. I wept and struggled so I would not feel. He ripped open my pants, not having found the invisible zipper my mother had artfully sewn into their side.

"Big white panties," he said.

I felt huge and bloated. I felt like a sea in which he stood and pissed and shat. I felt the corners of my body were turning in on themselves and out, like in cat's cradle, which I played with Lindsey just to make her happy. He started working himself over me.


"Susie! Susie!" I heard my mother calling. "Dinner is ready."

He was inside me. He was grunting.

"We're having string beans and lamb."

I was the mortar, he was the pestle.

"Your brother has a new finger painting, and I made apple crumb cake."


Mr. Harvey made me lie still underneath him and listen to the beating of his heart and the beating of mine. How mine skipped like a rabbit, and how his thudded, a hammer against cloth. We lay there with our bodies touching, and, as I shook, a powerful knowledge took hold. He had done this thing to me and I had lived. That was all. I was still breathing. I heard his heart. I smelled his breath. The dark earth surrounding us smelled like what it was, moist dirt where worms and animals lived their daily lives. I could have yelled for hours.

I knew he was going to kill me. I did not realize then that I was an animal already dying.

"Why don't you get up?" Mr. Harvey said as he rolled to the side and then crouched over me.

His voice was gentle, encouraging, a lover's voice on a late morning. A suggestion, not a command.

I could not move. I could not get up.

When I would not — was it only that, only that I would not follow his suggestion? — he leaned to the side and felt, over his head, across the ledge where his razor and shaving cream sat. He brought back a knife. Unsheathed, it smiled at me, curving up in a grin.

He took the hat from my mouth.

"Tell me you love me," he said.

Gently, I did.

The end came anyway.

# TWO

———

When I first entered heaven I thought everyone saw what I saw. That in everyone's heaven there were soccer goalposts in the distance and lumbering women throwing shot put and javelin. That all the buildings were like suburban northeast high schools built in the 1960s. Large, squat buildings spread out on dismally landscaped sandy lots, with overhangs and open spaces to make them feel modern. My favorite part was how the colored blocks were turquoise and orange, just like the blocks in Fairfax High. Sometimes, on Earth, I had made my father drive me by Fairfax High so I could imagine myself there.

Following the seventh, eighth, and ninth grades of middle school, high school would have been a fresh start. When I got to Fairfax High I would insist on being called Suzanne. I would wear my hair feathered or up in a bun. I would have a body that the boys wanted and the girls envied, but I'd be so nice on top of it all that they would feel too guilty to do anything but worship me. I liked to think of myself — having reached a sort of queenly

status — as protecting misfit kids in the cafeteria. When someone
taunted Clive Saunders for walking like a girl, I would deliver
swift vengeance with my foot to the taunter's less-protected parts.
When the boys teased Phoebe Hart for her sizable breasts, I
would give a speech on why boob jokes weren't funny. I had to
forget that I too had made lists in the margins of my notebook
when Phoebe walked by: Winnebagos, Hoo-has, Johnny Yellows.
At the end of my reveries, I sat in the back of the car as my father
drove. I was beyond reproach. I would overtake high school in a
matter of days, not years, or, inexplicably, earn an Oscar for Best
Actress during my junior year.

These were my dreams on Earth.


After a few days in heaven, I realized that the javelin-throwers
and the shot-putters and the boys who played basketball on the
cracked blacktop were all in their own version of heaven. Theirs
just fit with mine — didn't duplicate it precisely, but had a lot of
the same things going on inside.

I met Holly, who became my roommate, on the third day. She
was sitting on the swing set. (I didn't question that a high school
had swing sets: that's what made it heaven. And no flat-benched
swings — only bucket seats made out of hard black rubber that
cradled you and that you could bounce in a bit before swinging.)
Holly sat reading a book in a weird alphabet that I associated
with the pork-fried rice my father brought home from Hop Fat
Kitchen, a place Buckley loved the name of, loved so much
he yelled "Hop Fat!" at the top of his lungs. Now I know
Vietnamese, and I know that Vietnamese is not what Herman
Jade, who owned Hop Fat, was, and that Herman Jade was not
Herman Jade's real name but one he adopted when he came to
the U.S. from China. Holly taught me all this.

"Hi," I said. "My name is Susie."

Later she would tell me she picked her name from a movie, *Breakfast at Tiffany's*. But that day it rolled right off her tongue.

"I'm Holly," she said. Because she wanted no trace of an accent in her heaven, she had none.

I stared at her black hair. It was shiny like the promises in magazines. "How long have you been here?" I asked.

"Three days."

"Me too."

I sat down on the swing next to her and twisted my body around and around to tie up the chains. Then I let go and spun until I stopped.

"Do you like it here?" she asked.

"No."

"Me either."

So it began.

We had been given, in our heavens, our simplest dreams. There were no teachers in the school. We never had to go inside except for art class for me and jazz band for Holly. The boys did not pinch our backsides or tell us we smelled; our textbooks were *Seventeen* and *Glamour* and *Vogue*.

And our heavens expanded as our relationship grew. We wanted many of the same things.

Franny, my intake counselor, became our guide. Franny was old enough to be our mother—mid-forties—and it took Holly and me a while to figure out that this had been something we wanted: our mothers.

In Franny's heaven, she served and was rewarded by results and gratitude. On Earth she had been a social worker for the homeless and destitute. She worked out of a church named Saint Mary's that served meals to women and children only, and she did everything there from manning the phones to swatting the roaches—karate-chop style. She was shot in the face by a man looking for his wife.

Franny walked over to Holly and me on the fifth day. She

handed us two Dixie Cups of lime Kool-Aid and we drank. "I'm here to help," she said.

I looked into her small blue eyes surrounded by laugh lines and told her the truth. "We're bored."

Holly was busy trying to reach her tongue out far enough to see if it had turned green.

"What do you want?" Franny asked.

"I don't know," I said.

"All you have to do is desire it, and if you desire it enough and understand why — really know — it will come."

It seemed so simple and it was. That's how Holly and I got our duplex.

I hated our split-level on Earth. I hated my parents' furniture, and how our house looked out onto another house and another house and another — an echo of sameness riding up over the hill. Our duplex looked out onto a park, and in the distance, just close enough to know we weren't alone, but not too close, we could see the lights of other houses.

Eventually I began to desire more. What I found strange was how much I desired to know what I had not known on Earth. I wanted to be allowed to grow up.

"People grow up by living," I said to Franny. "I want to live."

"That's out," she said.

"Can we at least watch the living?" asked Holly.

"You already do," she said.

"I think she means whole lives," I said, "from beginning to end, to see how they did it. To know the secrets. Then we can pretend better."

"You won't experience it," Franny clarified.

"Thank you, Brain Central," I said, but our heavens began to grow.

There was the high school still, all the Fairfax architecture, but now there were roads leading out.

"Walk the paths," Franny said, "and you'll find what you need."

So that's when Holly and I set out. Our heaven had an ice cream shop where, when you asked for peppermint stick ice cream, no one ever said, "It's seasonal"; it had a newspaper where our pictures appeared a lot and made us look important; it had real men in it and beautiful women too, because Holly and I were devoted to fashion magazines. Sometimes Holly seemed like she wasn't paying attention, and other times she was gone when I went looking for her. That was when she went to a part of heaven we didn't share. I missed her then, but it was an odd sort of missing because by then I knew the meaning of forever.

I could not have what I wanted most: Mr. Harvey dead and me living. Heaven wasn't perfect. But I came to believe that if I watched closely, and desired, I might change the lives of those I loved on Earth.

My father was the one who took the phone call on December ninth. It was the beginning of the end. He gave the police my blood type, had to describe the lightness of my skin. They asked him if I had any identifying features. He began to describe my face in detail, getting lost in it. Detective Fenerman let him go on, the next news too horrible to interrupt with. But then he said it: "Mr. Salmon, we have found only a body part."

My father stood in the kitchen and a sickening shiver overtook him. How could he tell that to Abigail?

"So you can't be certain that she's dead?" he asked.

"Nothing is ever certain," Len Fenerman said.

That was the line my father said to my mother: "Nothing is ever certain."

For three nights he hadn't known how to touch my mother or what to say. Before, they had never found themselves broken together. Usually, it was one needing the other but not both needing each other, and so there had been a way, by touching, to borrow from the stronger one's strength. And they had never understood, as they did now, what the word *horror* meant.

"Nothing is ever certain," my mother said, clinging to it as he had hoped she might.

My mother had been the one who knew the meaning of each charm on my bracelet — where we had gotten it and why I liked it. She made a meticulous list of what I'd carried and worn. If found miles away and in isolation along a road, these clues might lead a policeman there to link it to my death.

In my mind I had wavered between the bittersweet joy of seeing my mother name all the things I carried and loved and her futile hope that these things mattered. That a stranger who found a cartoon character eraser or a rock star button would report it to the police.

After Len's phone call, my father reached out his hand and the two of them sat in the bed together, staring straight in front of them. My mother numbly clinging to this list of things, my father feeling as if he were entering a dark tunnel. At some point, it began to rain. I could feel them both thinking the same thing then, but neither of them said it. That I was out there somewhere, in the rain. That they hoped I was safe. That I was dry somewhere, and warm.

Neither of them knew who fell asleep first; their bones aching with exhaustion, they drifted off and woke guiltily at the same time. The rain, which had changed several times as the temperature dropped, was now hail, and the sound of it, of small stones of ice hitting the roof above them, woke them together.

They did not speak. They looked at each other in the small light cast from the lamp left on across the room. My mother began to cry, and my father held her, wiped her tears with the pad of his thumbs as they crested her cheekbones, and kissed her very gently on the eyes.

I looked away from them then, as they touched. I moved my

eyes into the cornfield, seeing if there was anything that in the morning the police might find. The hail bent the stalks and drove all the animals into their holes. Not so deep beneath the earth were the warrens of the wild rabbits I loved, the bunnies that ate the vegetables and flowers in the neighborhood nearby and that sometimes, unwittingly, brought poison home to their dens. Then, inside the earth and so far away from the man or woman who had laced a garden with toxic bait, an entire family of rabbits would curl into themselves and die.

On the morning of the tenth, my father poured the Scotch down the kitchen sink. Lindsey asked him why.

"I'm afraid I might drink it," he said.

"What was the phone call?" my sister asked.

"What phone call?"

"I heard you say that thing you always say about Susie's smile. About stars exploding."

"Did I say that?"

"You got kind of goofy. It was a cop, wasn't it?"

"No lies?"

"No lies," Lindsey agreed.

"They found a body part. It might be Susie's."

It was a hard sock in the stomach. "What?"

"Nothing is ever certain," my father tried.

Lindsey sat down at the kitchen table. "I'm going to be sick," she said.

"Honey?"

"Dad, I want you to tell me what it was. Which body part, and then I'm going to need to throw up."

My father got down a large metal mixing bowl. He brought it to the table and placed it near Lindsey before sitting down.

"Okay," she said. "Tell me."

"It was an elbow. The Gilberts' dog found it."

He held her hand and then she threw up, as she had promised, into the shiny silver bowl.

Later that morning the weather cleared, and not too far from my house the police roped off the cornfield and began their search. The rain, sleet, snow, and hail melting and mixing had left the ground sodden; still, there was an obvious area where the earth had been freshly manipulated. They began there and dug.

In places, the lab later found, there was a dense concentration of my blood mixed with the dirt, but at the time, the police grew more and more frustrated, plying the cold wet ground and looking for girl.

Along the border of the soccer field, a few of my neighbors kept a respectful distance from the police tape, wondering at the men dressed in heavy blue parkas wielding shovels and rakes like medical tools.

My father and mother remained at home. Lindsey stayed in her room. Buckley was nearby at his friend Nate's house, where he spent a lot of time these days. They had told him I was on an extended sleepover at Clarissa's.

I knew where my body was but I could not tell them. I watched and waited to see what they would see. And then, like a thunderbolt, late in the afternoon, a policeman held up his earth-caked fist and shouted.

"Over here!" he said, and the other officers ran to surround him.

The neighbors had gone home except for Mrs. Stead. After conferring around the discovering policeman, Detective Fenerman broke their dark huddle and approached her.

"Mrs. Stead?" he said over the tape that separated them.

"Yes."

"You have a child in the school?"

"Yes."

"Could you come with me, please?"

A young officer led Mrs. Stead under the police tape and over the bumpy, churned-up cornfield to where the rest of the men stood.

"Mrs. Stead," Len Fenerman said, "does this look familiar?" He held up a paperback copy of *To Kill a Mockingbird*. "Do they read this at the school?"

"Yes," she said, her face draining of color as she said the small word.

"Do you mind if I ask you . . ." he began.

"Ninth grade," she said, looking into Len Fenerman's slate blue eyes. "Susie's grade." She was a therapist and relied on her ability to hear bad news and discuss rationally the difficult details of her patients' lives, but she found herself leaning into the young policeman who had led her over. I could feel her wishing that she had gone home when the other neighbors had left, wishing that she was in the living room with her husband, or out in the back-yard with her son.

"Who teaches the class?"

"Mrs. Dewitt," Mrs. Stead said. "The kids find it a real relief after *Othello*."

"*Othello?*"

"Yes," she said, her knowledge of the school suddenly very im-portant right now—all the policemen listening. "Mrs. Dewitt likes to modulate her reading list, and she does a big push right before Christmas with Shakespeare. Then she passes out Harper Lee as a reward. If Susie was carrying around *To Kill a Mockingbird* it means she must have turned in her paper on *Othello* already."

All of this checked out.

The police made calls. I watched the circle widen. Mrs. Dewitt had my paper. Eventually, she sent it back to my parents, unmarked, through the mail. "Thought you would want to have this," Mrs.

Dewitt had written on a note attached to it. "I'm so very very sorry." Lindsey inherited the paper because it was too painful for my mother to read. "The Ostracized: One Man Alone," I had called it. Lindsey had suggested "The Ostracized," and I made up the other half. My sister punched three holes down the side of it and fastened each carefully handwritten page into an empty notebook. She put it in her closet under her Barbie case and the box that held her perfect-condition Raggedy Ann and Andy that I'd envied.

Detective Fenerman called my parents. They had found a schoolbook, they believed, that might have been given to me that last day.

"But it could be anyone's," my father said to my mother as they began another restless vigil. "Or she could have dropped it along the way."

Evidence was mounting, but they refused to believe.

Two days later, on December twelfth, the police found my notes from Mr. Botte's class. Animals had carried off the note-book from its original burial site — the dirt did not match the surrounding samples, but the graph paper, with its scribbled theories that I could never understand but still dutifully recorded, had been found when a cat knocked down a crow's nest. Shreds of the paper were laced among the leaves and twigs. The police unbraided the graph paper, along with strips of another kind of paper, thinner and brittle, that had no lines.

The girl who lived in the house where the tree stood recognized some of the handwriting. It was not my writing, but the writing of the boy who had a crush on me: Ray Singh. On his mother's special rice paper Ray had written me a love note, which I never read. He had tucked it into my notebook during our Wednesday lab. His hand was distinct. When the officers came they had to piece together the scraps of my biology notebook and of Ray Singh's love note.

"Ray is not feeling well," his mother said when a detective called his house and asked to speak to him. But they found out what they needed from her. Ray nodded to her as she repeated the policeman's questions to her son. Yes, he had written Susie Salmon a love note. Yes, he had put it in her notebook after Mr. Botte had asked her to collect the pop quiz. Yes, he had called himself the Moor.

Ray Singh became the first suspect.

"That sweet boy?" my mother said to my father.

"Ray Singh is nice," my sister said in a monotone at dinner that night.

I watched my family and knew they knew. It was not Ray Singh.

The police descended on his house, leaning heavily on him, insinuating things. They were fueled by the guilt they read into Ray's dark skin, by the rage they felt at his manner, and by his beautiful yet too exotic and unavailable mother. But Ray had an alibi. A whole host of nations could be called to testify on his behalf. His father, who taught postcolonial history at Penn, had urged his son to represent the teenage experience at a lecture he gave at the International House on the day I died.

At first Ray's absence from school had been seen as evidence of his guilt, but once the police were presented with a list of forty-five attendees who had seen Ray speak at "Suburbia: The American Experience," they had to concede his innocence. The police stood outside the Singh house and snapped small twigs from the hedges. It would have been so easy, so magical, their answer literally falling out of the sky from a tree. But rumors spread and, in school, what little headway Ray had made socially was reversed. He began to go home immediately after school.

All this made me crazy. Watching but not being able to steer the police toward the green house so close to my parents, where Mr. Harvey sat carving finials for a gothic dollhouse he was building. He watched the news and scanned the papers, but he wore his own innocence like a comfortable old coat. There had been a riot inside him and now there was calm.

I tried to take solace in Holiday, our dog. I missed him in a way

I hadn't yet let myself miss my mother and father, my sister and brother. That way of missing would mean that I had accepted that I would never be with them again; it might sound silly but I didn't believe it, would not believe it. Holiday stayed with Lindsey at night, stood by my father each time he answered the door to a new unknown. Gladly partook of any clandestine eating on the part of my mother. Let Buckley pull his tail and ears inside the house of locked doors.

There was too much blood in the earth.

On December fifteenth, among the knocks on the door that signaled to my family that they must numb themselves further before opening their house to strangers — the kind but awkward neighbors, the bumbling but cruel reporters — came the one that made my father finally believe.

It was Len Fenerman, who had been so kind to him, and a uniform.

They came inside, by now familiar enough with the house to know that my mother preferred them to come in and say what they had to say in the living room so that my sister and brother would not overhear.

"We've found a personal item that we believe to be Susie's," Len said. Len was careful. I could see him calculating his words. He made sure to specify so that my parents would be relieved of their first thought — that the police had found my body, that I was, for certain, dead.

"What?" my mother said impatiently. She crossed her arms and braced for another inconsequential detail in which others invested meaning. She was a wall. Notebooks and novels were nothing to her. Her daughter might survive without an arm. A lot of blood was a lot of blood. It was not a body. Jack had said it and she believed: Nothing is ever certain.

But when they held up the evidence bag with my hat inside, something broke in her. The fine wall of leaden crystal that had protected her heart — somehow numbed her into disbelief — shattered.

"The pompom," Lindsey said. She had crept into the living room from the kitchen. No one had seen her come in but me.

My mother made a sound and reached out her hand. The sound was a metallic squeak, a human-as-machine breaking down, uttering last sounds before the whole engine locks.

"We've tested the fibers," Len said. "It appears whoever accosted Susie used this during the crime."

"What?" my father asked. He was powerless. He was being told something he could not comprehend.

"As a way to keep her quiet."

"What?"

"It is covered with her saliva," the uniformed officer, who had been silent until now, volunteered. "He gagged her with it."

My mother grabbed it out of Len Fenerman's hands, and the bells she had sewn into the pompom sounded as she landed on her knees. She bent over the hat she had made me.

I saw Lindsey stiffen at the door. Our parents were unrecognizable to her; everything was unrecognizable.

My father led the well-meaning Len Fenerman and the uniformed officer to the front door.

"Mr. Salmon," Len Fenerman said, "with the amount of blood we've found, and the violence I'm afraid it implies, as well as other material evidence we've discussed, we must work with the assumption that your daughter has been killed."

Lindsey overheard what she already knew, had known since five days before, when my father told her about my elbow. My mother began to wail.

"We'll be working with this as a murder investigation from this point out," Fenerman said.

"But there is no body," my father tried.

"All evidence points to your daughter's death. I'm very sorry."

The uniformed officer had been staring to the right of my father's pleading eyes. I wondered if that was something they'd taught him in school. But Len Fenerman met my father's gaze. "I'll call to check in on you later today," he said.

By the time my father turned back to the living room, he was too devastated to reach out to my mother sitting on the carpet or my sister's hardened form nearby. He could not let them see him. He mounted the stairs, thinking of Holiday on the rug in the study. He had last seen him there. Into the deep ruff of fur surrounding the dog's neck, my father would let himself cry.

That afternoon the three of them crept forward in silence, as if the sound of footsteps might confirm the news. Nate's mother knocked on the door to return Buckley. No one answered. She stepped away, knowing something had changed inside the house, which looked exactly like the ones on either side of it. She made herself my brother's co-conspirator, telling him they would go out for ice cream and ruin his appetite.

At four, my mother and father ended up standing in the same room downstairs. They had come in from opposite doorways.

My mother looked at my father: "Mother," she said, and he nodded his head. He made the phone call to my only living grandparent, my mother's mother, Grandma Lynn.

I worried that my sister, left alone, would do something rash. She sat in her room on the old couch my parents had given up on and worked on hardening herself. *Take deep breaths and hold them. Try to stay still for longer and longer periods of time. Make yourself small and like a stone. Curl the edges of yourself up and fold them under where no one can see.*

My mother told her it was her choice whether she wanted to return to school before Christmas — there was only one week left — but Lindsey chose to go.

On Monday, in homeroom, everyone stared at her as she approached the front of the classroom.

"The principal would like to see you, dear," Mrs. Dewitt confided in a hush.

My sister did not look at Mrs. Dewitt when she was speaking. She was perfecting the art of talking to someone while looking through them. That was my first clue that something would have to give. Mrs. Dewitt was also the English teacher, but more importantly she was married to Mr. Dewitt, who coached boys' soccer and had encouraged Lindsey to try out for his team. My sister liked the Dewitts, but that morning she began looking into the eyes of only those people she could fight against.

As she gathered her things, she heard whispers everywhere. She was certain that right before she left the room Danny Clarke had whispered something to Sylvia Henley. Someone had dropped something near the back of the classroom. They did this, she believed, so that on their way to pick it up and back again, they could say a word or two to their neighbor about the dead girl's sister.

Lindsey walked through the hallways and in and out of the rows of lockers — dodging anyone who might be near. I wished I could walk with her, mimic the principal and the way he always started out a meeting in the auditorium: "Your principal is your pal with principles!" I would whine in her ear, cracking her up.

But while she was blessed with empty halls, when she reached the main office she was cursed with the drippy looks of consoling secretaries. No matter. She had prepared herself at home in her bedroom. She was armed to the teeth for any onslaught of sympathy.

"Lindsey," Principal Caden said, "I received a call from the police this morning. I'm sorry to hear of your loss."

She looked right at him. It was not so much a look as a laser. "What exactly is my loss?"

Mr. Caden felt he needed to address issues of children's crises directly. He walked out from behind his desk and ushered Lindsey onto what was commonly referred to by the students as The Sofa. Eventually he would replace The Sofa with two chairs, when politics swept through the school district and told him, *"It is not good to have a sofa here — chairs are better. Sofas send the wrong message."*

Mr. Caden sat on The Sofa and so did my sister. I like to think she was a little thrilled, in that moment, no matter how upset, to be on The Sofa itself. I like to think I hadn't robbed her of everything.

"We're here to help in any way we can," Mr. Caden said. He was doing his best.

"I'm fine," she said.

"Would you like to talk about it?"

"What?" Lindsey asked. She was being what my father called "petulant," as in, "Susie, don't speak to me in that petulant tone."

"Your loss," he said. He reached out to touch my sister's knee. His hand was like a brand burning into her.

"I wasn't aware I had lost anything," she said, and in a Herculean effort she made the motions of patting her shirt and checking her pockets.

Mr. Caden didn't know what to say. He had had Vicki Kurtz fall apart in his arms the year before. It had been difficult, yes, but now, in hindsight, Vicki Kurtz and her dead mother seemed an artfully handled crisis. He had led Vicki Kurtz to the couch — no, no, Vicki had just gone right over and sat down on it — he had said, "I'm sorry for your loss," and Vicki Kurtz had burst like an overinflated balloon. He held her in his arms as she sobbed, and sobbed, and that night he brought his suit to the dry cleaner's.

But Lindsey Salmon was another thing altogether. She was

gifted, one of the twenty students from his school who had been selected for the statewide Gifted Symposium. The only trouble in her file was a slight altercation early in the year when a teacher reprimanded her for bringing obscene literature — *Fear of Flying* — into the classroom.

"Make her laugh," I wanted to say to him. "Bring her to a Marx Brothers movie, sit on a fart cushion, show her the boxers you have on with the little devils eating hot dogs on them!" All I could do was talk, but no one on Earth could hear me.


The school district made everyone take tests and then decided who was gifted and who was not. I liked to suggest to Lindsey that I was much more pissed off by her hair than by my dumbo status. We had both been born with masses of blond hair, but mine quickly fell out and was replaced with a grudging growth of mousy brown. Lindsey's stayed and acquired a sort of mythical place. She was the only true blonde in our family.

But once called gifted, it had spurred her on to live up to the name. She locked herself in her bedroom and read big books. When I read *Are You There God? It's Me, Margaret,* she read Camus's *Resistance, Rebellion, and Death.* She might not have gotten most of it, but she carried it around, and that made people — including teachers — begin to leave her alone.

"What I'm saying, Lindsey, is that we all miss Susie," Mr. Caden said.

She did not respond.

"She was very bright," he tried.

She stared blankly back at him.

"It's on your shoulders now." He had no idea what he was saying, but he thought the silence might mean he was getting somewhere. "You're the only Salmon girl now."

Nothing.

"You know who came in to see me this morning?" Mr. Caden had held back his big finish, the one he was sure would work. "Mr. Dewitt. He's considering coaching a girls' team," Mr. Caden said. "The idea is all centered around you. He's watched how good you are, as competitive as his boys, and he thinks other girls would come out if you led the charge. What do you say?"

Inside, my sister's heart closed like a fist. "I'd say it would be pretty hard to play soccer on the soccer field when it's approximately twenty feet from where my sister was supposedly murdered."

*Score!*

Mr. Caden's mouth opened and he stared at her.

"Anything else?" Lindsey asked.

"No, I . . ." Mr. Caden reached out his hand again. There was a thread still — a desire to understand. "I want you to know how sorry we are," he said.

"I'm late for first period," she said.

In that moment she reminded me of a character in the Westerns my father loved, the ones we watched together on late-night TV. There was always a man who, after he shot his gun, raised the pistol to his lips and blew air across the opening.

Lindsey got up and took the walk out of Principal Caden's office slow. The walks away were her only rest time. Secretaries were on the other side of the door, teachers were at the front of the class, students in every desk, our parents at home, police coming by. She would not break. I watched her, felt the lines she repeated over and over again in her head. *Fine. All of it is fine.* I was dead, but that was something that happened all the time — people died. As she left the outer office that day, she appeared to be looking into the eyes of the secretaries, but she was focusing on their misapplied lipstick or two-piece paisley crepe de chine instead.

At home that night she lay on the floor of her room and braced her feet under her bureau. She did ten sets of sit-ups. Then she got into push-up position. Not the girl's kind. Mr. Dewitt had told her about the kind he had done in the Marines, head-up, or one-handed, clapping between. After she did ten push-ups, she went to her shelf and chose the two heaviest books — her dictionary and a world almanac. She did biceps curls until her arms ached. She focused only on her breathing. The in. The out.

I sat in the gazebo in the main square of my heaven (our neighbors, the O'Dwyers, had had a gazebo; I had grown up jealous for one), and watched my sister rage.

Hours before I died, my mother hung on the refrigerator a picture that Buckley had drawn. In the drawing a thick blue line separated the air and ground. In the days that followed I watched my family walk back and forth past that drawing and I became convinced that that thick blue line was a real place — an Inbetween, where heaven's horizon met Earth's. I wanted to go there into the cornflower blue of Crayola, the royal, the turquoise, the sky.

Often I found myself desiring simple things and I would get them. Riches in furry packages. Dogs.

Every day in my heaven tiny dogs and big dogs, dogs of every kind, ran through the park outside my room. When I opened the door I saw them fat and happy, skinny and hairy, lean and hairless even. Pitbulls rolled on their backs, the nipples of the females distended and dark, begging for their pups to come and suckle them, happy in the sun. Bassets tripped over their ears, ambling forward, nudging the rumps of dachshunds, the ankles of greyhounds, and the heads of the Pekingese. And when Holly took her tenor sax, set herself up outside the door that looked onto the park, and played the blues, the hounds all ran to form her chorus.

On their haunches they sat wailing. Other doors opened then, and women stepped out from where they lived alone or with roommates. I would step outside, Holly would go into an endless encore, the sun going down, and we would dance with the dogs — all of us together. We chased them, they chased us. We circled tail to tail. We wore spotted gowns, flowered gowns, striped gowns, plain. When the moon was high the music would stop. The dancing stopped. We froze.

Mrs. Bethel Utemeyer, the oldest resident of my heaven, would bring out her violin. Holly trod lightly on her horn. They would do a duet. One woman old and silent, one woman not past girl yet. Back and forth, a crazy schizoid solace they'd create.

All the dancers would slowly go inside. The song reverberated until Holly, for a final time, passed the tune over, and Mrs. Utemeyer, quiet, upright, historical, finished with a jig.

The house asleep by then; this was my Evensong.

# THREE

The odd thing about Earth was what we saw when we looked down. Besides the initial view that you might suspect, the old ants-from-the-skyscraper phenomenon, there were souls leaving bodies all over the world.

Holly and I could be scanning Earth, alighting on one scene or another for a second or two, looking for the unexpected in the most mundane moment. And a soul would run by a living being, touch them softly on the shoulder or cheek, and continue on its way to heaven. The dead are never exactly seen by the living, but many people seem acutely aware of something changed around them. They speak of a chill in the air. The mates of the deceased wake from dreams and see a figure standing at the end of their bed, or in a doorway, or boarding, phantomlike, a city bus.

On my way out of Earth, I touched a girl named Ruth. She went to my school but we'd never been close. She was standing in my path that night when my soul shrieked out of Earth. I could not help but graze her. Once released from life, having lost it in such violence, I couldn't calculate my steps. I didn't have time for contemplation. In violence, it is the getting away that you concentrate on. When you begin to go over the edge, life receding from you as a boat recedes inevitably from shore, you hold on to death tightly, like a rope that will transport you, and you swing out on it, hoping only to land away from where you are.

Like a phone call from the jail cell, I brushed by Ruth Connors — wrong number, accidental call. I saw her standing there near Mr. Botte's red and rusted Fiat. When I streaked by her, my hand leapt out to touch her, touch the last face, feel the last connection to Earth in this not-so-standard-issue teenage girl.

On the morning of December seventh, Ruth complained to her mother about having had a dream that seemed too real to be a dream. When her mother asked her what she meant, Ruth said, "I was crossing through the faculty parking lot, and suddenly, down out of the soccer field, I saw a pale running ghost coming toward me."

Mrs. Connors stirred the hardening oatmeal in its pot. She watched her daughter gesticulating with the long thin fingers of her hands — hands she had inherited from her father.

"It was female, I could sense that," Ruth said. "It flew up out of the field. Its eyes were hollow. It had a thin white veil over its body, as light as cheesecloth. I could see its face through it, the features coming up through it, the nose, the eyes, the face, the hair."

Her mother took the oatmeal off the stove and lowered the flame. "Ruth," she said, "you're letting your imagination get the best of you."

Ruth took the cue to shut up. She did not mention the dream that was not a dream again, even ten days later, when the story of my death began to travel through the halls of the school, receiving add-on nuances as all good horror stories do. They were hard-pressed, my peers, to make the horror any more horrible than it was. But the details were still missing—the what and when and who became hollow bowls to fill with their conjectures. Devil Worship. Midnight. Ray Singh.

Try as I might, I could not point Ruth strongly enough to what no one had found: my silver charm bracelet. I thought it might help her. It lay exposed, waiting for a hand to reach out, a hand that would recognize it and think, *Clue.* But it was no longer in the cornfield.

Ruth began writing poetry. If her mother or her more approachable teachers did not want to hear the darker reality she had experienced, she would cloak this reality in poetry.

How I wished Ruth could have gone to my family and talked to them. In all likelihood, no one but my sister would have even known her name. Ruth was the girl who got chosen next to last in gym. She was the girl who, when a volleyball sailed in her direction, cowered where she stood while the ball hit the gymnasium floor beside her, and her teammates and the gym teacher tried hard not to groan.

As my mother sat in the straight-backed chair in our hallway, watching my father run in and out on his various errands of responsibility—he would now be hyperaware of the movements and the whereabouts of his young son, of his wife, and of his remaining daughter—Ruth took our accidental meeting in the school parking lot and went underground.

She went through old yearbooks and found my class photos, as well as any activities photos like Chem Club, and cut them out with her mother's swan-shaped embroidery scissors. Even as her obsession grew I remained wary of her, until that last week before Christmas when she saw something in the hallway of our school.

It was my friend Clarissa and Brian Nelson. I'd dubbed Brian "the scarecrow" because even though he had incredible shoulders that all the girls mooned over, his face reminded me of a burlap sack stuffed with straw. He wore a floppy leather hippie hat and smoked hand-rolled cigarettes in the student smoking lounge. According to my mother, Clarissa's penchant for baby blue eye shadow was an early warning sign, but I'd always liked her for just this reason. She did things I wasn't allowed to do: she lightened her long hair, she wore platform shoes, she smoked cigarettes after school.

Ruth came upon the two of them, but they didn't see her. She had a pile of huge books she had borrowed from Mrs. Kaplan, the social science teacher. They were all early feminist texts, and she held them with their spines resting against her stomach so that no one could see what they were. Her father, a building contractor, had made her a gift of two super-strong elastic book bands. Ruth had placed two of them around the volumes she planned to read over vacation.

Clarissa and Brian were giggling. His hand was inside her shirt. As he inched it up, her giggling increased, but she thwarted his advances each time by twisting or moving an inch or two away. Ruth stood apart from this, as she did most things. She would have passed it in her usual manner, head down/eyes averted, but everyone knew Clarissa had been my friend. So she watched.

"Come on, honey," Brian said, "just a little mound of love. Just one."

I noticed Ruth's lip curl in disgust. Mine was curling up in heaven.

"Brian, I can't. Not here."

"How 'bout out in the cornfield?" he whispered.

Clarissa giggled nervously but nuzzled the space between his neck and shoulder. For now, she would deny him.

After that, Clarissa's locker was burgled.

Gone were her scrapbook, random photos stuck to the inside of her locker, and Brian's stash of marijuana, which he had hidden there without Clarissa's knowledge.

Ruth, who had never been high, spent that night emptying out the tobacco from her mother's long brown More 100s and stuffing them with pot. She sat in the toolshed with a flashlight, looking at photos of me and smoking more grass than even the potheads at school could suck down.

Mrs. Connors, standing at the kitchen window doing dishes, caught a whiff of the scent coming from the toolshed.

"I think Ruth is making friends at school," she said to her husband, who sat over his copy of the *Evening Bulletin* with a cup of coffee. At the end of his workday he was too tired even to speculate.

"Good," he said.

"Maybe there's hope for her yet."

"Always," he said.

When Ruth tottered in later that night, her eyes bleary from using the flashlight and from the eight More cigarettes she'd smoked, her mother greeted her with a smile and told her there was blueberry pie in the kitchen. It took a few days and some non-Susie-Salmon-focused research, but Ruth discovered why she had eaten the entire pie in one sitting.

The air in my heaven often smelled like skunk — just a hint of it. It was a smell that I had always loved on Earth. When I breathed it in, I could feel the scent as well as smell it. It was the animal's fear and power mixed together to form a pungent, lingering musk. In Franny's heaven it smelled like pure, grade-A tobacco. In Holly's it smelled like kumquats.

I would sit whole days and nights in the gazebo and watch. See Clarissa spin away from me, toward the comfort of Brian. See Ruth staring at her from behind a corner near the home ec room or outside the cafeteria near the nurse's station. At the start, the freedom I had to see the whole school was intoxicating. I would watch the assistant football coach leave anonymous chocolates for the married science teacher, or the head of the cheerleading squad trying to capture the attention of the kid who had been expelled so many times, from so many schools, even he had lost count. I watched the art teacher make love to his girlfriend in the kiln room and the principal moon over the assistant football coach. I concluded that this assistant football coach was a stud in the world of Kennet Junior High, even if his square jaw left me cold.

On the way back to the duplex each night I would pass under old-time street lamps that I had seen once in a play of *Our Town*. The globes of light hung down in an arc from an iron post. I had remembered them because when I saw the play with my family, I thought of them as giant, heavy berries full of light. I made a game in heaven of positioning myself so that my shadow plucked the berries as I made my way home.

After watching Ruth one night I met Franny in the midst of this. The square was deserted, and leaves began to swirl around in an eddy up ahead. I stood and looked at her—at the laugh lines that were clustered near her eyes and mouth.

"Why are you shivering?" Franny asked.

And though the air was damp and chilly I could not say that that was why.

"I can't help thinking of my mother," I said.

Franny took my left hand in both of hers and smiled.

I wanted to kiss her lightly on the cheek or have her hold me, but instead I watched her walk off in front of me, saw her blue dress trail away. I knew that she was not my mother; I could not play pretend.

I turned around and went back to the gazebo. I felt the moist air lace its way up along my legs and arms, lifting, ever so slightly, the ends of my hair. I thought of spider webs in the morning, how they held small jewels of dew, how, with a light movement of the wrist, I used to destroy them without thinking.

On the morning of my eleventh birthday I had woken up very early. No one else was up, or so I thought. I crept downstairs and looked into the dining room, where I assumed my presents would be. But there was nothing there. Same table as yesterday. But as I turned around I saw it lying on my mother's desk in the living room. The fancy desk with an always-clean surface. "The bill-paying desk" was what they called it. Swaddled in tissue paper but not yet wrapped was a camera — what I had asked for with a tinge of whining in my voice, so sure they would not get it for me. I went over to it and stared down. It was an Instamatic, and lying beside it were three cartridges of film and a box of four square flashbulbs. It was my first machine, my starter kit to becoming what I wanted to be. A wildlife photographer.

I looked around. No one. I saw through the front blinds, which my mother always kept at a half-slant — "inviting but discreet" — that Grace Tarking, who lived down the street and went to a private school, was walking with ankle weights strapped to her feet. Hurriedly I loaded the camera and I began to stalk Grace Tarking as I would, I imagined, when I grew older, stalk wild elephants and rhinos. Here I hid behind blinds and windows, there it would be high reeds. I was quiet, what I thought of as stealthy, gathering the long hem of my flannel nightgown up in my free hand. I traced her movements past our living room, front hall, into the den on the other side. As I watched her receding form I had a brainstorm — I would run into the backyard, where I could see her with no barriers.

So I ran on tiptoe into the back of the house, only to find the door to the porch wide open.

When I saw my mother, I forgot all about Grace Tarking. I wish I could explain it better than this, but I had never seen her sitting so still, so *not there* somehow. Outside the screened-in porch she was sitting on an aluminum fold-out chair that was facing the backyard. In her hand she held a saucer and in the saucer was her customary cup of coffee. That morning there were no lip-stick marks because there was no lipstick until she put it on for . . . who? I had never thought to ask the question. My father? Us?

Holiday was sitting near the birdbath, panting happily, but he did not notice me. He was watching my mother. She had a stare that stretched to infinity. She was, in that moment, not my mother but something separate from me. I looked at what I had never seen as anything but Mom and saw the soft powdery skin of her face — powdery without makeup — soft without help. Her eyebrows and eyes were a set-piece together. "Ocean Eyes," my father called her when he wanted one of her chocolate-covered cherries, which she kept hidden in the liquor cabinet as her private treat. And now I understood the name. I had thought it was because they were blue, but now I saw it was because they were bottomless in a way that I found frightening. I had an instinct then, not a developed thought, and it was that, before Holiday saw and smelled me, before the dewy mist hovering over the grass evaporated and the mother inside her woke as it did every morning, I should take a photograph with my new camera.

When the roll came back from the Kodak plant in a special heavy envelope, I could see the difference immediately. There was only one picture in which my mother was Abigail. It was that first one, the one taken of her unawares, the one captured before the click startled her into the mother of the birthday girl, owner of the happy dog, wife to the loving man, and mother again to another girl and a cherished boy. Homemaker. Gardener. Sunny neighbor. My mother's eyes were oceans, and inside them there was loss. I thought I had my whole life to understand them, but that was the only day I had. Once upon Earth I saw her as Abigail, and then I let it slip effortlessly back — my fascination held in check by wanting her to be that mother and envelop me as that mother.

I was in the gazebo thinking of the photo, thinking of my mother, when Lindsey got up in the middle of the night and crept across the hall. I watched her as I would a burglar circling a house in a movie. I knew when she turned the knob to my room it would give. I knew she would get in, but what would she do in there? Already my private territory had become a no man's land in the middle of our house. My mother had not touched it. My bed was still unmade from the hurried morning of my death. My flowered hippo lay among the sheets and pillows, and so did an outfit I'd discarded before I chose the yellow bell-bottoms.

Lindsey walked across the soft rug and touched the navy skirt and red and blue crocheted vest that were two separate, heatedly despised balls. She had an orange and green vest made from the same pattern. She took the vest and spread it out flat on the bed, smoothing it. It was ugly and precious all at once. I could see that. She petted it.

Lindsey traced the outline of the gold tray I kept on my dresser, filled with pins from elections and school. My favorite was a pink pin that said "Hippy-Dippy Says Love," which I'd found in the school parking lot but had had to promise my mother I wouldn't wear. I kept a lot of pins on that tray and pinned to a giant felt banner from Indiana University, where my father had gone to school. I thought she would steal them—take one or two to wear—but she didn't. She didn't even pick them up. She just swept her fingertips over everything on the tray. Then she saw it, a tiny white corner sticking out from underneath. She pulled.

It was the picture.

A deep breath rushed out of her, and she sat down on the floor, her mouth still open and her hand still holding the picture. The tethers were rushing and whipping around her, like a canvas tent come loose from its stakes. She too, like me until the morning of that photograph, had never seen the mother-stranger. She had seen the photos right after. My mother looking tired but smiling. My mother and Holiday standing in front of the dogwood tree as the sun shot through her robe and gown. But I had wanted to be the only one in the house that knew my mother was also someone else — someone mysterious and unknown to us.

The first time I broke through, it was an accident. It was December 23, 1973.

Buckley was sleeping. My mother had taken Lindsey to the dentist. That week they had agreed that each day, as a family, they would spend time trying to move forward. My father had assigned himself the task of cleaning the upstairs guest room, which long ago had become his den.

His own father had taught him how to build ships in bottles. They were something my mother, sister, and brother couldn't care less about. It was something I adored. The den was full of them.

All day at work he counted numbers — due diligence for a Chadds Ford insurance firm — and at night he built the ships or read Civil War books to unwind. He would call me in whenever he was ready to raise the sail. By then the ship would have been glued fast to the bottom of the bottle. I would come in and my father would ask me to shut the door. Often, it seemed, the dinner bell rang immediately, as if my mother had a sixth sense for things that didn't include her. But when this sense failed her, my job was to hold the bottle for him.

"Stay steady," he'd say. "You're my first mate."

Gently he would draw the one string that still reached out of the bottle's neck, and, voilà, the sails all rose, from simple mast to clipper ship. We had our boat. I couldn't clap because I held the bottle, but I always wanted to. My father worked quickly then, burning the end of the string off inside the bottle with a coat hanger he'd heated over a candle. If he did it improperly, the ship would be ruined, or, worse still, the tiny paper sails would catch on fire and suddenly, in a giant whoosh, I would be holding a bottle of flames in my hands.

Eventually my father built a balsa wood stand to replace me. Lindsey and Buckley didn't share my fascination. After trying to create enough enthusiasm for all three of them, he gave up and re-treated to his den. One ship in a bottle was equal to any other as far as the rest of my family was concerned.

But as he cleaned that day he talked to me.

"Susie, my baby, my little sailor girl," he said, "you always liked these smaller ones."

I watched him as he lined up the ships in bottles on his desk, bringing them over from the shelves where they usually sat. He used an old shirt of my mother's that had been ripped into rags and began dusting the shelves. Under his desk there were empty bottles — rows and rows of them we had collected for our future ship-building. In the closet were more ships — the ships he had built with his own father, ships he had built alone, and then those we had made together. Some were perfect, but their sails browned; some had sagged or toppled over after years. Then there was the one that had burst into flames in the week before my death.

He smashed that one first.

My heart seized up. He turned and saw all the others, all the years they marked and the hands that had held them. His dead fa-ther's, his dead child's. I watched him as he smashed the rest. He christened the walls and wooden chair with the news of my death, and afterward he stood in the guest room/den surrounded by green glass. The bottles, all of them, lay broken on the floor, the sails and boat bodies strewn among them. He stood in the wreck-age. It was then that, without knowing how, I revealed myself. In every piece of glass, in every shard and sliver, I cast my face. My father glanced down and around him, his eyes roving across the room. Wild. It was just for a second, and then I was gone. He was quiet for a moment, and then he laughed — a howl coming up from the bottom of his stomach. He laughed so loud and deep, I shook with it in my heaven.

He left the room and went down the two doors to my bedroom. The hallway was tiny, my door like all the others, hollow enough to easily punch a fist through. He was about to smash the mirror over my dresser, rip the wallpaper down with his nails, but instead he fell against my bed, sobbing, and balled the lavender sheets up in his hands.

"Daddy?" Buckley said. My brother held the doorknob with his hand.

My father turned but was unable to stop his tears. He slid to the floor with the sheets still in his fists, and then he opened up his arms. He had to ask my brother twice, which he had never had to do before, but Buckley came to him.

My father wrapped my brother inside the sheets that smelled of me. He remembered the day I'd begged him to paint and paper my room purple. Remembered moving in the old *National Geographic*s to the bottom shelves of my bookcases. (I had wanted to steep myself in wildlife photography.) Remembered when there was just one child in the house for the briefest of time until Lindsey arrived.

"You are so special to me, little man," my father said, clinging to him.

Buckley drew back and stared at my father's creased face, the fine bright spots of tears at the corners of his eyes. He nodded seriously and kissed my father's cheek. Something so divine that no one up in heaven could have made it up; the care a child took with an adult.

My father draped the sheets around Buckley's shoulders and remembered how I would fall out of the tall four-poster bed and onto the rug, never waking up. Sitting in his study in his green chair and reading a book, he would be startled by the sound of my body landing. He would get up and walk the short distance to my bedroom. He liked to watch me sleeping soundly, unchecked by nightmare or even hardwood floor. He swore in those moments that his children would be kings or rulers or artists or doctors or wildlife photographers. Anything they dreamed they could be.

A few months before I died, he had found me like this, but tucked inside my sheets with me was Buckley, in his pajamas, with his bear, curled up against my back, sucking sleepily on his thumb. My father had felt in that moment the first flicker of the strange sad mortality of being a father. His life had given birth to three children, so the number calmed him. No matter what happened to Abigail or to him, the three would have one another. In that way the line he had begun seemed immortal to him, like a strong steel filament threading into the future, continuing past him no matter where he might fall off. Even in deep snowy old age.

He would find his Susie now inside his young son. Give that love to the living. He told himself this — spoke it aloud inside his brain — but my presence was like a tug on him, it dragged him back back back. He stared at the small boy he held in his arms. *"Who are you?"* he found himself asking. *"Where did you come from?"*

I watched my brother and my father. The truth was very different from what we learned in school. The truth was that the line between the living and the dead could be, it seemed, murky and blurred.

# FOUR

In the hours after I was murdered, as my mother made phone calls and my father began going door to door in the neighborhood looking for me, Mr. Harvey had collapsed the hole in the cornfield and carried away a sack filled with my body parts. He passed within two houses of where my father stood talking to Mr. and Mrs. Tarking. He kept to the property line in between two rows of warring hedge — the O'Dwyers' boxwood and the Steads' goldenrod. His body brushed past the sturdy green leaves, leaving traces of me behind him, smells the Gilberts' dog would pick up and follow to find my elbow, smells the sleet and rain of the next three days would wash away before police dogs could even be thought of. He carried me back to his house, where, while he went inside to wash up, I waited for him.

After the house changed hands, the new owners tsk-tsked at the dark spot on the floor of their garage. As she brought prospective buyers through, the realtor said it was an oil stain, but it was me, seeping out of the bag Mr. Harvey carried and spilling onto the concrete. The beginning of my secret signals to the world.

It would be some time before I realized what you've undoubtedly already assumed, that I wasn't the first girl he'd killed. He knew to remove my body from the field. He knew to watch the weather and to kill during an arc of light-to-heavy precipitation because that would rob the police of evidence. But he was not as fastidious as the police liked to think. He forgot my elbow, he used a cloth sack for a bloody body, and if someone, anyone, had been watching, maybe they would have thought it strange to see their neighbor walk a property line that was a tight fit, even for children who liked to pretend the warring hedges were a hideout.

As he scoured his body in the hot water of his suburban bathroom—one with the identical layout to the one Lindsey, Buckley, and I shared—his movements were slow, not anxious. He felt a calm flood him. He kept the lights out in the bathroom and felt the warm water wash me away and he felt thoughts of me then. My muffled scream in his ear. My delicious death moan. The glorious white flesh that had never seen the sun, like an infant's, and then split, so perfectly, with the blade of his knife. He shivered under the heat, a prickling pleasure creating goose bumps up and down his arms and legs. He had put me in the waxy cloth sack and thrown in the shaving cream and razor from the mud ledge, his book of sonnets, and finally the bloody knife. They were tumbled together with my knees, fingers, and toes, but he made a note to extract them before my blood grew too sticky later that night. The sonnets and the knife, at least, he saved.

At Evensong, there were all sorts of dogs. And some of them, the ones I liked best, would lift their heads when they smelled an interesting scent in the air. If it was vivid enough, if they couldn't identify it immediately, or if, as the case may be, they knew exactly what it was — their brains going, "Um steak tartare" — they'd track it until they came to the object itself. In the face of the real article, the true story, they decided then what to do. That's how they operated. They didn't shut down their desire to know just because the smell was bad or the object was dangerous. They hunted. So did I.

Mr. Harvey took the waxy orange sack of my remains to a sinkhole eight miles from our neighborhood, an area that until recently had been desolate save for the railroad tracks and a nearby motorcycle repair shop. In his car he played a radio station that looped Christmas carols during the month of December. He whistled inside his huge station wagon and congratulated himself, felt full-up. Apple pie, cheeseburger, ice cream, coffee. Full. Better and better he was getting now, never using an old pattern that would bore him but making each kill a surprise to himself, a gift to himself.

The air inside the station wagon was cold and fragile. I could see the moist air when he exhaled, and this made me want to palpate my own stony lungs.

He drove the reed-thin road that cut between two new industrial lots. The wagon fishtailed coming up out of a particularly deep pothole, and the safe that held the sack that held my body smashed against the inside hub of the wagon's back wheel, cracking the plastic. "Damn," Mr. Harvey said. But he picked up his whistling again without pause.

I had a memory of going down this road with my father at the wheel and Buckley sitting nestled against me — one seat belt serving the two of us — in an illegal joyride away from the house.

My father had asked if any of us kids wanted to watch a refrigerator disappear.

"The earth will swallow it!" he said. He put on his hat and the dark cordovan gloves I coveted. I knew gloves meant you were an adult and mittens meant you weren't. (For Christmas 1973, my mother had bought me a pair of gloves. Lindsey ended up with them, but she knew they were mine. She left them at the edge of the cornfield one day on her way home from school. She was always doing that — bringing me things.)

"The earth has a mouth?" Buckley asked.

"A big round mouth but with no lips," my father said.

"Jack," my mother said, laughing, "stop it. Do you know I caught him outside growling at the snapdragons?"

"I'll go," I said. My father had told me that there was an abandoned underground mine and it had collapsed to create a sinkhole. I didn't care; I liked to see the earth swallow something as much as the next kid.

So when I watched Mr. Harvey take me out to the sinkhole, I couldn't help but think how smart he was. How he put the bag in a metal safe, placing me in the middle of all that weight.

It was late when he got there, and he left the safe in his Wagoneer while he approached the house of the Flanagans, who lived on the property where the sinkhole was. The Flanagans made their living by charging people to dump their appliances.

Mr. Harvey knocked on the door of the small white house and a woman came to answer it. The scent of rosemary and lamb filled my heaven and hit Mr. Harvey's nose as it trailed out from the back of the house. He could see a man in the kitchen.

"Good evening, sir," Mrs. Flanagan said. "Got an item?"

"Back of my wagon," Mr. Harvey said. He was ready with a twenty-dollar bill.

"What you got in there, a dead body?" she joked.

It was the last thing on her mind. She lived in a warm if small house. She had a husband who was always home to fix things and to be sweet on her because he never had to work, and she had a son who was still young enough to think his mother was the only thing in the world.

Mr. Harvey smiled, and, as I watched his smile break across his face, I would not look away.

"Old safe of my father's, finally got it out here," he said. "Been meaning to do it for years. No one remembers the combination."

"Anything in it?" she asked.

"Stale air."

"Back her up then. You need any help?"

"That would be lovely," he said.

The Flanagans never suspected for a moment that the girl they read about in the papers over the next few years — MISSING, FOUL PLAY SUSPECTED; ELBOW FOUND BY NEIGHBORING DOG; GIRL, 14, BELIEVED KILLED IN STOLFUZ CORNFIELD; WARNINGS TO OTHER YOUNG WOMEN; TOWNSHIP TO REZONE ADJOINING LOTS TO HIGH SCHOOL; LINDSEY SALMON, SISTER OF DEAD GIRL, GIVES VALEDIC-TORIAN SPEECH — could have been in the gray metal safe that a lonely man brought over one night and paid them twenty dollars to sink.

On the way back to the wagon Mr. Harvey put his hands in his pockets. There was my silver charm bracelet. He couldn't re-member taking it off my wrist. Had no memory of thrusting it into the pocket of his clean pants. He fingered it, the fleshy pad of his index finger finding the smooth gold metal of the Pennsylvania keystone, the back of the ballet slipper, the tiny hole of the minuscule thimble, and the spokes of the bicycle with wheels that worked. Down Route 202, he pulled over on the shoulder, ate a liverwurst sandwich he'd prepared earlier that day, then drove to an industrial park they were building south of Downingtown. No one was on the construction lot. In those days there was no security in the suburbs. He parked his car near a Port-o-John. His excuse was prepared in the unlikely event that he needed one.

It was this part of the aftermath that I thought of when I thought of Mr. Harvey — how he wandered the muddy excavations and got lost among the dormant bulldozers, their monstrous bulk frightening in the dark. The sky of the earth was dark blue on the night following my death, and out in this open area Mr. Harvey could see for miles. I chose to stand with him, to see those miles ahead as he saw them. I wanted to go where he would go. The snow had stopped. There was wind. He walked into what his builder's instincts told him would soon be a false pond, and he stood there and fingered the charms one last time. He liked the Pennsylvania keystone, which my father had had engraved with my initials — my favorite was the tiny bike — and he pulled it off and placed it in his pocket. He threw the bracelet, with its remaining charms, into the soon-to-be man-made lake.

Two days before Christmas, I watched Mr. Harvey read a book on the Dogon and Bambara of Mali. I saw the bright spark of an idea when he was reading of the cloth and ropes they used to build shelters. He decided he wanted to build again, to experiment as he had with the hole, and he settled on a ceremonial tent like the ones described in his reading. He would gather the simple materials and raise it in a few hours in his backyard.

After smashing all the ships in bottles, my father found him there.

It was cold out, but Mr. Harvey wore only a thin cotton shirt. He had turned thirty-six that year and was experimenting with hard contacts. They made his eyes perpetually bloodshot, and many people, my father among them, believed he had taken to drink.

"What's this?" my father asked.

Despite the Salmon men's heart disease, my father was hardy. He was a bigger man than Mr. Harvey, so when he walked around the front of the green shingled house and into the backyard, where he saw Harvey erecting things that looked like goalposts, he seemed bluff and able. He was buzzing from having seen me in the shattered glass. I watched him cut through the lawn, ambling as school kids did on their way toward the high school. He stopped just short of brushing Mr. Harvey's elderberry hedge with his palm.

"What's this?" he asked again.

Mr. Harvey stopped long enough to look at him and then turned back to his work.

"A mat tent."

"What's that?"

"Mr. Salmon," he said, "I'm sorry for your loss."

Drawing himself up, my father gave back what the ritual demanded.

"Thank you." It was like a rock perched in his throat.

There was a moment of quiet, and then Mr. Harvey, sensing my father had no intention of leaving, asked him if he wanted to help.

So it was that, from heaven, I watched my father build a tent with the man who'd killed me.

My father did not learn much. He learned how to lash arch pieces onto pronged posts and to weave more slender rods through these pieces to form semiarches in the other direction. He learned to gather the ends of these rods and lash them to the crossbars. He learned he was doing this because Mr. Harvey had been reading about the Imezzureg tribe and had wanted to replicate their tents. He stood, confirmed in the neighborhood opinion that the man was odd. So far, that was all.

But when the basic structure was done — a one-hour job — Mr. Harvey went toward the house without giving a reason. My father assumed it was breaktime. That Mr. Harvey had gone in to get coffee or brew a pot of tea.

He was wrong. Mr. Harvey went into the house and up the stairs to check on the carving knife that he had put in his bedroom. It was still in the nightstand, on top of which he kept his sketch pad where, often, in the middle of the night, he drew the designs in his dreams. He looked inside a crumpled paper grocery sack. My blood on the blade had turned black. Remembering it, remembering his act in the hole, made him remember what he had read about a particular tribe in southern Ayr. How, when a tent was made for a newly married couple, the women of the tribe made the sheet that would cover it as beautiful as they could.

It had begun to snow outside. It was the first snow since my death, and this was not lost on my father.

"I can hear you, honey," he said to me, even though I wasn't talking. "What is it?"

I focused very hard on the dead geranium in his line of vision. I thought if I could make it bloom he would have his answer. In my heaven it bloomed. In my heaven geranium petals swirled in eddies up to my waist. On Earth nothing happened.

But through the snow I noticed this: my father was looking toward the green house in a new way. He had begun to wonder.

Inside, Mr. Harvey had donned a heavy flannel shirt, but what my father noticed first was what he carried in his arms: a stack of white cotton sheets.

"What are those for?" my father asked. Suddenly he could not stop seeing my face.

"Tarps," said Mr. Harvey. When he handed a stack to my father, the back of his hand touched my father's fingers. It was like an electric shock.

"You know something," my father said.

He met my father's eyes, held them, but did not speak.

They worked together, the snow falling, almost wafting, down. And as my father moved, his adrenaline raced. He checked what he knew. Had anyone asked this man where he was the day I disappeared? Had anyone seen this man in the cornfield? He knew his neighbors had been questioned. Methodically, the police had gone from door to door.

My father and Mr. Harvey spread the sheets over the domed arch, anchoring them along the square formed by the crossbars that linked the forked posts. Then they hung the remaining sheets straight down from these crossbars so that the bottoms of the sheets brushed the ground.

By the time they had finished, the snow sat gingerly on the covered arches. It filled in the hollows of my father's shirt and lay in a line across the top of his belt. I ached. I realized I would never rush out into the snow with Holiday again, would never push Lindsey on a sled, would never teach, against my better judgment, my little brother how to compact snow by shaping it against the base of his palm. I stood alone in a sea of bright petals. On Earth the snowflakes fell soft and blameless, a curtain descending.

Standing inside the tent, Mr. Harvey thought of how the virgin bride would be brought to a member of the Imezzureg on a camel. When my father made a move toward him, Mr. Harvey put his palm up.

"That's enough now," he said. "Why don't you go on home?"

The time had come for my father to think of something to say. But all he could think of was this: "Susie," he whispered, the second syllable whipped like a snake.

"We've just built a tent," Mr. Harvey said. "The neighbors saw us. We're friends now."

"You know something," my father said.

"Go home. I can't help you."

Mr. Harvey did not smile or step forward. He retreated into the bridal tent and let the final monogrammed white cotton sheet fall down.

## FIVE

Part of me wished swift vengeance, wanted my father to turn into the man he could never have been — a man violent in rage. That's what you see in movies, that's what happens in the books people read. An everyman takes a gun or a knife and stalks the murderer of his family; he does a Bronson on them and everyone cheers.

What it *was* like:

Every day he got up. Before sleep wore off, he was who he used to be. Then, as his consciousness woke, it was as if poison seeped in. At first he couldn't even get up. He lay there under a heavy weight. But then only movement could save him, and he moved and he moved and he moved, no movement being enough to make up for it. The guilt on him, the hand of God pressing down on him, saying, *You were not there when your daughter needed you.*

Before my father left for Mr. Harvey's, my mother had been sitting in the front hall next to the statue they'd bought of St.

Francis. She was gone when he came back. He'd called for her, said her name three times, said it like a wish that she would not appear, and then he ascended the steps to his den to jot things down in a small spiral notebook: "A drinker? Get him drunk. Maybe he's a talker." He wrote this next: "I think Susie watches me." I was ecstatic in heaven. I hugged Holly, I hugged Franny. My father knew, I thought.

Then Lindsey slammed the front door more loudly than usual, and my father was glad for the noise. He was afraid of going further in his notes, of writing the words down. The slamming door echoed down the strange afternoon he'd spent and brought him into the present, into activity, where he needed to be so he would not drown. I understood this — I'm not saying I didn't resent it, that it didn't remind me of sitting at the dinner table and having to listen to Lindsey tell my parents about the test she'd done so well on, or about how the history teacher was going to recommend her for the district honors council, but Lindsey was living, and the living deserved attention too.

She stomped up the stairs. Her clogs slammed against the pine boards of the staircase and shook the house.

I may have begrudged her my father's attention, but I respected her way of handling things. Of everyone in the family, it was Lindsey who had to deal with what Holly called the Walking Dead Syndrome — when other people see the dead person and don't see you.

When people looked at Lindsey, even my father and mother, they saw me. Even Lindsey was not immune. She avoided mirrors. She now took her showers in the dark.

She would leave the dark shower and feel her way over to the towel rack. She would be safe in the dark — the moist steam from the shower still rising off the tiles encased her. If the house was quiet or if she heard murmurs below her, she knew she would be undisturbed. This was when she could think of me and she did so

in two ways: she either thought *Susie,* just that one word, and
cried there, letting her tears roll down her already damp cheeks,
knowing no one would see her, no one would quantify this dangerous substance as grief, or she would imagine me running,
imagine me getting away, imagine herself being taken instead,
fighting until she was free. She fought back the constant question,
*Where is Susie now?*

My father listened to Lindsey in her room. Bang, the door was
slammed shut. Thump, her books were thrown down. Squeak,
she fell onto her bed. Her clogs, boom, boom, were kicked off
onto the floor. A few minutes later he stood outside her door.

"Lindsey," he said upon knocking.

There was no answer.

"Lindsey, can I come in?"

"Go away," came her resolute answer.

"Come on now, honey," he pleaded.

"Go away!"

"Lindsey," my father said, sucking in his breath, "why can't you
let me in?" He placed his forehead gently against the bedroom
door. The wood felt cool and, for a second, he forgot the pounding of his temples, the suspicion he now held that kept repeating
itself. *Harvey, Harvey, Harvey.*

In sock feet, Lindsey came silently to the door. She unlocked it
as my father drew back and prepared a face that he hoped said
"Don't run."

"What?" she said. Her face was rigid, an affront. "What is it?"

"I want to know how you are," he said. He thought of the curtain falling between him and Mr. Harvey, how a certain capture,
a lovely blame, was lost to him. He had his family walking
through the streets, going to school, passing, on their way, Mr.
Harvey's green-shingled house. To get the blood back in his heart
he needed his child.

"I want to be alone," Lindsey said. "Isn't that obvious?"

"I'm here if you need me," he said.

"Look, Dad," my sister said, making her one concession for him, "I'm handling this alone."

What could he do with that? He could have broken the code and said, "I'm not, I can't, don't make me," but he stood there for a second and then retreated. "I understand," he said first, although he didn't.

I wanted to lift him up, like statues I'd seen in art history books. A woman lifting up a man. The rescue in reverse. Daughter to father saying, "It's okay. You're okay. Now I won't let anything hurt."

Instead, I watched him as he went to place a call to Len Fenerman.

The police in those first weeks were almost reverent. Missing dead girls were not a common occurrence in the suburbs. But with no leads coming in on where my body was or who had killed me, the police were getting nervous. There was a window of time during which physical evidence was usually found; that window grew smaller every day.

"I don't want to sound irrational, Detective Fenerman," my father said.

"Len, please." Tucked in the corner of his desk blotter was the school picture Len Fenerman had taken from my mother. He had known, before anyone said the words, that I was already dead.

"I'm certain there's a man in the neighborhood who knows something," my father said. He was staring out the window of his upstairs den, toward the cornfield. The man who owned it had told the press he was going to let it sit fallow for now.

"Who is it, and what led you to believe this?" Len Fenerman asked. He chose a stubby, chewed pencil from the front metal lip of his desk drawer.

My father told him about the tent, about how Mr. Harvey had told him to go home, about saying my name, about how weird the neighborhood thought Mr. Harvey was with no regular job and no kids.

"I'll check it out," Len Fenerman said, because he had to. That was the role he played in the dance. But what my father had given him offered him little or nothing to work with. "Don't talk to anyone and don't approach him again," Len warned.

When my father hung up the phone he felt strangely empty. Drained, he opened the door to his den and closed it quietly behind him. In the hallway, for the second time, he called my mother's name: "Abigail."

She was in the downstairs bathroom, sneaking bites from the macaroons my father's firm always sent us for Christmas. She ate them greedily; they were like suns bursting open in her mouth. The summer she was pregnant with me, she wore one gingham maternity dress over and over, refusing to spend money on another, and ate all she wanted, rubbing her belly and saying, "Thank you, baby," as she dribbled chocolate on her breasts.

There was a knock down low on the door.

"Momma?" She stuffed the macaroons back in the medicine cabinet, swallowing what was already in her mouth.

"Momma?" Buckley repeated. His voice was sleepy.

*"Mommmmm-maaa!"*

She despised the word.

When my mother opened the door, my little brother held on to her knees. Buckley pressed his face into the flesh above them.

Hearing movement, my father went to meet my mother in the kitchen. Together they took solace in attending to Buckley.

"Where's Susie?" Buckley asked as my father spread Fluffernutter on wheat bread. He made three. One for himself, one for my mother, and one for his four-year-old son.

"Did you put away your game?" my father asked Buckley,

wondering why he persisted in avoiding the topic with the one person who approached it head-on.

"What's wrong with Mommy?" Buckley asked. Together they watched my mother, who was staring into the dry basin of the sink.

"How would you like to go to the zoo this week?" my father asked. He hated himself for it. Hated the bribe and the tease — the deceit. But how could he tell his son that, somewhere, his big sister might lie in pieces?

But Buckley heard the word *zoo* and all that it meant — which to him was largely *Monkeys!* — and he began on the rippling path to forgetting for one more day. The shadow of years was not as big on his small body. He knew I was away, but when people left they always came back.

When Len Fenerman had gone door to door in the neighborhood he had found nothing remarkable at George Harvey's. Mr. Harvey was a single man who, it was said, had meant to move in with his wife. She had died sometime before this. He built dollhouses for specialty stores and kept to himself. That was all anyone knew. Though friendships had not exactly blossomed around him, the sympathy of the neighborhood had always been with him. Each split-level contained a narrative. To Len Fenerman especially, George Harvey's seemed a compelling one.

No, Harvey said, he didn't know the Salmons well. Had seen the children. Everyone knew who had children and who didn't, he noted, his head hanging down and to the left a bit. "You can see the toys in the yard. The houses are always more lively," he noted, his voice halting.

"I understand you had a conversation with Mr. Salmon recently," Len said on his second trip to the dark green house.

"Yes, is there something wrong?" Mr. Harvey asked. He

squinted at Len but then had to pause. "Let me get my glasses," he said. "I was doing some close work on a Second Empire."

"Second Empire?" Len asked.

"Now that my Christmas orders are done, I can experiment," Mr. Harvey said. Len followed him into the back, where a dining table was pushed against a wall. Dozens of small lengths of what looked like miniature wainscoting were lined up on top of it.

*A little strange,* Fenerman thought, *but it doesn't make the man a murderer.*

Mr. Harvey got his glasses and immediately opened up. "Yes, Mr. Salmon was on one of his walks and he helped me build the bridal tent."

"The bridal tent?"

"Each year it's something I do for Leah," he said. "My wife. I'm a widower."

Len felt he was intruding on this man's private rituals. "So I understand," he said.

"I feel terrible about what happened to that girl," Mr. Harvey said. "I tried to express that to Mr. Salmon. But I know from experience that nothing makes sense at a time like this."

"So you erect this tent every year?" Len Fenerman asked. This was something he could get confirmation on from neighbors.

"In the past, I've done it inside, but I tried to do it outside this year. We were married in the winter. Until the snow picked up, I thought it would work."

"Where inside?"

"The basement. I can show you if you want. I have all of Leah's things down there still."

But Len did not go further.

"I've intruded enough," he said. "I just wanted to sweep the neighborhood a second time."

"How's your investigation coming?" Mr. Harvey asked. "Are you finding anything?"

Len never liked questions like this, though he supposed they were the right of the people whose lives he was invading.

"Sometimes I think clues find their way in good time," he said. "If they want to be found, that is." It was cryptic, sort of a Confucius-says answer, but it worked on almost every civilian.

"Have you talked to the Ellis boy?" Mr. Harvey asked.

"We talked to the family."

"He's hurt some animals in the neighborhood, I hear."

"He sounds like a bad kid, I grant you," said Len, "but he was working in the mall at the time."

"Witnesses?"

"Yes."

"That's my only idea," Mr. Harvey said. "I wish I could do more."

Len felt him to be sincere.

"He's certainly a bit tweaked at an angle," Len said when he called my father, "but I have nothing on him."

"What did he say about the tent?"

"That he built it for Leah, his wife."

"I remember Mrs. Stead told Abigail his wife's name was Sophie," my father said.

Len checked his notes. "No, Leah. I wrote it down."

My father doubted himself. Where had he gotten the name Sophie? He was sure he had heard it too, but that was years ago, at a block party, where the names of children and wives flew about like confetti between the stories people told to be neighborly and the introductions to infants and strangers too vague to remember the following day.

He did remember that Mr. Harvey had not come to the block party. He had never come to any of them. This went to his strangeness by the standards of many in the neighborhood but not by my father's own standards. He had never felt completely comfortable at these forced efforts of conviviality himself.

My father wrote "Leah?" in his book. Then he wrote, "Sophie?" Though unaware of it, he had begun a list of the dead.

On Christmas Day, my family would have been more comfortable in heaven. Christmas was largely ignored in my heaven. Some people dressed all in white and pretended they were snowflakes, but other than that, nothing.

That Christmas, Samuel Heckler came to our house on an un-expected visit. He was not dressed like a snowflake. He wore his older brother's leather jacket and a pair of ill-fitting army fatigues.

My brother was in the front room with his toys. My mother blessed the fact that she had gone early to buy his gifts. Lindsey got gloves and cherry-flavored lip gloss. My father got five white handkerchiefs that she'd ordered months ago in the mail. Save Buckley, no one wanted anything anyway. In the days before Christmas the lights on the tree were not plugged in. Only the candle that my father kept in the window of his den burned. He lit it after dark, but my mother, sister, and brother had stopped leaving the house after four o'clock. Only I saw it.

"There's a man outside!" my brother shouted. He'd been play-ing Skyscraper and it had yet to collapse. "He's got a suitcase."

My mother left her eggnog in the kitchen and came to the front of the house. Lindsey was suffering the mandatory presence in the family room that all holidays required. She and my father played Monopoly, ignoring the more brutal squares for each other's sake. There was no Luxury Tax, and a bad Chance wasn't recognized.

In the front hall my mother pressed her hands down along her skirt. She placed Buckley in front of her and put her arms on his shoulders.

"Wait for the man to knock," she said.

"Maybe it's Reverend Strick," my father said to Lindsey,

collecting his fifteen dollars for winning second prize in a beauty contest.

"For Susie's sake, I hope not," Lindsey ventured.

My father held on to it, on to my sister saying my name. She rolled doubles and moved to Marvin Gardens.

"That's twenty-four dollars," my father said, "but I'll take ten."

"Lindsey," my mother called. "It's a visitor for you."

My father watched my sister get up and leave the room. We both did. I sat with my father then. I was the ghost on the board. He stared at the old shoe lying on its side in the box. If only I could have lifted it up, made it hop from Boardwalk to Baltic, where I always claimed the better people lived. "That's because you're a purple freak," Lindsey would say. My father would say, "I'm proud I didn't raise a snob."

"Railroads, Susie," he said. "You always liked owning those railroads."

To accentuate his widow's peak and tame his cowlick, Samuel Heckler insisted on combing his hair straight back. This made him look, at thirteen and dressed in black leather, like an adolescent vampire.

"Merry Christmas, Lindsey," he said to my sister, and held out a small box wrapped in blue paper.

I could see it happen: Lindsey's body began to knot. She was working hard keeping everyone out, everyone, but she found Samuel Heckler cute. Her heart, like an ingredient in a recipe, was reduced, and regardless of my death she was thirteen, he was cute, and he had visited her on Christmas Day.

"I heard you made gifted," he said to her, because no one was talking. "Me too."

My mother remembered then, and she switched on her auto-pilot hostess. "Would you like to come sit?" she managed. "I have some eggnog in the kitchen."

"That would be wonderful," Samuel Heckler said and, to Lindsey's amazement and mine, offered my sister his arm.

"What's that?" asked Buckley, trailing behind and pointing to what he thought was a suitcase.

"An alto," Samuel Heckler said.

"What?" asked Buckley.

Lindsey spoke then. "Samuel plays the alto saxophone."

"Barely," Samuel said.

My brother did not ask what a saxophone was. He knew what Lindsey was being. She was being what I called snooty-wooty, as in "Buckley, don't worry, Lindsey's being snooty-wooty." Usually I'd tickle him as I said the word, sometimes burrowing into his stomach with my head, butting him and saying "snooty-wooty" over and over until his trills of laughter flowed down over me.

Buckley followed the three of them into the kitchen and asked, as he had at least once a day, "Where's Susie?"

They were silent. Samuel looked at Lindsey.

"Buckley," my father called from the adjoining room, "come play Monopoly with me."

My brother had never been invited to play Monopoly. Everyone said he was too young, but this was the magic of Christmas. He rushed into the family room, and my father picked him up and sat him on his lap.

"See this shoe?" my father said.

Buckley nodded his head.

"I want you to listen to everything I say about it, okay?"

"Susie?" my brother asked, somehow connecting the two.

"Yes, I'm going to tell you where Susie is."

I began to cry up in heaven. What else was there for me to do?

"This shoe was the piece Susie played Monopoly with," he said. "I play with the car or sometimes the wheelbarrow. Lindsey plays with the iron, and when your mother plays, she likes the cannon."

"Is that a dog?"

"Yes, that's a Scottie."

"Mine!"

"Okay," my father said. He was patient. He had found a way to explain it. He held his son in his lap, and as he spoke, he felt Buckley's small body on his knee — the very human, very warm, very alive weight of it. It comforted him. "The Scottie will be your piece from now on. Which piece is Susie's again?"

"The shoe," Buckley said.

"Right, and I'm the car, your sister's the iron, and your mother is the cannon."

My brother concentrated very hard.

"Now let's put all the pieces on the board, okay? You go ahead and do it for me."

Buckley grabbed a fist of pieces and then another, until all the pieces lay between the Chance and Community Chest cards.

"Let's say the other pieces are our friends."

"Like Nate?"

"Right, we'll make your friend Nate the hat. And the board is the world. Now if I were to tell you that when I rolled the dice, one of the pieces would be taken away, what would that mean?"

"They can't play anymore?"

"Right."

"Why?" Buckley asked.

He looked up at my father; my father flinched.

"Why?" my brother asked again.

My father did not want to say "because life is unfair" or "because that's how it is." He wanted something neat, something that could explain death to a four-year-old. He placed his hand on the small of Buckley's back.

"Susie is dead," he said now, unable to make it fit in the rules of any game. "Do you know what that means?"

Buckley reached over with his hand and covered the shoe. He looked up to see if his answer was right.

My father nodded. "You won't see Susie anymore, honey. None of us will." My father cried. Buckley looked up into the eyes of our father and did not fully understand.

Buckley kept the shoe on his dresser, until one day it wasn't there anymore and no amount of looking for it could turn it up.

In the kitchen my mother finished her eggnog and excused herself. She went into the dining room and counted silverware, methodically laying out the three kinds of forks, the knives, and the spoons, making them "climb the stairs" as she'd been taught when she worked in Wanamaker's bridal shop before I was born. She wanted a cigarette and for her children who were living to disappear for a little while.

"Are you going to open your gift?" Samuel Heckler asked my sister.

They stood at the counter, leaning against the dishwasher and the drawers that held napkins and towels. In the room to their right sat my father and brother; on the other side of the kitchen, my mother was thinking Wedgwood Florentine, Cobalt Blue; Royal Worcester, Mountbatten; Lenox, Eternal.

Lindsey smiled and pulled at the white ribbon on top of the box.

"My mom did the ribbon for me," Samuel Heckler said.

She tore the blue paper away from the black velvet box. Carefully she held it in her palm once the paper was off. In heaven I was excited. When Lindsey and I played Barbies, Barbie and Ken got married at sixteen. To us there was only one true love in everyone's life; we had no concept of compromise, or retries.

"Open it," Samuel Heckler said.

"I'm scared."

"Don't be."

He put his hand on her forearm and—Wow!—what I felt

when he did that. Lindsey had a cute boy in the kitchen, vampire or no! This was news, this was a bulletin — I was suddenly privy to everything. She never would have told me any of this stuff.

What the box held was typical or disappointing or miraculous depending on the eye. It was typical because he was a thirteen-year-old boy, or it was disappointing because it was not a wedding ring, or it was miraculous. He'd given her a half a heart. It was gold and from inside his Hukapoo shirt, he pulled out the other side. It hung around his neck on a rawhide cord.

Lindsey's face flushed; mine flushed up in heaven.

I forgot my father in the family room and my mother counting silver. I saw Lindsey move toward Samuel Heckler. She kissed him; it was glorious. I was almost alive again.

———

Two weeks before my death, I left the house later than usual, and by the time I reached the school, the blacktop circle where the school buses usually hovered was empty.

A hall monitor from the discipline office would write down your name if you tried to get in the front doors after the first bell rang, and I didn't want to be paged during class to come and sit on the hard bench outside Mr. Peterford's room, where, it was widely known, he would bend you over and paddle your behind with a board. He'd asked the shop teacher to drill holes into it for less wind resistance on the downstroke and more pain when it landed against your jeans.

I had never been late enough or done anything bad enough to meet the board, but in my mind as in every other kid's I could visualize it so well my butt would sting. Clarissa had told me that the baby stoners, as they were called in junior high, used the back door to the stage, which was always left open by Cleo, the janitor, who had dropped out of high school as a full-blown stoner.

So that day I crept into the backstage area, watching my step, careful not to trip over the various cords and wires. I paused near some scaffolding and put down my book bag to brush my hair. I'd taken to leaving the house in the jingle-bell cap and then switching, as soon as I gained cover behind the O'Dwyers' house, to an old black watch cap of my father's. All this left my hair full of static electricity, and my first stop was usually the girls' room, where I would brush it flat.

"You are beautiful, Susie Salmon."

I heard the voice but could not place it immediately. I looked around me.

"Here," the voice said.

I looked up and saw the head and torso of Ray Singh leaning out over the top of the scaffold above me.

"Hello," he said.

I knew Ray Singh had a crush on me. He had moved from England the year before but Clarissa said he was born in India. That someone could have the face of one country and the voice of another and then move to a third was too incredible for me to fathom. It made him immediately cool. Plus, he seemed eight hundred times smarter than the rest of us, and he had a crush on me. What I finally realized were affectations—the smoking jacket that he sometimes wore to school and his foreign cigarettes, which were actually his mother's—I thought were evidence of his higher breeding. He knew and saw things that the rest of us didn't see. That morning when he spoke to me from above, my heart plunged to the floor.

"Hasn't the first bell rung?" I asked.

"I have Mr. Morton for homeroom," he said. This explained everything. Mr. Morton had a perpetual hangover, which was at its peak during homeroom. He never called roll.

"What are you doing up there?"

"Climb up and see," he said, removing his head and shoulders from my view.

I hesitated.

"Come on, Susie."

It was my one day in life of being a bad kid — of at least feigning the moves. I placed my foot on the bottom rung of the scaffold and reached my arms up to the first crossbar.

"Bring your stuff," Ray advised.

I went back for my book bag and then climbed unsteadily up.

"Let me help you," he said and put his hands under my armpits, which, even though covered by my winter parka, I was self-conscious about. I sat for a moment with my feet dangling over the side.

"Tuck them in," he said. "That way no one will see us."

I did what he told me, and then I stared at him for a moment. I felt suddenly stupid — unsure of why I was there.

"Will you stay up here all day?" I asked.

"Just until English class is over."

"You're cutting English!" It was as if he said he'd robbed a bank.

"I've seen every Shakespeare play put on by the Royal Shakespeare Company," Ray said. "That bitch has nothing to teach me."

I felt sorry for Mrs. Dewitt then. If part of being bad was calling Mrs. Dewitt a bitch, I wasn't into it.

"I like *Othello*," I ventured.

"It's condescending twaddle the way she teaches it. A sort of *Black Like Me* version of the Moor."

Ray was smart. This combined with being an Indian from England had made him a Martian in Norristown.

"That guy in the movie looked pretty stupid with black makeup on," I said.

"You mean Sir Laurence Olivier."

Ray and I were quiet. Quiet enough to hear the bell for the end of homeroom ring and then, five minutes later, the bell that meant we should be on the first floor in Mrs. Dewitt's class. As each second passed after that bell, I could feel my skin heat up and Ray's look lengthen out over my body, taking in my royal blue parka and my kelly green miniskirt with my matching Danskin tights. My real shoes sat beside me inside my bag. On my feet I had a pair of fake sheepskin boots with dirty synthetic shearing spilling out like animal innards around the tops and seams. If I had known this was to be the sex scene of my life, I might have prepared a bit, reapplied my Strawberry-Banana Kissing Potion as I came in the door.

I could feel Ray's body leaning toward me, the scaffolding underneath us squeaking from his movement. *He is from England,* I was thinking. His lips moved closer, the scaffold listed. I was dizzy—about to go under the wave of my first kiss, when we both heard something. We froze.

Ray and I lay down side by side and stared at the lights and wires overhead. A moment later, the stage door opened and in walked Mr. Peterford and the art teacher, Miss Ryan, who we recognized by their voices. There was a third person with them.

"We are not taking disciplinary action at this time, but we will if you persist," Mr. Peterford was saying. "Miss Ryan, did you bring the materials?"

"Yes." Miss Ryan had come to Kennet from a Catholic school and taken over the art department from two ex-hippies who had been fired when the kiln exploded. Our art classes had gone from wild experiments with molten metals and throwing clay to day after day of drawing profiles of wooden figures she placed in stiff positions at the beginning of each class.

"I'm only doing the assignments." It was Ruth Connors. I recognized the voice and so did Ray. We all had Mrs. Dewitt's English class first period.

"This," Mr. Peterford said, "was not the assignment."

Ray reached for my hand and squeezed. We knew what they

were talking about. A xeroxed copy of one of Ruth's drawings had been passed around in the library until it had reached a boy at the card catalog who was overtaken by the librarian.

"If I'm not mistaken," said Miss Ryan, "there are no breasts on our anatomy model."

The drawing had been of a woman reclining with her legs crossed. And it was no wooden figure with eyehooks connecting the limbs. It was a real woman, and the charcoal smudges of her eyes — whether by accident or intent — had given her a leering look that made every kid who saw it either highly uncomfortable or quite happy, thank you.

"There isn't a nose or mouth on that wooden model either," Ruth said, "but you encouraged us to draw in faces."

Again Ray squeezed my hand.

"That's enough, young lady," Mr. Peterford said. "It is the attitude of repose in this particular drawing that clearly made it something the Nelson boy would xerox."

"Is that my fault?"

"Without the drawing there would be no problem."

"So it's my fault?"

"I invite you to realize the position this puts the school in and to assist us by drawing what Miss Ryan instructs the class to draw without making unnecessary additions."

"Leonardo da Vinci drew cadavers," Ruth said softly.

"Understood?"

"Yes," said Ruth.

The stage doors opened and shut, and a moment later Ray and I could hear Ruth Connors crying. Ray mouthed the word *go,* and I moved to the end of the scaffold, dangling my foot over the side to find a hold.

That week Ray would kiss me by my locker. It didn't happen up on the scaffold when he'd wanted it to. Our only kiss was like an accident — a beautiful gasoline rainbow.

I climbed down off the scaffold with my back to her. She didn't move or hide, just looked at me when I turned around. She was sitting on a wooden crate near the back of the stage. A pair of old curtains hung to her left. She watched me walk toward her but didn't wipe her eyes.

"Susie Salmon," she said, just to confirm it. The possibility of my cutting first period and hiding backstage in the auditorium was, until that day, as remote as the smartest girl in our class being bawled out by the discipline officer.

I stood in front of her, hat in hand.

"That's a stupid hat," she said.

I lifted the jingle-bell cap and looked at it. "I know. My mom made it."

"So you heard?"

"Can I see?"

Ruth unfolded the much-handled xerox and I stared.

Using a blue ballpoint pen, Brian Nelson had made an obscene hole where her legs were crossed. I recoiled and she watched me. I could see something flicker in her eyes, a private wondering, and then she leaned over and brought out a black leather sketchbook from her knapsack.

Inside, it was beautiful. Drawings of women mostly, but of animals and men too. I'd never seen anything like it before. Each page was covered in her drawings. I realized how subversive Ruth was then, not because she drew pictures of nude women that got misused by her peers, but because she was more talented than her teachers. She was the quietest kind of rebel. Helpless, really.

"You're really good, Ruth," I said.

"Thank you," she said, and I kept looking through the pages of her book and drinking it in. I was both frightened and excited by what existed underneath the black line of the navel in those drawings — what my mother called the "baby-making machinery."

I told Lindsey I'd never have one, and when I was ten I'd spent the better part of six months telling any adult who would listen that I intended on getting my tubes tied. I didn't know what this meant, exactly, but I knew it was drastic, required surgery, and it made my father laugh out loud.

Ruth went from weird to special for me then. The drawings were so good that in that moment I forgot the rules of school, all the bells and whistles, which as kids we were supposed to respond to.

After the cornfield was roped off, searched, then abandoned, Ruth went walking there. She would wrap a large wool shawl of her grandmother's around her under the ratty old peacoat of her father's. Soon she noted that teachers in subjects besides gym didn't report her if she cut. They were happy not to have her there: her intelligence made her a problem. It demanded attention and rushed their lesson plans forward.

And she began to take rides from her father in the mornings to avoid the bus. He left very early and brought his red metal, sloped-top lunchbox, which he had allowed her to pretend was a barn for her Barbies when she was little, and in which he now tucked bourbon. Before he let her out in the empty parking lot, he would stop his truck but keep the heater running.

"Going to be okay today?" he always asked.

Ruth nodded.

"One for the road?"

And without nodding this time she handed him the lunchbox. He opened it, unscrewed the bourbon, took a deep swallow, and then passed it to her. She threw her head back dramatically and either placed her tongue against the glass so very little would make it to her mouth, or took a small, wincing gulp if he was watching her.

She slid out of the high cab. It was cold, bitterly cold, before the sun rose. Then she remembered a fact from one of our classes:

people moving are warmer than people at rest. So she began to walk directly to the cornfield, keeping a good pace. She talked to herself, and sometimes she thought about me. Often she would rest a moment against the chain-link fence that separated the soccer field from the track, while she watched the world come alive around her.

So we met each morning in those first few months. The sun would come up over the cornfield and Holiday, let loose by my father, would come to chase rabbits in and out of the tall dry stalks of dead corn. The rabbits loved the trimmed lawns of the athletic fields, and as Ruth approached she'd see their dark forms line up along the white chalk of the farthest boundaries like some sort of tiny sports team. She liked the idea of this and I did too. She believed stuffed animals moved at night when humans went to sleep. She still thought in her father's lunchbox there might be minute cows and sheep that found time to graze on the bourbon and baloney.

When Lindsey left the gloves from Christmas for me, in between the farthest boundary of the soccer field and the cornfield, I looked down one morning to see the rabbits investigate: sniff at the corners of the gloves lined with their own kin. Then I saw Ruth pick them up before Holiday grabbed them. She turned the bottom of one glove so the fur faced out and held it up to her cheek. She looked up to the sky and said, "Thank you." I liked to think she was talking to me.

I grew to love Ruth on those mornings, feeling that in some way we could never explain on our opposite sides of the Inbetween, we were born to keep each other company. Odd girls who had found each other in the strangest way — in the shiver she had felt when I passed.


Ray was a walker, like me, living at the far end of our development, which surrounded the school. He had seen Ruth Connors walking alone out on the soccer fields. Since Christmas he had come and gone to school as quickly as he could, never lingering. He wanted my killer to be caught almost as much as my parents did. Until he was, Ray could not wipe the traces of suspicion off himself, despite his alibi.

He chose a morning when his father was not going to work at the university and filled his father's thermos with his mother's sweet tea. He left early to wait for Ruth and made a little camp of the cement shot-put circle, sitting on the metal curve against which the shot-putters braced their feet.

When he saw her walking on the other side of the chain-link fence that separated the school from the soccer field and inside which was the most revered of the sports fields — the football one — he rubbed his hands together and prepared what he wanted to say. His bravery this time came not from having kissed me — a goal he'd set himself a full year before its completion — but from being, at fourteen, intensely lonely.

I watched Ruth approach the soccer field, thinking she was alone. In an old home her father had gone to scavenge, he had found her a treat to go along with her new hobby — an anthology of poems. She held them close.

She saw Ray stand up when she was still some distance away.

"Hello, Ruth Connors!" he called and waved his arms.

Ruth looked over, and his name came into her head: Ray Singh. But she didn't know much more than that. She had heard the rumors about the police being over at his house, but she believed what her father had said — "No kid did that" — and so she walked over to him.

"I prepared tea and have it in my thermos here," Ray said. I blushed for him up in heaven. He was smart when it came to *Othello,* but now he was acting like a geek.

"No thank you," Ruth said. She stood near him but with a definite few feet more than usual still in between. Her fingernails were pressed into the worn cover of the poetry anthology.

"I was there that day, when you and Susie talked backstage," Ray said. He held the thermos out to her. She made no move closer and didn't respond.

"Susie Salmon," he clarified.

"I know who you mean," she said.

"Are you going to the memorial service?"

"I didn't know there was one," she said.

"I don't think I'm going."

I was staring hard at his lips. They were redder than usual from the cold. Ruth took a step forward.

"Do you want some lip balm?" Ruth asked.

Ray lifted his wool gloves up to his lips, where they snagged briefly on the chapped surface that I had kissed. Ruth dug her hands in the peacoat pocket and pulled out her Chap Stick. "Here," she said, "I have tons of them. You can keep it."

"That's so nice," he said. "Will you at least sit with me until the buses come?"

They sat together on the shot-putters' cement platform. Again I was seeing something I never would have seen: the two of them together. It made Ray more attractive to me than he had ever been. His eyes were the darkest gray. When I watched him from heaven I did not hesitate to fall inside of them.

It became a ritual for the two of them. On the days that his father taught, Ruth brought him a little bourbon in her father's flask; otherwise they had sweet tea. They were cold as hell, but that didn't seem to matter to them.

They talked about what it was like to be a foreigner in Norristown. They read poems aloud from Ruth's anthology. They talked about how to become what they wanted to be. A doctor for Ray. A painter/poet for Ruth. They made a secret club of the other oddballs they could point out in our class. There were the obvious ones like Mike Bayles, who had taken so much acid no one understood how he was still in school, or Jeremiah, who was from Louisiana and so just as much a foreigner as Ray. Then there were the quiet ones. Artie, who talked excitedly to anyone about the effects of formaldehyde. Harry Orland, who was so painfully shy he wore his gym shorts over his jeans. And Vicki Kurtz, who everyone thought was okay after the death of her mother, but whom Ruth had seen sleeping in a bed of pine needles behind the junior high's regulating plant. And, sometimes, they would talk about me.

"It's so strange," Ruth said. "I mean, it's like we were in the same class since kindergarten but that day backstage in the auditorium was the first time we ever looked at each other."

"She was great," Ray said. He thought of our lips brushing past one another as we stood alone in a column of lockers. How I had smiled with my eyes closed and then almost run away. "Do you think they'll find him?"

"I guess so. You know, we're only like one hundred yards away from where it happened."

"I know," he said.

They both sat on the thin metal rim of the shot-putters' brace, holding tea in their gloved hands. The cornfield had become a place no one went. When a ball strayed from the soccer field, a boy took a dare to go in and get it. That morning the sun was slicing right through the dead stalks as it rose, but there was no heat from it.

"I found these here," she said, indicating the leather gloves.

"Do you ever think about her?" he asked.

They were quiet again.

"All the time," Ruth said. A chill ran down my spine. "Sometimes I think she's lucky, you know. I hate this place."

"Me too," Ray said. "But I've lived other places. This is just a temporary hell, not a permanent one."

"You're not implying . . ."

"She's in heaven, if you believe in that stuff."

"You don't?"

"I don't think so, no."

"I do," Ruth said. "I don't mean la-la angel-wing crap, but I do think there's a heaven."

"Is she happy?"

"It *is* heaven, right?"

"But what does that mean?"

The tea was stone-cold and the first bell had already rung. Ruth smiled into her cup. "Well, as my dad would say, it means she's out of this shithole."


When my father knocked on the door of Ray Singh's house, he was struck dumb by Ray's mother, Ruana. It was not that she was immediately welcoming, and she was far from sunny, but something about her dark hair, and her gray eyes, and even the strange way she seemed to step back from the door once she opened it, all of these things overwhelmed him.

He had heard the offhand comments the police made about her. To their mind she was cold and snobbish, condescending, odd. And so that was what he imagined he would find.

"Come in and sit," she'd said to him when he pronounced his name. Her eyes, on the word *Salmon,* had gone from closed to open doorways — dark rooms where he wanted to travel firsthand.

He almost lost his balance as she led him into the small cramped front room of their house. There were books on the floor with their spines facing up. They came out three rows deep from the wall. She was wearing a yellow sari and what looked like gold lamé capri pants underneath. Her feet were bare. She padded across the wall-to-wall and stopped at the couch. "Something to drink?" she asked, and he nodded his head.

"Hot or cold?"

"Hot."

As she turned the corner into a room he couldn't see, he sat down on the brown plaid couch. The windows across from him under which the books were lined were draped with long muslin curtains, which the harsh daylight outside had to fight to filter through. He felt suddenly very warm, almost close to forgetting why that morning he had double-checked the Singhs' address.

A little while later, as my father was thinking of how tired he was and how he had promised my mother to pick up some long-held dry cleaning, Mrs. Singh returned with tea on a tray and put it down on the carpet in front of him.

"We don't have much furniture, I'm afraid. Dr. Singh is still looking for tenure."

She went into an adjoining room and brought back a purple floor pillow for herself, which she placed on the floor to face him.

"Dr. Singh is a professor?" my father asked, though he knew this already, knew more than he was comfortable with about this beautiful woman and her sparsely furnished home.

"Yes," she said, and poured the tea. It was quiet. She held out a cup to him, and as he took it she said, "Ray was with him the day your daughter was killed."

He wanted to fall over into her.

"That must be why you've come," she continued.

"Yes," he said, "I want to talk to him."

"He's at school right now," she said. "You know that." Her legs in the gold pants were tucked to her side. The nails on her toes were long and unpolished, their surface gnarled from years of dancing.

"I wanted to come by and assure you I mean him no harm," my father said. I watched him. I had never seen him like this before. The words fell out of him like burdens he was delivering, back-logged verbs and nouns, but he was watching her feet curl against the dun-colored rug and the way the small pool of numbed light from the curtains touched her right cheek.

"He did nothing wrong and loved your little girl. A schoolboy crush, but still."

Schoolboy crushes happened all the time to Ray's mother. The teenager who delivered the paper would pause on his bike, hoping that she would be near the door when she heard the thump of the *Philadelphia Inquirer* hit the porch. That she would come out and, if she did, that she would wave. She didn't even have to smile, and she rarely did outside her house — it was the eyes, her dancer's carriage, the way she seemed to deliberate over the smallest movement of her body.

When the police had come they had stumbled into the dark front hall in search of a killer, but before Ray even reached the top of the stairs, Ruana had so confused them that they were agreeing to tea and sitting on silk pillows. They had expected her to fall into the grooves of the patter they relied on with all attractive women, but she only grew more erect in posture as they tried harder and harder to ingratiate themselves, and she stood upright by the windows while they questioned her son.

"I'm glad Susie had a nice boy like her," my father said. "I'll thank your son for that."

She smiled, not showing teeth.

"He wrote her a love note," he said.

"Yes."

"I wish I had known enough to do the same," he said. "Tell her I loved her on that last day."

"Yes."

"But your son did."

"Yes."

They stared at each other for a moment.

"You must have driven the policemen nuts," he said and smiled more to himself than to her.

"They came to accuse Ray," she said. "I wasn't concerned with how they felt about me."

"I imagine it's been hard for him," my father said.

"No, I won't allow that," she said sternly and placed her cup back on the tray. "You cannot have sympathy for Ray or for us."

My father tried to stutter out a protest.

She placed her hand in the air. "You have lost a daughter and come here for some purpose. I will allow you that and that only, but trying to understand our lives, no."

"I didn't mean to offend," he said. "I only . . ."

Again, the hand up.

"Ray will be home in twenty minutes. I will talk to him first and prepare him, then you may talk to my son about your daughter."

"What did I say?"

"I like that we don't have much furniture. It allows me to think that someday we might pack up and leave."

"I hope you'll stay," my father said. He said it because he had been trained to be polite from an early age, a training he passed on to me, but he also said it because part of him wanted more of her, this cold woman who was not exactly cold, this rock who was not stone.

"With all gentleness," she said, "you don't even know me. We'll wait together for Ray."

My father had left our house in the midst of a fight between Lindsey and my mother. My mother was trying to get Lindsey to go with her to the Y to swim. Without thinking, Lindsey had blared, "I'd rather die!" at the top of her lungs. My father watched as my mother froze, then burst, fleeing to their bedroom to wail behind the door. He quietly tucked his notebook in his jacket pocket, took the car keys off the hook by the back door, and snuck out.

In those first two months my mother and father moved in opposite directions from each other. One stayed in, the other went out. My father fell asleep in his den in the green chair, and when he woke he crept carefully into the bedroom and slid into bed. If my mother had most of the sheets he would lie without them, his body curled up tight, ready to spring at a moment's notice, ready for anything.

"I know who killed her," he heard himself say to Ruana Singh.

"Have you told the police?"

"Yes."

"What do they say?"

"They say that for now there is nothing but my suspicion to link him to the crime."

"A father's suspicion . . ." she began.

"Is as powerful as a mother's intuition."

This time there were teeth in her smile.

"He lives in the neighborhood."

"What are you doing?"

"I'm investigating all leads," my father said, knowing how it sounded as he said it.

"And my son . . ."

"Is a lead."

"Perhaps the other man frightens you too much."

"But I have to do something," he protested.

"Here we are again, Mr. Salmon," she said. "You misinterpret me. I am not saying you are doing the wrong thing by coming here. It is the right thing in its way. You want to find something soft, something warm in all this. Your searching led you here. That's a good thing. I am only concerned that it be good, too, for my son."

"I mean no harm."

"What is the man's name?"

"George Harvey." It was the first time he'd said it aloud to anyone but Len Fenerman.

She paused and stood. Turning her back to him, she walked over to first one window and then the other and drew the curtains back. It was the after-school light that she loved. She watched for Ray as he walked up the road.

"Ray will come now. I will go to meet him. If you'll excuse me I need to put on my coat and boots." She paused. "Mr. Salmon," she said, "I would do exactly what you are doing: I would talk to everyone I needed to, I would not tell too many people his name. When I was sure," she said, "I would find a quiet way, and I would kill him."

He could hear her in the hallway, the metal clank of hangers as she got her coat. A few minutes later the door was opened and closed. A cold breeze came in from the outside and then out on the road he could see a mother greet her son. Neither of them smiled. Their heads bent low. Their mouths moved. Ray took in the fact that my father was waiting for him inside his home.

At first my mother and I thought it was just the obvious that marked Len Fenerman as different from the rest of the force. He was smaller than the hulking uniforms who frequently accompanied him. Then there were the less obvious traits too — the way he often seemed to be thinking to himself, how he wasn't much for joking or trying to be anything but serious when he talked about me and the circumstances of the case. But, talking with my mother, Len Fenerman had shown himself for what he was: an optimist. He believed my killer would be caught.

"Maybe not today or tomorrow," he said to my mother, "but someday he'll do something uncontrollable. They are too uncontrolled in their habits not to."

My mother was left to entertain Len Fenerman until my father arrived home from the Singhs'. On the table in the family room Buckley's crayons were scattered across the butcher paper my mother had laid down. Buckley and Nate had drawn until their heads began to nod like heavy flowers, and my mother had plucked them up in her arms, first one and then the other, and brought them over to the couch. They slept there end to end with their feet almost touching in the center.

Len Fenerman knew enough to talk in hushed whispers, but he wasn't, my mother noted, a worshiper of children. He watched her carry the two boys but did not stand to help or comment on them the way the other policemen always did, defining her by her children, both living and dead.

"Jack wants to talk to you," my mother said. "But I'm sure you're too busy to wait."

"Not too busy."

I saw a black strand of her hair fall from where she had tucked it behind her ear. It softened her face. I saw Len see it too.

"He went over to that poor Ray Singh's house," she said and tucked the fallen hair back in its proper place.

"I'm sorry we had to question him," Len said.

"Yes," she said. "No young boy is capable of . . ." She couldn't say it, and he didn't make her.

"His alibi was airtight."

My mother took up a crayon from the butcher paper.

Len Fenerman watched my mother draw stick figures and stick dogs. Buckley and Nate made quiet sounds of sleep on the couch. My brother curled up into a fetal position and a moment later placed his thumb in his mouth to suck. It was a habit my mother had told us all we must help him break. Now she envied such easy peace.

"You remind me of my wife," Len said after a long silence, during which my mother had drawn an orange poodle and what looked like a blue horse undergoing electroshock treatment.

"She can't draw either?"

"She wasn't much of a talker when there was nothing to say."

A few more minutes passed. A yellow ball of sun. A brown house with flowers outside the door — pink, blue, purple.

"You used the past tense."

They both heard the garage door. "She died soon after we were married," he said.

"Daddy!" Buckley yelled, and leapt up, forgetting Nate and everyone else.

"I'm sorry," she said to Len.

"I am too," he said, "about Susie. Really."

In the back hall my father greeted Buckley and Nate with high cheers and calls for "Oxygen!" as he always did when we besieged him after a long day. Even if it felt false, elevating his mood for my brother was often the favorite part of his day.

My mother stared at Len Fenerman while my father walked toward the family room from the back. *Rush to the sink,* I felt like saying to her, stare down the hole and look into the earth. I'm down there waiting; I'm up here watching.

Len Fenerman had been the one that first asked my mother for my school picture when the police thought I might be found alive. In his wallet, my photo sat in a stack. Among these dead children and strangers was a picture of his wife. If a case had been solved he had written the date of its resolution on the back of the photo. If the case was still open — in his mind if not in the official files of the police — it was blank. There was nothing on the back of mine. There was nothing on his wife's.

"Len, how are you?" my father asked. Holiday up and wiggling back and forth for my father to pet him.

"I hear you went to see Ray Singh," Len said.

"Boys, why don't you go play up in Buckley's room?" my mother suggested. "Detective Fenerman and Daddy need to talk."

## SEVEN

D o you see her?" Buckley asked Nate as they climbed the stairs, Holiday in tow. "That's my sister."

"No," Nate said.

"She was gone for a while, but now she's back. Race!"

And the three of them — two boys and a dog — raced the rest of the way up the long curve of the staircase.

I had never even let myself yearn for Buckley, afraid he might see my image in a mirror or a bottle cap. Like everyone else I was trying to protect him. "Too young," I said to Franny. "Where do you think imaginary friends come from?" she said.

For a few minutes the two boys sat under the framed grave rubbing outside my parents' room. It was from a tomb in a London graveyard. My mother had told Lindsey and me the story of how my father and she had wanted things to hang on their walls and an old woman they met on their honeymoon had taught them how to do grave rubbings. By the time I was in double digits most of the grave rubbings had been put down in the basement for storage, the spots on our suburban walls replaced with bright graphic prints meant to stimulate children. But Lindsey and I loved the grave rubbings, particularly the one under which Nate and Buckley sat that afternoon.

Lindsey and I would lie down on the floor underneath it. I would pretend to be the knight that was pictured, and Holiday was the faithful dog curled up at his feet. Lindsey would be the wife he'd left behind. It always dissolved into giggles no matter how solemn the start. Lindsey would tell the dead knight that a wife had to move on, that she couldn't be trapped for the rest of her life by a man who was frozen in time. I would act stormy and mad, but it never lasted. Eventually she would describe her new lover: the fat butcher who gave her prime cuts of meat, the agile blacksmith who made her hooks. "You are dead, knight," she would say. "Time to move on."

"Last night she came in and kissed me on the cheek," Buckley said.

"Did not."

"Did too."

"Really?"

"Yeah."

"Have you told your mom?"

"It's a secret," Buckley said. "Susie told me she isn't ready to talk to them yet. Do you want to see something else?"

"Sure," said Nate.

The two of them stood up to go to the children's side of the house, leaving Holiday asleep under the grave rubbing.

"Come look," Buckley said.

They were in my room. The picture of my mother had been taken by Lindsey. After reconsideration, she had come back for the "Hippy-Dippy Says Love" button too.

"Susie's room," Nate said.

Buckley put his fingers to his lips. He'd seen my mother do this when she wanted us to be quiet, and now he wanted that from Nate. He got down on his belly and gestured for Nate to follow, and they wriggled like Holiday as they made their way beneath the dust ruffle of my bed into my secret storage space.

In the material that was stretched on the underside of the box spring, there was a hole, and stuffed up inside were things I didn't want anyone else to see. I had to guard it from Holiday or he would scratch at it to try and pry the objects loose. This had been exactly what happened twenty-four hours after I went missing. My parents had searched my room hoping to find a note of explanation and then left the door open. Holiday had carried off the licorice I kept there. Strewn beneath my bed were the objects I'd kept hidden, and one of them only Buckley and Nate would recognize. Buckley unwrapped an old handkerchief of my father's and there it was, the stained and bloody twig.

The year before, a three-year-old Buckley had swallowed it. Nate and he had been shoving rocks up their noses in our backyard, and Buckley had found a small twig under the oak tree where my mother strung one end of the clothesline. He put the stick in his mouth like a cigarette. I watched him from the roof outside my bedroom window, where I was sitting painting my toenails with Clarissa's Magenta Glitter and reading *Seventeen*.

I was perpetually assigned the job of watching out for little brother. Lindsey was not thought to be old enough. Besides, she was a burgeoning brain, which meant she got to be free to do things like spend that summer afternoon drawing detailed pictures of a fly's eye on graph paper with her 130-pack of Prisma Colors.

It was not too hot out and it was summer, and I was going to spend my internment at home beautifying. I had begun the morning by showering, shampooing, and steaming myself. On the roof I air-dried and applied lacquer.

I had on two coats of Magenta Glitter when a fly landed on the bottle's applicator. I heard Nate making dare and threat sounds, and I squinted at the fly to try to make out all the quadrants of his eyes that Lindsey was coloring inside the house. A breeze came up, blowing the fringe on my cutoffs against my thighs.

"Susie, Susie!" Nate was yelling.

I looked down to see Buckley on the ground.

It was this day that I always told Holly about when we talked about rescue. I believed it was possible; she did not.

I swung my legs around and scrambled through my open window, one foot landing on the sewing stool and the other immediately in front of that one and on the braided rug and then down on my knees and out of the blocks like an athlete. I ran down the hall and slid down the banister as we'd been forbidden to do. I called Lindsey's name and then forgot her, ran out to the backyard through the screened-in porch, and jumped over the dog fence to the oak tree.

Buckley was choking, his body bucking, and I carried him with Nate trailing into the garage, where my father's precious Mustang sat. I had watched my parents drive, and my mother had shown me how a car went from park to reverse. I put Buckley in the back and grabbed the keys from the unused terra-cotta pots where my father hid them. I sped all the way to the hospital. I burned out the emergency brake, but no one seemed to care.

"If she hadn't been there," the doctor later told my mother, "you would have lost your little boy."

Grandma Lynn predicted I'd have a long life because I had saved my brother's. As usual, Grandma Lynn was wrong.

"Wow," Nate said, holding the twig and marveling at how over time red blood turned black.

"Yeah," said Buckley. His stomach felt queasy with the memory of it. How much pain he had been in, how the faces of the adults changed as they surrounded him in the huge hospital bed. He had seen them that serious only one other time. But whereas in the hospital, their eyes had been worried and then later not, shot through with so much light and relief that they'd enveloped him, now our parents' eyes had gone flat and not returned.

I felt faint in heaven that day. I reeled back in the gazebo, and my eyes snapped open. It was dark, and across from me stood a large building that I had never been in.

I had read *James and the Giant Peach* when I was little. The building looked like the house of his aunts. Huge and dark and Victorian. It had a widow's walk. For a moment, as I readjusted to the darkness, I thought I saw a long row of women standing on the widow's walk and pointing my way. But a moment later, I saw differently. Crows were lined up, their beaks holding crooked twigs. As I stood to go back to the duplex, they took wing and followed me. Had my brother really seen me somehow, or was he merely a little boy telling beautiful lies?

_____

## EIGHT

For three months Mr. Harvey dreamed of buildings. He saw a slice of Yugoslavia where thatched-roofed dwellings on stilts gave way to rushing torrents of water from below. There were blue skies overhead. Along the fjords and in the hidden valleys of Norway, he saw wooden stave churches, the timbers of which had been carved by Viking boat-builders. Dragons and local heroes made from wood. But there was one building, from the Vologda, that he dreamed about most: the Church of the Transfiguration. And it was this dream — his favorite — that he had on the night of my murder and on the nights following until the others came back. The *not still* dreams — the ones of women and children.

I could see all the way back to Mr. Harvey in his mother's arms, staring out over a table covered with pieces of colored glass. His father sorted them into piles by shape and size, depth and weight. His father's jeweler's eyes looked deeply into each specimen for cracks and flaws. And George Harvey would turn his attention to the single jewel that hung from his mother's neck, a large oval piece of amber framed by silver, inside of which sat a whole and perfect fly.

"A builder" was all Mr. Harvey said when he was young. Then he stopped answering the question of what his father did. How could he say he worked in the desert, and that he built shacks of broken glass and old wood? He lectured George Harvey on what made a good building, on how to make sure you were construct- ing things to last.

So it was his father's old sketchbooks that Mr. Harvey looked at when the not still dreams came back. He would steep himself in the images of other places and other worlds, trying to love what he did not. And then he would begin to dream dreams of his mother the last time he had seen her, running through a field on the side of the road. She had been dressed in white. White capri pants and a tight white boat-neck shirt, and his father and she had fought for the last time in the hot car outside of Truth or Consequences, New Mexico. He had forced her out of the car. George Harvey sat still as stone in the back seat — eyes wide, no more afraid than a stone, watching it all as he did everything by then — in slow-mo. She had run without stopping, her white body thin and fragile and disappearing, while her son clung on to the amber necklace she had torn from her neck to hand him. His father had watched the road. "She's gone now, son," he said. "She won't be coming back."

# N I N E

My grandmother arrived on the evening before my memorial in her usual style. She liked to hire limousines and drive in from the airport sipping champagne while wearing what she called her "thick and fabulous animal" — a mink she had gotten secondhand at the church bazaar. My parents had not so much invited her as included her if she wanted to be there. In late January, Principal Caden had initiated the idea. "It will be good for your children and all the students at school," he had said. He took it upon himself to organize the event at our church. My parents were like sleepwalkers saying yes to his questions, nodding their heads to flowers or speakers. When my mother mentioned it on the phone to her mother, she was surprised to hear the words "I'm coming."

"But you don't have to, Mother."

There was a silence on my grandmother's end. "Abigail," she said, "this is Susan's funeral."

\* \* \*

Grandma Lynn embarrassed my mother by insisting on wearing her used furs on walks around the block and by once attending a block party in high makeup. She would ask my mother questions until she knew who everyone was, whether or not my mother had seen the inside of their house, what the husband did for a living, what cars they drove. She made a solid catalog of the neighbors. It was a way, I now realized, to try to understand her daughter better. A miscalculated circling, a sad, partnerless dance.

"Jack-y," my grandmother said as she approached my parents on the front porch, "we need some stiff drinks!" She saw Lindsey then, trying to sneak up the stairs and gain a few more minutes before the required visitation. "Kid hates me," Grandma Lynn said. Her smile was frozen, her teeth perfect and white.

"Mother," my mother said. And I wanted to rush into those ocean eyes of loss. "I'm sure Lindsey is just going to make herself presentable."

"An impossibility in this house!" said my grandmother.

"Lynn," said my father, "this is a different house than last time you were here. I'll get you a drink, but I ask you to respect that."

"Still handsome as hell, Jack," my grandmother said.

My mother took my grandmother's coat. Holiday had been closed up in my father's den as soon as Buckley had yelled from his post at the upstairs window — "It's Grandma!" My brother bragged to Nate or anyone who would listen that his grandmother had the biggest cars in the whole wide world.

"You look lovely, Mother," my mother said.

"Hmmmm." While my father was out of earshot, my grandmother said, "How is he?"

"We're all coping, but it's hard."

"Is he still muttering about that man having done it?"

"He still thinks so, yes."

"You'll be sued, you know," she said.

"He hasn't told anyone but the police."

What they couldn't see was that my sister was sitting above them on the top step.

"And he shouldn't. I realize he has to blame someone, but . . ."

"Lynn, 7 & 7 or a martini?" my father said, coming back out into the hallway.

"What are you having?"

"I'm not drinking these days, actually," my father said.

"Now there's your problem. I'll lead the way. No one has to tell me where the liquor is!"

Without her thick and fabulous animal, my grandmother was rail thin. "Starved down" was how she put it when she'd counseled me at age eleven. "You need to get yourself starved down, honey, before you keep fat on for too long. Baby fat is just another way to say ugly." She and my mother had fought about whether I was old enough for benzedrine—her own personal savior, she called it, as in, "I am offering your daughter my own personal savior and you deny her?"

When I was alive, everything my grandmother did was bad. But an odd thing happened when she arrived in her rented limo that day, opened up our house, and barged in. She was, in all her obnoxious finery, dragging the light back in.

"You need help, Abigail," my grandmother said after having eaten the first real meal my mother had cooked since my disappearance. My mother was stunned. She had donned her blue dishwashing gloves, filled the sink with sudsy water, and was preparing to do every dish. Lindsey would dry. Her mother, she assumed, would call upon Jack to pour her an after-dinner drink.

"Mother, that is so nice of you."

"Don't mention it," she said. "I'll just run out to the front hall and get my bag o' magic."

"Oh no," I heard my mother say under her breath.

"Ah, yes, the bag o' magic," said Lindsey, who had not spoken the whole meal.

"Please, Mother!" my mother protested when Grandma Lynn came back.

"Okay, kids, clear off the table and get your mother over here. I'm doing a makeover."

"Mother, that's crazy. I have all these dishes to do."

"Abigail," my father said.

"Oh no. She may get you to drink, but she's not getting those instruments of torture near me."

"I'm not drunk," he said.

"You're smiling," my mother said.

"So sue him," Grandma Lynn said. "Buckley, grab your mother's hand and drag her over here." My brother obliged. It was fun to see his mother be bossed and prodded.

"Grandma Lynn?" Lindsey asked shyly.

My mother was being led by Buckley to a kitchen chair my grandmother had turned to face her.

"What?"

"Could you teach me about makeup?"

"My God in heaven, praise the Lord, yes!"

My mother sat down and Buckley climbed up into her lap. "What's wrong, Mommy?"

"Are you laughing, Abbie?" My father smiled.

And she was. She was laughing and she was crying too.

"Susie was a good girl, honey," Grandma Lynn said. "Just like you." There was no pause. "Now lift up your chin and let me have a look at those bags under your eyes."

Buckley got down and moved onto a chair. "This is an eyelash curler, Lindsey," my grandmother instructed. "I taught your mother all of these things."

"Clarissa uses those," Lindsey said.

My grandmother set the rubber curler pads on either side of my mother's eyelashes, and my mother, knowing the ropes, looked upward.

"Have you talked to Clarissa?" my father asked.

"Not really," said Lindsey. "She's hanging out a lot with Brian Nelson. They cut class enough times to get a three-day suspension."

"I don't expect that of Clarissa," my father said. "She may not have been the brightest apple in the bunch, but she was never a troublemaker."

"When I ran into her she reeked of pot."

"I hope you're not getting into that," Grandma Lynn said. She finished the last of her 7 & 7 and slammed the highball glass down on the table. "Now, see this, Lindsey, see how when the lashes are curled it opens up your mother's eyes?"

Lindsey tried to imagine her own eyelashes, but instead saw the star-clumped lashes of Samuel Heckler as his face neared hers for a kiss. Her pupils dilated, pulsing in and out like small, ferocious olives.

"I stand amazed," Grandma Lynn said, and put her hands, one still twisted into the awkward handles of the eyelash curler, on her hips.

"What?"

"Lindsey Salmon, you have a boyfriend," my grandmother announced to the room.

My father smiled. He was liking Grandma Lynn suddenly. I was too.

"Do not," Lindsey said.

My grandmother was about to speak when my mother whispered, "Do too."

"Bless you, honey," my grandmother said, "you should have a boyfriend. As soon as I'm done with your mother, I'm giving you the grand Grandma Lynn treatment. Jack, make me an apéritif."

"An apéritif is something you . . ." my mother began.

"Don't correct me, Abigail."

My grandmother got sloshed. She made Lindsey look like a

clown or, as Grandma Lynn said herself, "a grade-A 'tute." My father got what she called "finely drunkened." The most amazing thing was that my mother went to bed and left the dirty dishes in the sink.

While everyone else slept, Lindsey stood at the mirror in the bathroom, looking at herself. She wiped off some of the blush, blotted her lips, and ran her fingers over the swollen, freshly plucked parts of her formerly bushy eyebrows. In the mirror she saw something different and so did I: an adult who could take care of herself. Under the makeup was the face she'd always known as her own, until very recently, when it had become the face that reminded people of me. With lip pencil and eyeliner, she now saw, the edges of her features were delineated, and they sat on her face like gems imported from some far-off place where the colors were richer than the colors in our house had ever been. It was true what our grandmother said — the makeup brought out the blue of her eyes. The plucking of the eyebrows changed the shape of her face. The blush highlighted the hollows beneath her cheekbones ("The hollows that could stand some more hollowing," our grandmother pointed out). And her lips — she practiced her facial expressions. She pouted, she kissed, she smiled wide as if she too had had a cocktail, she looked down and pretended to pray like a good girl but cocked one eye up to see how she looked being good. She went to bed and slept on her back so as not to mess up her new face.

Mrs. Bethel Utemeyer was the only dead person my sister and I ever saw. She moved in with her son to our development when I was six and Lindsey five.

My mother said that she had lost part of her brain and that

sometimes she left her son's house and didn't know where she was. She would often end up in our front yard, standing under the dogwood tree and looking out at the street as if waiting for a bus. My mother would sit her down in the kitchen and make tea for the two of them, and after she calmed her she would call her son's house to tell them where she was. Sometimes no one was home and Mrs. Utemeyer would sit at our kitchen table and stare into the centerpiece for hours. She would be there when we came home from school. Sitting. She smiled at us. Often she called Lindsey "Natalie" and reached out to touch her hair.

When she died, her son encouraged my mother to bring Lindsey and me to the funeral. "My mother seemed to have a special fondness for your children," he wrote.

"She didn't even know my name, Mom," Lindsey whined, as our mother buttoned up the infinite number of round buttons on Lindsey's dress coat. *Another impractical gift from Grandma Lynn,* my mother thought.

"At least she *called* you a name," I said.

It was after Easter, and a spring heat wave had set in that week. All but the most stubborn of that winter's snow had seeped into the earth, and in the graveyard of the Utemeyers' church snow clung to the base of the headstones, while, nearby, buttercup shoots were making their way up.

The Utemeyers' church was fancy. "High Catholic," my father had said in the car. Lindsey and I thought this was very funny. My father hadn't wanted to come but my mother was so pregnant that she couldn't drive. For the last few months of her pregnancy with Buckley she was unable to fit behind the wheel. She was so uncomfortable most of the time that we avoided being near her for fear we'd be thrown into servitude.

But her pregnancy allowed her to get out of what Lindsey and I couldn't stop talking about for weeks and what I kept dreaming about for long after that: viewing the body. I could tell my father and mother didn't want this to happen, but Mr. Utemeyer made a beeline for the two of us when it was time to file past the casket. "Which one of you is the one she called Natalie?" he asked. We stared at him. I pointed to Lindsey.

"I'd like you to come say goodbye," he said. He smelled of a perfume sweeter than what my mother sometimes wore, and the sting of it in my nose, and my sense of exclusion, made me want to cry. "You can come too," he said to me, extending his hands so we would flank him in the aisle.

It wasn't Mrs. Utemeyer. It was something else. But it *was* Mrs. Utemeyer too. I tried to keep my eyes focused on the gleaming gold rings on her fingers.

"Mother," Mr. Utemeyer said, "I brought the little girl you called Natalie."

Lindsey and I both admitted later that we expected Mrs. Utemeyer to speak and that we had decided, individually, that if she did we were going to grab the other one and run like hell.

An excruciating second or two and it was over and we were released back to our mother and father.

I wasn't very surprised when I first saw Mrs. Bethel Utemeyer in my heaven, nor was I shocked when Holly and I found her walking hand in hand with a small blond girl she introduced as her daughter, Natalie.


The morning of my memorial Lindsey stayed in her room for as long as she could. She didn't want my mother to see the still-applied makeup until it would be too late to make her wash it off. She had also told herself it would be okay to take a dress from my closet. That I wouldn't mind.

But it was weird to watch.

She opened the door to my room, a vault that by February was being disturbed more and more, though no one, not my mother or father, nor Buckley or Lindsey, confessed to entering, nor to taking things that they didn't plan on returning. They were blind to the clues that each of them came and visited me there. Any disturbance, even if it could not possibly be blamed on Holiday, was blamed on him.

Lindsey wanted to look nice for Samuel. She opened the double doors to my closet and reviewed the mess. I hadn't been exactly orderly, so every time my mother told us to clean up, I'd shoved whatever was on the floor or bed into my closet.

Lindsey had always wanted the clothes I owned first-run but had gotten them all as hand-me-downs.

"Gosh," she said, whispering into the darkness of my closet. She realized with guilt and glee that everything she saw before her was hers now.

"Hello? Knock-knock," said Grandma Lynn.

Lindsey jumped.

"Sorry to disturb you, hon," she said. "I thought I heard you in here."

My grandmother stood in what my mother called one of her Jackie Kennedy dresses. She had never understood why unlike the rest of us her mother had no hips — she could slide into a straight-cut dress and fill it out just enough, even at sixty-two, to look perfect in it.

"What are you doing in here?" Lindsey asked.

"I need help with this zipper." Grandma Lynn turned, and Lindsey could see what she had never seen on our own mother. The back of Grandma Lynn's black bra, the top of her half-slip. She walked the step or two over to our grandmother and, trying not to touch anything but the zipper tab, zipped her up.

"How about that hook and eye up there," said Grandma Lynn. "Can you get that?"

There were powdery smells and Chanel No. 5 sprinkled all around our grandmother's neck.

"It's one of the reasons for a man — you can't do this stuff yourself."

Lindsey was as tall as our grandmother and still growing. As she took the hook and eye in either hand, she saw the fine wisps of dyed blond hair at the base of my grandmother's skull. She saw the downy gray hair trailing along her back and neck. She hooked the dress and then stood there.

"I've forgotten what she looked like," Lindsey said.

"What?" Grandma Lynn turned.

"I can't remember," Lindsey said. "I mean her neck, you know, did I ever look at it?"

"Oh honey," Grandma Lynn said, "come here." She opened up her arms, but Lindsey turned into the closet.

"I need to look pretty," she said.

"You are pretty," Grandma Lynn said.

Lindsey couldn't get her breath. One thing Grandma Lynn never did was dole out compliments. When they came, they were unexpected gold.

"We'll find you a nice outfit in here," Grandma Lynn said and strode toward my clothes. No one could shop a rack like Grandma Lynn. On the rare occasions that she visited near the start of the school year she would take the two of us out. We marveled at her as we watched her nimble fingers play the hangers like so many keys. Suddenly, hesitating only for a moment, she would pull out a dress or shirt and hold it up to us. "What do you think?" she'd ask. It was always perfect.

As she considered my separates, plucked and posed them against my sister's torso, she talked:

"Your mother's a wreck, Lindsey. I've never seen her like this before."

"Grandma."

"Hush, I'm thinking." She held up my favorite church dress. It was blackwatch wool with a Peter Pan collar. I liked it mostly

because the skirt was so big I could sit in the pew cross-legged
and flounce the hem down to the ground. "Where did she get *this*
sack?" my grandmother asked. "Your dad, he's a mess too, but
he's mad about it."

"Who was that man you asked Mom about?"

She stiffened on the question. "What man?"

"You asked Mom if Dad still was saying that *that* man did it.
What man?"

"Voilà!" Grandma Lynn held up a dark blue minidress that my
sister had never seen. It was Clarissa's.

"It's so short," Lindsey said.

"I'm shocked at your mother," Grandma Lynn said. "She let
the kid get something stylish!"

My father called up from the hallway that he expected everyone downstairs in ten minutes.

Grandma Lynn went into preparation overdrive. She helped
Lindsey get the dark blue dress over her head, and then they
ran back to Lindsey's room for shoes, and then, finally, in the
hallway, under the overhead light, she fixed the smudged
eyeliner and mascara on my sister's face. She finished her off
with firmly pressed powder, whisking the cotton pad lightly in
an upward direction along either side of Lindsey's face. It wasn't
until my grandmother came downstairs and my mother commented on the shortness of Lindsey's dress while looking suspi-
ciously at Grandma Lynn that my sister and I realized Grandma
Lynn didn't have a spot of makeup on her own face. Buckley
rode between them in the back seat, and as they neared the
church he looked at Grandma Lynn and asked what she was
doing.

"When you don't have time for rouge, this puts a little life into
them," she said, and so Buckley copied her and pinched his
cheeks.

*   *   *

Samuel Heckler was standing by the stone posts that marked the path to the church door. He was dressed all in black, and beside him his older brother, Hal, stood wearing the beat-up leather jacket Samuel had worn on Christmas Day.

His brother was like a darker print of Samuel. He was tanned, and his face was weathered from riding his motorcycle full-tilt down country roads. As my family approached, Hal turned quickly and walked away.

"This must be Samuel," my grandmother said. "I'm the evil grandma."

"Shall we go in?" my father said. "It's nice to see you, Samuel."

Lindsey and Samuel led the way, while my grandmother dropped back and walked on the other side of my mother. A united front.

Detective Fenerman was standing by the doorway in an itchy-looking suit. He nodded at my parents and seemed to linger on my mother. "Will you join us?" my father asked.

"Thank you," he said, "but I just want to be in the vicinity."

"We appreciate that."

They walked into the cramped vestibule of our church. I wanted to snake up my father's back, circle his neck, whisper in his ear. But I was already there in his every pore and crevice.

He had woken up with a hangover and turned over on his side to watch my mother's shallow breathing against the pillow. His lovely wife, his lovely girl. He wanted to place his hand on her cheek, smooth her hair back from her face, kiss her — but sleeping, she was at peace. He hadn't woken a day since my death when the day wasn't something to get through. But the truth was, the memorial service day was not the worst kind. At least it was honest. At least it was a day shaped around what they were so pre-occupied by: my absence. Today he would not have to pretend he was getting back to normal — whatever normal was. Today he could walk tall with grief and so could Abigail. But he knew that as soon as she woke up he would not really look at her for the rest of the day, not really look into her and see the woman he had known her to be before the day they had taken in the news of my death. At nearly two months, the idea of it as news was fading away in the hearts of all but my family—and Ruth.

She came with her father. They were standing in the corner near the glass case that held a chalice used during the Revolutionary War, when the church had been a hospital. Mr. and Mrs. Dewitt were making small talk with them. At home on her desk, Mrs. Dewitt had a poem of Ruth's. On Monday she was going to the guidance counselor with it. It was a poem about me.

"My wife seems to agree with Principal Caden," Ruth's father was saying, "that the memorial will help allow the kids to accept it."

"What do you think?" Mr. Dewitt asked.

"I think let bygones be bygones and leave the family to their own. But Ruthie wanted to come."

Ruth watched my family greet people and noted in horror my sister's new look. Ruth did not believe in makeup. She thought it demeaned women. Samuel Heckler was holding Lindsey's hand. A word from her readings popped into her head: *subjugation*. But then I saw her notice Hal Heckler through the window. He was standing out by the oldest graves in the front and pulling on a cigarette butt.

"Ruthie," her father asked, "what is it?"

She focused again and looked at him. "What's what?"

"You were staring off into space just now," he said.

"I like the way the graveyard looks."

"Ah kid, you're my angel," he said. "Let's grab a seat before the good ones get taken."

Clarissa was there, with a sheepish-looking Brian Nelson, who was wearing a suit of his father's. She made her way up to my family, and when Principal Caden and Mr. Botte saw her they fell away and let her approach.

She shook hands with my father first.

"Hello, Clarissa," he said. "How are you?"

"Okay," she said. "How are you and Mrs. Salmon?"

"We're fine, Clarissa," he said. *What an odd lie,* I thought. "Would you like to join us in the family pew?"

"Um"—she looked down at her hands—"I'm with my boyfriend."

My mother had entered some trancelike state and was staring hard at Clarissa's face. Clarissa was alive and I was dead. Clarissa began to feel it, the eyes boring into her, and she wanted to get away. Then Clarissa saw the dress.

"Hey," she said, reaching out toward my sister.

"What is it, Clarissa?" my mother snapped.

"Um, nothing," she said. She looked at the dress again, knew she could never ask for it back now.

"Abigail?" my father said. He was attuned to her voice, her anger. Something was off.

Grandma Lynn, who stood just a bit behind my mother, winked at Clarissa.

"I was just noticing how good Lindsey looked," Clarissa said. My sister blushed.

The people in the vestibule began to stir and part. It was the Reverend Strick, walking in his vestments toward my parents.

Clarissa faded back to look for Brian Nelson. When she found him, she joined him out among the graves.


Ray Singh stayed away. He said goodbye to me in his own way: by looking at a picture—my studio portrait—that I had given him that fall.

He looked into the eyes of that photograph and saw right through them to the backdrop of marbleized suede every kid had to sit in front of under a hot light. What did dead mean, Ray wondered. It meant lost, it meant frozen, it meant gone. He knew that no one ever really looked the way they did in photos. He knew he didn't look as wild or as frightened as he did in his own. He came to realize something as he stared at my photo—that it was not me. I was in the air around him, I was in the cold mornings he had now with Ruth, I was in the quiet time he spent alone between studying. I was the girl he had chosen to kiss. He wanted, somehow, to set me free. He didn't want to burn my photo or toss it away, but he didn't want to look at me anymore, either. I watched him as he placed the photograph in one of the giant volumes of Indian poetry in which he and his mother had pressed dozens of fragile flowers that were slowly turning to dust.

At the service they said nice things about me. Reverend Strick. Principal Caden. Mrs. Dewitt. But my father and mother sat through it numbed. Samuel kept squeezing Lindsey's hand, but she didn't seem to notice him. She barely blinked. Buckley sat in a small suit borrowed for the occasion from Nate, who had attended a wedding that year. He fidgeted and watched my father. It was Grandma Lynn who did the most important thing that day.

During the final hymn, as my family stood, she leaned over to Lindsey and whispered, "By the door, that's him."

Lindsey looked over.

Standing just behind Len Fenerman, who was now inside the doorway and singing along, stood a man from the neighborhood. He was dressed more casually than anyone else, wearing flannel-lined khaki trousers and a heavy flannel shirt. For a moment Lindsey thought she recognized him. Their eyes locked. Then she passed out.

In all the commotion of attending to her, George Harvey slipped between the Revolutionary War gravestones behind the church and walked away without being noticed.

## TEN

A t the statewide Gifted Symposium each summer, the gifted kids from seventh to ninth grade would get together for a four-week retreat to, as I always thought of it, hang out in the trees and pick one another's brains. Around the campfire they sang oratorios instead of folk songs. In the girls' showers they would swoon over the physique of Jacques d'Amboise or the frontal lobe of John Kenneth Galbraith.

But even the gifted had their cliques. There were the Science Nerds and the Math Brains. They formed the superior, if somewhat socially crippled, highest rung of the gifted ladder. Then came the History Heads, who knew the birth and death dates of every historical figure anyone had ever heard of. They would pass by the other campers voicing cryptic, seemingly meaningless life spans: "1769 to 1821," "1770 to 1831." When Lindsey passed the History Heads she would think the answers to herself. "Napoleon." "Hegel."

There were also the Masters of Arcane Knowledge. Everyone begrudged their presence among the gifteds. These were the kids that could break down an engine and build it back again — no diagrams or instructions needed. They understood things in a real, not theoretical, way. They seemed not to care about their grades.

Samuel was a Master. His heroes were Richard Feynman and his brother, Hal. Hal had dropped out of high school and now ran the bike shop near the sinkhole, where he serviced everyone from Hell's Angels to the elderly who rode motorized scooters around the parking lots of their retirement homes. Hal smoked, lived at home over the Hecklers' garage, and conducted a variety of romances in the back of his shop.

When people asked Hal when he was going to grow up, he said, "Never." Inspired by this, when the teachers asked Samuel what he wanted to be, he would say: "I don't know. I just turned fourteen."

Almost fifteen now, Ruth Connors knew. Out in the aluminum toolshed behind her house, surrounded by the doorknobs and hardware her father had found in old houses slated for demolition, Ruth sat in the darkness and concentrated until she came away with a headache. She would run into the house, past the living room, where her father sat reading, and up to her room, where in fits and bursts she would write her poetry. "Being Susie," "After Death," "In Pieces," "Beside Her Now," and her favorite — the one she was most proud of and carried with her to the symposium folded and refolded so often that the creases were close to cuts — "The Lip of the Grave."

Ruth had to be driven to the symposium because that morning, when the bus was leaving, she was still at home with an acute attack of gastritis. She was trying weird all-vegetable regimes and the night before had eaten a whole head of cabbage for dinner. Her mother refused to kowtow to the vegetarianism Ruth had taken up after my death.

"This is not Susie, for Chrissakes!" her mother would say, plunking down an inch-thick sirloin in front of her daughter.

Her father drove her first to the hospital at three A.M. and then to the symposium, stopping home on the way to pick up the bag her mother had packed and left at the end of their driveway.

As the car pulled up into the camp, Ruth scanned the crowd of kids lining up for nametags. She spotted my sister among an all-male group of Masters. Lindsey had avoided putting her last name on her nametag, choosing to draw a fish instead. She wasn't exactly lying that way, but she hoped to meet a few kids from the surrounding schools who didn't know the story of my death or at least wouldn't connect her to it.

All spring she'd worn the half-a-heart pendant while Samuel wore the other half. They were shy about their affection for each other. They did not hold hands in the hallways at school, and they did not pass notes. They sat together at lunch; Samuel walked her home. On her fourteenth birthday he brought her a cupcake with a candle in it. Other than that, they melted into the gender-subdivided world of their peers.

The following morning Ruth was up early. Like Lindsey, Ruth was a floater at gifted camp. She didn't belong to any one group. She had gone on a nature walk and collected plants and flowers she needed help naming. When she didn't like the answers one of the Science Nerds provided, she decided to start naming the plants and flowers herself. She drew a picture of the leaf or blossom in her journal, and then what sex she thought it was, and then gave it a name like "Jim" for a simple-leaved plant and "Pasha" for a more downy flower.

By the time Lindsey stumbled into the dining hall, Ruth was in line for a second helping of eggs and sausage. She had made a big stink about no meat at home and she had to hold to it, but no one at the symposium knew of the oath she'd sworn.

Ruth hadn't talked to my sister since before my death, and then it was only to excuse herself in the hallway at school. But she'd seen Lindsey walking home with Samuel and seen her smile with him. She watched as my sister said yes to pancakes and no to everything else. She had tried to imagine herself being my sister as she had spent time imagining being me.

As Lindsey walked blindly to the next open spot in line, Ruth interceded. "What's the fish for?" Ruth asked, nodding her head toward my sister's nametag. "Are you religious?"

"Notice the direction of the fish," Lindsey said, wishing simultaneously that they had vanilla puddings at breakfast. They would go great with her pancakes.

"Ruth Connors, poet," Ruth said, by way of introduction.

"Lindsey," Lindsey said.

"Salmon, right?"

"Please don't," Lindsey said, and for a second Ruth could feel the feeling a little more vividly — what it was like to claim me. How people looked at Lindsey and imagined a girl covered in blood.


Even among the gifteds, who distinguished themselves by doing things differently, people paired off within the first few days. It was mostly pairs of boys or pairs of girls — few serious relationships had begun by fourteen — but there was one exception that year. Lindsey and Samuel.

"K-I-S-S-I-N-G!" greeted them wherever they went. Unchaperoned, and with the heat of the summer, something grew in them like weeds. It was lust. I'd never felt it so purely or seen it move so hotly into someone I knew. Someone whose gene pool I shared.

They were careful and followed the rules. No counselor could say he had flashed a light under the denser shrubbery by the boys' dorm and found Salmon and Heckler going at it. They set up little meetings outside in back of the cafeteria or by a certain tree that they'd marked up high with their initials. They kissed. They wanted to do more but couldn't. Samuel wanted it to be special. He was aware that it should be perfect. Lindsey just wanted to get it over with. Have it behind her so she could achieve adulthood — transcend the place and the time. She thought of sex as the *Star Trek* transport. You vaporized and found yourself navigating another planet within the second or two it took to realign.

"They're going to do it," Ruth wrote in her journal. I had pinned hopes on Ruth's writing everything down. She told her journal about me passing by her in the parking lot, about how on that night I had touched her — literally, she felt, reached out. What I had looked like then. How she dreamed about me. How she had fashioned the idea that a spirit could be a sort of second skin for someone, a protective layer somehow. How maybe if she was assiduous she could free us both. I would read over her shoulder as she wrote down her thoughts and wonder if anyone might believe her one day.

When she was imagining me, she felt better, less alone, more connected to something out there. To someone out there. She saw the cornfield in her dreams, and a new world opening, a world where maybe she could find a foothold too.

"You're a really good poet, Ruth," she imagined me saying, and her journal would release her into a daydream of being such a good poet that her words had the power to resurrect me.

I could see back to an afternoon when Ruth watched her teenage cousin undress to take a bath while Ruth sat on the bathroom rug, locked in the bathroom so her cousin could babysit her as she'd been told. Ruth had longed to touch her cousin's skin and hair, longed to be held. I wondered if this longing in a three-year-old had sparked what came at eight. That fuzzy feeling of difference, that her crushes on female teachers or her cousin were more real than the other girls' crushes. Hers contained a desire beyond sweetness and attention, it fed a longing, beginning to flower green and yellow into a crocuslike lust, the soft petals opening into her awkward adolescence. It was not so much, she would write in her journal, that she wanted to have sex with women, but that she wanted to disappear inside of them forever. To hide.

The last week of the symposium was always spent developing a final project, which the various schools would present in competition on the night before the parents returned to pick the students up. The competition wasn't announced until the Saturday breakfast of that final week, but the kids had already begun planning for it anyway. It was always a better-mousetrap competition, and so the stakes were raised year after year. No one wanted to repeat a mousetrap that had already been built.

Samuel went in search of the kids with braces. He needed the tiny rubber bands orthodontists doled out. They would work to keep the tension tight on the guiding arm of his mousetrap. Lindsey begged clean tinfoil from the retired army cook. Their trap involved reflecting light in order to confuse the mice.

"What happens if they like the way they look?" Lindsey asked Samuel.

"They can't see that clearly," Samuel said. He was stripping the paper off the wire twists from the camp garbage bag supply. If a kid looked strangely at ordinary objects around the camp, he or she was most likely thinking of how it would serve the ultimate mousetrap.

"They're pretty cute," Lindsey said one afternoon.

Lindsey had spent the better part of the night before gathering field mice with string lures and putting them under the wire mesh of an empty rabbit hutch.

Samuel watched them intently. "I could be a vet, I guess," he said, "but I don't think I'd like cutting them open."

"Do we have to kill them?" Lindsey asked. "It's a better mouse*trap,* not a better mouse death camp."

"Artie's contributing little coffins made out of balsa wood," Samuel said, laughing.

"That's sick."

"That's Artie."

"He supposedly had a crush on Susie," Lindsey said.

"I know."

"Does he talk about her?" Lindsey took a long thin stick and poked it through the mesh.

"He's asked about you, actually," Samuel said.

"What did you tell him?"

"That you're okay, that you'll be okay."

The mice kept running from the stick into the corner, where they crawled on top of one another in a useless effort to flee. "Let's build a mousetrap with a little purple velvet couch in it and we can rig up a latch so that when they sit on the couch, a door drops and little balls of cheese fall down. We can call it Wild Rodent Kingdom."

Samuel didn't press my sister like the adults did. He would talk in detail about mouse couch upholstery instead.

By that summer I had begun to spend less time watching from the gazebo because I could still see Earth as I walked the fields of heaven. The night would come and the javelin-throwers and shot-putters would leave for other heavens. Heavens where a girl like me didn't fit in. Were they horrific, these other heavens? Worse than feeling so solitary among one's living, growing peers? Or were they the stuff I dreamed about? Where you could be caught in a Norman Rockwell world forever. Turkey constantly being brought to a table full of family. A wry and twinkling relative carving up the bird.

If I walked too far and wondered loud enough the fields would change. I could look down and see horse corn and I could hear it then — singing — a kind of low humming and moaning warning me back from the edge. My head would throb and the sky would darken and it would be that night again, that perpetual yesterday lived again. My soul solidifying, growing heavy. I came up to the lip of my grave this way many times but had yet to stare in.

I did begin to wonder what the word *heaven* meant. I thought, if this were heaven, truly heaven, it would be where my grandparents lived. Where my father's father, my favorite of them all, would lift me up and dance with me. I would feel only joy and have no memory, no cornfield and no grave.

"You can have that," Franny said to me. "Plenty of people do."

"How do you make the switch?" I asked.

"It's not as easy as you might think," she said. "You have to stop desiring certain answers."

"I don't get it."

"If you stop asking why you were killed instead of someone else, stop investigating the vacuum left by your loss, stop wondering what everyone left on Earth is feeling," she said, "you can be free. Simply put, you have to give up on Earth."

This seemed impossible to me.


Ruth crept into Lindsey's dorm that night.

"I had a dream about her," she whispered to my sister.

Lindsey blinked sleepily at her. "Susie?" she asked.

"I'm sorry about the incident in the dining hall," Ruth said.

Lindsey was on the bottom of a three-tiered aluminum bunk bed. Her neighbor directly above her stirred.

"Can I get into bed with you?" Ruth asked.

Lindsey nodded.

Ruth crawled in next to Lindsey in the narrow sliver of the bed.

"What happened in your dream?" Lindsey whispered.

Ruth told her, turning her face so that Lindsey's eyes could make out the silhouette of Ruth's nose and lips and forehead. "I was inside the earth," Ruth said, "and Susie walked over me in the cornfield. I could feel her walking over me. I called out to her but my mouth filled with dirt. She couldn't hear me no matter how much I tried to yell. Then I woke up."

"I don't dream about her," Lindsey said. "I have nightmares about rats nibbling at the ends of my hair."

Ruth liked the comfort she felt next to my sister — the heat their bodies created.

"Are you in love with Samuel?"

"Yes."

"Do you miss Susie?"

Because it was dark, because Ruth was facing away from her, because Ruth was almost a stranger, Lindsey said what she felt. "More than anyone will ever know."

The principal of Devon Junior High was called away on a family matter, and it was left up to the newly appointed assistant principal of Chester Springs School to create, overnight, that year's challenge. She wanted to do something different from mousetraps.

CAN YOU GET AWAY WITH CRIME? HOW TO COMMIT THE PERFECT MURDER, announced her hurriedly drawn-up flier.

The kids loved it. The musicians and poets, the History Heads and artists, were teeming and bubbling about how to begin. They shoveled down their bacon and eggs at breakfast and compared the great unsolved murders of the past or thought of ordinary objects that could be used for fatal wounds. They began to think of whom they could plot to kill. It was all in good fun until 7:15, when my sister walked in.

Artie watched her get in line. She was still unaware, just picking up on the excitement in the air — figuring the mousetrap competition had been announced.

He kept his eye on Lindsey and saw the closest flier was posted at the end of the food line over the utensils tray. He was listening to a story about Jack the Ripper that someone at the table was relaying. He stood to return his tray.

When he reached my sister, he cleared his throat. All my hopes were pinned on this wobbly boy. "Catch her," I said. A prayer going down to Earth.

"Lindsey," Artie said.

Lindsey looked at him. "Yes?"

Behind the counter the army cook held out a spoon full of scrambled eggs to plop on her tray.

"I'm Artie, from your sister's grade."

"I don't need any coffins," Lindsey said, moving her tray down the metalwork to where there was orange juice and apple juice in big plastic pitchers.

"What?"

"Samuel told me you were building balsa wood coffins for the mice this year. I don't want any."

"They changed the competition," he said.

That morning Lindsey had decided she would take the bottom off of Clarissa's dress. It would be perfect for the mouse couch.

"To what?"

"Do you want to go outside?" Artie used his body to shadow her and block her passage to the utensils. "Lindsey," he blurted. "The competition is about murder."

She stared at him.

Lindsey held on to her tray. She kept her eyes locked on Artie.

"I wanted to tell you before you read the flier," he said.

Samuel rushed into the tent.

"What's going on?" Lindsey looked helplessly at Samuel.

"This year's competition is how to commit the perfect murder," Samuel said.

Samuel and I saw the tremor. The inside shakeoff of her heart. She was getting so good the cracks and fissures were smaller and smaller. Soon, like a sleight-of-hand trick perfected, no one would see her do it. She could shut out the whole world, including herself.

"I'm fine," she said.

But Samuel knew she wasn't.

He and Artie watched her back as she departed.

"I was trying to warn her," Artie said weakly.

Artie returned to his table. He drew hypodermics, one after another. His pen pressed harder and harder as he colored in the embalming fluid inside, as he perfected the trajectory of the three drops squirting out.

*Lonely,* I thought, *on Earth as it is in heaven.*


"You kill people by stabbing and cutting and shooting," Ruth said. "It's sick."

"Agreed," Artie said.

Samuel had taken my sister away to talk. Artie had seen Ruth at one of the outside picnic tables with her big blank book.

"But there are good reasons to kill," Ruth said.

"Who do you think did it?" Artie asked. He sat on the bench and braced his feet up under the table on the crossbar.

Ruth sat almost motionless, right leg crossed over left, but her foot jiggled ceaselessly.

"How did you hear?" she asked.

"My father told us," Artie said. "He called my sister and me into the family room and made us sit down."

"Shit, what did he say?"

"First he said that horrible things happened in the world and my sister said, 'Vietnam,' and he was quiet because they always fight about that whenever it comes up. So he said, 'No, honey, horrible things happen close to home, to people we know.' She thought it was one of her friends."

Ruth felt a raindrop.

"Then my dad broke down and said a little girl had been killed. I was the one who asked who. I mean, when he said 'little girl,' I pictured *little,* you know. Not us."

It was a definite drop, and they began to land on the redwood tabletop.

"Do you want to go in?" Artie asked.

"Everyone else will be inside," Ruth said.

"I know."

"Let's get wet."

They sat still for a while and watched the drops fall around them, heard the sound against the leaves of the tree above.

"I knew she was dead. I sensed it," Ruth said, "but then I saw a mention of it in my dad's paper and I was sure. They didn't use her name at first. Just 'Girl, fourteen.' I asked my dad for the page but he wouldn't give it to me. I mean, who else and her sister hadn't been in school all week?"

"I wonder who told Lindsey?" Artie said. The rain picked up. Artie slipped underneath the table. "We're going to get soaked," he yelled up.

And then as quickly as the rain had started, it ceased. Sun came through the branches of the tree above her, and Ruth looked up past them. "I think she listens," she said, too softly to be heard.

It became common knowledge at the symposium who my sister was and how I had died.

"Imagine being stabbed," someone said.

"No thanks."

"I think it's cool."

"Think of it—she's famous."

"Some way to get famous. I'd rather win the Nobel Prize."

"Does anyone know what she wanted to be?"

"I dare you to ask Lindsey."

And they listed the dead they knew.

Grandmother, grandfather, uncle, aunt, some had a parent, rarer was a sister or brother lost young to an illness — a heart irregularity — leukemia — an unpronounceable disease. No one knew anyone who had been murdered. But now they knew me.

Under a rowboat that was too old and worn to float, Lindsey lay down on the earth with Samuel Heckler, and he held her.

"You know I'm okay," she said, her eyes dry. "I think Artie was trying to help me," she offered.

"You can stop now, Lindsey," he said. "We'll just lie here and wait until things quiet down."

Samuel's back was flush against the ground, and he brought my sister close in to his body to protect her from the dampness of the quick summer rain. Their breath began to heat the small space beneath the boat, and he could not stop it — his penis stiffened inside his jeans.

Lindsey reached her hand over.

"I'm sorry . . ." He began.

"I'm ready," my sister said.

At fourteen, my sister sailed away from me into a place I'd never been. In the walls of my sex there was horror and blood, in the walls of hers there were windows.

"How to Commit the Perfect Murder" was an old game in heaven. I always chose the icicle: the weapon melts away.

# ELEVEN

When my father woke up at four A.M., the house was quiet. My mother lay beside him, lightly snoring. My brother, the only child, what with my sister attending the symposium, was like a rock with a sheet pulled up over him. My father marveled at what a sound sleeper he was — just like me. While I was still alive, Lindsey and I had had fun with that, clapping, dropping books, and even banging pot lids to see if Buckley would wake up.

Before leaving the house, my father checked on Buckley — to make sure, to feel the warm breath against his palm. Then he suited up in his thin-soled sneakers and light jogging outfit. His last task was to put Holiday's collar on.

It was still early enough that he could almost see his breath. He could pretend at that early hour that it was still winter. That the seasons had not advanced.

The morning dog walk gave him an excuse to pass by Mr. Harvey's house. He slowed only slightly — no one would have noticed save me or, if he had been awake, Mr. Harvey. My father was sure that if he just stared hard enough, just looked long enough, he would find the clues he needed in the casements of the windows, in the green paint coating the shingles, or along the driveway, where two large stones sat, painted white.

By late summer 1974, there had been no movement on my case. No body. No killer. Nothing.

My father thought of Ruana Singh: "When I was sure, I would find a quiet way, and I would kill him." He had not told this to Abigail because the advice made a sort of baseline sense that would frighten her into telling someone, and he suspected that someone might be Len.

Ever since the day he'd seen Ruana Singh and then had come home to find Len waiting for him, he'd felt my mother leaning heavily on the police. If my father said something that contradicted the police theories — or, as he saw them, the lack of them — my mother would immediately rush to fill the hole left open by my father's idea. "Len says that doesn't mean anything," or, "I trust the police to find out what happened."

Why, my father wondered, did people trust the police so much? Why not trust instinct? It was Mr. Harvey and he knew it. But what Ruana had said was *when I was sure*. Knowing, the deep-soul knowing that my father had, was not, in the law's more literal mind, incontrovertible proof.

The house that I grew up in was the same house where I was born. Like Mr. Harvey's, it was a box, and because of this I nurtured useless envies whenever I visited other people's homes. I dreamed about bay windows and cupolas, balconies, and slanted attic ceilings in a bedroom. I loved the idea that there could be trees in a yard taller and stronger than people, slanted spaces under stairs, thick hedges grown so large that inside there were hollows of dead branches where you could crawl and sit. In my heaven there were verandas and circular staircases, window ledges with iron rails, and a campanile housing a bell that tolled the hour.

I knew the floor plan of Mr. Harvey's by heart. I had made a warm spot on the floor of the garage until I cooled. He had brought my blood into the house with him on his clothes and skin. I knew the bathroom. Knew how in my house my mother had tried to decorate it to accommodate Buckley's late arrival by stenciling battleships along the top of the pink walls. In Mr. Harvey's house the bathroom and kitchen were spotless. The porcelain was yellow and the tile on the floor was green. He kept it cold. Upstairs, where Buckley, Lindsey, and I had our rooms, he had almost nothing. He had a straight chair where he would go to sit sometimes and stare out the window over at the high school, listen for the sound of band practice wafting over from the field, but mostly he spent his hours in the back on the first floor, in the kitchen building dollhouses, in the living room listening to the radio or, as his lust set in, sketching blueprints for follies like the hole or the tent.

No one had bothered him about me for several months. By that summer he only occasionally saw a squad car slow in front of his house. He was smart enough not to alter his pattern. If he was walking out to the garage or the mailbox, he kept on going.

He set several clocks. One to tell him when to open the blinds, one when to close them. In conjunction with these alarms, he would turn lights on and off throughout the house. When an occasional child happened by to sell chocolate bars for a school competition or inquire if he would like to subscribe to the *Evening Bulletin,* he was friendly but businesslike, unremarkable.

He kept things to count, and this counting reassured him. They were simple things. A wedding ring, a letter sealed in an envelope, the heel of a shoe, a pair of glasses, an eraser in the shape of a cartoon character, a small bottle of perfume, a plastic bracelet, my Pennsylvania keystone charm, his mother's amber pendant. He would take them out at night long after he was certain that no newsboy or neighbor would knock on his door. He would count them like the beads on a rosary. For some he had forgotten the names. I knew the names. The heel of the shoe was from a girl named Claire, from Nutley, New Jersey, whom he had convinced to walk into the back of a van. She was littler than me. (I like to think I wouldn't have gone into a van. Like to think it was my curiosity about how he could make a hole in the earth that wouldn't collapse.) He had ripped the heel off her shoe before he let Claire go. That was all he did. He got her into the van and took her shoes off. She started crying, and the sound drove into him like screws. He pleaded with her to be quiet and just leave. Step magically out of the van barefoot and uncomplaining while he kept her shoes. But she wouldn't. She cried. He started working on one of the heels of the shoes, prying it loose with his penknife, until someone pounded on the back of the van. He heard men's voices and a woman yelling something about calling the police. He opened the door.

"What the hell are you doing to that kid?" one of the men yelled. This man's buddy caught the little girl as she flew, bawling, out of the back.

"I'm trying to repair her shoe."

The little girl was hysterical. Mr. Harvey was all reason and calm. But Claire had seen what I had—his look bearing down—his wanting something unspoken that to give him would equal our oblivion.

Hurriedly, as the men and woman stood confused, unable to see what Claire and I knew, Mr. Harvey handed the shoes to one of the men and said his goodbyes. He kept the heel. He liked to hold the small leather heel and rub it between his thumb and forefinger—a perfect worry stone.

\* \* \*

I knew the darkest place in our house. I had climbed inside of it and stayed there for what I told Clarissa was a whole day but was really about forty-five minutes. It was the crawlspace in the basement. Inside ours there were pipes coming down that I could see with a flashlight and tons and tons of dust. That was it. There were no bugs. My mother, like her own, employed an exterminator for the slightest infestation of ants.

When the alarm had gone off to tell him to shut the blinds and then the next alarm, which told him to shut off most of the lights because the suburbs were asleep after that, Mr. Harvey would go down into the basement, where there were no cracks that light could peek through and people could point to, to say he was strange. By the time he killed me he had tired of visiting the crawlspace, but he still liked to hang out in the basement in an easy chair that faced the dark hole beginning halfway up the wall and reaching to the exposed baseboards of his kitchen floor. He would often drift off to sleep there, and there he was asleep when my father passed the green house at around 4:40 A.M.

Joe Ellis was an ugly little tough. He had pinched Lindsey and me under water in the pool and kept us from going to swim parties because we hated him so much. He had a dog that he dragged around no matter what the dog wanted. It was a small dog and couldn't run very fast, but Ellis didn't care. He would hit it or lift it painfully by the tail. Then one day it was gone, and so was a cat that Ellis had been seen taunting. And then animals from all over the neighborhood began disappearing.

What I discovered, when I followed Mr. Harvey's stare to the crawlspace, were these animals that had gone missing for more than a year. People thought it stopped because the Ellis boy had been sent to military school. When they let their pets loose in the morning, they returned in the evening. This they held as proof. No one could imagine an appetite like the one in the green house. Someone who would spread quicklime on the bodies of cats and dogs, the sooner for him to have nothing left but their bones. By counting the bones and staying away from the sealed letter, the wedding ring, the bottle of perfume, he tried to stay away from what he wanted most—from going upstairs in the dark to sit in the straight chair and look out toward the high school, from imagining the bodies that matched the cheerleaders' voices, which pulsated in waves on fall days during football games, or from watching the buses from the grammar school unload two houses down. Once he had taken a long look at Lindsey, the lone girl on the boys' soccer team out running laps in our neighborhood near dark.

What I think was hardest for me to realize was that he had tried each time to stop himself. He had killed animals, taking lesser lives to keep from killing a child.

By August, Len wanted to establish some boundaries for his sake and for my father's. My father had called the precinct too many times and frustrated the police into irritation, which wouldn't help anyone be found and just might make the whole place turn against him.

The final straw had been a call that came in the first week of July. Jack Salmon had detailed to the operator how, on a morning walk, his dog had stopped in front of Mr. Harvey's house and started howling. No matter what Salmon had done, went the story, the dog wouldn't budge from the spot and wouldn't stop howling. It became a joke at the station: Mr. Fish and his Huckleberry Hound.

Len stood on the stoop of our house to finish his cigarette. It was still early, but the humidity from the day before had intensified. All week rain had been promised, the kind of thunder and lightning rainstorm the area excelled at, but so far the only moisture of which Len was aware was that covering his body in a damp sweat. He had made his last easy visit to my parents' house.

Now he heard humming—a female voice from inside. He stubbed out his cigarette against the cement under the hedge and lifted the heavy brass knocker. The door opened before he let go.

"I smelled your cigarette," Lindsey said.

"Was that you humming?"

"Those things will kill you."

"Is your father home?"

Lindsey stood aside to let him in.

"Dad!" my sister yelled into the house. "It's Len!"

"You were away, weren't you?" Len asked.

"I just got back."

My sister was wearing Samuel's softball shirt and a pair of strange sweatpants. My mother had accused her of returning home without one single item of her own clothing.

"I'm sure your parents missed you."

"Don't bet on it," Lindsey said. "I think they were happy to have me out of their hair."

Len knew she was right. He was certainly sure my mother had seemed less frantic when he had visited the house.

Lindsey said, "Buckley's made you the head of the police squad in the town he built under his bed."

"That's a promotion."

The two of them heard my father's footsteps in the hallway above and then the sounds of Buckley begging. Lindsey could tell that whatever he'd asked for our father had finally granted.

My father and brother descended the stairs, all smiles.

"Len," he said, and he shook Len's hand.

"Good morning, Jack," Len said. "And how are you this morning, Buckley?"

My father took Buckley's hand and stood him in front of Len, who solemnly bent down to my brother.

"I hear you've made me chief of police," Len said.

"Yes sir."

"I don't think I deserve the job."

"You more than anyone," my father said breezily. He loved it when Len Fenerman dropped by. Each time he did, it verified for my father that there was a consensus — a group behind him — that he wasn't alone in all this.

"I need to talk to your father, kids."

Lindsey took Buckley back into the kitchen with the promise of cereal. She herself was thinking of what Samuel had shown her; it was a drink called a jellyfish, which involved a maraschino cherry at the bottom of some sugar and gin. Samuel and Lindsey had sucked the cherries up through the sugar and booze until their heads hurt and their lips were stained red.

"Should I get Abigail? Can I make you some coffee or something?"

"Jack," Len said, "I'm not here with any news — just the opposite. Can we sit?"

I watched my father and Len head into the living room. The living room seemed to be where no living ever actually occurred. Len sat on the edge of a chair and waited for my father to take a seat.

"Listen, Jack," he said. "It's about George Harvey."

My father brightened. "I thought you said you had no news."

"I don't. I have something I need to say on behalf of the station and myself."

"Yes."

"We need you to stop making calls about George Harvey."

"But . . ."

"*I* need you to stop. There is nothing, no matter how much we stretch it, to connect him to Susie's death. Howling dogs and bridal tents are not evidence."

"I know he did it," my father said.

"He's odd, I agree, but as far as we know he isn't a killer."

"How could you possibly know that?"

Len Fenerman talked, but all my father could hear was Ruana Singh saying what she had to him, and of standing outside Mr. Harvey's house and feeling the energy radiating out to him, the coldness at the core of the man. Mr. Harvey was at once unknowable and the only person in the world who could have killed me. As Len denied it, my father grew more certain.

"You are stopping your investigation of him," my father said flatly.

Lindsey was in the doorway, hovering as she'd done on the day Len and the uniformed officer had brought my hat with the jingle bell, the twin of which she owned. That day she had quietly shoved this second hat into a box of old dolls in the back of her closet. She never wanted my mother to hear the sound of those beadlike bells again.

There was our father, the heart we knew held all of us. Held us heavily and desperately, the doors of his heart opening and closing with the rapidity of stops on an instrument, the quiet felt closures, the ghostly fingering, practice and practice and then, incredibly, sound and melody and warmth. Lindsey stepped forward from her place by the door.

"Hello again, Lindsey," Len said.

"Detective Fenerman."

"I was just telling your father . . ."

"That you're giving up."

"If there was any good reason to suspect the man . . ."

"Are you done?" Lindsey asked. She was suddenly the wife to our father, as well as the oldest, most responsible child.

"I just want you all to know that we've investigated every lead."

My father and Lindsey heard her, and I saw her. My mother coming down the stairs. Buckley raced out of the kitchen and charged, propelling his full weight into my father's legs.

"Len," my mother said, pulling her terry-cloth robe tighter when she saw him, "has Jack offered you coffee?"

My father looked at his wife and Len Fenerman.

"The cops are punting," Lindsey said, taking Buckley gently by the shoulders and holding him against her.

"Punting?" Buckley asked. He always rolled a sound around in his mouth like a sourball until he had its taste and feel.

"What?"

"Detective Fenerman is here to tell Dad to stop bugging them."

"Lindsey," Len said, "I wouldn't put it like that."

"Whatever," she said. My sister wanted out, now, into a place where gifted camp continued, where Samuel and she, or even Artie, who at the last minute had won the Perfect Murder competition by entering the icicle-as-murder-weapon idea, ruled her world.

"Come on, Dad," she said. My father was slowly fitting something together. It had nothing to do with George Harvey, nothing to do with me. It was in my mother's eyes.

That night, as he had more and more often, my father stayed up by himself in his study. He could not believe the world falling down around him — how unexpected it all was after the initial blast of my death. "I feel like I'm standing in the wake of a volcano eruption," he wrote in his notebook. "Abigail thinks Len Fenerman is right about Harvey."

As he wrote, the candle in the window kept flickering, and despite his desk lamp the flickering distracted him. He sat back in the old wooden school chair he'd had since college and heard the reassuring squeak of the wood under him. At the firm he was failing to even register what was needed of him. Daily now he faced column after column of meaningless numbers he was supposed to make square with company claims. He was making mistakes with a frequency that was frightening, and he feared, more than he had in the first days following my disappearance, that he would not be able to support his two remaining children.

He stood up and stretched his arms overhead, trying to concentrate on the few exercises that our family doctor had suggested. I watched his body bend in uneasy and surprising ways I had never seen before. He could have been a dancer rather than a businessman. He could have danced on Broadway with Ruana Singh.

He snapped off the desk light, leaving only the candle.

In his low green easy chair he now felt the most comfortable. It was where I often saw him sleep. The room like a vault, the chair like a womb, and me standing guard over him. He stared at the candle in the window and thought about what to do; how he had tried to touch my mother and she had pulled away over to the edge of the bed. But how in the presence of the police she seemed to bloom.

He had grown used to the ghostly light behind the candle's flame, that quivering reflection in the window. He stared at the two of them — real flame and ghost — and began to work toward a doze, dozing in thought and strain and the events of the day.

As he was about to let go for the night, we both saw the same thing: another light. Outside.

It looked like a penlight from that distance. One white beam slowly moving out across the lawns and toward the junior high. My father watched it. It was after midnight now, and the moon was not full enough, as it often was, to see the outlines of the trees and houses. Mr. Stead, who rode his bike late at night with a flashing light on the front powered by his pedals, would never degrade the lawns of his neighbors that way. It was too late for Mr. Stead anyway.

My father leaned forward in the green chair in his study and watched the flashlight move in the direction of the fallow cornfield.

"Bastard," he whispered. "You murderous bastard."

He dressed quickly from the storage closet in his study, putting on a hunting jacket that he hadn't had on since an ill-fated hunting trip ten years earlier. Downstairs he went into the front hall closet and found the baseball bat he'd bought for Lindsey before she favored soccer.

First he shut off the porch light they kept on all night for me and that, even though it had been eight months since the police said I would not be found alive, they could not bring themselves to stop leaving on. With his hand on the doorknob, he took a deep breath.

He turned the knob and found himself out on the dark front porch. Closed the door and found himself standing in his front yard with a baseball bat and these words: *find a quiet way.*

He walked through his front yard and across the street and then into the O'Dwyers' yard, where he had first seen the light. He passed their darkened swimming pool and the rusted-out swing set. His heart was pumping, but he could not feel anything but the knowledge in his brain. George Harvey had killed his last little girl.

He reached the soccer field. To his right, far into the cornfield but not in the vicinity he knew by heart—the area that had been roped off and cleared and combed and bulldozed—he saw the small light. He clenched his fingers tighter around the bat by his side. For just a second he could not believe what he was about to do, but then, with everything in him, he knew.

The wind helped him. It swept along the soccer field alongside the cornfield and whipped his trousers around the front of his legs; it pushed him forward despite himself. Everything fell away. Once he was among the rows of corn, his focus solely on the light, the wind disguised his presence. The sound of his feet crushing the stalks was swept up in the whistle and bustle of the wind against the broken plants.

Things that made no sense flooded his head—the hard rubber sound of children's roller skates on pavement, the smell of his father's pipe tobacco, Abigail's smile when he met her, like light piercing his confused heart—and then the flashlight shut off and everything went equal and dark.

He took a few more steps, then stopped.

"I know you're here," he said.

I flooded the cornfield, I flashed fires through it to light it up, I sent storms of hail and flowers, but none of it worked to warn him. I was relegated to heaven: I watched.

"I'm here for it," my father said, his voice trembling. That heart bursting in and out, blood gorging the rivers of his chest and then cinching up. Breath and fire and lungs seizing, releasing, adrenaline saving what was left. My mother's smile in his mind gone, mine taking its place.

"Nobody's awake," my father said. "I'm here to finish it."

He heard whimpering. I wanted to cast down a spotlight like they did in the school auditorium, awkwardly, the light not always hitting the right place on the stage. There she would be, crouching and whimpering and now, despite her blue eye shadow and Western-style boots from Bakers', wetting her pants. A child.

She didn't recognize my father's voice infused with hate. "Brian?" Clarissa's quavering voice came out. "Brian?" It was hope like a shield.

My father's hand loosened on the bat, letting it fall.

"Hello? Who's there?"

With wind in his ears, Brian Nelson, the beanstalk scarecrow, parked his older brother's Spyder Corvette in the school lot. Late, always late, sleeping in class and at the dinner table but never when a boy had a *Playboy* or a cute girl walked by, never on a night when he had a girl waiting for him out in the cornfield. Still, he took his time. The wind, glorious blanket and cover for what he had planned, whipped past his ears.

Brian moved toward the cornfield with his giant torch light from his mother's under-the-sink disaster kit. Finally he heard what he would later say were Clarissa's cries for help.

My father's heart was like a stone there, heavy, carried inside his chest as he ran and fumbled toward the sound of the girl's whimpering. His mother was knitting him mittens, Susie was asking for gloves, so cold in the cornfield in winter. Clarissa! Susie's silly friend. Makeup, prissy jam sandwiches, and her tropical tan skin.

He ran blind into her and knocked her down in the darkness. Her screaming filled his ear and poured into the empty spaces, ricocheting inside of him. "Susie!" he screamed back.

Brian ran when he heard my name — full-speed-ahead awake. His light hopped over the cornfield, and, for one bright second, there was Mr. Harvey. No one but me saw him. Brian's light hit his back as he crawled into the high stalks and listened, again, for the sound of whimpering.

And then the light hit target and Brian dragged my father up and off Clarissa to hit him. Hit him on the head and back and face with the survival-kit flashlight. My father shouted and yelped and moaned.

And then Brian saw the bat.

I pushed and pushed against the unyielding borders of my heaven. I wanted to reach out and lift my father up, away, to me.

Clarissa ran and Brian swung. My father's eyes caught Brian's but he could barely breathe.

"You fucker!" Brian was black and white with blame.

I heard mumblings in the dirt. I heard my name. I thought I could taste the blood on my father's face, reach out to draw my fingers across his cut lips, lie down with him in my grave.

But I had to turn my back in heaven. I could do nothing —

trapped in my perfect world. The blood I tasted was bitter. Acid. I wanted my father's vigil, his tight love for me. But also I wanted him to go away and leave me be. I was granted one weak grace. Back in the room where the green chair was still warm from his body, I blew that lonely, flickering candle out.

# TWELVE

I stood in the room beside him and watched him sleep. During the night the story had come unwound and spun down so that the police understood: Mr. Salmon was crazy with grief and had gone out to the cornfield seeking revenge. It fit what they knew of him, his persistent phone calls, his obsession with the neighbor, and Detective Fenerman having visited that same day to tell my parents that for all intents and purposes my murder investigation had entered a sort of hiatus. No clues were left to pursue. No body had been found.

The surgeon had to operate on his knee to replace the cap with a purselike suture that partially disabled the joint. As I watched the operation I thought of how much like sewing it seemed, and I hoped that my father was in more capable hands than if he had been brought to me. In home ec my hands had been clumsy. Zipper foot or baster, I got them all confused.

But the surgeon had been patient. A nurse had filled him in on the story as he washed and scrubbed his hands. He remembered reading about what had happened to me in the papers. He was my father's age and had children of his own. He shivered as he stretched his gloves out over his hands. How alike he and this man were. How very different.

In the dark hospital room, a fluorescent bar light buzzed just behind my father's bed. As dawn approached it was the only light in the room until my sister walked in.

My mother and sister and brother woke to the sounds of the police sirens and came down into the dark kitchen from their bedrooms.

"Go wake your father," my mother said to Lindsey. "I can't believe he slept through this."

And so my sister had gone up. Everyone now knew where to look for him: in only six months, the green chair had become his true bed.

"Dad's not here!" my sister yelled as soon as she realized. "Dad's gone. Mom! Mom! Dad's gone!" For a rare moment Lindsey was a frightened child.

"Damn!" my mother said.

"Mommy?" Buckley said.

Lindsey rushed into the kitchen. My mother faced the stove. Her back was a riddled mass of nerves as she went about making tea.

"Mom?" Lindsey asked. "We have to do something."

"Don't you see . . . ?" my mother said, stopping for a moment with a box of Earl Grey suspended in the air.

"What?"

She put the tea down, switched on the burner, and turned around. She saw something herself then: Buckley had gone to cling to my sister as he anxiously sucked his thumb.

"He's gone off after that man and gotten himself in trouble."

"We should go out, Mom," Lindsey said. "We should go help him."

"No."

"Mom, we have to help Daddy."

"Buckley, stop milking your thumb!"

My brother burst into hot panicked tears, and my sister reached her arms down to pull him in tighter. She looked at our mother.

"I'm going out to find him," Lindsey said.

"You are doing no such thing," my mother said. "He'll come home in good time. We're staying out of this."

"Mom," Lindsey said, "what if he's hurt?"

Buckley stopped crying long enough to look back and forth from my sister to my mother. He knew what hurt meant and who was missing from the house.

My mother gave Lindsey a meaningful look. "We are not discussing this further. You can go up to your room and wait or wait with me. Your choice."

Lindsey was dumbfounded. She stared at our mother and knew what she wanted most: to flee, to run out into the cornfield where my father was, where I was, where she felt suddenly that the heart of her family had moved. But Buckley stood warm against her.

"Buckley," she said, "let's go back upstairs. You can sleep in my bed."

He was beginning to understand: you were treated special and, later, something horrible would be told to you.

When the call came from the police, my mother went immediately to the front closet. "He's been hit with our own baseball bat!" she said, grabbing her coat and keys and lipstick. My sister felt more alone than she had ever been but also more responsible. Buckley couldn't be left by himself, and Lindsey wasn't even able to drive. Besides, it made the clearest sense in the world. Didn't the wife belong most at the husband's side?

But when my sister was able to get Nate's mother on the line—after all, the commotion in the cornfield had awakened the whole neighborhood—she knew what she would do. She called Samuel next. Within an hour, Nate's mother arrived to take Buckley, and Hal Heckler pulled up to our house on his motorcycle. It should have been exciting—clutching on to Samuel's gorgeous older brother, riding on a motorcycle for the first time—but all she could think of was our father.

My mother was not in his hospital room when Lindsey entered; it was just my father and me. She came up and stood on the other side of his bed and started to cry quietly.

"Daddy?" she said. "Are you okay, Daddy?"

The door opened a crack. It was Hal Heckler, a tall handsome slash of a man.

"Lindsey," he said, "I'll wait for you out in the visitors' area in case you need a ride home."

He saw her tears when she turned around. "Thanks, Hal. If you see my mother . . ."

"I'll tell her you're in here."

Lindsey took my father's hand and watched his face for movement. My sister was growing up before my eyes. I listened as she whispered the words he had sung to the two of us before Buckley was born:

> Stones and bones;
> snow and frost;
> seeds and beans and polliwogs.
> Paths and twigs, assorted kisses,
> We all know who Daddy misses!

His two little frogs of girls, that's who.
They know where they are, do you, do you?

I wish a smile had come curling up onto my father's face, but he was deep under, swimming against drug and nightmare and waking dream. For a time leaden weights had been tied by anesthesia to the four corners of his consciousness. Like a firm waxen cover it had locked him away tight into the hard-blessed hours where there was no dead daughter and no gone knee, and where there was also no sweet daughter whispering rhymes.

"When the dead are done with the living," Franny said to me, "the living can go on to other things."

"What about the dead?" I asked. "Where do we go?"

She wouldn't answer me.

Len Fenerman had rushed to the hospital as soon as they put the call through. Abigail Salmon, the dispatcher said, requesting him.

My father was in surgery, and my mother was pacing back and forth near the nurses' station. She had driven to the hospital in her raincoat with only her thin summer nightgown beneath it. She had her beating-around-the-yard ballet flats on her feet. She hadn't bothered to pull her hair back, and there hadn't been any hair elastics in her pockets or purse. In the dark foggy parking lot of the hospital she had stopped to check her face and applied her stock red lipstick with a practiced hand.

When she saw Len approaching from the end of the long white corridor, she relaxed.

"Abigail," he said when he grew closer.

"Oh, Len," she said. Her face puzzled up on what she could say next. His name had been the sigh she needed. Everything that came next was not words.

The nurses at their station turned their heads away as Len and my mother touched hands. They extended this privacy veil habitually, as a matter of course, but even so they could see this man meant something to this woman.

"Let's talk in the visitors' area," Len said and led my mother down the corridor.

As they walked she told him my father was in surgery. He filled her in on what had happened in the cornfield.

"Apparently he said he thought the girl was George Harvey."

"He thought Clarissa was George Harvey?" My mother stopped, incredulous, just outside the visitors' area.

"It was dark out, Abigail. I think he only saw the girl's flashlight. My visit today couldn't have helped much. He's convinced that Harvey is involved."

"Is Clarissa all right?"

"She was treated for scratches and released. She was hysterical. Crying and screaming. It was a horrible coincidence, her being Susie's friend."

Hal was slumped down in a darkened corner of the visitors' area with his feet propped up on the helmet he'd brought for Lindsey. When he heard the voices approaching he stirred.

It was my mother and a cop. He slumped back down and let his shoulder-length hair obscure his face. He was pretty sure my mother wouldn't remember him.

But she recognized the jacket as Samuel's and for a moment thought, *Samuel's here,* but then thought, *His brother.*

"Let's sit," Len said, indicating the connected modular chairs on the far side of the room.

"I'd rather keep walking," my mother said. "The doctor said it will be an hour at least before they have anything to tell us."

"Where to?"

"Do you have cigarettes?"

"You know I do," Len said, smiling guiltily. He had to seek out her eyes. They weren't focusing on him. They seemed to be preoccupied, and he wished he could reach up and grab them and train them on the here and now. On him.

"Let's find an exit, then."

They found a door to a small concrete balcony near my father's room. It was a service balcony for a heating unit, so even though it was cramped and slightly chilly, the noise and the hot exhaust of the humming hydrant beside them shut them into a capsule that felt far away. They smoked cigarettes and looked at each other as if they had suddenly and without preparation moved on to a new page, where the pressing business had already been highlighted for prompt attention.

"How did your wife die?" my mother asked.

"Suicide."

Her hair was covering most of her face, and watching her I was reminded of Clarissa at her most self-conscious. The way she behaved around boys when we went to the mall. She would giggle too much and flash her eyes over at them to see where they were looking. But I was also struck by my mother's red mouth with the cigarette going up and away from it and smoke trailing out. I had seen this mother only once before—in the photograph. This mother had never had us.

"Why did she kill herself?"

"That's the question that preoccupies me most when I'm not preoccupied by things like your daughter's murder."

A strange smile came across my mother's face.

"Say that again," she said.

"What?" Len looked at her smile, wanted to reach out and trace the corners of it with his fingertips.

"My daughter's murder," my mother said.

"Abigail, are you okay?"

"No one says it. No one in the neighborhood talks about it. People call it the 'horrible tragedy' or some variation on that. I just want it to be spoken out loud by somebody. To have it said aloud. I'm ready—I wasn't ready before."

My mother dropped her cigarette onto the concrete and let it burn. She took Len's face in her hands.

"Say it," she said.

"Your daughter's murder."

"Thank you."

And I watched that flat red mouth move across an invisible line that separated her from the rest of the world. She pulled Len in to her and slowly kissed him on the mouth. He seemed to hesitate at first. His body tensed, telling him NO, but that NO became vague and cloudy, became air sucked into the intake fan of the humming hydrant beside them. She reached up and unbuttoned her raincoat. He placed his hand against the thin gauzy material of her summer gown.

My mother was, in her need, irresistible. As a child I had seen her effect on men. When we were in grocery stores, stockers volunteered to find the items on her list and would help us out to the car. Like Ruana Singh, she was known as one of the pretty mothers in the neighborhood; no man who met her could help but smile. When she asked a question, their beating hearts gave in.

But still, it had only ever been my father who stretched her laughter out into the rooms of the house and made it okay, somehow, for her to let go.

By tacking on extra hours here and there and skipping lunches, my father had managed to come home early from work every Thursday when we were little. But whereas the weekends were family time, they called that day "Mommy and Daddy time." Lindsey and I thought of it as good-girl time. It meant no peeps out of us as we stayed quiet on the other side of the house, while we used my father's then sparsely filled den as our playroom.

My mother would start preparing us around two.

"Bath time," she sang, as if she were saying we could go out to play. And in the beginning that was how it felt. All three of us would rush up to our rooms and put on bathrobes. We would meet in the hallway — three girls — and my mother would take us by the hands and lead us into our pink bathroom.

Back then she talked to us about mythology, which she had studied in school. She liked to tell us stories about Persephone and Zeus. She bought us illustrated books on the Norse gods, which gave us nightmares. She had gotten her master's in English — having fought tooth and nail with Grandma Lynn to go so far in school — and still held on to vague ideas of teaching when the two of us were old enough to be left on our own.

Those bath times blur together, as do all the gods and goddesses, but what I remember most is watching things hit my mother while I looked at her, how the life she had wanted and the loss of it reached her in waves. As her firstborn, I thought it was me who took away all those dreams of what she had wanted to be.

My mother would lift Lindsey out of the tub first, dry her, and listen to her chatter about ducks and cuts. Then she would get me out of the tub and though I tried to be quiet the warm water made my sister and me drunk, and we talked to my mother about everything that mattered to us. Boys that teased us or how another family down the block had a puppy and why couldn't we have one too. She would listen seriously as if she were mentally noting the points of our agenda on a steno pad to which she would later refer.

"Well, first things first," she summed up. "Which means a nice nap for the two of you!"

She and I would tuck Lindsey in together. I stood by the bed as she kissed my sister on her forehead and brushed back her hair from her face. I think competition started there for me. Who got the better kiss, the longer time after the bath with Mom.

Luckily, I always won this. When I look back now I see that my mother had become — and very quickly after they moved into that house — lonely. Because I was the oldest, I became her closest friend.

I was too little to know what she was really saying to me, but I loved to be hushed to sleep by the soft lullaby of her words. One of the blessings of my heaven is that I can go back to these moments, live them again, and be with my mother in a way I never could have been. I reach my hand across the Inbetween and take the hand of that young lonely mother in mine.

What she said to a four-year-old about Helen of Troy: "A feisty woman who screwed things up." About Margaret Sanger: "She was judged by her looks, Susie. Because she looked like a mouse, no one expected her to last." Gloria Steinem: "I feel horrible, but I wish she'd trim those nails." Our neighbors: "An idiot in tight pants; oppressed by that prig of a husband; typically provincial and judgmental of everyone."

"Do you know who Persephone is?" she asked me absently one Thursday. But I didn't answer. By then I'd learned to hush when she brought me into my room. My sister's and my time was in the bathroom as we were being toweled off. Lindsey and I could talk about anything then. In my bedroom it was Mommy's time.

She took the towel and draped it over the spindle knob of my four-poster bed. "Imagine our neighbor Mrs. Tarking as Persephone," she said. She opened the drawer of the dresser and handed me my underpants. She always doled out my clothes piecemeal, not wanting to pressure me. She understood my needs early. If I was aware I would have to tie laces I would not have been able to put my feet into socks.

"She's wearing a long white robe, like a sheet draped over her shoulders, but made out of some nice shiny or light fabric, like silk. And she has sandals made of gold and she's surrounded by torches which are light made out of flames . . ."

She went to the drawer to get my undershirt and absentmind-edly put it over my head instead of leaving it to me. Once my mother was launched I could take advantage of it—be the baby again. I never protested and claimed to be grown up or a big girl. Those afternoons were about listening to my mysterious mother.

She pulled back the tough-cord Sears bedspread, and I scooted over to the far side along the wall. She always checked her watch then and afterward she would say, "Just for a little while," and slide off her shoes and slip in between the sheets with me.

For both of us it was about getting lost. She got lost in her story. I got lost in her talk.

She would tell me about Persephone's mother, Demeter, or Cupid and Psyche, and I would listen to her until I fell asleep. Sometimes my parents' laughter in the room beside me or the sounds of their late-afternoon lovemaking would wake me up. I would lie there in half-sleep, listening. I liked to pretend that I was in the warm hold of a ship from one of the stories my father read to us, and that all of us were on the ocean and the waves were rolling gently up against the sides of the ship. The laughter, the small sounds of muffled moaning, would usher me back under into sleep.

But then my mother's escape, her half-measure return to the outside world, had been smashed when I was ten and Lindsey nine. She'd missed her period and had taken the fateful car trip to the doctor. Underneath her smile and exclamations to my sis-ter and me were fissures that led somewhere deep inside her. But because I didn't want to, because I was a child, I chose not to follow them. I grabbed the smile like a prize and entered the land of wonder of whether I would be the sister to a little boy or to a little girl.

If I had paid attention, I would have noticed signs. Now I see the shifting, how the stack of books on my parents' bedside table changed from catalogs for local colleges, encyclopedias of mythology, novels by James, Eliot, and Dickens, to the works of Dr. Spock. Then came gardening books and cookbooks until for her birthday two months before I died, I thought the perfect gift was *Better Homes and Gardens Guide to Entertaining.* When she realized she was pregnant the third time, she sealed the more mysterious mother off. Bottled up for years behind that wall, that needy part of her had grown, not shrunk, and in Len, the greed to get out, to smash, destroy, rescind, overtook her. Her body led, and in its wake would be the pieces left to her.

It was not easy for me to witness, but I did.

Their first embrace was hurried, fumbled, passionate.

"Abigail," Len said, his two hands now on either side of her waist underneath the coat, the gauzy gown barely a veil between them. "Think of what you're doing."

"I'm tired of thinking," she said. Her hair was floating above her head because of the fan beside them — in an aureole. Len blinked as he looked at her. Marvelous, dangerous, wild.

"Your husband," he said.

"Kiss me," she said. "Please."

I was watching a beg for leniency on my mother's part. My mother was moving physically through time to flee from me. I could not hold her back.

Len kissed her forehead hard and closed his eyes. She took his hand and placed it on her breast. She whispered in his ear. I knew what was happening. Her rage, her loss, her despair. The whole life lost tumbling out in an arc on that roof, clogging up her being. She needed Len to drive the dead daughter out.

He pushed her back into the stucco surface of the wall as they kissed, and my mother held on to him as if on the other side of his kiss there could be a new life.

\*    \*    \*

On my way home from the junior high, I would sometimes stop at the edge of our property and watch my mother ride the ride-on mower, looping in and out among the pine trees, and I could remember then how she used to whistle in the mornings as she made her tea and how my father, rushing home on Thursdays, would bring her marigolds and her face would light up yellowy in delight. They had been deeply, separately, wholly in love—apart from her children my mother could reclaim this love, but with them she began to drift. It was my father who grew toward us as the years went by; it was my mother who grew away.

Beside his hospital bed, Lindsey had fallen asleep while holding our father's hand. My mother, still mussed, passed by Hal Heckler in the visitors' area, and a moment later so did Len. Hal didn't need more than this. He grabbed his helmet and went off down the hall.

After a brief visit to the ladies' room, my mother was heading in the direction of my father's room when Hal stopped her.

"Your daughter's in there," Hal called out. She turned.

"Hal Heckler," he said, "Samuel's brother. I was at the memorial service."

"Oh, yes, I'm sorry. I didn't recognize you."

"Not your job," he said.

There was an awkward pause.

"So, Lindsey called me and I brought her here an hour ago."

"Oh."

"Buckley's with a neighbor," he said.

"Oh." She was staring at him. In her eyes she was climbing back to the surface. She used his face to climb back to.

"Are you okay?"

"I'm a little upset—that's understandable, right?"

"Perfectly," he said, speaking slowly. "I just wanted to let you know that your daughter is in there with your husband. I'll be in the visitors' area if you need me."

"Thank you," she said. She watched him turn away and paused for a moment to listen to the worn heels of his motorcycle boots reverberate down the linoleum hall.

She caught herself then, shook herself back to where she was, never guessing for a second that that had been Hal's purpose in greeting her.

Inside the room it was dark now, the fluorescent light behind my father flickering so slightly it lit only the most obvious masses in the room. My sister was in a chair pulled up alongside the bed, her head resting on the side of it with her hand extended out to touch my father. My father, deep under, was lying on his back. My mother could not know that I was there with them, that here were the four of us so changed now from the days when she tucked Lindsey and me into bed and went to make love to her husband, our father. Now she saw the pieces. She saw that my sister and father, together, had become a piece. She was glad of it.

I had played a hide-and-seek game of love with my mother as I grew up, courting her attention and approval in a way that I had never had to with my father.

I didn't have to play hide-and-seek anymore. As she stood in the darkened room and watched my sister and father, I knew one of the things that heaven meant. I had a choice, and it was not to divide my family in my heart.


Late at night the air above hospitals and senior citizen homes was often thick and fast with souls. Holly and I watched sometimes on the nights when sleep was lost to us. We came to realize how these deaths seemed choreographed from somewhere far away. Not our heaven. And so we began to suspect that there was a place more all-encompassing than where we were.

Franny came to watch with us in the beginning.

"It's one of my secret pleasures," she admitted. "After all these years I still love to watch the souls that float and spin in masses, all of them clamoring at once inside the air."

"I don't see anything," I said that first time.

"Watch closely," she said, "and hush."

But I felt them before I saw them, small warm sparks along my arms. Then there they were, fireflies lighting up and expanding in howls and swirls as they abandoned human flesh.

"Like snowflakes," Franny said, "none of them the same and yet each one, from where we stand, exactly like the one before."

# THIRTEEN

When she returned to junior high in the fall of 1974, Lindsey was not only the sister of the murdered girl but the child of a "crackpot," "nutcase," "looney-tunes," and the latter hurt her more because it wasn't true.

The rumors Lindsey and Samuel heard in the first weeks of the school year wove in and out of the rows of student lockers like the most persistent of snakes. Now the swirl had grown to include Brian Nelson and Clarissa who, thankfully, had both entered the high school that year. At Fairfax Brian and Clarissa clung to each other, exploiting what had happened to them, using my father's debasement as a varnish of cool they could coat themselves with by retelling throughout the school what had happened that night in the cornfield.

Ray and Ruth walked by on the inside of the glass wall that looked out on the outdoor lounge. On the false boulders where the supposed bad kids sat, they would see Brian holding court. His walk that year went from anxious scarecrow to masculine strut. Clarissa, giggly with both fear and lust, had unlocked her privates and slept with Brian. However haphazardly, everyone I'd known was growing up.

Buckley entered kindergarten that year and immediately arrived home with a crush on his teacher, Miss Koekle. She held his hand so gently whenever she had to lead him to the bathroom or help explain an assignment that her force was irresistible. In one way he profited—she would often sneak him an extra cookie or a softer sit-upon—but in another he was held aloft and apart from his fellow kindergartners. By my death he was made different among the one group—children—in which he might have been anonymous.

Samuel would walk Lindsey home and then go down the main road and thumb his way to Hal's bike shop. He counted on buddies of his brother's to recognize him, and he reached his destination in various pasted-together bikes and trucks that Hal would fine-tune for the driver when they pulled up.

He did not go inside our house for a while. No one but family did. By October my father was just beginning to get up and around. His doctors had told him that his right leg would always be stiff, but if he stretched and stayed limber it wouldn't present too much of an obstacle. "No running bases, but everything else," the surgeon said the morning after his surgery, when my father woke to find Lindsey beside him and my mother standing by the window staring out at the parking lot.

Buckley went right from basking in the shine of Miss Koekle home to burrow in the empty cave of my father's heart. He asked ceaseless questions about the "fake knee," and my father warmed to him.

"The knee came from outer space," my father would say. "They brought pieces of the moon back and carved them up and now they use them for things like this."

"Wow," Buckley would say, grinning. "When can Nate see?"

"Soon, Buck, soon," my father said. But his smile grew weak.

When Buckley took these conversations and brought them to our mother — "Daddy's knee is made out of moonbone," he would tell her, or "Miss Koekle said my colors were really good" — she would nod her head. She had become aware of what she did. She cut carrots and celery into edible lengths. She washed out thermoses and lunchboxes, and when Lindsey decided she was too old for a lunchbox, my mother caught herself actually happy when she found wax-lined bags that would keep her daughter's lunch from seeping through and staining her clothes. Which she washed. Which she folded. Which she ironed when necessary and which she straightened on hangers. Which she picked up from the floor or retrieved from the car or untangled from the wet towel left on the bed that she made every morning, tucking the corners in, and fluffing the pillows, and propping up stuffed animals, and opening the blinds to let the light in.

In the moments when Buckley sought her out, she often made a barter of it. She would focus on him for a few minutes, and then she would allow herself to drift away from her house and home and think of Len.


By November, my father had mastered what he called an "adroit hobble," and when Buckley egged him on he would do a contorted skip that, as long as it made his son laugh, didn't make him think of how odd and desperate he might look to an outsider or to my mother. Everyone save Buckley knew what was coming: the first anniversary.

Buckley and my father spent the crisp fall afternoons out in the fenced-in yard with Holiday. My father would sit in the old iron lawn chair with his leg stretched out in front of him and propped up slightly on an ostentatious boot scraper that Grandma Lynn had found in a curio shop in Maryland.

Buckley threw the squeaky cow toy while Holiday ran to get it. My father took pleasure in the agile body of his five-year-old son and Buckley's peals of delight when Holiday knocked him over and nudged him with his nose or licked his face with his long pink tongue. But he couldn't rid himself of one thought: this too — this perfect boy — could be taken from him.

It had been a combination of things, his injury not the least among them, that had made him stay inside the house on an extended sick leave from his firm. His boss acted differently around him now, and so did his coworkers. They trod gently outside his office and would stop a few feet from his desk as if, should they be too relaxed in his presence, what had happened to him would happen to them — as if having a dead child were contagious. No one knew how he continued to do what he did, while simultaneously they wanted him to shut all signs of his grief away, place it in a file somewhere and tuck it in a drawer that no one would be asked to open again. He called in regularly, and his boss just as easily agreed that he could take another week, another month if he had to, and he counted this as a blessing of always having been on time or willing to work late. But he stayed away from Mr. Harvey and tried to curb even the thought of him. He would not use his name except in his notebook, which he kept hidden in his study, where it was surprisingly easily agreed with my mother that she would no longer clean. He had apologized to me in his notebook. "I need to rest, honey. I need to understand how to go after this man. I hope you'll understand."

But he had set his return to work for December 2, right after Thanksgiving. He wanted to be back in the office by the anniversary of my disappearance. Functioning and catching up on work—in as public and distracting a place as he could think of. And away from my mother, if he was honest with himself.

How to swim back to her, how to reach her again. She was pulling and pulling away—all her energy was against the house, and all his energy was inside it. He settled on building back his strength and finding a strategy to pursue Mr. Harvey. Placing blame was easier than adding up the mounting figures of what he'd lost.

Grandma Lynn was due for Thanksgiving, and Lindsey had kept to a beautifying regime Grandma had set up for her through letters. She'd felt silly when she first put cucumbers on her eyes (to diminish puffiness), or oatmeal on her face (to cleanse the pores and absorb excess oils), or eggs yolks in her hair (to make it shine). Her use of groceries had even made my mother laugh, then wonder if she too should start to beautify. But that was only for a second, because she was thinking of Len, not because she was in love with him but because being with him was the fastest way she knew to forget.

Two weeks before Grandma Lynn's arrival, Buckley and my father were out in the yard with Holiday. Buckley and Holiday were romping from one large pile of burnished oak leaves to another in an increasingly hyper game of tag. "Watch out, Buck," my father said. "You'll make Holiday nip." And sure enough.

My father said he wanted to try something out.

"We have to see if your old dad can carry you piggyback style again. Soon you'll be too big."

So, awkwardly, in the beautiful isolation of the yard, where if my father fell only a boy and a dog who loved him would see, the two of them worked together to make what they both wanted—this return to father/son normalcy—happen. When Buckley stood on the iron chair—"Now scoot up my back," my father said, stooping forward, "and grab on to my shoulders," not knowing if he'd have the strength to lift him up from there—I crossed my fingers hard in heaven and held my breath. In the cornfield, yes, but, in this moment, repairing the most basic fabric of their previous day-to-day lives, challenging his injury to take a moment like this back, my father became my hero.

"Duck, now duck again," he said as they galumphed through the downstairs doorways and up the stairs, each step a balance my father negotiated, a wincing pain. And with Holiday rushing past them on the stairs, and Buckley joyous on his mount, he knew that in this challenge to his strength he had done the right thing.

When the two of them—with dog—discovered Lindsey in the upstairs bathroom, she whined a loud complaint.

*"Daaaaddd!"*

My father stood up straight. Buckley reached up and touched the light fixture with his hand.

"What are you doing?" my father said.

"What does it look like I'm doing?"

She sat on the toilet lid wrapped in a large white towel (the towels my mother bleached, the towels my mother hung on the line to dry, the towels she folded, and placed in a basket and brought up to the linen closet . . .). Her left leg was propped up on the edge of the tub, covered with shaving cream. In her hand she held my father's razor.

"Don't be petulant," my father said.

"I'm sorry," my sister said, looking down. "I just want a little privacy is all."

My father lifted Buckley up and over his head. "The counter, the counter, son," he said, and Buckley thrilled at the illegal halfway point of the bathroom counter and how his muddy feet soiled the tile.

"Now hop down." And he did. Holiday tackled him.

"You're too young to shave your legs, sweetie," my father said.

"Grandma Lynn started shaving at eleven."

"Buckley, will you go in your room and take the dog? I'll be in in a while."

"Yes, Daddy."

Buckley was still a little boy who my father could, with patience and a bit of maneuvering, get up on his shoulders so they could be a typical father and son. But he now saw in Lindsey what brought a double pain. I was a little girl in the tub, a toddler being held up to the sink, a girl who had forever stopped just short of sitting as my sister did now.

When Buckley was gone, he turned his attention to my sister. He would care for his two daughters by caring for one: "Are you being careful?" he asked.

"I just started," Lindsey said. "I'd like to be alone, Dad."

"Is that the same blade that was on it when you got it from my shaving kit?"

"Yes."

"Well, my beard stubble dulls the blade. I'll go get you a fresh one."

"Thanks, Dad," my sister said, and again she was his sweet, piggyback-riding Lindsey.

He left the room and went down the hallway to the other side of the house and the master bathroom that he and my mother still shared, though they no longer slept in the same room together. As he reached up into the cabinet for the package of fresh razors, he felt a tear in his chest. He ignored it and focused on the task. There was only a flicker of a thought then: *Abigail should be doing this.*

He brought the razor blades back, showed Lindsey how to change them, and gave her a few pointers on how best to shave. "Watch out for the ankle and the knee," he said. "Your mother always called those the danger spots."

"You can stay if you want," she said, ready now to let him in.

"But I might be a bloody mess." She wanted to hit herself. "Sorry, Dad," she said. "Here, I'll move — you sit."

She got up and went to sit on the edge of the tub. She ran the tap, and my father lowered himself onto the toilet lid.

"It's okay, honey," he said. "We haven't talked about your sister in a while."

"Who needs to?" my sister said. "She's everywhere."

"Your brother seems to be all right."

"He's glued to you."

"Yes," he said, and he realized he liked it, this father-courting his son was doing.

"Ouch," Lindsey said, a fine trickle of blood beginning to spread into the white foam of the shaving cream. "This is a total hassle."

"Press down on the nick with your thumb. It stops the bleeding. You could do just to the top of your knee," he offered. "That's what your mother does unless we're going to the beach."

Lindsey paused. "You guys never go to the beach."

"We used to."

My father had met my mother when they were both working at Wanamaker's during the summer break from college. He had just made a nasty comment about how the employee's lounge reeked of cigarettes when she smiled and brought out her then-habitual pack of Pall Malls. "Touché," he said, and he stayed beside her despite the reeking stink of her cigarettes enveloping him from head to toe.

"I've been trying to decide who I look like," Lindsey said, "Grandma Lynn or Mom."

"I've always thought both you and your sister looked like my mother," he said.

"Dad?"

"Yes."

"Are you still convinced that Mr. Harvey had something to do with it?"

It was like a stick finally sparking against another stick—the friction took.

"There is no doubt in my mind, honey. None."

"Then why doesn't Len arrest him?"

She drew the razor sloppily up and finished her first leg. She hesitated there, waiting.

"I wish it was easy to explain," he said, the words coiling out of him. He had never talked at length about his suspicion to anyone. "When I met him that day, in his backyard, and we built that tent—the one he claimed he built for his wife, whose name I thought was Sophie and Len took down as Leah—there was something about his movements that made me sure."

"Everyone thinks he's kind of weird."

"True, I understand that," he said. "But then everyone hasn't had much to do with him either. They don't know whether his weirdness is benign or not."

"Benign?"

"Harmless."

"Holiday doesn't like him," Lindsey offered.

"Exactly. I've never seen that dog bark so hard. The fur on his back stood straight up that morning."

"But the cops think you're nuts."

" 'No evidence' is all they can say. Without evidence and with-out—excuse me, honey—a body, they have nothing to move on and no basis for an arrest."

"What would be a basis?"

"I guess something to link him to Susie. If someone had seen him in the cornfield or even lurking around the school. Something like that."

"Or if he had something of hers?" Both my father and Lindsey were heatedly talking, her second leg lathered but left unshaved, because what radiated as the two sticks of their interest sparked flame was that I was in that house somewhere. My body—in the

basement, first floor, second floor, attic. To keep from acknowl-
edging that horrible — but oh, if it were true, so blatant so perfect
so conclusive as evidence — thought, they remembered what I
wore that day, remembered what I carried, the Frito Bandito
eraser I prized, the David Cassidy button I'd pinned inside my
bag, the David Bowie one I had pinned on the outside. They
named all the clutter and accessories that surrounded what would
be the best, most hideous evidence anyone could find — my
corpse cut up, my blank and rotting eyes.

My eyes: the makeup Grandma Lynn had given her helped but
did not solve the problem of how much everyone could see my
eyes in Lindsey's. When they presented themselves — a compact
flashing past her when in use by a girl at a neighboring desk, or
an unexpected reflection in the window of a store — she looked
away. It was particularly painful with my father. What she realized
as they talked was that as long as they were on this subject — Mr.
Harvey, my clothes, my book bag, my body, me — the vigilance to
my memory made my father see her as Lindsey and not as a tragic
combination of his two daughters.

"So you would want to be able to get in his house?" she said.

They stared at each other, a flicker of recognition of a dangerous idea. In his hesitation, before he finally said that that would
be illegal, and no, he hadn't thought of that, she knew he was
lying. She also knew he needed someone to do it for him.

"You should finish shaving, honey," he said.

She agreed with him and turned away, knowing what she'd
been told.


Grandma Lynn arrived on the Monday before Thanksgiving.
With the same laser-beam eyes that immediately sought out any
unsightly blemish on my sister, she now saw something beneath
the surface of her daughter's smile, in her placated, tranquilized

movements and in how her body responded whenever Detective
Fenerman or the police work came up.

When my mother refused my father's help in cleaning up after
dinner that night, the laser eyes were certain. Adamantly, and to
the shock of everyone at the table and the relief of my sister —
Grandma Lynn made an announcement.

"Abigail, I am going to help you clean up. It will be a
mother/daughter thing."

"What?"

My mother had calculated that she could let Lindsey off easily
and early and then she would spend the rest of the night over the
sink, washing slowly and staring out the window until the darkness brought her own reflection back to her. The sounds of the
TV would fade away and she would be alone again.

"I just did my nails yesterday," Grandma Lynn said after tying
on an apron over her camel-colored A-line dress, "so I'll dry."

"Mother, really. This isn't necessary."

"It is necessary, believe me, sweetie," my grandmother said.
There was something sober and curt in that *sweetie*.

Buckley led my father by the hand into the adjoining room
where the TV sat. They took up their stations and Lindsey, having been given a reprieve, went upstairs to call Samuel.

It was such a strange thing to see. So out of the ordinary. My
grandmother in an apron, holding a dish towel up like a mata-
dor's red flag in anticipation of the first dish coming her way.

They were quiet as they worked, and the silence — the only
sounds being the splash of my mother's hands plunging into the
scalding water, the squeak of plates, and the clank of the silver —
made a tension fill the room which grew unbearable. The noises
of the game from the nearby room were just as odd to me. My father had never watched football; basketball his only sport.
Grandma Lynn had never done dishes; frozen meals and takeout
menus were her weapons of choice.

"Oh Christ," she finally said. "Take this." She handed the just-washed dish back to my mother. "I want to have a real conversation but I'm afraid I'm going to drop these things. Let's take a walk."

"Mother, I need to . . ."

"You need to take a walk."

"After the dishes."

"Listen," my grandmother said, "I know I'm whatever I am and you're whatever you are, which isn't me, which makes you happy, but I know some things when I see them and I know something is going on that isn't kosher. *Capisce?*"

My mother's face was wavering, soft and malleable — almost as soft and malleable as the image of her that floated on the sullied water in the sink.

"What?"

"I have suspicions and I don't want to talk about them here."

*Ten-four, Grandma Lynn,* I thought. I'd never seen her nervous before.

It would be easy for the two of them to leave the house alone. My father, with his knee, would never think to join them, and, these days, where my father went or did not go, my brother, Buckley, followed.

My mother was silent. She saw no other option. As an afterthought they removed their aprons in the garage and piled them on the roof of the Mustang. My mother bent down and lifted the garage door.

It was still early enough so the light would hold for the beginning of their walk. "We could take Holiday," my mother tried.

"Just you and your mother," my grandmother said. "The most frightening pairing imaginable."

They had never been close. They both knew it, but it wasn't something they acknowledged very much. They joked around it like two children who didn't particularly like each other but were the only children in a large, barren neighborhood. Now, never having tried to before, having always let her daughter run as fast as she could in whatever direction she wished, my grandmother found that she was suddenly catching up.

They had passed by the O'Dwyers' and were near the Tarkings' before my grandmother said what she had to say.

"My humor buried my acceptance," my grandmother said. "Your father had a long-term affair in New Hampshire. Her first initial was F and I never knew what it stood for. I found a thousand options for it over the years."

"Mother?"

My grandmother kept walking, didn't turn. She found that the crisp fall air helped, filling her lungs until they felt cleaner than they had just minutes before.

"Did you know that?"

"No."

"I guess I never told you," she said. "I didn't think you needed to know. Now you do, don't you think?"

"I'm not sure why you're telling me this."

They had come to the bend in the road that would lead them back around the circle. If they went that way and did not stop, eventually they would find themselves in front of Mr. Harvey's house. My mother froze.

"My poor, poor sweetie," my grandmother said. "Give me your hand."

They were awkward. My mother could count on her fingers how many times her tall father had leaned down and kissed her as a child. The scratchy beard that smelled of a cologne that, after years of searching, she could never identify. My grandmother took her hand and held on as they walked the other way.

They walked into an area of the neighborhood where newer families seemed to be moving in more and more. The anchor houses, I remembered my mother calling them, because they

lined the street that led into the whole development — anchored
the neighborhood to an original road built before the township
was a township. The road that led to Valley Forge, to George
Washington and the Revolution.

"Susie's death brought your father's back to me," my grandmother said. "I never let myself mourn him properly."

"I know," my mother said.

"Do you resent me for it?"

My mother paused. "Yes."

My grandmother patted the back of my mother's hand with her
free one. "Good, see, that's a nugget."

"A nugget?"

"Something that's coming out of all this. You and me. A nugget
of truth between us."

They passed the one-acre lots on which trees had been growing
for twenty years. If not exactly towering, they were still twice as
tall as the fathers who had first held them and stomped the dirt
around them with their weekend work shoes.

"Do you know how alone I've always felt?" my mother asked
her mother.

"That's why we're walking, Abigail," Grandma Lynn said.

My mother focused her eyes in front of her but stayed connected to her mother with her hand. She thought of the solitary
nature of her childhood. How, when she had watched her two
daughters tie string between paper cups and go to separate rooms
to whisper secrets to each other, she could not really say she knew
how that felt. There had been no one else in the house with her
but her mother and father, and then her father had gone.

She stared at the tops of the trees, which, miles from our development, were the tallest things around. They stood on a high
hill that had never been cleared for houses and on which a few
old farmers still dwelled.

"I can't describe what I'm feeling," she said. "To anyone."

They reached the end of the development just as the sun was going down over the hill in front of them. A moment passed without either of them turning around. My mother watched the last light flicker in a drain-off puddle at the end of the road.

"I don't know what to do," she said. "It's all over now."

My grandmother was not sure what she meant by "it," but she did not press harder.

"Shall we head back?" my grandmother offered.

"How?" my mother said.

"To the house, Abigail. Head back to the house."

They turned and began walking again. The houses one after another, identical in structure. Only what my grandmother thought of as their accessories marked them as different. She had never understood places like this — places where her own child had chosen to live.

"When we get to the turn to the circle," my mother said, "I want to walk past it."

"His house?"

"Yes."

I watched Grandma Lynn turn when my mother turned.

"Would you promise me not to see the man anymore?" my grandmother asked.

"Who?"

"The man you're involved with. That's what I've been talking about."

"I'm not involved with anyone," my mother said. Her mind flew like a bird from one rooftop to the next. "Mother?" she said, and turned.

"Abigail?"

"If I needed to get away for a while, could I use Daddy's cabin?"

"Have you been listening to me?"

They could smell something in the air, and again my mother's anxious, agile mind slipped away. "Someone is smoking," she said.

Grandma Lynn was staring at her child. The pragmatic, prim mistress that my mother had always been was gone. She was flighty and distracted. My grandmother had nothing left to say to her.

"They're foreign cigarettes," my mother said. "Let's go find them!"

And in the fading light my grandmother stared, flabbergasted, as my mother began to follow the scent to its source.

"I'm heading back," my grandmother said.

But my mother kept walking.

She found the source of the smoke soon enough. It was Ruana Singh, standing behind a tall fir tree in her backyard.

"Hello," my mother said.

Ruana did not start as I thought she would. Her calmness had become something practiced. She could make a breath last through the most startling event, whether it was her son being accused of murder by the police or her husband running their dinner party as if it were an academic committee meeting. She had told Ray he could go upstairs, and then she had disappeared out the back door and not been missed.

"Mrs. Salmon," Ruana said, exhaling the heady smell of her cigarettes. In a rush of smoke and warmth my mother met Ruana's extended hand. "I'm so glad to see you."

"Are you having a party?" my mother asked.

"My husband is having a party. I am the hostess."

My mother smiled.

"This is a weird place we both live," Ruana said.

Their eyes met. My mother nodded her head. Back on the road somewhere was her own mother, but for right now she, like Ruana, was on a quiet island off the mainland.

"Do you have another cigarette?"

"Absolutely, Mrs. Salmon, yes." Ruana fished into the pocket of her long black cardigan and held out the pack and her lighter. "Dunhills," she said. "I hope that's all right."

My mother lit her cigarette and handed the blue package with its golden foil back to Ruana. "Abigail," she said as she exhaled. "Please call me Abigail."

Up in his room with his lights off, Ray could smell his mother's cigarettes, which she never accused him of pilfering, just as he never let on that he knew she had them. He heard voices down-stairs — the loud sounds of his father and his colleagues speaking six different languages and laughing delightedly over the oh-so-American holiday to come. He did not know that my mother was out on the lawn with his mother or that I was watching him sit in his window and smell their sweet tobacco. Soon he would turn away from the window and switch on the small light by his bed to read. Mrs. McBride had told them to find a sonnet they'd like to write a paper on, but as he read the lines of those available to him in his *Norton Anthology* he kept drifting back to the moment he wished he could take back and do over again. If he had just kissed me on the scaffold, maybe everything would have turned out differently.

Grandma Lynn kept on the course she had set with my mother, and, eventually, there it was — the house they tried to forget while living two houses down. *Jack was right,* my grandmother thought. She could even feel it in the dark. The place radiated something malevolent. She shivered and began to hear the crickets and see the fireflies gathering in a swarm above his front flower beds. She thought suddenly that she would do nothing but sympathize with her daughter. Her child was living inside the middle of a ground zero to which no affair on her own husband's part could offer her insight. She would tell my mother in the morning that the keys to the cabin would always be there for her if she needed them.

That night my mother had what she considered a wonderful

dream. She dreamed of the country of India, where she had never been. There were orange traffic cones and beautiful lapis lazuli insects with mandibles of gold. A young girl was being led through the streets. She was taken to a pyre where she was wound in a sheet and placed up on a platform built from sticks. The bright fire that consumed her brought my mother into that deep, light, dreamlike bliss. The girl was being burned alive, but, first, there had been her body, clean and whole.

# FOURTEEN

For a week Lindsey cased my killer's house. She was doing exactly what he did to everyone else.

She had agreed to train with the boys' soccer team all year in preparation for the challenge Mr. Dewitt and Samuel encouraged her to take on: qualifying to play in the all-male high school soccer league. And Samuel, to show his support, trained alongside her with no hope of qualifying for anything, he said, other than "fastest guy in shorts."

He could run, even if kicking and fielding and noticing a ball anywhere within his vicinity were all beyond him. And so, while they did laps around the neighborhood, each time Lindsey shot a look toward Mr. Harvey's house, Samuel was out in front, setting the pace for her — unaware of anything else.

Inside the green house, Mr. Harvey was looking out. He saw her watching and he began to itch. It had been almost a year now, but the Salmons remained bent on crowding him.

It had happened before in other towns and states. The family of a girl suspected him but no one else did. He had perfected his patter to the police, a certain obsequious innocence peppered with wonder about their procedures or useless ideas that he presented as if they might help. Bringing up the Ellis boy with Fenerman had been a good stroke, and the lie that he was a widower always helped. He fashioned a wife out of whichever victim he'd recently been taking pleasure in in his memory, and to flesh her out there was always his mother.

He left the house every day for an hour or two in the afternoon. He would pick up any supplies he needed and then drive out to Valley Forge Park and walk the paved roads and the unpaved trails and find himself suddenly surrounded by school tours at George Washington's log cabin or the Washington Memorial Chapel. This would buoy him up — these moments when the children were eager to see history, as if they might actually find a long silver hair from Washington's wig caught on the rough end of a log post.

Occasionally one of the tour guides or teachers would notice him standing there, unfamiliar even if amiable, and he would be met with a questioning stare. He had a thousand lines to give them: "I used to bring my children here." "This is where I met my wife." He knew to ground whatever he said in connection to some imagined family, and then the women would smile at him. Once an attractive, heavy woman tried to engage him in conversation while the park guide told the children about the winter of 1776 and the Battle of the Clouds.

He had used the story of widowhood and talked about a woman named Sophie Cichetti, making her his now-deceased wife and true love. It had been like luscious food to this woman, and, as he listened to her tell him about her cats and her brother, who had three children, whom she loved, he pictured her sitting on the chair in his basement, dead.

After that, when he met a teacher's questioning glare he would shyly back off and go somewhere else inside the park. He watched mothers with their children still in strollers walk briskly along the exposed paths. He saw teenagers who were cutting school necking in the uncut fields or along the interior trails. And at the highest point of the park was a small wood beside which he sometimes parked. He would sit in his Wagoneer and watch lonely men pull up beside him and get out of their cars. Men in suits on their lunch hour or men in flannel and jeans would walk quickly into that wood. Sometimes they would cast a look back in his direction — an inquiry. If they were close enough, these men could see, through his windshield, what his victims saw — his wild and bottomless lust.

On November 26, 1974, Lindsey saw Mr. Harvey leaving the green house, and she began to hang back from the pack of running boys. Later she could claim she had gotten her period and all of them would hush up, even be satisfied that this was proof that Mr. Dewitt's unpopular plan — a girl at regionals! — would never work out.

I watched my sister and marveled. She was becoming everything all at once. A woman. A spy. A jock. The Ostracized: One Man Alone.

She walked, clutching her side in a false cramp, and waved the boys on when they turned to notice her. She kept walking with her hand on her waist until they turned the corner at the far end of the block. At the edge of Mr. Harvey's property was a row of tall, thick pines that had been left untrimmed for years. She sat down by one of them, still feigning exhaustion in case any neighbor was looking out, and then, when she felt the moment was right, she curled up in a ball and rolled in between two pines. She waited. The boys had one more lap. She watched them pass her and followed them with her eyes as they cut up through the vacant lot and back to the high school. She was alone. She calcu-lated she had forty-five minutes before our father would begin to wonder when she'd be home. The agreement had been that if she trained with the boys' soccer team, Samuel would escort her home and have her back by five o'clock.

The clouds had hung heavy in the sky all day, and the late-fall cold raised goose bumps along her legs and arms. The team runs always warmed her, but when she reached the locker room where she shared the showers with the field hockey team, she would begin to shiver until the hot water hit her body. But on the lawn of the green house, her goose bumps were also from fear.

When the boys cut up the path, she scrambled over to the base-ment window at the side of Mr. Harvey's house. She had already thought of a story if she was caught. She was chasing a kitten that she'd seen dart in between the pine trees. She would say it was gray, that it was fast, that it had run toward Mr. Harvey's house and she'd followed it without thinking.

She could see inside to the basement, where it was dark. She tried the window, but the latch lock was pushed in. She would have to break the glass. Her mind racing, she worried about the noise, but she was too far along to stop now. She thought of my father at home, ever mindful of the clock near his chair, and took her sweatshirt off and balled it around her feet. Sitting down, she braced her body with her arms and then kicked once, twice, three times with both feet until the window smashed—a muffled cracking.

Carefully, she lowered herself down, searching the wall for a foothold but having to jump the final few feet onto the broken glass and concrete.

The room appeared tidy and swept, different from our own basement, where heaps of holiday-marked boxes—EASTER EGGS AND GREEN GRASS, CHRISTMAS STAR/ORNAMENTS—never made it back on the shelves my father had built.

The cold air from outside came in, and she felt the draft along her neck pushing her out of the shimmering semicircle of shattered glass and into the rest of the room. She saw the easy chair and a little table beside it. She saw the large alarm clock with luminous numbers sitting on the metal shelving. I wanted to guide her eyes to the crawlspace, where she would find the bones of the animals, but I knew, too, that regardless of drawing a fly's eyes on graph paper and excelling that fall in Mr. Botte's biology class, she would imagine the bones were mine. For this, I was glad she went nowhere near them.

Despite my inability to appear or whisper, push or usher, Lindsey, all alone, felt something. Something charged the air in the cold, dank basement and made her cringe. She stood only a few feet from the open window, knowing that she would, no matter what, be walking farther in and that she had to, no matter what, calm and focus herself to look for clues; but right then, for one moment, she thought of Samuel running ahead, having thought he would find her on his last lap, then running back toward the school, thinking he would find her outside, and then assuming, but with the first trace of a doubt, that she was showering, and so he too would be showering now, and then waiting for her before he did anything else. How long would he wait? As her eyes mounted the stairs to the first floor before her feet followed, she wished that Samuel were there to climb down after her and trace her movements, erasing her solitude as he went, fitting into her limbs. But she had not told him on purpose—had told no one. What she was doing was beyond the pale—criminal— and she knew it.

If she thought about it later, she would say that she had needed air and so that was what had gotten her up the stairs. Small flecks of white dust collected at the tips of her shoes as she mounted the stairs, but she didn't notice them.

She twisted the knob of the basement door and reached the

first floor. Only five minutes had passed. She had forty left, or so she thought. There was still a bit of light seeping in through the closed blinds. As she stood, again, hesitating, in this house identical to our own, she heard the thwack of the *Evening Bulletin* hit the stoop and the delivery boy ring the bell on his bike as he passed.

My sister told herself that she was inside a series of rooms and spaces that, gone through methodically, might yield what she needed, provide her the trophy she could take home to our father, earning her freedom from me that way. Competition always, even between the living and the dead. She saw the flagstones in the hall—the same dark green and gray as ours—and imagined crawling after me when she was a baby and I was just learning to walk. Then she saw my toddler body running delightedly away from her and into the next room, and she remembered her own sense of reaching out, of taking her first steps as I teased her from the living room.

But Mr. Harvey's house was much emptier than ours, and there were no rugs to lend warmth to the decor. Lindsey stepped from the flagstones onto the polished pine floors of what in our house was the living room. She made echoes up the open front hall, the sound of every movement reaching back for her.

She couldn't stop the memories slamming into her. Every one had a brutal report. Buckley riding piggyback on my shoulders down the stairs. Our mother steadying me as Lindsey looked on, jealous that I could reach, with the silver star in my hands, the top of the Christmas tree. Me sliding down the banister and asking her to join. Both of us begging the comics off our father after dinner. All of us running after Holiday as he barked and barked. And the countless exhausted smiles awkwardly dressing our faces for photos at birthdays, and holidays, and after school. Two sisters dressed identically in velvet or plaid or Easter yellows. We held baskets of bunnies and eggs we had sunk in dye. Patent leather shoes with straps and hard buckles. Smiling hard as our mother tried to focus her camera. The photos always fuzzy, our eyes bright red spots. None of them, these artifacts left to my sister, would hold for posterity the moments before and the moments after, when we two girls played in the house or fought over toys. When we were sisters.

Then she saw it. My back darting into the next room. Our dining room, the room that held his finished dollhouses. I was a child running just ahead of her.

She hurried after me.

She chased me through the downstairs rooms and though she was training hard for soccer, when she returned to the front hall she was unable to catch her breath. She grew dizzy.

I thought of what my mother had always said about a boy at our bus stop who was twice as old as us but still in the second grade. "He doesn't know his own strength, so you need to be careful around him." He liked to give bear hugs to anyone who was nice to him, and you could see this dopey love drop into his features and ignite his desire to touch. Before he was removed from regular school and sent somewhere else no one talked about, he had picked up a little girl named Daphne and squeezed her so hard that she fell into the road when he let go. I was pushing so hard on the Inbetween to get to Lindsey that I suddenly felt I might hurt her when I meant to help.

My sister sat down on the wide steps at the bottom of the front hall and closed her eyes, focused on regaining her breath, on why she was in Mr. Harvey's house in the first place. She felt encased in something heavy, a fly trapped in a spider's funnel web, the thick silk binding up around her. She knew that our father had walked into the cornfield possessed by something that was creeping into her now. She had wanted to bring back clues he could use as rungs to climb back to her on, to anchor him with facts, to ballast his sentences to Len. Instead she saw herself falling after him into a bottomless pit.

She had twenty minutes.

Inside that house my sister was the only living being, but she was not alone, and I was not her only company. The architecture of my murderer's life, the bodies of the girls he'd left behind, began to reveal itself to me now that my sister was in that house. I stood in heaven. I called their names:

Jackie Meyer. Delaware, 1967. Thirteen.

A chair knocked over, its underside facing the room. Lying curled toward it, she wore a striped T-shirt and nothing else. Near her head, a small pool of blood.

Flora Hernandez. Delaware, 1963. Eight.

He'd only wanted to touch her, but she screamed. A small girl for her age. Her left sock and shoe were found later. The body, unrecovered. The bones lay in the earthen basement of an old apartment house.

Leah Fox. Delaware, 1969. Twelve.

On a slipcovered couch under a highway on-ramp, he killed her, very quietly. He fell asleep on top of her, lulled by the sound of cars rushing above them. Not until ten hours later, when a vagrant knocked on the small shack Mr. Harvey had built out of discarded doors — did he begin to pack himself and Leah Fox's body up.

Sophie Cichetti, Pennsylvania, 1960. Forty-nine.

A landlady, she had divided her upstairs apartment into two by erecting a Sheetrock wall. He liked the half-circle window this created, and the rent was cheap. But she talked too much about her son and insisted on reading him poems from a book of sonnets. He made love to her on her side of the divided room, smashed her skull in when she started to talk, and brought her body to the bank of a creek nearby.

Leidia Johnson. 1960. Six.

Buck's County, Pennsylvania. He dug an arched cave inside a hill near the quarry and waited. She was the youngest one.

Wendy Richter. Connecticut, 1971. Thirteen.

She was waiting for her father outside a bar. He raped her in the bushes and then strangled her. That time, as he grew conscious, coming up out of the stupor that often clung on, he heard noises. He turned the dead girl's face toward his, and as the voices grew closer he bit down on her ear. "Sorry, man," he heard two drunk men say as they walked into the nearby bushes to take a leak.

I saw now that town of floating graves, cold and whipped by winds, where the victims of murder went in the minds of the living. I could see his other victims as they occupied his house — those trace memories left behind before they fled this earth — but I let them go that day and went to my sister.

Lindsey stood up the moment I focused back on her. Together the two of us walked the stairs. She felt like the zombies in the movies Samuel and Hal loved. One foot in front of the other and staring blankly straight ahead. She reached what was my parents' bedroom in our house and found nothing. She circled the hallway upstairs. Nothing. Then she went into what had been my bedroom in our house, and she found my killer's.

It was the least barren room in the house, and she did her best not to displace anything. To move her hand in between the sweaters stacked on the shelf, prepared to find anything in their warm insides — a knife, a gun, a Bic pen chewed on by Holiday. Nothing. But then, as she heard something but could not identify what it was, she turned toward the bed and saw the bedside table and, lying in the circle of light from a reading lamp left on, his sketchbook. She walked toward it and heard another sound, again, not putting the sounds together. Car pulling up. Car braking with a squeak. Car door slamming shut.

She turned the pages of the sketchbook and looked at the inky drawings of crossbeams and braces or turrets and buttresses, and she saw the measurements and notes, none of which meant anything to her. Then, as she flipped a final page, she thought she heard footsteps outside and very close.

As Mr. Harvey turned the key in the lock of his front door, she saw the light pencil sketch on the page in front of her. It was a small drawing of stalks above a sunken hole, a detail off to the side of a shelf and how a chimney could draw out smoke from a fire, and the thing that sunk into her: in a spidery hand he had written "Stolfuz cornfield." If it were not for the articles in the paper after the discovery of my elbow, she would not have known that the cornfield was owned by a man named Stolfuz. Now she saw what I wanted her to know. I had died inside that hole; I had screamed and fought and lost.

She ripped out the page. Mr. Harvey was in the kitchen making something to eat — the liverwurst he favored, a bowl of sweet green grapes. He heard a board creak. He stiffened. He heard another and his back rose and blossomed with sudden understanding.

The grapes dropped on the floor to be crushed by his left foot, while my sister in the room above sprang to the aluminum blinds and unlocked the stubborn window. Mr. Harvey mounted the stairs two at a time, and my sister smashed out the screen, scrambling onto the porch roof and rolling down it as he gained the upstairs hall and came barreling toward her. The gutter broke when her body tipped past it. As he reached his bedroom, she fell into the bushes and brambles and muck.

But she was not hurt. Gloriously not hurt. Gloriously young. She stood up as he reached the window to climb out. But he stopped. He saw her running toward the elderberry. The silk-screened number on her back screamed out at him. 5! 5! 5!

Lindsey Salmon in her soccer shirt.


Samuel was sitting with my parents and Grandma Lynn when Lindsey reached the house.

"Oh my God," my mother said, the first to see her through the small square windows that lined either side of our front door.

And by the time my mother opened it Samuel had rushed to fill the space, and she walked, without looking at my mother or even my father hobbling forward, right into Samuel's arms.

"My God, my God, my God," my mother said as she took in the dirt and the cuts.

My grandmother came to stand beside her.

Samuel put his hand on my sister's head and smoothed her hair back.

"Where have you been?"

But Lindsey turned to our father, lessened so now — smaller, weaker, than this child who raged. How alive she was consumed me whole that day.

"Daddy?"

"Yes, sweetheart."

"I did it. I broke into his house." She was shaking slightly and trying not to cry.

My mother balked: "You what?"

But my sister didn't look at her, not once.

"I brought you this. I think it might be important."

She had kept the drawing in her hand, crumpled tightly into a ball. It had made her landing harder, but she had come away anyway.

A phrase my father had read that day appeared in his mind now. He spoke it aloud as he looked into Lindsey's eyes.

"There is no condition one adjusts to so quickly as a state of war."

Lindsey handed him the drawing.

"I'm going to pick up Buckley," my mother said.

"Don't you even want to look at this, Mom?"

"I don't know what to say. Your grandmother is here. I have shopping to do, a bird to cook. No one seems to realize that we have a family. We have a family, a family and a son, and I'm going."

Grandma Lynn walked my mother to the back door but did not try to stop her.

My mother gone, my sister reached her hand out to Samuel. My father saw what Lindsey did in Mr. Harvey's spidery hand: the possible blueprint of my grave. He looked up.

"Do you believe me now?" he asked Lindsey.

"Yes, Daddy."

My father — so grateful — had a call to make.

"Dad," she said.

"Yes."

"I think he saw me."

I could never have imagined a blessing greater to me than the physical safety of my sister that day. As I walked back from the gazebo I shivered with the fear that had held me, the possibility of her loss on Earth not just to my father, my mother, Buckley, and Samuel, but, selfishly, the loss of her on Earth to me.

Franny walked toward me from the cafeteria. I barely raised my head.

"Susie," she said. "I have something to tell you."

She drew me under one of the old-fashioned lampposts and then out of the light. She handed me a piece of paper folded into four.

"When you feel stronger, look at it and go there."

Two days later, Franny's map led me to a field that I had always walked by but which, though beautiful, I'd left unexplored. The drawing had a dotted line to indicate a path. Searching nervously, I looked for an indentation in the rows and rows of wheat. Just ahead I saw it, and as I began to walk between the rows the paper dissolved in my hand.

I could see an old and beautiful olive tree just up ahead.

The sun was high, and in front of the olive tree was a clearing. I waited only a moment until I saw the wheat on the other side begin to pulse with the arrival of someone who did not crest the stalks.

She was small for her age, as she had been on Earth, and she wore a calico dress that was frayed at the hem and the cuffs.

She paused and we stared at each other.

"I come here almost every day," she said. "I like to listen to the sounds."

All around us, I realized, the wheat was rustling as it moved against itself in the wind.

"Do you know Franny?" I asked.

The little girl nodded solemnly.

"She gave me a map to this place."

"Then you must be ready," she said, but she was in *her* heaven too, and that called for twirling and making her skirt fly out in a circle. I sat on the ground under the tree and watched her.

When she was done she came toward me and breathlessly sat herself down. "I was Flora Hernandez," she said. "What was your name?"

I told her, and then I began to cry with comfort, to know another girl he had killed.

"The others will be here soon," she said.

And as Flora twirled, other girls and women came through the field in all directions. Our heartache poured into one another like water from cup to cup. Each time I told my story, I lost a bit, the smallest drop of pain. It was that day that I knew I wanted to tell the story of my family. Because horror on Earth is real and it is every day. It is like a flower or like the sun; it cannot be contained.

---

## FIFTEEN

At first no one stopped them, and it was something his mother enjoyed so much, the trill of her laughter when they ducked around the corner from whatever store and she uncovered and presented the pilfered item to him, that George Harvey joined in her laughter and, spying an opportunity, would hug her while she was occupied with her newest prize.

It was a relief for both of them, getting away from his father for the afternoon and driving into the nearby town to get food or other supplies. They were scavengers at best and made their money by collecting scrap metal and old bottles and hauling them into town on the back of the elder Harvey's ancient flatbed truck.

When his mother and he were caught for the first time, the two of them were treated graciously by the woman at the cash register. "If you can pay for it, do. If you can't, leave it on the counter as good as new," she said brightly and winked at the eight-year-old George Harvey. His mother took the small glass bottle of aspirin out of her pocket and placed it sheepishly on the counter.

Her face sank. "No better than the child," his father often repri-manded her.

Getting caught became another moment in his life that brought fear—that sick feeling curling into his stomach like eggs being folded into a bowl—and he could tell by the closed faces and hard eyes when the person walking down the aisle toward them was a store employee who had seen a woman stealing.

And she began handing him the stolen items to hide on his body, and he did it because she wanted him to. If they got outside and away in the truck, she would smile and bang the steering wheel with the flat of her hand and call him her little accomplice. The cab would fill with her wild, unpredictable love, and for a lit-tle while—until it wore off and they spied something glinting on the side of the road that they would have to investigate for what his mother called its "possibilities"—he did feel free. Free and warm.


He remembered the advice she gave him the first time they drove a stretch of road in Texas and saw a white wooden cross along the road. Around the base of it were clusters of fresh and dead flowers. His scavenger's eye had been drawn immediately by the colors.

"You have to be able to look past the dead," his mother said. "Sometimes there are good trinkets to take away from them."

Even then, he could sense they were doing something wrong. The two of them got out of the truck and went up to the cross, and his mother's eyes changed into the two black points that he was used to seeing when they were searching. She found a charm in the shape of an eye and one in the shape of a heart and held them out for George Harvey to see.

"Don't know what your father would make of them, but we can keep them, just you and me."

She had a secret stash of things that she never showed his father.

"Do you want the eye or the heart?"

"The eye," he said.

"I think these roses are fresh enough to save, nice for the truck."

That night they slept in the truck, unable to make the drive back to where his father was working a temporary job splitting and riving boards by hand.

The two of them slept curled into each other as they did with some frequency, making the inside of the cab an awkward nest. His mother, like a dog worrying a blanket, moved around in her seat and fidgeted. George Harvey had realized after earlier struggles that it was best to go limp and let her move him as she wished. Until his mother was comfortable, no one slept.

In the middle of the night, as he was dreaming about the soft insides of the palaces in picture books he'd seen in public libraries, someone banged on the roof, and George Harvey and his mother sat bolt upright. It was three men, looking through the windows in a way George Harvey recognized. It was the way his own father looked when he was drunk sometimes. It had a double effect: the whole gaze was leveled at his mother and simultaneously absented his son.

He knew not to cry out.

"Stay quiet. They aren't here for you," she whispered to him. He began to shiver underneath the old army blankets that covered them.

One of the three men was standing in front of the truck. The other two were banging on either side of the truck's roof, laughing and lolling their tongues.

His mother shook her head vehemently, but this only enraged them. The man blocking the truck started rocking his hips back and forth against the front end, which caused the other two men to laugh harder.

"I'm going to move slow," his mother whispered, "and pretend I'm getting out of the truck. I want you to reach forward and turn the keys in the ignition when I say so."

He knew he was being told something very important. That she needed him. Despite her practiced calm, he could hear the metal in her voice, the iron breaking up through fear now.

She smiled at the men, and as they sent up whoops and their bodies relaxed, she used her elbow to knock the gear shift into place. "Now," she said in a flat monotone, and George Harvey reached forward and turned the keys. The truck came to life with its rumbling old engine.

The faces of the men changed, fading from an acquisitive joy and then, as she reversed back to a good degree and they stared after her, uncertainty. She switched into drive and screamed, "On the floor!" to her son. He could feel the bump of the man's body hitting the truck only a few feet from where he lay curled up inside. Then the body was pitched up onto the roof. It lay there for a second until his mother reversed again. He had had a moment of clarity about how life should be lived: not as a child or as a woman. They were the two worst things to be.

His heart had beat wildly as he watched Lindsey make for the elderberry hedge, but then immediately he had calmed. It was a skill his mother, not his father, had taught him — to take action only after calculating the worst possible outcome of each choice available. He saw the notebook disturbed and the missing page in his sketchbook. He checked the bag with the knife. He took the knife with him to the basement and dropped it down the square hole that was drilled through the foundation. From the metal shelving, he retrieved the group of charms that he kept from the women. He took the Pennsylvania keystone charm from my bracelet and held it in his hand. Good luck. The others he spread out on his white handkerchief, and then he brought the four ends together to form a small hobo sack. He put his hand inside the hole under the foundation and got down on the floor on his stomach to push his arm in all the way to the shoulder. He groped, feeling with the free fingers of his hand as the other held the hobo sack, until he found a rusty jut of a metal support over which the workmen had poured the cement. He hung his trophy bag there and then withdrew his arm and stood. The book of sonnets he had buried earlier that summer in the woods of Valley Forge Park, shedding evidence slowly as he always did; now, he had to hope, not too slowly.

Five minutes at the most had gone by. That could be accounted for by shock and anger. By checking what everyone else thought to be valuables — his cuff links, his cash, his tools. But he knew no more time than that could be overlooked. He had to call the police.

He worked himself up. He paced briefly, drew his breath in and out rapidly, and when the operator answered he set his voice on edge.

"My home has been broken into. I need the police," he said, scripting the opening of his version of the story as inside he calculated how quickly he could leave and what he would carry with him.


When my father called the station, he requested Len Fenerman. But Fenerman couldn't be located. My father was informed that two uniforms had already been sent out to investigate. What they found when Mr. Harvey answered his door was a man who was tearfully upset and who in every aspect, save a certain repellent quality that the officers attributed to the sight of a man allowing himself to cry, seemed to be responding rationally to the reported events.

Even though the information about the drawing Lindsey had taken had come in over the radio, the officers were more impressed by Mr. Harvey's readily volunteering to have his home searched. He also seemed sincere in his sympathy for the Salmon family.

The officers grew uncomfortable. They searched the house perfunctorily and found nothing except both the evidence of what they took to be extreme loneliness and a room full of beautiful dollhouses on the second floor, where they switched topics and asked him how long he had been building them.

They noticed, they said later, an immediate and friendly change in his demeanor. He went into his bedroom and got the sketchbook, not mentioning any stolen drawing. The police took note of his increasing warmth as he showed them the sketches for the dollhouses. They asked their next question delicately.

"Sir," an officer said, "we can take you down to the station for further questioning, and you do have the right to have a lawyer present but —"

Mr. Harvey interrupted him. "I would be happy to answer anything here. I am the wronged party, though I have no wish to press charges against that poor girl."

"The young woman that broke in," the other officer began, "she did take something. It was a drawing of the cornfield and a sort of structure in it . . ."

The way it hit Harvey, the officers would tell Detective Fenerman, was all at once and very convincing. He had an explanation that fit so perfectly, they did not see him as a flight risk — largely because they did not see him first and foremost as a murderer.

"Oh, the poor girl," he said. He placed his fingers to his pursed lips. He turned to his sketchbook and flipped through it until he came to a drawing that was very much like the one Lindsey had taken.

"There, it was a drawing similar to this one, correct?" The officers — now audience — nodded. "I was trying to figure it out," Mr. Harvey confessed. "I admit the horror of it has obsessed me. I think everyone in the neighborhood has tried to think how they could have prevented it. Why they didn't hear something, see something. I mean, surely the girl screamed.

"Now here," he said to the two men, pointing to his drawing with a pen. "Forgive me, but I think in structures, and after hearing about how much blood there was in the cornfield and the churned-up nature of that area where it was found, I decided that perhaps . . ." He looked at them, checking their eyes. Both officers were following him. They wanted to follow him. They had had no leads, no body, no clues. Perhaps this strange man had a workable theory. "Well, that the person who did it had built something underground, a hole, and then I confess I began to worry at it and detail it the way I do the dollhouses, and I gave it a chimney and a shelf, and, well, that's just my habit." He paused. "I have a lot of time to myself."

"So, did it work out?" one of the two officers asked.

"I always did think I had something there."

"Why didn't you call us?"

"I wasn't bringing back their daughter. When Detective Fenerman interviewed me I mentioned how I suspected the Ellis boy, and I turned out to be dead wrong. I didn't want to meddle with any more of my amateur theories."

The officers apologized for the fact that the following day Detective Fenerman would be calling again, most likely wanting to go over the same material. See the sketchbook, hear Mr. Harvey's assertions about the cornfield. All of this Mr. Harvey took as part of being a dutiful civilian, even if it had been he who was victimized. The officers documented my sister's path of break-in from the basement window and then out through the bedroom window. They discussed the damages, which Mr.

Harvey said he would take care of out-of-pocket, stressing his awareness of the overwhelming grief the Salmon father had displayed several months ago, and how it now seemed to be infecting the poor girl's sister.


I saw the chances of Mr. Harvey's capture diminish as I watched the end of my family as I had known it ignite.

After picking up Buckley from Nate's house, my mother stopped at a payphone outside the 7-Eleven on Route 30. She told Len to meet her at a loud and raucous store in the mall near the grocery store. He left immediately. As he pulled out of his driveway, the phone in his house was ringing but he didn't hear it. He was inside the capsule of his car, thinking of my mother, of how wrong it all was and then of how he could not say no to her for reasons he couldn't hold on to long enough to analyze or disclaim.

My mother drove the short distance from the grocery store to the mall and led Buckley by the hand through the glass doors to a sunken circle where parents could leave their children to play while they shopped.

Buckley was elated. "The circle! Can I?" he said, as he saw his peers jumping off the jungle gym and turning somersaults on the rubber-covered floor.

"Do you really want to, honey?" she asked him.

"Please," he said.

She phrased it as a motherly concession. "All right," she said. And he went off in the direction of a red metal slide. "Be good," she called after him. She had never allowed him to play there without her.

She left his name with the monitor who watched over the play circle and said that she would be shopping on the lower level near Wanamaker's.

While Mr. Harvey was explaining his theory of my murder, my mother felt a hand brush across the back of her shoulders inside a trashy store called Spencer's. She turned with expectant relief, only to see Len Fenerman's back as he made his way out of the store. Passing glow-in-the-dark masks, black plastic eight balls, fuzzy troll keychains, and a large laughing skull, my mother followed after him.

He did not turn around. She kept following him, at first excited and then annoyed. In between footfalls there was enough time to think, and she did not want to think.

Finally, she saw him unlock a white door that was set flush into the wall, which she had never noticed before.

She could tell by the noises up ahead in the dark corridor that Len had brought her into the inner workings of the mall — the air filtration system or the water pumping plant. She didn't care. In the darkness she imagined herself to be within her own heart, and a vision of the enlarged drawing from her doctor's office entered her head and simultaneously she saw my father, in his paper gown and black socks, perched on the edge of the examining table as the doctor had explained to them the dangers of congestive heart failure. Just as she was about to let go into grief, cry out, and stumble and fall into confusion, she came to the end of the corridor. It opened into a huge room three stories high that throbbed and buzzed and throughout which there were tiny lights mounted higgledy-piggledy on metal tanks and drums. She paused and listened for any sound other than the deafening thrumming of air being sucked out of the mall and reconditioned to be pushed back in. Nothing.

I saw Len before she did. Standing alone in the almost-darkness he watched her for a moment, locating the need in her eyes. He was sorry for my father, for my family, but he fell into those eyes. "I could drown in those eyes, Abigail," he wanted to say to her, but he knew that this he would not be allowed.

My mother began to make out more and more shapes within the bright interconnected jumble of metal, and for a moment I could feel the room begin to be enough for her, the foreign territory enough to soothe her. It was the feeling of being unreachable.

If it had not been for Len's hand stretching out and grazing her fingers with the tips of his own, I might have kept her to myself there. The room could have remained simply a brief vacation from her life as Mrs. Salmon.

But he did touch her, and she did turn. Still, she could not really look at him. He accepted this absence on her part.

I swirled as I watched it and held on to the bench in the gazebo, gulping air. She could never know, I thought, that while she was clutching Len's hair and he was reaching his hand around to the small of her back, bringing her in closer, that the man who had murdered me was escorting two officers out his front door.

I felt the kisses as they came down my mother's neck and onto her chest, like the small, light feet of mice, and like the flower petals falling that they were. Ruinous and marvelous all at once. They were whispers calling her away from me and from her family and from her grief. She followed with her body.

While Len took her hand and brought her away from the wall into the tangle of pipes where the noise overhead added its chorus, Mr. Harvey began to pack his belongings; my brother met a small girl playing Hula-Hoop in the circle; my sister and Samuel lay beside each other on her bed, fully dressed and nervous; my grandmother downed three shots in the empty dining room. My father watched the phone.

My mother grabbed at Len's coat and shirt greedily, and he helped her. He watched as she tugged at her own clothes, pulling her sweater over her head, then her mother-jumper, and her turtleneck, until she was left in her underpants and camisole. He stared at her.

Samuel kissed the back of my sister's neck. She smelled of soap and Bactine, and he wanted, even then, never to leave her.

Len was about to say something; I could see my mother notice his lips just as they parted. She shut her eyes and commanded the world to shut up — screaming the words inside her skull. She opened her eyes again and looked at him. He was silent, his mouth set. She took her cotton camisole over the top of her head and stepped out of her underwear. My mother had my body as it would never become. But she had her own moonlit skin, her ocean eyes. She was hollow and lost and abandoned up.

Mr. Harvey left his house for the final time while my mother was granted her most temporal wish. To find a doorway out of her ruined heart, in merciful adultery.

# SIXTEEN

A year to the day after my death, Dr. Singh called to say he would not be home for dinner. But Ruana would do her exercises no matter what. If, as she stretched out on the rug in the one warm spot that the house seemed to hold in the winter, she could not help but turn over and over again her husband's absences in her mind, she would let them consume her until her body pled for her to let him go and to focus — as she leaned forward, her arms outstretched toward her toes now — and move, to shut her brain off and forget everything but the slight and pleasant yearning of muscles stretching and her own body bending.

Reaching almost to the floor, the window in the dining room was interrupted only by the metal baseboard for the heat, which Ruana liked to keep turned off because the noises it made disturbed her. Outside, she could see the cherry tree, its leaves and flowers all gone. The empty bird feeder swung slightly on its branch.

She stretched until she was quite warm and she'd forgotten herself, and the home she stood in fell away from her. Her age.

Her son. But still, creeping in on her was the figure of her husband. She had a premonition. She did not believe it was a woman, or even a student who worshiped him, that made him late more and more often. She knew what it was because it was something she too had had and had severed herself from after having been injured long ago. It was ambition.

She heard sounds now. Holiday barking two streets over and the Gilberts' dog answering him and Ray moving around upstairs. Blessedly, in another moment, Jethro Tull erupted again, shutting out all else.

Except for the occasional cigarette, which she smoked as secretly as she could so as not to give Ray license, she had kept herself in good health. Many of the women in the neighborhood commented on how well she kept herself and some had asked her if she would mind showing them how, though she had always taken these entreaties merely as their way of making conversation with their lone foreign-born neighbor. But as she sat in Sukhasana and her breath slowed to a deep rhythm, she could not fully release and let go. The niggling idea of what she would do as Ray grew older and her husband worked increasingly long hours crept up the inside of her foot and along her calf to the back of her knee and began to climb into her lap.

The doorbell rang.

Ruana was happy for the escape, and though she was someone to whom order was also a sort of meditation, she hopped up, wrapped a shawl that was hanging on the back of a chair around her waist, and, with Ray's music barreling down the stairs, walked to the door. She thought only for a moment that it might be a neighbor. A complaining neighbor—the music—and she, dressed in a red leotard and shawl.

Ruth stood on the stoop, holding a grocery sack.

"Hello," Ruana said. "May I help you?"

"I'm here to see Ray."

"Come in."

All of this had to be half-shouted over the noise coming from upstairs. Ruth stepped into the front hall.

"Go on up," Ruana shouted, pointing to the stairs.

I watched Ruana take in Ruth's baggy overalls, her turtleneck, her parka. *I could start with her,* Ruana thought to herself.


Ruth had been standing in the grocery store with her mother when she saw the candles among the paper plates and plastic forks and spoons. At school that day she had been acutely aware of what day it was and even though what she had done so far — lain in bed reading *The Bell Jar,* helped her mother clean out what her father insisted on calling his toolshed and what she thought of as the poetry shed, and tagged along to the grocery store — hadn't consisted of anything that might mark the anniversary of my death, she had been determined to do something.

When she saw the candles she knew immediately that she would find her way over to Ray's house and ask him to come with her. Because of their meetings at the shot-put circle, the kids at school had made them a couple despite all evidence to the contrary. Ruth could draw as many female nudes as she might wish and fashion scarves on her head and write papers on Janis Joplin and loudly protest the oppression of shaving her legs and armpits. In the eyes of her classmates at Fairfax, she remained a weird girl who had been found K-I-S-S-I-N-G a weird boy.

What no one understood — and they could not begin to tell anyone — was that it had been an experiment between them. Ray had kissed only me, and Ruth had never kissed anyone, so, united, they had agreed to kiss each other and see.

"I don't feel anything," Ruth had said afterward, as they lay in the maple leaves under a tree behind the teachers' parking lot.

"I don't either," Ray admitted.

"Did you feel something when you kissed Susie?"

"Yes."

"What?"

"That I wanted more. That night I dreamed of kissing her again and wondered if she was thinking the same thing."

"And sex?"

"I hadn't really gotten that far yet," Ray said. "Now I kiss you and it's not the same."

"We could keep trying," Ruth said. "I'm game if you don't tell anyone."

"I thought you liked girls," Ray said.

"I'll make you a deal," Ruth said. "You can pretend I'm Susie and I will too."

"You are so entirely screwed up," Ray said, smiling.

"Are you saying you don't want to?" Ruth teased.

"Show me your drawings again."

"I may be screwed up," Ruth said, dragging out her sketchbook from her book bag—it was now full of nudes she'd copied out of *Playboy,* scaling various parts up or down and adding hair and wrinkles where they had been airbrushed out—"but at least I'm not a perv for charcoal."

Ray was dancing around his bedroom when Ruth walked in. He wore his glasses, which at school he tried to do without because they were thick and his father had only sprung for the least expensive, hard-to-break frames. He had on a pair of jeans that were baggy and stained and a T-shirt that Ruth imagined, and I knew, had been slept in.

He stopped dancing as soon as he saw her standing at the doorway holding the grocery bag. His hands went up immediately and collected his glasses, and then, not knowing what to do with them, he waved them at her and said, "Hello."

"Can you turn it down?" Ruth screamed.

"Sure!"

When the noise ceased her ears rang for a second, and in that second she saw something flicker across Ray's eyes.

He now stood on the other side of the room, and in between them was his bed, where sheets were rumpled and balled and over which hung a drawing Ruth had done of me from memory.

"You hung it up," Ruth said.

"I think it's really good."

"You and me and nobody else."

"My mom thinks it's good."

"She's intense, Ray," Ruth said, putting down the bag. "No wonder you're so freak-a-delic."

"What's in the bag?"

"Candles," said Ruth. "I got them at the grocery store. It's December sixth."

"I know."

"I thought we might go to the cornfield and light them. Say goodbye."

"How many times can you say it?"

"It was an idea," Ruth said. "I'll go alone."

"No," Ray said. "I'll go."

Ruth sat down in her jacket and overalls and waited for him to change his shirt. She watched him with his back toward her, how thin he was but also how the muscles seemed to pop on his arms the way they were supposed to and the color of his skin, like his mother's, so much more inviting than her own.

"We can kiss for a while if you want."

And he turned, grinning. He had begun to like the experiments. He was not thinking of me anymore—though he couldn't tell that to Ruth.

He liked the way she cursed and hated school. He liked how smart she was and how she tried to pretend that it didn't matter to her that his father was a doctor (even though not a real doctor, as she pointed out) and her father scavenged old houses, or that the Singhs had rows and rows of books in their house while she was starved for them.

He sat down next to her on the bed.

"Do you want to take your parka off?"

She did.

And so on the anniversary of my death, Ray mashed himself against Ruth and the two of them kissed and at some point she looked him in the face. "Shit!" she said. "I think I feel something."

When Ray and Ruth arrived at the cornfield, they were silent and he was holding her hand. She didn't know whether he was holding it because they were observing my death together or because he liked her. Her brain was a storm, her usual insight gone.

Then she saw she had not been the only one to think of me. Hal and Samuel Heckler were standing in the cornfield with their hands jammed in their pockets and their backs turned toward her. Ruth saw yellow daffodils on the ground.

"Did you bring those?" Ruth asked Samuel.

"No," Hal said, answering for his brother. "They were already here when we got here."

Mrs. Stead watched from her son's upstairs bedroom. She decided to throw on her coat and walk out to the field. It was not something she even tried to judge, whether or not she belonged there.

Grace Tarking was walking around the block when she saw Mrs. Stead leaving her house with a poinsettia. They talked briefly in the street. Grace said that she was going to stop at home but she would come and join them.

Grace made two phone calls, one to her boyfriend, who lived a short distance away in a slightly richer area, and one to the

Gilberts. They had not yet recovered from their strange role in the discovery of my death—their faithful lab having found the first evidence. Grace offered to escort them, since they were older and cutting across neighbors' lawns and over the bumpy earth of the cornfield would be a challenge to them, but yes, Mr. Gilbert had said, he wanted to come. They needed this, he told Grace Tarking, his wife particularly—though I could see how crushed he was. He always covered his pain by being attentive to his wife. Though they had thought briefly of giving their dog away, he was too much comfort to both of them.

Mr. Gilbert wondered if Ray, who ran errands for them and was a sweet boy who had been badly judged, knew, and so he called the Singh household. Ruana said she suspected her son must already be there but that she would be along herself.

Lindsey was looking out the window when she saw Grace Tarking with her arm in Mrs. Gilbert's and Grace's boyfriend steadying Mr. Gilbert as the four of them cut across the O'Dwyers' lawn.

"Something's going on in the cornfield, Mom," she said.

My mother was reading Molière, whom she had studied so intensely in college but hadn't looked at since. Beside her were the books that had marked her as an avant-garde undergraduate: Sartre, Colette, Proust, Flaubert. She had pulled them off the shelves in her bedroom and promised herself she would reread them that year.

"I'm not interested," she said to Lindsey, "but I'm sure your father will be when he gets home. Why don't you go up and play with your brother?"

My sister had dutifully hovered for weeks now, paying court to our mother regardless of the signals she gave. There was something on the other side of the icy surface. Lindsey was sure of it. She stayed by my mother, sitting by her chair and watching our neighbors outside the window.

*     *     *

By the time darkness fell, the candles the latecomers had had the foresight to bring lit the cornfield. It seemed like everyone I'd ever known or sat next to in a classroom from kindergarten to eighth grade was there. Mr. Botte saw that something was happening when he'd come out of the school after preparing his classroom for the next day's annual animal digestion experiment. He'd strolled over, and, when he realized what it was, he let himself back into the school and made some calls. There had been a secretary who had been overcome by my death. She came with her son. There had been some teachers who hadn't come to the official school memorial.

The rumors of Mr. Harvey's suspected guilt had begun to make their way from neighbor to neighbor on Thanksgiving night. By the next afternoon it was the only thing the neighbors could talk about — was it possible? Could that strange man who had lived so quietly among them have killed Susie Salmon? But no one had dared approach my family to find out the details. Cousins of friends or fathers of the boys who cut their lawn were asked if they knew anything. Anyone who might know what the police were doing had been buddied up to in the past week, and so my memorial was both a way to mark my memory and a way for the neighbors to seek comfort from one another. A murderer had lived among them, passed them on the street, bought Girl Scout cookies from their daughters and magazine subscriptions from their sons.

In my heaven I buzzed with heat and energy as more and more people reached the cornfield and lit their candles and began to hum a low, dirgelike song for which Mr. O'Dwyer called back to the distant memory of his Dublin grandfather. My neighbors were awkward at first, but the secretary from the school clung to Mr. O'Dwyer as his voice gave forth, and she added her less melodious one. Ruana Singh stood stiffly in an outer circle away from her son. Dr. Singh had called as she was leaving to say he would be sleeping overnight in his office. But other fathers, coming home from their offices, parked their cars in their driveways only to get out and follow their neighbors. How could they both work to support their families and watch their children to make sure they were safe? As a group they would learn it was impossible, no matter how many rules they laid down. What had happened to me could happen to anyone.

No one had called my house. My family was left undisturbed. The impenetrable barrier that surrounded the shingles, the chimney, the woodpile, the driveway, the fence, was like a layer of clear ice that coated the trees when it rained and then froze. Our house looked the same as every other one on the block, but it was not the same. Murder had a blood red door on the other side of which was everything unimaginable to everyone.

When the sky had turned a dappled rose, Lindsey realized what was happening. My mother never lifted her eyes from her book.

"They're having a ceremony for Susie," Lindsey said. "Listen." She cracked the window open. In rushed the cold December air and the distant sound of singing.

My mother used all her energy. "We've had the memorial," she said. "That's done for me."

"What's done?"

My mother's elbows were on the armrests of the yellow winged-back chair. She leaned slightly forward and her face moved into shadow, making it harder for Lindsey to see the expression on her face. "I don't believe she's waiting for us out there. I don't think lighting candles and doing all that stuff is honoring her memory. There are other ways to honor it."

"Like what?" Lindsey said. She sat cross-legged on the rug in front of my mother, who sat in her chair with her finger marking her place in Molière.

"I want to be more than a mother."

Lindsey thought she could understand this. She wanted to be more than a girl.

My mother put the Molière book on top of the coffee table and scooted forward on the chair until she lowered herself down onto the rug. I was struck by this. My mother did not sit on the floor, she sat at the bill-paying desk or in the wing chairs or sometimes on the end of the couch with Holiday curled up beside her.

She took my sister's hand in hers.

"Are you going to leave us?" Lindsey asked.

My mother wobbled. How could she say what she already knew? Instead, she told a lie. "I promise I won't leave you."

What she wanted most was to be that free girl again, stacking china at Wanamaker's, hiding from her manager the Wedgwood cup with the handle she broke, dreaming of living in Paris like de Beauvoir and Sartre, and going home that day laughing to herself about the nerdy Jack Salmon, who was pretty cute even if he hated smoke. The cafés in Paris were full of cigarettes, she'd told him, and he'd seemed impressed. At the end of that summer when she invited him in and they had, both for the first time, made love, she'd smoked a cigarette, and for the joke he said he'd have one too. When she handed him the damaged blue china to use as an ashtray, she used all her favorite words to embellish the story of breaking and then hiding, inside her coat, the now homely Wedgwood cup.

"Come here, baby," my mother said, and Lindsey did. She leaned her back into my mother's chest, and my mother rocked her awkwardly on the rug. "You are doing so well, Lindsey; you are keeping your father alive." And they heard his car pull into the drive.

Lindsey let herself be held while my mother thought of Ruana Singh out behind her house, smoking. The sweet scent of Dunhills had drifted out onto the road and taken my mother far away. Her last boyfriend before my father had loved Gauloises. He had been a pretentious little thing, she thought, but he had also been oh-so-serious in a way that let her be oh-so-serious as well.

"Do you see the candles, Mom?" Lindsey asked, as she stared out the window.

"Go get your father," my mother said.

My sister met my father in the mud room, hanging up his keys and coat. Yes, they would go, he said. Of course they would go.

"Daddy!" My brother called from the second floor, where my sister and father went to meet him.

"Your call," my father said as Buckley bodychecked him.

"I'm tired of protecting him," Lindsey said. "It doesn't feel real not to include him. Susie's gone. He knows that."

My brother stared up at her.

"There is a party for Susie," Lindsey said. "And me and Daddy are taking you."

"Is Mommy sick?" Buckley asked.

Lindsey didn't want to lie to him, but she also felt it was an accurate description of what she knew.

"Yes."

Lindsey agreed to meet our father downstairs while she brought Buckley into his room to change his clothes.

"I see her, you know," Buckley said, and Lindsey looked at him.

"She comes and talks to me, and spends time with me when you're at soccer."

Lindsey didn't know what to say, but she reached out and grabbed him and squeezed him to her, the way he often squeezed Holiday.

"You are so special," she said to my brother. "I'll always be here, no matter what."

My father made his slow way down the stairs, his left hand tightening on the wooden banister, until he reached the flagstone landing.

His approach was loud. My mother took her Molière book and crept into the dining room, where he wouldn't see her. She read her book, standing in the corner of the dining room and hiding from her family. She waited for the front door to open and close.

My neighbors and teachers, friends and family, circled an arbitrary spot not far from where I'd been killed. My father, sister, and brother heard the singing again once they were outside. Everything in my father leaned and pitched toward the warmth and light. He wanted so badly to have me remembered in the minds and hearts of everyone. I knew something as I watched: almost everyone was saying goodbye to me. I was becoming one of many little-girl-losts. They would go back to their homes and put me to rest, a letter from the past never reopened or reread. And I could say goodbye to them, wish them well, bless them somehow for their good thoughts. A handshake in the street, a dropped item picked up and retrieved and handed back, or a friendly wave from a distant window, a nod, a smile, a moment when the eyes lock over the antics of a child.

Ruth saw my three family members first, and she tugged on Ray's sleeve. "Go help him," she whispered. And Ray, who had met my father on his first day of what would prove a long journey to try to find my killer, moved forward. Samuel came away too. Like youthful pastors, they brought my father and sister and brother into the group, which made a wide berth for them and grew silent.

My father had not been outside the house except to drive back and forth to work or sit out in the backyard, for months, nor had he seen his neighbors. Now he looked at them, from face to face, until he realized I had been loved by people he didn't even recognize. His heart filled up, warm again as it had not been in what seemed so long to him—save small forgotten moments with Buckley, the accidents of love that happened with his son.

He looked at Mr. O'Dwyer. "Stan," he said, "Susie used to stand at the front window during the summer and listen to you singing in your yard. She loved it. Will you sing for us?"

And in the kind of grace that is granted but rarely, and not when you wish it most—to save a loved one from dying—Mr. O'Dwyer wobbled only a moment on his first note, then sang loud and clear and fine.

Everyone joined in.


I remembered those summer nights my father spoke of. How the darkness would take forever to come and with it I always hoped for it to cool down. Sometimes, standing at the open window in the front hall, I would feel a breeze, and on that breeze was the music coming from the O'Dwyers' house. As I listened to Mr. O'Dwyer run through all the Irish ballads he had ever learned, the breeze would begin to smell of earth and air and a mossy scent that meant only one thing: a thunderstorm.

There was a wonderful temporary hush then, as Lindsey sat in her room on the old couch studying, my father sat in his den reading his books, my mother downstairs doing needlepoint or washing up.

I liked to change into a long cotton nightgown and go out onto the back porch, where, as the rain began falling in heavy drops against the roof, breezes came in the screens from all sides and swept my gown against me. It was warm and wonderful and the lightning would come and, a few moments later, the thunder.

My mother would stand at the open porch door, and, after she said her standard warning, "You're going to catch your death of cold," she grew quiet. We both listened together to the rain pour down and the thunder clap and smelled the earth rising to greet us.

"You look invincible," my mother said one night.

I loved these times, when we seemed to feel the same thing. I turned to her, wrapped in my thin gown, and said:

"I am."

# SNAPSHOTS

W ith the camera my parents gave me, I took dozens of candids of my family. So many that my father forced me to choose which rolls I thought should be developed. As the cost of my obsession mounted, I began keeping two boxes in my closet. "Rolls to be sent out" and "Rolls to hold back." It was, my mother said, the only hint of any organizational skills I possessed.

I loved the way the burned-out flashcubes of the Kodak Instamatic marked a moment that had passed, one that would now be gone forever except for a picture. When they were spent, I took the cubed four-corner flashbulbs and passed them from hand to hand until they cooled. The broken filaments of the flash would turn a molten marble blue or sometimes smoke the thin glass black. I had rescued the moment by using my camera and in that way had found a way to stop time and hold it. No one could take that image away from me because I owned it.

\*   \*   \*

On a summer evening in 1975, my mother turned to my father and said:

"Have you ever made love in the ocean?"

And he said, "No."

"Neither have I," my mother said. "Let's pretend it is the ocean and that I am going away and we might never see each other again."

The next day she left for her father's cabin in New Hampshire.

That same summer, Lindsey or Buckley or my father would open the front door and find a casserole or a bundt cake on the front stoop. Sometimes an apple pie — my father's favorite. The food was unpredictable. The casseroles Mrs. Stead made were horrible. The bundt cakes Mrs. Gilbert made were overly moist but bearable. The apple pies from Ruana: heaven on Earth.

In his study during the long nights after my mother left, my father would try to lose himself by rereading passages from the Civil War letters of Mary Chestnut to her husband. He tried to let go of any blame, of any hope, but it was impossible. He did manage a small smile once.

"Ruana Singh bakes a mean apple pie," he wrote in his notebook.

In the fall he picked up the phone one afternoon to hear Grandma Lynn.

"Jack," my grandmother announced, "I am thinking of coming to stay."

My father was silent, but the line was riddled with his hesitation.

"I would like to make myself available to you and the children. I've been knocking around in this mausoleum long enough."

"Lynn, we're just beginning to start over again," he stammered. Still, he couldn't depend on Nate's mother to watch Buckley forever. Four months after my mother left, her temporary absence was beginning to take on the feel of permanence.

My grandmother insisted. I watched her resist the remaining slug of vodka in her glass. "I will contain my drinking until" — she thought hard here — "after five o'clock, and," she said, "what the hell, I'll stop altogether if you should find it necessary."

"Do you know what you're saying?"

My grandmother felt a clarity from her phone hand down to her pump-encased feet. "Yes, I do. I think."

It was only after he got off the phone that he let himself wonder, *Where will we PUT her?*

It was obvious to everyone.


By December 1975, a year had passed since Mr. Harvey had packed his bags, but there was still no sign of him. For a while, until the tape dirtied or the paper tore, store owners kept a scratchy sketch of him taped to their windows. Lindsey and Samuel walked in the neighborhood or hung out at Hal's bike shop. She wouldn't go to the diner where the other kids went. The owner of the diner was a law and order man. He had blown up the sketch of George Harvey to twice its size and taped it to the front door. He willingly gave the grisly details to any customer who asked — young girl, cornfield, found only an elbow.

Finally Lindsey asked Hal to give her a ride to the police station. She wanted to know what exactly they were doing.

They bid farewell to Samuel at the bike shop and Hal gave Lindsey a ride through a wet December snow.

From the start, Lindsey's youth and purpose had caught the police off guard. As more and more of them realized who she was, they gave her a wider and wider berth. Here was this girl, focused, mad, fifteen. Her breasts were perfect small cups, her legs gangly but curved, her eyes like flint and flower petals.

While Lindsey and Hal waited outside the captain's office on a wooden bench, she thought she saw something across the room that she recognized. It was on Detective Fenerman's desk and it stood out in the room because of its color. What her mother had always distinguished as Chinese red, a harsher red than rose red, it was the red of classic lipsticks, rarely found in nature. Our mother was proud of her ability to wear Chinese red, noting each time she tied a particular scarf around her neck that it was a color even Grandma Lynn dared not wear.

"Hal," she said, every muscle tense as she stared at the increasingly familiar object on Fenerman's desk.

"Yes."

"Do you see that red cloth?"

"Yes."

"Can you go and get it for me?"

When Hal looked at her, she said: "I think it's my mother's."

As Hal stood to retrieve it, Len entered the squad room from behind where Lindsey sat. He tapped her on the shoulder just as he realized what Hal was doing. Lindsey and Detective Fenerman stared at each other.

"Why do you have my mother's scarf?"

He stumbled. "She might have left it in my car one day."

Lindsey stood and faced him. She was clear-eyed and driving fast toward the worst news yet. "What was she doing in your car?"

"Hello, Hal," Len said.

Hal held the scarf in his hand. Lindsey grabbed it away, her voice growing angry. "Why do you have my mother's scarf?"

And though Len was the detective, Hal saw it first—it arched over her like a rainbow—Prismacolor understanding. The way it happened in algebra class or English when my sister was the first person to figure out the sum of *x* or point out the double entendres to her peers. Hal put his hand on Lindsey's shoulder to guide her. "We should go," he said.

And later she cried out her disbelief to Samuel in the back room of the bike shop.


When my brother turned seven, he built a fort for me. It was something the two of us had said we would always do together and something my father could not bring himself to do. It reminded him too much of building the tent with the disappeared Mr. Harvey.

A family with five little girls had moved into Mr. Harvey's house. Laughter traveled over into my father's study from the built-in pool they had poured the spring after George Harvey ran. The sound of little girls — girls to spare.

The cruelty of it became like glass shattering in my father's ears. In the spring of 1976, with my mother gone, he would shut the window of his den on even the hottest evenings to avoid the sound. He watched his solitary little boy in among the three pussy-willow bushes, talking to himself. Buckley had brought empty terra-cotta pots from the garage. He hauled the boot scraper out from where it lay forgotten at the side of the house. Anything to make walls for the fort. With the help of Samuel and Hal and Lindsey, he edged two huge boulders from the front of the driveway into the backyard. This was such an unexpected windfall that it prompted Samuel to ask, "How are you going to make a roof?"

And Buckley looked at him in wonder as Hal mentally scanned the contents of his bike shop and remembered two scrap sheets of corrugated tin he had leaning up against the back wall.

So one hot night my father looked down and didn't see his son anymore. Buckley was nestled inside his fort. On his hands and knees, he would pull the terra-cotta pots in after him and then prop a board against them that reached almost up to the wavy roof. Just enough light came in to read by. Hal had obliged him and painted in big black spray paint letters KEEP OUT on one side of the plywood door.

Mostly he read the Avengers and the X-Men. He dreamed of being Wolverine, who had a skeleton made of the strongest metal in the universe and who could heal from any wound overnight. At the oddest moments he would think about me, miss my voice, wish I would come out from the house and pound on the roof of his fort and demand to be let in. Sometimes he wished Samuel and Lindsey hung out more or that my father would play with him as he once had. Play without that always-worried look underneath the smile, that desperate worry that surrounded everything now like an invisible force field. But my brother would not let himself miss my mother. He tunneled into stories where weak men changed into strong half-animals or used eye beams or magic hammers to power through steel or climb up the sides of skyscrapers. He was the Hulk when angry and Spidey the rest of the time. When he felt his heart hurt he turned into something stronger than a little boy, and he grew up this way. A heart that flashed from heart to stone, heart to stone. As I watched I thought of what Grandma Lynn liked to say when Lindsey and I rolled our eyes or grimaced behind her back. "Watch out what faces you make. You'll freeze that way."

One day, Buckley came home from the second grade with a story he'd written: "Once upon a time there was a kid named Billy. He liked to explore. He saw a hole and went inside but he never came out. The End."

My father was too distracted to see anything in this. Mimicking my mother, he taped it to the fridge in the same place Buckley's long-forgotten drawing of the Inbetween had been. But my brother knew something was wrong with his story. Knew it by how his teacher had reacted, doing a double take like they did in his comic books. He took the story down and brought it to my old room while Grandma Lynn was downstairs. He folded it into a tiny square and put it inside the now-empty insides of my four-poster bed.

On a hot day in the fall of 1976, Len Fenerman visited the large safety box in the evidence room. The bones of the neighborhood animals he had found in Mr. Harvey's crawlspace were there, along with the lab confirmation of evidence of quicklime. He had supervised the investigation, but no matter how much they dug, or how deep, no other bones or bodies had been found on his property. The blood stain on the floor of his garage was my only calling card. Len had spent weeks, then months, poring over a xerox of the sketch Lindsey had stolen. He had led a team back into the field, and they had dug and then dug again. Finally they found an old Coke bottle at the opposite end of the field. There it was, a solid link: fingerprints matching Mr. Harvey's prints, which were all over his house, and fingerprints matching those on my birth certificate. There was no question in his mind: Jack Salmon had been right from the beginning.

But no matter how hard he looked for the man himself, it was as if George Harvey had evaporated into thin air when he hit the property line. He could find no records with that name attached. Officially, he did not exist.

What he had left behind were his dollhouses. So Len called the man who sold them for him, and who took commissions from se-lect stores, and the wealthy people who ordered replicas of their own homes. Nothing. He had called the makers of the miniature chairs, the tiny doors and windows with beveled glass and brass hardware, and the manufacturer of the cloth shrubs and trees. Nothing.

He sat down among the evidence at a barren communal desk in the basement of the station. He looked through the stack of extra fliers that my father had made up. He had memorized my face, but still he looked at them. He had come to believe that the best hope in my case might be the recent rise in development in the area. With all the land churning and changing, perhaps other clues would be found that would provide the answer he needed.

In the bottom of the box was the bag with my jingle-bell hat. When he'd handed it to my mother, she had collapsed on the rug. He still couldn't pinpoint the moment he'd fallen in love with her. I knew it was the day he'd sat in our family room while my mother drew stick figures on butcher paper and Buckley and Nate slept toe to toe on the couch. I felt sorry for him. He had tried to solve my murder and he had failed. He had tried to love my mother and he had failed.

Len looked at the drawing of the cornfield that Lindsey had stolen and forced himself to acknowledge this: in his cautiousness, he had allowed a murderer to get away. He could not shake his guilt. He knew, if no one else did, that by being with my mother in the mall that day he was the one to blame for George Harvey's freedom.

He took his wallet out of his back pocket and laid down the photos of all the unsolved cases he had ever worked on. Among them was his wife's. He turned them all face-down. "Gone," he wrote on each one of them. He would no longer wait for a date to mark an understanding of who or why or how. He would never understand all the reasons why his wife had killed herself. He would never understand how so many children went missing. He placed these photos in the box with my evidence and turned the lights off in the cold room.

But he did not know this:

In Connecticut on September 10, 1976, a hunter on his way back to his car saw something shiny on the ground. My

Pennsylvania keystone charm. Then he saw that the ground nearby had been partially dug up by a bear. Exposed by the bear were the unmistakable bones of a child's foot.

My mother made it through only one winter in New Hampshire before she got the idea of driving all the way to California. It was something she had always thought she would do but had never done. A man she met in New Hampshire had told her about the work to be had in wineries in the valleys above San Francisco. It was easy to get, it was physical, and it could be, if you wanted it to be, very anonymous. All three sounded good to her.

This man had also wanted to sleep with her, but she said no. By then, she knew this wasn't the road out anymore. From the first night with Len in the innards of the mall she had known the two of them weren't building anything. She could not even really feel him.

She packed her bags for California and sent cards to my brother and sister from every town she stopped in. "Hello, I'm in Dayton. Ohio's state bird is the cardinal." "Reached the Mississippi last night at sunset. It certainly is a big river."

In Arizona, when she was eight states beyond the farthest she had ever been, she paid for her room and brought a bucket of ice with her from the machine outside. The next day she would reach California, and to celebrate she had bought herself a bottle of champagne. She thought of what the man in New Hampshire had said, how he had spent one whole year scraping the mold out of the giant casks that held wine. He had lain flat on his back and had to use a knife to peel back the layers of mold. The mold had the color and consistency of liver, and no matter how hard he bathed he would still attract fruit flies for hours afterward.

She sipped champagne from a plastic cup and looked at herself in the mirror. She forced herself to look.

She remembered sitting in our living room then, with me and my sister, my brother and father, on the first New Year's Eve that all five of us had stayed up. She had shaped the day around making sure Buckley got enough sleep.

When he woke up after dark he was sure that someone better than Santa would come that night. In his mind he held a big bang image of the ultimate holiday, when he would be transported to toyland.

Hours later, as he yawned and leaned into my mother's lap and she finger-combed his hair, my father ducked into the kitchen to make cocoa and my sister and I served German chocolate cake. When the clock struck twelve and there was only distant screaming and a few guns shot into the air in our neighborhood, my brother was unbelieving. Disappointment so swiftly and thoroughly overtook him that my mother was at a loss for what to do. She thought of it as sort of an infant Peggy Lee's "Is that all there is?" and then bawling.

She remembered my father had lifted Buckley up into his arms and started singing. The rest of us joined in. "Let ole acquaintance be forgot and never brought to mind, should ole acquaintance be forgot and days of auld lang syne!"

And Buckley had stared at us. He captured the foreign words like bubbles floating above him in the air. "Lang syne?" he said with a look of wonder.

"What does that mean?" I asked my parents.

"The old days," my father said.

"Days long past," my mother said. But then, suddenly, she had started pinching the crumbs of her cake together on her plate.

"Hey, Ocean Eyes," my father said. "Where'd you go on us?"

And she remembered that she had met his question with a closing off, as though her spirit had a tap—twist to the right and she was up on her feet asking me to help her clean up.

In the fall of 1976, when she reached California, she drove

directly to the beach and stopped her car. She felt like she had
driven through nothing but families for four days—squabbling
families, bawling families, screaming families, families under the
miraculous strain of the day by day—and she was relieved to see
the waves from the windshield of her car. She couldn't help thinking of the books she had read in college. *The Awakening.* And
what had happened to one writer, Virginia Woolf. It all seemed
so wonderful back then—filmy and romantic—stones in the
pocket, walk into the waves.

She climbed down the cliffs after tying her sweater loosely
around her waist. Down below she could see nothing but jagged
rocks and waves. She was careful, but I watched her feet more
than the view she saw—I worried about her slipping.

My mother's desire to reach those waves, touch her feet to another ocean on the other side of the country, was all she was
thinking of—the pure baptismal goal of it. Whoosh and you can
start over again. Or was life more like the horrible game in gym
that has you running from one side of an enclosed space to another, picking up and setting down wooden blocks without end?
She was thinking *reach the waves, the waves, the waves,* and I was
watching her feet navigate the rocks, and when we heard her we
did so together—looking up in shock.

It was a baby on the beach.

In among the rocks was a sandy cove, my mother now saw, and
crawling across the sand on a blanket was a baby in knitted pink
cap and singlet and boots. She was alone on the blanket with a
stuffed white toy—my mother thought a lamb.

With their backs to my mother as she descended were a group
of adults—very official and frantic-looking—wearing black and
navy with cool slants to their hats and boots. Then my wildlife
photographer's eye saw the tripods and silver circles rimmed by
wire, which, when a young man moved them left or right,
bounced light off or on the baby on her blanket.

My mother started laughing, but only one assistant turned to notice her up among the rocks; everyone else was too busy. This was an ad for something, I imagined, but what? New fresh infant girls to replace your own? As my mother laughed and I watched her face light up, I also saw it fall into strange lines.

She saw the waves behind the girl child and how both beautiful and intoxicating they were—they could sweep up so softly and remove this girl from the beach. All the stylish people could chase after her, but she would drown in a moment—no one, not even a mother who had every nerve attuned to anticipate disaster, could have saved her if the waves leapt up, if life went on as usual and freak accidents peppered a calm shore.

That same week she found work at the Krusoe Winery, in a valley above the bay. She wrote my sister and brother postcards filled with the bright fragments of her life, hoping in a postcard's limited space she would sound cheery.

On her days off, she would walk down the streets of Sausalito or Santa Rosa—tiny upscale towns where everyone was a stranger—and, no matter how hard she tried to focus on the hopeful unfamiliar, when she walked inside a gift shop or café the four walls around her would begin to breathe like a lung. She would feel it then, creeping up the side of her calves and into her gut, the onslaught, the grief coming, the tears like a small relentless army approaching the front lines of her eyes, and she would breathe in, taking a large gulp of air to try to stop herself from crying in a public place. She asked for coffee and toast in a restaurant and buttered it with tears. She went into a flower shop and asked for daffodils, and when there were none she felt robbed. It was such a small wish—a bright yellow flower.

The first impromptu memorial in the cornfield opened in my father the need for more. Yearly now, he organized a memorial, to which fewer and fewer neighbors and friends came. There were the regulars, like Ruth, and the Gilberts, but more and more the group was filled out by kids from the high school who, as time went by, knew only my name and even that only as a large dark rumor invoked as a warning to any student that might prove too much a loner. Especially girls.

Each time my name was said by these strangers it felt like a pin-prick. It was not the pleasant sensation that it could be when my father said it or when Ruth wrote it in her journal. It was the sensation of being simultaneously resurrected and buried within the same breath. As if in an economics class I had been ushered over into a column of transmutable commodities: the Murdered. A few teachers, like Mr. Botte, remembered me as a real girl. Sometimes on his lunch hour he would go and sit in his red Fiat and think about the daughter he had lost to leukemia. In the distance, out past his window, the cornfield loomed. Often, he would say a prayer for me.

In just a few short years, Ray Singh grew so handsome that a spell radiated from him when he walked into a crowd. His adult face had still not settled on him, but, now that he was seventeen, it was just around the corner. He exuded a dreamy asexuality that made him attractive to both men and women, with his long lashes and hooded eyelids, his thick black hair, and the same delicate features that were still a boy's.

I would watch Ray with a longing different from that which I had for anyone else. A longing to touch and hold him, to understand the very body that he examined with the coldest of eyes. He would sit at his desk and read his favorite book — *Gray's Anatomy* — and depending on what he was reading about he would use his fingers to palpate his carotid artery or his thumb to press down and follow the longest muscle in his body — the sartorius, which ran from the outside of his hip to the inside of his knee. His thinness was a boon to him then, the bones and muscles clearly distinguished beneath the skin.

By the time he packed his bags for Penn, he had committed so many words and their definitions to memory that I grew worried. With all that, how could his mind contain anything else? Ruth's friendship, his mother's love, my memory would be pushed to the back as he made way for the eye's crystalline lens and its capsule, the semicircular canals of the ear, or my favorite, the qualities of the sympathetic nervous system.

I need not have worried. Ruana cast about the house for something, anything, that her son might bring with him that was equal in heft and weight to *Gray's* and that would, she hoped, keep the flower-gathering side of him alive. Without his knowing, she tucked the book of Indian poetry into his luggage. Inside was the long-forgotten photo of me. When he unpacked inside Hill House dormitory, my picture fell on the floor by his bed. Despite how he could dissect it — the vessels of the globe of my eye, the surgical anatomy of my nasal fossae, the light tincture of my epidermis — he could not avoid them, the lips he had once kissed.


In June 1977, on the day of what would have been my graduation, Ruth and Ray were already gone. The day classes ended at Fairfax, Ruth moved to New York City with her mother's old red suitcase full of new black clothes. Having graduated early, Ray was already at the end of his freshman year at Penn.

In our kitchen that same day, Grandma Lynn gave Buckley a book on gardening. She told him about how plants came from seeds. That radishes, which he hated, grew fastest, but that flowers, which he loved, could grow from seeds as well. And she began to teach him the names: zinnias and marigolds, pansies and lilacs, carnations and petunias, and morning glory vines.

\*   \*   \*

Occasionally my mother called from California. My parents had hurried and difficult conversations. She asked after Buckley and Lindsey and Holiday. She asked how the house was holding up and whether there was anything he needed to tell her.

"We still miss you," he said in December 1977, when the leaves had all fallen and been blown or raked away but even still, with the ground waiting to receive it, there had been no snow.

"I know that," she said.

"What about teaching? I thought that was your plan."

"It was," she conceded. She was on the phone in the office of the winery. Things had slowed up after the lunch crowd, but five limos of old ladies, three sheets to the wind, were soon due in. She was silent and then she said something that no one, least of all my father, could have argued with. "Plans change."


In New York, Ruth was living in an old woman's walk-in closet on the Lower East Side. It was the only thing she could afford, and she had no intention of spending much time there anyway. Daily she rolled her twin-sized futon into the corner so she could have a little floor space in which to dress. She visited the closet only once a day, and she never spent any time there if she could help it. The closet was for sleeping and having an address, a solid if tiny perch in the city.

She worked service bar and walked every inch of Manhattan on her off hours. I watched her pound the cement in her defiant boots, sure that women were being murdered wherever she went. Down in stairwells and up inside beautiful highrises. She would linger at streetlights and scan the facing street. She wrote small prayers in her journal at the cafés and the bars, where she stopped to use the bathroom after ordering the cheapest thing on the menu.

She had become convinced that she had a second sight that no one else had. She didn't know what she would do with it, save taking copious notes for the future, but she had grown unafraid. The world she saw of dead women and children had become as real to her as the world in which she lived.

In the library at Penn, Ray read about the elderly under the bold-face heading "The Conditions of Death." It described a study done in nursing homes in which a large percentage of patients reported to the doctors and nurses that they saw someone standing at the end of their bed at night. Often this person tried to talk to them or call their name. Sometimes the patients were in such a high state of agitation during these delusions that they had to be given a sedative or strapped to their beds.

The text went on to explain that these visions were a result of small strokes that often preceded death. "What is commonly thought of by the layman as the Angel of Death, when discussed at all with the patient's family, should be presented to them as a small series of strokes compounding an already precipitous state of decline."

For a moment, with his finger marking the place in the book, Ray imagined what it would be like if, standing over the bed of an elderly patient, remaining as open as he could to possibility, he might feel something brush past him as Ruth had so many years ago in the parking lot.

Mr. Harvey had been living wild within the Northeast Corridor from the outlying areas of Boston down to the northern tips of the southern states, where he would go to find easier work and fewer questions and make an occasional attempt to reform. He had always liked Pennsylvania and had crisscrossed the long state, camping sometimes behind the 7-Eleven just down the local high-

way from our development, where a ridge of woods survived between the all-night store and the railroad tracks, and where he
found more and more tin cans and cigarette butts each time he
passed through. He still liked to drive close to the old neighborhood when he could. He took these risks early in the morning or
late at night, when the wild pheasants that had once been plentiful still traversed the road and his headlights would catch the hollow glowing of their eye sockets as they skittered from one side of
the road to the other. There were no longer teenagers and young
children sent to pick blackberries just up to the edge of our development, because the old farm fence that had hung so heavily
with them had been torn down to make room for more houses.
He had learned to pick wild mushrooms over time and gorged on
them sometimes when staying overnight in the overgrown fields
of Valley Forge Park. On a night like this I saw him come upon
two novice campers who had died after eating the mushrooms'
poisonous look-alikes. He tenderly stripped their bodies of any
valuables and then moved on.


Hal and Nate and Holiday were the only ones Buckley had ever
allowed into his fort. The grass died underneath the boulders and
when it rained, the insides of the fort were a fetid puddle, but it
stayed there, though Buckley went there less and less, and it was
Hal who finally begged him to make improvements.

"We need to waterproof it, Buck," Hal said one day. "You're
ten — that's old enough to work a caulking gun."

And Grandma Lynn couldn't help herself, she loved men. She
encouraged Buck to do what Hal said, and when she knew Hal
would be coming to visit, she dressed up.

"What are you doing?" my father said one Saturday morning,
lured out of his den by the sweet smell of lemons and butter and
golden batter rising in pans.

"Making muffins," Grandma Lynn said.

My father did a sanity check, staring at her. He was still in his robe and it was almost ninety degrees at ten in the morning, but she had pantyhose and makeup on. Then he noticed Hal in an undershirt out in the yard.

"My God, Lynn," he said. "That boy is young enough . . ."

"But he's de-lec-ta-ble!"

My father shook his head and sat down at the kitchen table. "When will the love muffins be done, Mata Hari?"


In December 1981, Len did not want to get the call he got from Delaware, where a murder in Wilmington had been connected to a girl's body found in 1976 in Connecticut. A detective, working overtime, had painstakingly traced the keystone charm in the Connecticut case back to a list of lost property from my murder.

"It's a dead file," Len told the man on the other end.

"We'd like to see what you have."

"George Harvey," Len said out loud, and the detectives at neighboring desks turned toward him. "The crime was in December 1973. The murder victim was Susie Salmon, fourteen."

"Any body for the Simon girl?"

"Salmon, like the fish. We found an elbow," Len said.

"She have a family?"

"Yes."

"Connecticut has teeth. Do you have her dentals?"

"Yes."

"That may save the family some grief," the man told Len.

Len trekked back to the evidence box he had hoped never to look at again. He would have to make a phone call to my family. But he would wait as long as possible, until he was certain the detective in Delaware had something.

\*   \*   \*

For almost eight years after Samuel told Hal about the drawing Lindsey had stolen, Hal had quietly worked through his network of biker friends to track George Harvey down. But he, like Len, had vowed not to report anything until he was sure it might be a lead. And he had never been sure. When late one night a Hell's Angel named Ralph Cichetti, who admitted freely he had spent some time in prison, said that he thought his mother had been killed by a man she rented a room to, Hal began asking his usual questions. Questions that held elements of elimination about height and weight and preoccupations. The man hadn't gone by the name George Harvey, though that didn't mean anything. But the murder itself seemed too different. Sophie Cichetti was forty-nine. She was killed in her home with a blunt object and her body had been found intact nearby. Hal had read enough crime books to know that killers had patterns, peculiar and important ways they did things. So as Hal adjusted the timing chain of Cichetti's cranky Harley, they moved on to other topics, then fell silent. It was only when Cichetti mentioned something else that every hair on Hal's neck stood up.

"The guy built dollhouses," Ralph Cichetti said.

Hal placed a call to Len.

Years passed. The trees in our yard grew taller. I watched my family and my friends and neighbors, the teachers whom I'd had or imagined having, the high school I had dreamed about. As I sat in the gazebo I would pretend instead that I was sitting on the topmost branch of the maple under which my brother had swallowed a stick and still played hide-and-seek with Nate, or I would perch on the railing of a stairwell in New York and wait for Ruth to pass near. I would study with Ray. Drive the Pacific Coast Highway on a warm afternoon of salty air with my mother. But I would end each day with my father in his den.

I would lay these photographs down in my mind, those gathered from my constant watching, and I could trace how one thing—my death—connected these images to a single source. No one could have predicted how my loss would change small moments on Earth. But I held on to those moments, hoarded them. None of them were lost as long as I was there watching.

At Evensong one night, while Holly played her sax and Mrs. Bethel Utemeyer joined in, I saw him: Holiday, racing past a fluffy white Samoyed. He had lived to a ripe old age on Earth and slept at my father's feet after my mother left, never wanting to let him out of his sight. He had stood with Buckley while he built his fort and had been the only one permitted on the porch while Lindsey and Samuel kissed. And in the last few years of his life, every Sunday morning, Grandma Lynn had made him a skillet-sized peanut butter pancake, which she would place flat on the floor, never tiring of watching him try to pick it up with his snout.

I waited for him to sniff me out, anxious to know if here, on the other side, I would still be the little girl he had slept beside. I did not have to wait long: he was so happy to see me, he knocked me down.

## SEVENTEEN

A t twenty-one Lindsey was many things I would never become, but I barely grieved this list anymore. Still, I roved where she roved. I collected my college diploma and rode on the back of Samuel's bike, clinging on to him with my arms wrapped around his waist, pressing into his back for warmth . . .

Okay, it was Lindsey. I realized that. But in watching her I found I could get lost more than with anyone else.

On the night of their graduation from Temple University, she and Samuel rode his bike back to my parents' house, having promised my father and Grandma Lynn repeatedly that they would not touch the champagne tucked inside the bike's pannard until they reached the house. "After all, we're college graduates!" Samuel had said. My father was soft in his trust with Samuel — years had gone by when the boy had done nothing but right by his surviving daughter.

But on the ride back from Philadelphia down Route 30, it began to rain. Lightly at first, small pinpricks flashing into my sister and Samuel at fifty miles per hour. The cool rain hit the hot dry tar of the road and lifted up smells that had been baked in all day under the hot June sun. Lindsey liked to rest her head between Samuel's shoulder blades and take in the scent of the road and the scrappy shrubs and bushes on either side. She had been remembering how the breeze in the hours before the storm had filled all the white gowns of the graduating seniors as they stood outside Macy Hall. Everyone looked poised, for just a moment, to float away.

Finally, eight miles away from the turnoff that led to our house, the rain grew heavy enough to hurt, and Samuel shouted back to Lindsey that he was going to pull off.

They passed into a slightly more overgrown stretch of road, the kind that existed between two commercial areas and that gradually, by accretion, would be eliminated by another strip mall or auto parts store. The bike wobbled but did not fall on the wet gravel of the shoulder. Samuel used his feet to help brake the bike, then waited, as Hal had taught him, for my sister to get off and step a few feet away before he got off himself.

He opened the visor of his helmet to yell to her. "This is no good," he said, "I'm going to roll her under those trees."

Lindsey followed behind him, the sound of rain hushed inside her padded helmet. They picked their way through the gravel and mud, stepping over branches and litter that had gathered at the side of the road. The rain seemed to be getting heavier still, and my sister was glad she had changed out of the dress she'd worn to commencement and into the leather pants and jacket that Hal had insisted on getting her despite her protests that she looked like a pervert.

Samuel wheeled the bike into the stand of oaks close to the road, and Lindsey followed. They had gone the week before to get haircuts at the same barber shop on Market Street, and though Lindsey's hair was lighter and finer than Samuel's, the barber had given them identical short, spiky cuts. Within a moment of removing their helmets their hair caught the large drops that filtered through the trees, and Lindsey's mascara began to bleed. I watched as Samuel used his thumb to wipe the traces from Lindsey's cheek. "Happy graduation," he said in the darkness, and stooped to kiss her.

Since their first kiss in our kitchen two weeks after my death, I had known that he was — as my sister and I had giggled with our Barbies or while watching Bobby Sherman on TV — her one and only. Samuel had pressed himself into her need, and the cement between the two of them had begun to set immediately. They had gone to Temple together, side by side. He had hated it and she had pushed him through. She had loved it and this had allowed him to survive.

"Let's try and find the densest part of this underbrush," he said.

"What about the bike?"

"Hal will probably have to rescue us when the rain stops."

"Shit!" Lindsey said.

Samuel laughed and grabbed her hand to start walking. The moment they did, they heard the first thunderclap and Lindsey jumped. He tightened his hold on her. The lightning was in the distance still, and the thunder would grow louder on its heels. She had never felt about it the way I did. It made her jumpy and nervous. She imagined trees split down the middle and houses on fire and dogs cowering in basements throughout the suburbs.

They walked through the underbrush, which was getting soaked despite the trees. Even though it was the middle of the afternoon, it was dark except for Samuel's safety light. Still they felt the evidence of people. Their boots crunched down on top of tin cans and pushed up against empty bottles. And then, through the thick weeds and darkness both of them saw the broken window panes that ran along the top of an old Victorian house. Samuel shut off the safety light immediately.

"Do you think there's someone inside?" Lindsey asked.

"It's dark."

"It's spooky."

They looked at each other, and my sister said what they both were thinking. "It's dry!"

They held hands in the heavy rain and ran toward the house as fast as they could, trying not to trip or slide in the increasing mud.

As they drew closer, Samuel could make out the steep pitch of the roof and the small wooden cross work that hung down from the gables. Most of the windows on the bottom floor had been covered over with wood, but the front door swung back and forth on its hinges, banging against the plaster wall on the inside. Though part of him wanted to stand outside in the rain and stare up at the eaves and cornices, he rushed into the house with Lindsey. They stood a few feet inside the doorway, shivering and staring out into the pre-suburban forest that surrounded them. Quickly I scanned the rooms of the old house. They were alone. No scary monsters lurked in corners, no wandering men had taken root.

More and more of these undeveloped patches were disappearing, but they, more than anything, had marked my childhood. We lived in one of the first developments to be built on the converted farmland in the area—a development that became the model and inspiration for what now seemed a limitless number—but my imagination had always rested on the stretch of road that had not been filled in with the bright colors of shingles and drainpipes, paved driveways and super-size mailboxes. So too had Samuel's.

"Wow!" Lindsey said. "How old do you think this is?"

Lindsey's voice echoed off the walls as if they stood alone in a church.

"Let's explore," said Samuel.

The boarded-up windows on the first floor made it hard to see anything, but with the help of Samuel's safety light they could pick out both a fireplace and the chair rail along the walls.

"Look at the floor," Samuel said. He knelt down, taking her with him. "Do you see the tongue and groove work? These people had more money than their neighbors."

Lindsey smiled. Just as Hal cared only for the inner workings of motorcycles, Samuel had become obsessed with carpentry.

He ran his fingers over the floor and had Lindsey do it too. "This is a gorgeous old wreck," he said.

"Victorian?" Lindsey asked, making her best guess.

"It blows my mind to say this," Samuel said, "but I think it's gothic revival. I noticed cross-bracing on the gable trim, so that means it was after 1860."

"Look," said Lindsey.

In the center of the floor someone had once, long ago, set a fire.

"And *that* is a tragedy," Samuel said.

"Why didn't they use the fireplace? There's one in every room."

But Samuel was busy looking up through the hole the fire had burned into the ceiling, trying to make out the patterns of the woodwork along the window frames.

"Let's go upstairs," he said.

"I feel like I'm in a cave," said Lindsey as they climbed the stairs. "It's so quiet in here you can barely hear the rain."

Samuel bounced the soft side of his fist off the plaster as he went. "You could wall someone into this place."

And suddenly it was one of those awkward moments that they had learned to let pass and I lived to anticipate. It begged a central question. Where was I? Would I be mentioned? Brought up and discussed? Usually now the answer was a disappointing no. It was no longer a Susie-fest on Earth.

But something about the house and the night — markers like graduations and birthdays always meant that I was more alive, higher up in the register of thoughts — made Lindsey dwell on me more in that moment than she normally might. Still, she didn't mention it. She remembered the heady feeling she had had in Mr.

Harvey's house and that she had often felt since — that I was with her somehow, in her thoughts and limbs — moving with her like a twin.

At the top of the stairs they found the entrance to the room they had stared up at.

"I want this house," Samuel said.

"What?"

"This house needs me, I can feel it."

"Maybe you should wait until the sun comes out to decide," she said.

"It's the most beautiful thing I've ever seen," he said.

"Samuel Heckler," my sister said, "fixer of broken things."

"One to talk," he said.

They stood for a moment in silence and smelled the damp air coming through the chimney and flooding the room. Even with the sound of rain, Lindsey still felt hidden away, tucked safely in an outside corner of the world with the one person she loved more than anyone else.

She took his hand, and I traveled with them up to the doorway of a small room at the very front. It jutted out over what would be the entrance hall of the floor below and was octagonal in shape.

"Oriels," Samuel said. "The windows" — he turned to Lindsey — "when they're built out like that, like a tiny room, that's called an oriel."

"Do they turn you on?" Lindsey asked, smiling.

I left them in the rain and darkness. I wondered if Lindsey noticed that when she and Samuel began to unzip their leathers the lightning stopped and the rumble in the throat of God — that scary thunder — ceased.

In his den, my father reached out to hold the snow globe in his hand. The cold glass against his fingers comforted him, and he shook it to watch the penguin disappear and then slowly be un-covered by the gently falling snow.

Hal had made it back from the graduation ceremonies on his motorcycle but instead of calming my father—providing some assurance that if one motorcycle could maneuver the storm and deliver its rider safe to his door, another one could too—it seemed to stack the probabilities in the reverse in his mind.

He had taken what could be called a painful delight in Lindsey's graduation ceremony. Buckley had sat beside him, du-tifully prompting him when to smile and react. He often *knew* when, but his synapses were never as quick now as normal peo-ple's—or at least that was how he explained it to himself. It was like reaction time in the insurance claims he reviewed. There was an average number of seconds for most people between when they saw something coming—another car, a rock rolling down an embankment—and when they reacted. My father's response times were slower than most, as if he moved in a world where a crushing inevitability had robbed him of any hope of accurate perception.

Buckley tapped on the half-open door of my father's den.

"Come in," he said.

"They'll be okay, Dad." At twelve, my brother had become se-rious and considerate. Even if he didn't pay for the food or cook the meals, he managed the house.

"You looked good in your suit, son," my father said.

"Thanks." This mattered to my brother. He had wanted to make my father proud and had taken time with his appearance, even asking Grandma Lynn that morning to help trim the bangs that fell in his eyes. My brother was in the most awkward stage of adolescence—not boy, not man. Most days he hid his body in big T-shirts and sloppy jeans, but he had liked wearing the suit that day. "Hal and Grandma are waiting for us downstairs," he said.

"I'll be down in a minute."

Buckley closed the door all the way this time, letting the latch snap into place.

That fall my father had developed the last roll of film that I'd kept in my closet in my "rolls to hold back" box, and now, as he often did when he begged just a minute before dinner or saw something on TV or read an article in the paper that made his heart ache, he drew back his desk drawer and gingerly lifted the photos in his hand.

He had lectured me repeatedly that what I called my "artistic shots" were foolhardy, but the best portrait he ever had was one I took of him at an angle so his face filled the three-by-three square when you held it so it was a diamond.

I must have been listening to his hints on camera angles and composition when I took the pictures he held now. He had had no idea what order the rolls were in or what they were of when he had them developed. There were an inordinate number of photos of Holiday, and many a shot of my feet or the grass. Gray balls of blurs in the air which were birds, and a grainy attempt at a sunset over the pussy-willow tree. But at some point I had decided to take portraits of my mother. When he'd picked the roll up at the photo lab my father sat in the car staring at photos of a woman he felt he barely knew anymore.

Since then he had taken these photos out too many times to count, but each time he looked into the face of this woman he had felt something growing inside him. It took him a long time to re-alize what it was. Only recently had his wounded synapses al-lowed him to name it. He had been falling in love all over again.

He didn't understand how two people who were married, who saw each other every day, could forget what each other looked like, but if he had had to name what had happened — this was it. And the last two photos in the roll provided the key. He had come home from work — I remember trying to keep my mother's at-tention as Holiday barked when he heard the car pull into the garage.

"He'll come out," I said. "Stay still." And she did. Part of what I loved about photography was the power it gave me over the people on the other side of the camera, even my own parents.

Out of the corner of my eye I saw my father walk through the side door into the yard. He carried his slim briefcase, which, years before, Lindsey and I had heatedly investigated only to find very little of interest to us. As he set it down I snapped the last solitary photo of my mother. Already her eyes had begun to seem distracted and anxious, diving under and up into a mask somehow. In the next photo, the mask was almost, but not quite, in place and the final photo, where my father was leaning slightly down to give her a kiss on the cheek — there it was.

"Did I do that to you?" he asked her image as he stared at the pictures of my mother, lined up in a row. "How did that happen?"


"The lightning stopped," my sister said. The moisture of the rain on her skin had been replaced by sweat.

"I love you," Samuel said.

"I know."

"No, I mean I love you, and I want to marry you, and I want to live in this house!"

"What?"

"That hideous, hideous college shit is over!" Samuel screamed. The small room absorbed his voice, barely bouncing back an echo from its thick walls.

"Not for me, it isn't," my sister said.

Samuel got up off the floor, where he had been lying beside my sister, and came to his knees in front of her. "Marry me."

"Samuel?"

"I'm tired of doing all the right things. Marry me and I'll make this house gorgeous."

"Who will support us?"

"We will," he said, "somehow."

She sat up and then joined him kneeling. They were both half-dressed and growing colder as their heat began to dissipate.

"Okay."

"Okay?"

"I think I can," my sister said. "I mean, yes!"

Some clichés I understood only when they came into my heaven full speed. I had never seen a chicken with its head cut off. It had never meant much to me except something else that had been treated much the same as me. But that moment I ran around my heaven like . . . a chicken with its head cut off! I was so happy I screamed over and over and over again. My sister! My Samuel! My dream!

She was crying, and he held her in his arms, rocking her against him.

"Are you happy, sweetheart?" he asked.

She nodded against his bare chest. "Yes," she said, then froze. "My dad." She raised her head and looked at Samuel. "I know he's worried."

"Yes," he said, trying to switch gears with her.

"How many miles is it to the house from here?"

"Ten maybe," Samuel said. "Maybe eight."

"We could do that," she said.

"You're nuts."

"We have sneakers in the other pannard."

They could not run in leather, so they wore their underwear and T-shirts, as close to streakers as anyone in my family would ever be. Samuel, as he had for years, set a pace just ahead of my sister to keep her going. There were hardly any cars on the road, but when one passed by a wall of water would come up from the puddles near the side of the road and make the two of them gasp to get air back in their lungs. Both of them had run in rain before but never rain this heavy. They made a game of who could gain the most shelter as they ran the miles, waltzing in and out to gain cover under any overhanging trees, even as the dirt and grime of the road covered their legs. But by mile three they were silent, pushing their feet forward in a natural rhythm they had both known for years, focusing on the sound of their own breath and the sound of their wet shoes hitting the pavement.

At some point as she splashed through a large puddle, no longer trying to avoid them, she thought of the local pool of which we had been members until my death brought the comfortably public existence of my family to a close. It had been somewhere along this road, but she did not lift her head to find the familiar chain-link fence. Instead, she had a memory. She and I were under water in our bathing suits with their small ruffled skirts. Both of our eyes were open under water, a new skill—newer for her—and we were looking at each other, our separate bodies suspended under water. Hair floating, small skirts floating, our cheeks bulging with captured air. Then, together, we would grab on to each other and shoot up out of the water, breaking the surface. We sucked air into our lungs—ears popping—and laughed together.

I watched my beautiful sister running, her lungs and legs pumping, and the skill from the pool still there—fighting to see through the rain, fighting to keep her legs lifting at the pace set by Samuel, and I knew she was not running away from me or toward me. Like someone who has survived a gut-shot, the wound had been closing, closing—braiding into a scar for eight long years.

By the time the two of them were within a mile of my house, the rain had lightened and people were beginning to look out their windows toward the street.

Samuel slowed his pace and she joined him. Their T-shirts were locked onto their bodies like paste.

Lindsey had fought off a cramp in her side, but as the cramp lifted she ran with Samuel full-out. Suddenly she was covered in goose bumps and smiling ear to ear.

"We're getting married!" she said, and he stopped short, grabbed her up in his arms, and they were still kissing when a car passed them on the road, the driver honking his horn.


When the doorbell rang at our house it was four o'clock and Hal was in the kitchen wearing one of my mother's old white chef's aprons and cutting brownies for Grandma Lynn. He liked being put to work, feeling useful, and my grandmother liked to use him. They were a simpatico team. While Buckley, the boy-guard, loved to eat.

"I'll get it," my father said. He had been propping himself up during the rain with highballs, mixed, not measured, by Grandma Lynn.

He was spry now with a thin sort of grace, like a retired ballet dancer who favored one leg over the other after long years of one-footed leaps.

"I was so worried," he said when he opened the door.

Lindsey was holding her arms over her chest, and even my father had to laugh while he looked away and hurriedly got the extra blankets kept in the front closet. Samuel draped one around Lindsey first, as my father covered Samuel's shoulders as best he could and puddles collected on the flagstone floor. Just as Lindsey had covered herself up, Buckley and Hal and Grandma Lynn came forward into the hallway.

"Buckley," Grandma Lynn said, "go get some towels."

"Did you manage the bike in this?" Hal asked, incredulous.

"No, we ran," Samuel said.

"You what?"

"Get into the family room," my father said. "We'll set a fire going."

\* \* \*

While the two of them sat with their backs to the fire, shivering at first and drinking the brandy shots Grandma Lynn had Buckley serve them on a silver tray, everyone heard the story of the bike and the house and the octagonal room with windows that had made Samuel euphoric.

"And the bike's okay?" Hal asked.

"We did the best we could," Samuel said, "but we'll need a tow."

"I'm just happy that the two of you are safe," my father said.

"We ran home for you, Mr. Salmon."

My grandmother and brother had taken seats at the far end of the room, away from the fire.

"We didn't want anyone to worry," Lindsey said.

"Lindsey didn't want you to worry, specifically."

The room was silent for a moment. What Samuel had said was true, of course, but it also pointed too clearly to a certain fact — that Lindsey and Buckley had come to live their lives in direct proportion to what effect it would have on a fragile father.

Grandma Lynn caught my sister's eye and winked. "Hal and Buckley and I made brownies," she said. "And I have some frozen lasagna I can break out if you'd like." She stood and so did my brother — ready to help.

"I'd love some brownies, Lynn," Samuel said.

"Lynn? I like that," she said. "Are you going to start calling Jack 'Jack'?"

"Maybe."

Once Buckley and Grandma Lynn had left the room, Hal felt a new nervousness in the air. "I think I'll pitch in," he said.

Lindsey, Samuel, and my father listened to the busy noises of the kitchen. They could all hear the clock ticking in the corner, the one my mother had called our "rustic colonial clock."

"I know I worry too much," my father said.

"That's not what Samuel meant," Lindsey said.

Samuel was quiet and I was watching him.

"Mr. Salmon," he finally said—he was not quite ready to try "Jack." "I've asked Lindsey to marry me."

Lindsey's heart was in her throat, but she wasn't looking at Samuel. She was looking at my father.

Buckley came in with a plate of brownies, and Hal followed him with champagne glasses hanging from his fingers and a bottle of 1978 Dom Perignon. "From your grandmother, on your graduation day," Hal said.

Grandma Lynn came through next, empty-handed except for her highball. It caught the light and glittered like a jar of icy diamonds.

For Lindsey, it was as if no one but herself and my father were there. "What do you say, Dad?" she asked.

"I'd say," he managed, standing up to shake Samuel's hand, "that I couldn't wish for a better son-in-law."

Grandma Lynn exploded on the final word. "My God, oh, honey! Congratulations!"

Even Buckley let loose, slipping out of the knot that usually held him and into a rare joy. But I saw the fine, wavering line that still tied my sister to my father. The invisible cord that can kill.

The champagne cork popped.

"Like a master!" my grandmother said to Hal, who was pouring.

It was Buckley, as my father and sister joined the group and listened to Grandma Lynn's countless toasts, who saw me. He saw me standing under the rustic colonial clock and stared. He was drinking champagne. There were strings coming out from all around me, reaching out, waving in the air. Someone passed him a brownie. He held it in his hands but did not eat. He saw my shape and face, which had not changed—the hair still parted down the middle, the chest still flat and hips undeveloped—and wanted to call out my name. It was only a moment, and then I was gone.

*   *   *

Over the years, when I grew tired of watching, I often sat in the back of the trains that went in and out of Suburban Station in Philadelphia. Passengers would get on and off as I listened to their conversations mix with the sounds of the train doors opening and closing, the conductors yelling their stops, and the shuffle and staccato of shoe soles and high heels going from pavement to metal to the soft *thump thump* on the carpeted train aisles. It was what Lindsey, in her workouts, called an active rest; my muscles were still engaged but my focus relaxed. I listened to the sounds and felt the train's movement and sometimes, by doing this, I could hear the voices of those who no longer lived on Earth. Voices of others like me, the watchers.

Almost everyone in heaven has someone on Earth they watch, a loved one, a friend, or even a stranger who was once kind, who offered warm food or a bright smile when one of us had needed it. And when I wasn't watching I could hear the others talking to those they loved on Earth: just as fruitlessly as me, I'm afraid. A one-sided cajoling and coaching of the young, a one-way loving and desiring of their mates, a single-sided card that could never be signed.

The train would be still or stop-starting from 30th Street to near Overbrook, and I could hear them say names and sentences: "Now be careful with that glass." "Mind your father." "Oh, look how big she looks in that dress." "I'm with you, Mother," ". . . Esmeralda, Sally, Lupe, Keesha, Frank . . ." So many names. And then the train would gain speed, and as it did the volume of all these unheard phrases coming from heaven would grow louder and louder; at its height between stations, the noise of our longing became so deafening that I had to open my eyes.

I saw women hanging or collecting wash as I peered from the windows of the suddenly silent trains. They stooped over baskets and then spread white or yellow or pink sheets along the line. I counted men's underwear and boys' underwear and the familiar lollipop cotton of little girls' drawers. And the sound of it that I craved and missed—the sound of life—replaced the endless calling of names.

Wet laundry: the snap, the yank, the wet heaviness of double- and queen-sized sheets. The real sounds bringing back the remembered sounds of the past when I had lain under the dripping clothes to catch water on my tongue or run in between them as if they were traffic cones through which I chased Lindsey or was chased by Lindsey back and forth. And this would be joined by the memory of our mother attempting to lecture us about the peanut butter from our hands getting on the good sheets, or the sticky lemon-candy patches she had found on our father's shirts. In this way the sight and smell of the real, of the imagined, and of the remembered all came together for me.

After I turned away from Earth that day, I rode the trains until I could think of only one thing:

"Hold still," my father would say, while I held the ship in the bottle and he burned away the strings he'd raised the mast with and set the clipper ship free on its blue putty sea. And I would wait for him, recognizing the tension of that moment when the world in the bottle depended, solely, on me.

## EIGHTEEN

When her father mentioned the sinkhole on the phone, Ruth was in the walk-in closet that she rented on First Avenue. She twirled the phone's long black cord around her wrist and arm and gave short, clipped answers of acknowledgment. The old woman that rented her the closet liked to listen in, so Ruth tried not to talk much on the phone. Later, from the street, she would call home collect and plan a visit.

She had known she would make a pilgrimage to see it before the developers closed it up. Her fascination with places like the sinkhole was a secret she kept, as was my murder and our meeting in the faculty parking lot. They were all things she would not give away in New York, where she watched others tell their drunken bar stories, prostituting their families and their traumas for popularity and booze. These things, she felt, were not to be passed around like disingenuous party favors. She kept an honor code with her journals and her poems. "Inside, inside," she would whisper quietly to herself when she felt the urge to tell, and she would end up taking long walks through the city, seeing instead the Stolfuz cornfield or an image of her father staring at his pieces of rescued antique molding. New York provided a perfect background for her thoughts. Despite her willed stomping and pitching in its streets and byways, the city itself had very little to do with her interior life.

She no longer looked haunted, as she had in high school, but still, if you looked closely at her eyes you could see the skittery rabbit energy that often made people nervous. She had an expression of someone who was constantly on the lookout for something or someone that hadn't yet arrived. Her whole body seemed to slant forward in inquiry, and though she had been told at the bar where she worked that she had beautiful hair or beautiful hands or, on the rare occasions when any of her patrons saw her come out from behind the bar, beautiful legs, people never said anything about her eyes.

She dressed hurriedly in black tights, a short black skirt, black boots, and a black T-shirt, all of them stained from serving double-duty as work clothes and real clothes. The stains could be seen only in the sunlight, so Ruth was never really aware of them until later, when she would stop at an outdoor café for a cup of coffee and look down at her skirt and see the dark traces of spilled vodka or whiskey. The alcohol had the effect of making the black cloth blacker. This amused her; she had noted in her journal: "booze affects material as it does people."

Once outside the apartment, on her way for a cup of coffee on First Avenue, she made up secret conversations with the bloated lap dogs — Chihuahuas and Pomeranians — that the Ukrainian women held on their laps as they sat on their stoops. Ruth liked the antagonistic little dogs, who barked ardently as she passed.

Then she walked, walked flat out, walked with an ache coming up through the earth and into the heel of her striking foot. No one said hello to her except creeps, and she made a game of how many streets she could navigate without having to stop for traffic. She would not slow down for another person and would vivisect crowds of NYU students or old women with their laundry carts, creating a wind on either side of her. She liked to imagine that when she passed the world looked after her, but she also knew how anonymous she was. Except when she was at work, no one knew where she was at any time of day and no one waited for her. It was an immaculate anonymity.

She would not know that Samuel had proposed to my sister and, unless it trickled down to her through Ray, the sole person she had kept in touch with from school, she would never find out. While still at Fairfax she had heard my mother had left. A fresh ripple of whispers had gone through the high school, and Ruth had watched my sister cope with them as best she could. Occasionally the two of them would meet up in the hallway. Ruth would say a few words of support if she could manage them without doing what she thought of as harming Lindsey by talking to her. Ruth knew her status as a freak at school and knew that their one night at the gifted symposium had been exactly what it felt like — a dream, where elements let loose came together unbidden outside the damning rules of school.

But Ray was different. Their kisses and early pushing and rubbings were objects under glass to her — memories that she kept preserved. She saw him every time she visited her parents and had known immediately that it would be Ray she took when she went back to see the sinkhole. He would be happy for the vacation from his constant studying grind, and, if she was lucky, he would describe, as he often did, a medical procedure that he had observed. Ray's way of describing such things made her feel as if she knew exactly what it felt like — not just what it looked like. He could evoke everything for her, with small verbal pulse points of which he was completely unaware.

Heading north on First, she could tick off all the places she'd formerly stopped and stood, certain that she had found a spot where a woman or girl had been killed. She tried to list them in her journal at the end of each day, but often she was so consumed with what she thought might have happened in this or that dark overhang or tight alleyway that she neglected the simpler, more obvious ones, where she had read about a death in the paper and visited what had been a woman's grave.

She was unaware that she was somewhat of a celebrity up in heaven. I had told people about her, what she did, how she observed moments of silence up and down the city and wrote small individual prayers in her journal, and the story had traveled so quickly that women lined up to know if she had found where they'd been killed. She had fans in heaven, even though she would have been disappointed to know that often these fans, when they gathered, resembled more a bunch of teenagers poring over an issue of *TeenBeat* than Ruth's image of low dirgelike whisperings set to a celestial timpani.

I was the one who got to follow and watch, and, as opposed to the giddy choir, I often found these moments as painful as they were amazing. Ruth would get an image and it would burn into her memory. Sometimes they were only bright flashes—a fall down the stairs, a scream, a shove, the tightening of hands around a neck—and at other times it was as if an entire scenario spun out in her head in just the amount of time that it took the girl or woman to die.

No one on the street thought anything of the downtown girl dressed in black who had paused in the middle of midtown foot traffic. In her art student camouflage she could walk the entire length of Manhattan and, if not blend in, be classified and therefore ignored. Meanwhile, for us, she was doing important work, work that most people on Earth were too frightened even to contemplate.

The day after Lindsey and Samuel's graduation I joined her on her walk. By the time she got up to Central Park it was well past lunchtime, but the park was still busy. Couples sat on the clipped grass of the Sheep Meadow. Ruth peered at them. Her ardentness was off-putting on a sunny afternoon, and when the open faces of young men caught sight of her they closed down or looked away.

She zigzagged up and across the park. There were obvious places where she could go, like the Rambles, to document the history of violence there without even leaving the trees, but she preferred those places people considered safe. The cool shimmering surface of the duck pond tucked into the busy southeast corner of the park, or the placid man-made lake, where old men sailed beautiful hand-carved boats.

She sat on a bench on a path leading to the Central Park Zoo and looked out across the gravel at children with their nannies and lone adults reading books in various patches of shade or sun. She was tired from the walk uptown, but still she took her journal out from her bag. She placed it open on her lap, holding the pen as her thinking prop. It was better to look like you were doing something when you stared into the distance, Ruth had learned. Otherwise it was likely that strange men would come over and try to talk to you. Her journal was her closest and most important relationship. It held everything.

Across from her a little girl had strayed from the blanket where her nanny slept. She was making her way for the bushes that lined a small rise before giving way to a fence separating the park from Fifth Avenue. Just as Ruth was about to enter the world of human beings whose lives impinged on one another by calling out to the nanny, a thin cord, which Ruth had not seen, warned the nanny to wake. She immediately sat bolt upright and barked an order at the little girl to return.

In moments like this she thought of all the little girls who grew into adulthood and old age as a sort of cipher alphabet for all of those who didn't. Their lives would somehow be inextricably attached to all the girls who had been killed. It was then, as the nanny packed up her bag and rolled up the blanket, preparing for whatever came next in their day, that Ruth saw her—a little girl who had strayed for the bushes one day and disappeared.

She could tell by the clothes that it had happened some time ago, but that was all. There was nothing else—no nanny or mother, no idea of night or day, only a little girl gone.

I stayed with Ruth. Her journal open, she wrote it down. "Time? Little girl in C.P. strays toward bushes. White lace collar, fancy." She closed the journal and tucked it into her bag. Close at hand was a place that soothed her. The penguin house at the zoo.

We spent the afternoon together there, Ruth sitting on the carpeted seat that ran the length of the exhibit, her black clothes making only her face and hands visible in the room. The penguins tottered and clucked and dived, slipping off the habitat rocks like amiable hams but living under water like tuxedoed muscles. Children shouted and screamed and pressed their faces against the glass. Ruth counted the living just as much as she counted the dead, and in the close confines of the penguin house the joyous screams of the children echoed off the walls with such vibrancy that, for a little while, she could drown out the other kinds of screams.

That weekend my brother woke early, as he always did. He was in the seventh grade and bought his lunch at school and was on the debate team and, like Ruth had been, was always picked either last or second to last in gym. He had not taken to athletics as Lindsey had. He practiced instead what Grandma Lynn called his "air of dignification." His favorite teacher was not really a teacher at all but the school librarian, a tall, frail woman with wiry hair who drank tea from her thermos and talked about having lived in England when she was young. After this he had affected an

English accent for a few months and shown a heightened interest when my sister watched *Masterpiece Theatre.*

When he had asked my father that year if he could reclaim the garden my mother had once kept, my father had said, "Sure, Buck, go crazy."

And he had. He had gone extraordinarily, insanely crazy, reading old Burpee catalogs at night when he was unable to sleep and scanning the few books on gardening that the school library kept. Where my grandmother had suggested respectful rows of parsley and basil and Hal had suggested "some plants that really matter" — eggplants, cantaloupes, cucumbers, carrots, and beans — my brother had thought they were both right.

He didn't like what he read in books. He saw no reason to keep flowers separated from tomatoes and herbs segregated in a corner. He had slowly planted the whole garden with a spade, daily begging my father to bring him seeds and taking trips to the grocery with Grandma Lynn, where the price of his extreme helpfulness in fetching things would be a quick stop at the greenhouse for a small flowering plant. He was now awaiting his tomatoes, his blue daisies, his petunias, and pansies and salvias of all kinds. He had made his fort a sort of work shed for the garden, where he kept his tools and supplies.

But my grandmother was preparing for the moment when he realized that they couldn't grow all together and that some seeds would not come up at certain times, that the fine downy tendrils of cucumber might be abruptly stopped by the thickening underground bosses of carrot and potato, that the parsley might be camouflaged by the more recalcitrant weeds, and bugs that hopped about could blight the tender flowers. But she was waiting patiently. She no longer believed in talk. It never rescued anything. At seventy she had come to believe in time alone.

Buckley was hauling up a box of clothes from the basement and into the kitchen when my father came down for his coffee.

"What ya got there, Farmer Buck?" my father said. He had always been at his best in the morning.

"I'm making stakes for my tomato plants," my brother said.

"Are they even above ground yet?"

My father stood in the kitchen in his blue terry-cloth robe and bare feet. He poured his coffee from the coffee maker that Grandma Lynn set up each morning, and sipped at it as he looked at his son.

"I just saw them this morning," my brother said, beaming. "They curl up like a hand unfolding."

It wasn't until my father was repeating this description to Grandma Lynn as he stood at the counter that he saw, through the back window, what Buckley had taken from the box. They were my clothes. My clothes, which Lindsey had picked through for anything she might save. My clothes, which my grandmother, when she had moved into my room, had quietly boxed while my father was at work. She had put them down in the basement with a small label that said, simply, SAVE.

My father put down his coffee. He walked out through the screened-in porch and strode forward, calling Buckley's name.

"What is it, Dad?" He was alert to my father's tone.

"Those clothes are Susie's," my father said calmly when he reached him.

Buckley looked down at my blackwatch dress that he held in his hand.

My father stepped closer, took the dress from my brother, and then, without speaking, he gathered the rest of my clothes, which Buckley had piled on the lawn. As he turned in silence toward the house, hardly breathing, clutching my clothes to him, it sparked.

I was the only one to see the colors. Just near Buckley's ears and on the tips of his cheeks and chin he was a little orange somehow, a little red.

"Why can't I use them?" he asked.

It landed in my father's back like a fist.

"Why can't I use those clothes to stake my tomatoes?"

My father turned around. He saw his son standing there, behind him the perfect plot of muddy, churned-up earth spotted with tiny seedlings. "How can you ask me that question?"

"You have to choose. It's not fair," my brother said.

"Buck?" My father held my clothes against his chest.

I watched Buckley flare and light. Behind him was the sun of the goldenrod hedge, twice as tall as it had been at my death.

"I'm tired of it!" Buckley blared. "Keesha's dad died and she's okay!"

"Is Keesha a girl at school?"

"Yes!"

My father was frozen. He could feel the dew that had gathered on his bare ankles and feet, could feel the ground underneath him, cold and moist and stirring with possibility.

"I'm sorry. When did this happen?"

"That's not the point, Dad! You don't get it." Buckley turned around on his heel and started stomping the tender tomato shoots with his foot.

"Buck, stop!" my father cried.

My brother turned.

"You don't get it, Dad," he said.

"I'm sorry," my father said. "These are Susie's clothes and I just ... It may not make sense, but they're hers — something she wore."

"You took the shoe, didn't you?" my brother said. He had stopped crying now.

"What?"

"You took the shoe. You took it from my room."

"Buckley, I don't know what you're talking about."

"I saved the Monopoly shoe and then it was gone. You took it! You act like she was yours only!"

"Tell me what you want to say. What's this about your friend Keesha's dad?"

"Put the clothes down."

My father laid them gently on the ground.

"It isn't about Keesha's dad."

"Tell me what it is about." My father was now all immediacy. He went back to the place he had been after his knee surgery, coming up out of the druggie sleep of painkillers to see his then-five-year-old son sitting near him, waiting for his eyes to flicker open so he could say, "Peek-a-boo, Daddy."

"She's dead."

It never ceased to hurt. "I know that."

"But you don't act that way. Keesha's dad died when she was six. Keesha said she barely even thinks of him."

"She will," my father said.

"But what about us?"

"Who?"

"Us, Dad. Me and Lindsey. Mom left because she couldn't take it."

"Calm down, Buck," my father said. He was being as generous as he could as the air from his lungs evaporated out into his chest. Then a little voice in him said, *Let go, let go, let go.* "What?" my father said.

"I didn't say anything."

*Let go. Let go. Let go.*

"I'm sorry," my father said. "I'm not feeling very well." His feet had grown unbelievably cold in the damp grass. His chest felt hollow, bugs flying around an excavated cavity. There was an echo in there, and it drummed up into his ears. *Let go.*

My father dropped down to his knees. His arm began to tingle on and off as if it had fallen asleep. Pins and needles up and down. My brother rushed to him.

"Dad?"

"Son." There was a quaver in his voice and a grasping outward toward my brother.

"I'll get Grandma." And Buckley ran.

My father whispered faintly as he lay on his side with his face twisted in the direction of my old clothes: "You can never choose. I've loved all three of you."

That night my father lay in a hospital bed, attached to monitors that beeped and hummed. Time to circle around my father's feet and along his spine. Time to hush and usher him. But where?

Above his bed the clock ticked off the minutes and I thought of the game Lindsey and I had played in the yard together: "he loves me/he loves me not" picked out on a daisy's petals. I could hear the clock casting my own two greatest wishes back to me in this same rhythm: "Die for me/don't die for me, die for me/don't die for me." I could not help myself, it seemed, as I tore at his weakening heart. If he died, I would have him forever. Was this so wrong to want?

At home, Buckley lay in bed in the dark and pulled the sheet up to his chin. He had not been allowed past the emergency room where Lindsey had driven them, following the shrieking ambulance inside which lay our father. My brother had felt a huge burden of guilt descend in the silences from Lindsey. In her two repeated questions: "What were you talking about? Why was he so upset?"

My little brother's greatest fear was that the one person who meant so much to him would go away. He loved Lindsey and Grandma Lynn and Samuel and Hal, but my father kept him stepping lightly, son gingerly monitoring father every morning and every evening as if, without such vigilance, he would lose him.

We stood — the dead child and the living — on either side of my father, both wanting the same thing. To have him to ourselves forever. To please us both was an impossibility.

My father had only missed nighttimes twice in Buckley's life. Once after he had gone into the cornfield at night looking for Mr. Harvey and now as he lay in the hospital and they monitored him in case of a second heart attack.

Buckley knew he should be too old for it to matter, but I sympathized with him. The good-night kiss was something at which my father excelled. As my father stood at the end of the bed after closing the venetian blinds and running his hands down them to make sure they were all down at the same slant — no rebel venetian stuck to let the sunlight in on his son before he came to wake him — my brother would often get goose bumps on his arms and legs. The anticipation was so sweet.

"Ready, Buck?" my father would say, and sometimes Buckley said "Roger," or sometimes he said "Takeoff," but when he was most frightened and giddy and waiting for peace he just said "Yes!" And my father would take the thin cotton top sheet and bunch it up in his hands while being careful to keep the two corners between his thumb and forefinger. Then he would snap it out so the pale blue (if they were using Buckley's) or lavender (if they were using mine) sheet would spread out like a parachute above him and gently, what felt wonderfully slowly, it would waft down and touch along his exposed skin — his knees, his forearms, his cheeks and chin. Both air and cover somehow there in the same space at the same time — it felt like the ultimate freedom and protection. It was lovely, left him vulnerable and quivering on some edge and all he could hope was that if he begged him, my father would oblige and do it again. Air and cover, air and cover — sustaining the unspoken connection between them: little boy, wounded man.

That night his head lay on the pillow while his body was curled in the fetal position. He had not thought to close the blinds himself, and the lights from the nearby houses spotted the hill. He stared across his room at the louvered doors of his closet, out of which he had once imagined evil witches would escape to join the dragons beneath his bed. He no longer feared these things.

"Please don't let Daddy die, Susie," he whispered. "I need him."

When I left my brother, I walked out past the gazebo and under the lights hanging down like berries, and I saw the brick paths branching out as I advanced.

I walked until the bricks turned to flat stones and then to small, sharp rocks and then to nothing but churned earth for miles and miles around me. I stood there. I had been in heaven long enough to know that something would be revealed. And as the light began to fade and the sky turn a dark, sweet blue as it had on the night of my death, I saw someone walking into view, so far away I could not at first make out if it was man or woman, child or adult. But as moonlight reached this figure I could make out a man and, frightened now, my breathing shallow, I raced just far enough to see. Was it my father? Was it what I had wanted all this time so desperately?

"Susie," the man said as I approached and then stopped a few feet from where he stood. He raised his arms up toward me.

"Remember?" he said.

I found myself small again, age six and in a living room in Illinois. Now, as I had done then, I placed my feet on top of his feet.

"Grandaddy," I said.

And because we were all alone and both in heaven, I was light enough to move as I had moved when I was six and he was fifty-six and my father had taken us to visit. We danced so slowly to a song that on Earth had always made my grandfather cry.

"Do you remember?" he asked.

"Barber!"

"Adagio for Strings," he said.

But as we danced and spun—none of the herky-jerky awkwardness of Earth—what I remembered was how I'd found him crying to this music and asked him why.

"Sometimes you cry, Susie, even when someone you love has been gone a long time." He had held me against him then, just briefly, and then I had run outside to play again with Lindsey in what seemed like my grandfather's huge backyard.

We didn't speak any more that night, but we danced for hours in that timeless blue light. I knew as we danced that something was happening on Earth and in heaven. A shifting. The sort of slow-to-sudden movement that we'd read about in science class one year. Seismic, impossible, a rending and tearing of time and space. I pressed myself into my grandfather's chest and smelled the old-man smell of him, the mothball version of my own father, the blood on Earth, the sky in heaven. The kumquat, skunk, grade-A tobacco.

When the music stopped, it could have been forever since we'd begun. My grandfather took a step back, and the light grew yellow at his back.

"I'm going," he said.

"Where?" I asked.

"Don't worry, sweetheart. You're so close."

He turned and walked away, disappearing rapidly into spots and dust. Infinity.

# NINETEEN

When she reached Krusoe Winery that morning, my mother found a message waiting for her, scrawled in the imperfect English of the caretaker. The word *emergency* was clear enough, and my mother bypassed her morning ritual of an early coffee drunk while staring out at the grapevines grafted on row upon row of sturdy white crosses. She opened up the part of the winery reserved for public tastings. Without turning on the overhead, she located the phone behind the wooden bar and dialed the number in Pennsylvania. No answer.

Then she dialed the operator in Pennsylvania and asked for the number of Dr. Akhil Singh.

"Yes," Ruana said, "Ray and I saw an ambulance pull up a few hours ago. I imagine they're all at the hospital."

"Who was it?"

"Your mother, perhaps?"

But she knew from the note that her mother had been the one who *called.* It was one of the children or it was Jack. She thanked

Ruana and hung up. She grabbed the heavy red phone and lifted it up from underneath the bar. A ream of color sheets that they passed out to customers — "Lemon Yellow = Young Chardonnay, Straw-colored = Sauvignon Blanc . . ." — fell down and around her feet from where they had been kept weighted by the phone. She had habitually arrived early ever since taking the job, and now she gave a quick thanks that this was so. After that, all she could think of were the names of the local hospitals, so she called the ones to which she had rushed her young children with unexplained fevers or possible broken bones from falls. At the same hospital where I had once rushed Buckley: "A Jack Salmon was seen in emergency and is still here."

"Can you tell me what happened?"

"What is your relationship to Mr. Salmon?"

She said the words she had not said in years: "I'm his wife."

"He had a heart attack."

She hung up the phone and sat down on the rubber-and-cork mats that covered the floor on the employee side. She sat there until the shift manager arrived and she repeated the strange words: *husband, heart attack.*

When she looked up later she was in the caretaker's truck, and he, this quiet man who barely ever left the premises, was barreling toward San Francisco International Airport.

She paid for her ticket and boarded a flight that would connect to another in Chicago and finally land her in Philadelphia. As the plane gained height and they were buried in the clouds, my mother listened distantly to the signature bells of the plane which told the crew what to do or what to prepare for, and she heard the cocktail cart jiggling past, but instead of her fellow passengers she saw the cool stone archway at the winery, behind which the empty oak barrels were stored, and instead of the men who often sat inside there to get out of the sun she imagined my father sitting there, holding the broken Wedgwood cup out toward her.

By the time she landed in Chicago with a two-hour wait, she had steadied herself enough to buy a toothbrush and a pack of cigarettes and place a call to the hospital, this time asking to speak to Grandma Lynn.

"Mother," my mother said. "I'm in Chicago and on my way."

"Abigail, thank God," my grandmother said. "I called Krusoe again and they said you were headed for the airport."

"How is he?"

"He's asking for you."

"Are the kids there?"

"Yes, and Samuel. I was going to call you today and tell you. Samuel has asked Lindsey to marry him."

"That's wonderful," my mother said.

"Abigail?"

"Yes." She could hear her mother's hesitation, which was always rare.

"Jack's asking for Susie, too."


She lit a cigarette as soon as she walked outside the terminal at O'Hare, a school tour flooding past her with small overnight bags and band instruments, each of which had a bright yellow nametag on the side of the case. HOME OF THE PATRIOTS, they read.

It was muggy and humid in Chicago, and the smoky exhaust of double-parked cars made the heavy air noxious.

She burned through the cigarette in record time and lit another, keeping one arm tucked hard across her chest and the other one extended on each exhale. She was wearing her winery outfit: a pair of faded but clean jeans and a pale orange T-shirt with KRUSOE WINERY embroidered over the pocket. Her skin was darker now, which made her pale blue eyes seem even bluer in contrast, and she had taken to wearing her hair in a loose ponytail at the base of her neck. I could see small wisps of salt and pepper hair near her ears and at her temples.

She held on to two sides of an hourglass and wondered how this could be possible. The time she'd had alone had been gravitationally circumscribed by when her attachments would pull her back. And they had pulled now — double-fisted. A marriage. A heart attack.

Standing outside the terminal, she reached into the back pocket of her jeans, where she kept the man's wallet she had started carrying when she got the job at Krusoe because it was easier not to worry about stowing a purse beneath the bar. She flicked her cigarette into the cab lane and turned to find a seat on the edge of a concrete planter, inside of which grew weeds and one sad sapling choked by fumes.

In her wallet were pictures, pictures she looked at every day. But there was one that she kept turned upside down in a fold of leather meant for a credit card. It was the same one that rested in the evidence box at the police station, the same one Ray had put in his mother's book of Indian poetry. My class photo that had made the papers and been put on police fliers and in mailboxes.

After eight years it was, even for my mother, like the ubiquitous photo of a celebrity. She had encountered it so many times that I had been neatly buried inside of it. My cheeks never redder, my eyes never bluer than they were in the photograph.

She took the photo out and held it face-up and slightly cupped in her hand. She had always missed my teeth — their small rounded serrations had fascinated her as she watched me grow. I had promised my mother a wide-open smile for that year's picture, but I was so self-conscious in front of the photographer that I had barely managed a close-lipped grin.

She heard the announcement for the connecting flight over the outdoor speaker. She stood. Turning around she saw the tiny, struggling tree. She left my class portrait propped up against its trunk and hurried inside the automatic doors.


On the flight to Philadelphia, she sat alone in the middle of a row of three seats. She could not help but think of how, if she were a mother traveling, there would be two seats filled beside her. One for Lindsey. One for Buckley. But though she was, by definition, a mother, she had at some point ceased to be one too. She couldn't claim that right and privilege after missing more than half a decade of their lives. She now knew that being a mother was a calling, something plenty of young girls dreamed of being. But my mother had never had that dream, and she had been punished in the most horrible and unimaginable way for never having wanted me.

I watched her on the plane, and I sent a wish into the clouds for her release. Her body grew heavy with the dread of what would come but in this heaviness was at least relief. The stewardess handed her a small blue pillow and for a little while she fell asleep.

When they reached Philadelphia, the airplane taxied down the runway and she reminded herself both where she was and what year it was. She hurriedly clicked through all the things she might say when she saw her children, her mother, Jack. And then, when they finally shivered to a halt, she gave up and focused only on getting off the plane.

She barely recognized her own child waiting at the end of the long ramp. In the years that had passed, Lindsey had become angular, thin, every trace of body fat gone. And standing beside my sister was what looked like her male twin. A bit taller, a little more meat. Samuel. She was staring so hard at the two of them, and they were staring back, that at first she didn't even see the chubby boy sitting off to the side on the arm of a row of waiting-area seats.

And then, just before she began walking toward them — for they all seemed suspended and immobile for the first few moments, as if they had been trapped in a viscous gelatin from which only her movement might free them — she saw him.

She began walking down the carpeted ramp. She heard announcements being made in the airport and saw passengers, with their more normal greetings, rushing past her. But it was as if she were entering a time warp as she took him in. 1944 at Camp Winnekukka. She was twelve, with chubby cheeks and heavy legs — all the things she'd felt grateful her daughters had escaped had been her son's to endure. So many years she had been away, so much time she could never recover.

If she had counted, as I did, she would have known that in seventy-three steps she had accomplished what she had been too afraid to do for almost seven years.

It was my sister who spoke first:

"Mom," she said.

My mother looked at my sister and flashed forward thirty-eight years from the lonely girl she'd been at Camp Winnekukka.

"Lindsey," my mother said.

Lindsey stared at her. Buckley was standing now, but he looked first down at his shoes and then over his shoulder, out past the window to where the planes were parked, disgorging their passengers into accordioned tubes.

"How is your father?" my mother asked.

My sister had spoken the word *Mom* and then frozen. It tasted soapy and foreign in her mouth.

"He's not in the greatest shape, I'm afraid," Samuel said. It was the longest sentence anyone had said, and my mother found herself disproportionately grateful for it.

"Buckley?" my mother said, preparing no face for him. Being who she was — whoever that was.

He turned his head toward her like a racheted gun. "Buck," he said.

"Buck," she repeated softly and looked down at her hands.

Lindsey wanted to ask, *Where are your rings?*

"Shall we go?" Samuel asked.

The four of them entered the long carpeted tunnel that would bring them from her gate into the main terminal. They were headed toward the cavernous baggage claim when my mother said, "I didn't bring any bags."

They stood in an awkward cluster, Samuel looking for the right signs to redirect them back to the parking garage.

"Mom," my sister tried again.

"I lied to you," my mother said before Lindsey could say anything further. Their eyes met, and in that hot wire that went from one to the other I swore I saw it, like a rat bulging, undigested, inside a snake: the secret of Len.

"We go back up the escalator," Samuel said, "and then we can take the overhead walkway into the parking lot."

Samuel called for Buckley, who had drifted off in the direction of a cadre of airport security officers. Uniforms had never lost the draw they held for him.

They were on the highway when Lindsey spoke next. "They won't let Buckley in to see Dad because of his age."

My mother turned around in her seat. "I'll try and do something about that," she said, looking at Buckley and attempting her first smile.

"Fuck you," my brother whispered without looking up.

My mother froze. The car opened up. Full of hate and tension — a riptide of blood to swim through.

"Buck," she said, remembering the shortened name just in time, "will you look at me?"

He glared over the front seat, boring his fury into her.

Eventually my mother turned back around and Samuel, Lindsey, and my brother could hear the sounds from the passenger seat that she was trying hard not to make. Little peeps and a choked sob. But no amount of tears would sway Buckley. He had been keeping, daily, weekly, yearly, an underground storage room of hate. Deep inside this, the four-year-old sat, his heart flashing. Heart to stone, heart to stone.

"We'll all feel better after seeing Mr. Salmon," Samuel said, and then, because even he could not bear it, he leaned forward toward the dash and turned on the radio.

It was the same hospital that she had come to eight years ago in the middle of the night. A different floor painted a different color, but she could feel it encasing her as she walked down the hall—what she'd done there. The push of Len's body, her back pressed into the sharp stucco wall. Everything in her wanted to run—fly back to California, back to her quiet existence working among strangers. Hiding out in the folds of tree trunks and tropical petals, tucked away safely among so many foreign plants and people.

Her mother's ankles and oxford pumps, which she saw from the hallway, brought her back. One of the many simple things she'd lost by moving so far away, just the commonplace of her mother's feet—their solidity and humor—seventy-year-old feet in ridiculously uncomfortable shoes.

But as she walked forward into the room, everyone else—her son, her daughter, her mother—fell away.

My father's eyes were weak but fluttered open when he heard her enter. He had tubes and wires coming out of his wrist and shoulder. His head seemed so fragile on the small square pillow.

She held his hand and cried silently, letting the tears come freely.

"Hello, Ocean Eyes," he said.

She nodded her head. This broken, beaten man — her husband.

"My girl," he breathed out heavily.

"Jack."

"Look what it took to get you home."

"Was it worth it?" she said, smiling bleakly.

"We'll have to see," he said.

To see them together was like a tenuous belief made real.

My father could see glimmers, like the colored flecks inside my mother's eyes — things to hold on to. These he counted among the broken planks and boards of a long-ago ship that had struck something greater than itself and sunk. There were only remnants and artifacts left to him now. He tried to reach up and touch her cheek, but his arm felt too weak. She moved closer and laid her cheek in his palm.

My grandmother knew how to move silently in heels. She tiptoed out of the room. As she resumed her normal stride and approached the waiting area, she intercepted a nurse with a message for Jack Salmon in Room 582. She had never met the man but knew his name. "Len Fenerman, will visit soon. Wishes you well." She folded the note neatly. Just before she came upon Lindsey and Buckley, who had gone to join Samuel in the waiting room, she popped open the metal lip of her purse and placed it between her powder and comb.

## TWENTY

By the time Mr. Harvey reached the tin-roofed shack in Connecticut that night, it promised rain. He had killed a young waitress inside the shack several years before and then bought some new slacks with the tips he'd found in the front pocket of her apron. By now the rot would have been eclipsed, and it was true, as he approached the area, that no rank smell greeted him. But the shack was open and inside he could see the earth had been dug up. He breathed in and approached the shack warily.

He fell asleep beside her empty grave.

At some point, to counter the list of the dead, I had begun keeping my own list of the living. It was something I noticed Len Fenerman did too. When he was off duty he would note the young girls and elderly women and every other female in the rainbow in between and count them among the things that sustained him. That young girl in the mall whose pale legs had grown too long for her now-too-young dress and who had an aching vulnerability that went straight to both Len's and my own heart. Elderly women, wobbling with walkers, who insisted on dyeing their hair unnatural versions of the colors they had in youth. Middle-aged single mothers racing around in grocery stores while their children pulled bags of candy off the shelves. When I saw them, I took count. Living, breathing women. Sometimes I saw the wounded—those who had been beaten by husbands or raped by strangers, children raped by their fathers—and I would wish to intervene somehow.

Len saw these wounded women all the time. They were regulars at the station, but even when he went somewhere outside his jurisdiction he could sense them when they came near. The wife in the bait-'n'-tackle shop had no bruises on her face but cowered like a dog and spoke in apologetic whispers. The girl he saw walk the road each time he went upstate to visit his sisters. As the years passed she'd grown leaner, the fat from her cheeks had drained, and sorrow had loaded her eyes in a way that made them hang heavy and hopeless inside her mallowed skin. When she was not there it worried him. When she was there it both depressed and revived him.

He had not had much to write in my file for a long time, but a few items had joined the log of old evidence in the last few months: the name of another potential victim, Sophie Cichetti, the name of her son, and an alias of George Harvey's. There was also what he held in his hands: my Pennsylvania keystone charm. He moved it around inside the evidence bag, using his fingers, and found, again, my initials. The charm had been checked for any clues it could provide, and, besides its presence at the scene of another girl's murder, it had come up clean under the microscope.

He had wanted to give the charm back to my father from the first moment he was able to confirm it was mine. Doing so was breaking the rules, but he had never had a body for them, just a sodden schoolbook and the pages from my biology book mixed in with a boy's love note. A Coke bottle. My jingle-bell hat. These he had cataloged and kept. But the charm was different, and he meant to give it back.

A nurse he'd dated in the years after my mother left had called him when she noticed the name Jack Salmon on a list of patients admitted. Len had determined that he would visit my father in the hospital and bring my charm along with him. In Len's mind he saw the charm as a talisman that might speed my father's recovery.

I couldn't help but think, as I watched him, of the barrels of toxic fluids that had accrued behind Hal's bike shop where the scrub lining the railroad tracks had offered local companies enough cover to dump a stray container or two. Everything had been sealed up, but things were beginning to leak out. I had come to both pity and respect Len in the years since my mother left. He followed the physical to try to understand things that were impossible to comprehend. In that, I could see, he was like me.


Outside the hospital, a young girl was selling small bouquets of daffodils, their green stems tied with lavender ribbons. I watched as my mother bought out the girl's whole stock.

Nurse Eliot, who remembered my mother from eight years ago, volunteered to help her when she saw her coming down the hall, her arms full of flowers. She rounded up extra water pitchers from a supply closet and together she and my mother filled them with water and placed the flowers around my father's room while he slept. Nurse Eliot thought that if loss could be used as a measure of beauty in a woman, my mother had grown even more beautiful.

Lindsey, Samuel, and Grandma Lynn had taken Buckley home

earlier in the evening. My mother was not ready to see the house yet. She focused solely on my father. Everything else would have to wait, from the house and its silent reproach to her son and daughter. She needed something to eat and time to think. Instead of going to the hospital cafeteria, where the bright lights made her think only of all the futile efforts that hospitals contained to keep people awake for more bad news — the weak coffee, the hard chairs, the elevators that stopped on every floor — she left the building and walked down the sloped sidewalk leading away from the entrance.

It was dark out now, and the parking lot where she had once driven in the middle of the night in her nightgown was spotted with only a few cars. She hugged the cardigan her mother had left behind tightly to her.

She crossed the parking lot, looking into the dark cars for signs of who the people inside the hospital were. There were cassette tapes spread out on the passenger seat of one car, the bulky shape of a baby's carseat in another. It became a game to her then, seeing what she could in each car. A way not to feel so alone and alien, as if she were a child playing a spy game in the house of her parents' friends. Agent Abigail to Mission Control. I see a fuzzy dog toy, I see a soccer ball, I see a woman! There she was, a stranger sitting in the driver's side behind the wheel. The woman did not see my mother looking at her, and as soon as she saw her face my mother turned her attention away, focusing on the bright lights of the old diner she had as her goal. She did not have to look back to know what the woman was doing. She was girding herself up to go inside. She knew the face. It was the face of someone who wanted more than anything to be anywhere but where she was.

She stood on the landscaped strip between the hospital and the emergency room entrance and wished for a cigarette. She had not questioned anything that morning. Jack had had a heart attack;

she would go home. But now here, she didn't know what she was supposed to do anymore. How long would she have to wait, what would have to happen, before she could leave again? Behind her in the parking lot, she heard the sound of a car door opening and closing—the woman going in.

The diner was a blur to her. She sat in a booth alone and ordered the kind of food—chicken-fried steak—that didn't seem to exist in California.

She was thinking about this when a man directly across from her gave her the eye. She registered every detail of his appearance. It was automatic and something she didn't do out west. While living in Pennsylvania after my murder, when she saw a strange man whom she didn't trust, she did an immediate breakdown in her mind. It was quicker—honoring the pragmatics of fear—than pretending she shouldn't think this way. Her dinner arrived, the chicken-fried steak and tea, and she focused on her food, on the gritty breading around the rubbery meat, on the metallic taste of old tea. She did not think she could handle being home more than a few days. Everywhere she looked she saw me, and at the booth across from her she saw the man who could have murdered me.

She finished the food, paid for it, and walked out of the diner without raising her eyes above waist level. A bell mounted on the door jingled above her, and she started, her heart jumping up in her chest.

She made it back across the highway in one piece, but she was breathing shallowly as she passed back across the parking lot. The car of the apprehensive visitor was still there.

In the main lobby, where people rarely sat, she decided to sit down and wait for her breathing to come back again.

She would spend a few hours with him and when he woke, she would say goodbye. As soon as her decision was made, a welcome coolness flew through her. The sudden relief of responsibility. Her ticket to a far-away land.

It was late now, after ten, and she took an empty elevator to the fifth floor, where the hall lights had been dimmed. She passed the nurses' station, behind which two nurses were quietly gossiping. She could hear the lilt and glee of nuanced rumors being exchanged between them, the sound of easy intimacy in the air. Then, just as one nurse was unable to suppress a high-pitched laugh, my mother opened my father's door and let it swing shut again.

Alone.

It was as if there was a vacuum hush when the door closed. I felt I did not belong, that I should go too. But I was glued.

Seeing him sleeping in the dark, with only the low-wattage fluorescent light on at the back of the bed, she remembered standing in this same hospital and taking steps to sever herself from him.

As I saw her take my father's hand, I thought of my sister and me sitting underneath the grave rubbing in the upstairs hallway. I was the dead knight gone to heaven with my faithful dog and she was the live wire of a wife. "How can I be expected to be trapped for the rest of my life by a man frozen in time?" Lindsey's favorite line.

My mother sat with my father's hand in hers for a long while. She thought how wonderful it would be to climb up on the fresh hospital sheets and lie beside him. And how impossible.

She leaned close. Even under the smells of antiseptics and alcohol, she could smell the grassy smell of his skin. When she'd left, she had packed her favorite shirt of my father's and would sometimes wrap it around her just to have something of his on. She never wore it outside, so it kept his scent longer than it might have. She remembered one night, when she missed him most, buttoning it over a pillow and hugging it to her as if she were still a high school girl.

In the distance beyond the closed window she could hear the hum of far-off traffic on the highway, but the hospital was shutting down for the night. Only the rubber soles of the night nurses' shoes made sounds as they passed in the hallway.

Just that winter she had found herself saying to a young woman who worked with her at the tasting bar on Saturdays that between a man and a woman there was always one person who was stronger than the other one. "That doesn't mean the weaker one doesn't love the stronger," she'd pleaded. The girl looked at her blankly. But for my mother what mattered was that as she spoke, she had suddenly identified herself as the weaker one. This revelation sent her reeling. What had she thought all those years but the opposite?

She pulled her chair as close to his head as she could and laid her face on the edge of his pillow to watch him breathing, to see the flutter of his eye beneath his eyelid when he dreamed. How could it be that you could love someone so much and keep it secret from yourself as you woke daily so far from home? She had put billboards and roads in between them, throwing roadblocks behind her and ripping off the rearview mirror, and thought that that would make him disappear? erase their life and children?

It was so simple, as she watched him, as his regular breathing calmed her, that she did not even see it happening at first. She began to think of the rooms in our house and the hours that she had worked so hard to forget spent inside of them. Like fruit put up in jars and forgotten about, the sweetness seemed even more distilled as she returned. There on that shelf were all the dates and silliness of their early love, the braid that began to form of their dreams, the solid root of a burgeoning family. The first solid evidence of it all. Me.

She traced a new line on my father's face. She liked the silvering of his temples.

Shortly after midnight, she fell asleep after trying as hard as she could to keep her eyes open. To hold on to everything all at once while she looked at that face, so that when he woke she could say goodbye.

When her eyes were closed and they both slept silently together, I whispered to them:

> Stones and bones;
> snow and frost;
> seeds and beans and polliwogs.
> Paths and twigs, assorted kisses,
> We all know who Susie misses . . .

Around two A.M. it began to rain, and it rained down on the hospital and on my old home and in my heaven. On the tin-roofed shack where Mr. Harvey slept, it was raining too. As the rain beat its tiny hammers above his head, he dreamed. He did not dream of the girl whose remains had been removed and were now being analyzed but of Lindsey Salmon, of the 5! 5! 5! hitting the border of elderberry. He had this dream whenever he felt threatened. It had been in the flash of her soccer shirt that his life had begun to spin out of control.

It was near four when I saw my father's eyes open and saw him feel the warmth of my mother's breath on his cheek even before he knew she was asleep. We wished together that he could hold her, but he was too weak. There was another way and he took it. He would tell her the things he had felt after my death — the things that came into his mind so frequently but that no one knew but me.

But he did not want to wake her. The hospital was silent except for the sound of rain. Rain was following him, he felt, darkness and damp — he thought of Lindsey and Samuel at the doorway, soaked and smiling, having run all that way to relieve him. He often found himself repeatedly commanding himself back to center. Lindsey. Lindsey. Lindsey. Buckley. Buckley. Buckley.

The way the rain looked outside the windows, lit up in circular patches by the lights in the hospital parking lot, reminded him of the movies he had gone to see as a boy—Hollywood rain. He closed his eyes with the breath of my mother reassuringly exhaling against his cheek and listened to it, the slight patter on the slim metal window sills, and then he heard the sound of birds—small birds chirping, but he could not see them. And the idea of this, that there might be a nest right outside his window where baby birds had woken in the rain and found their mother gone, made him want to rescue them. He felt my mother's limp fingers, which had loosened their hold on his hand in sleep. She was here, and this time, despite all, he was going to let her be who she was.

It was then that I slipped inside the room with my mother and father. I was present somehow, as a person, in a way I had never been. I had always hovered but had never stood beside them.

I made myself small in the darkness, unable to know if I could be seen. I had left him for hours every day for eight and a half years as I had left my mother or Ruth and Ray, my brother and sister, and certainly Mr. Harvey, but he, I now saw, had never left me. His devotion to me had made me know again and again that I had been beloved. In the warm light of my father's love I had remained Susie Salmon—a girl with my whole life in front of me.

"I thought if I was very quiet I would hear you," he whispered. "If I was still enough you might come back."

"Jack?" my mother said, waking. "I must have fallen asleep."

"It's wonderful to have you back," he said.

And my mother looked at him. Everything stripped away. "How do you do it?" she asked.

"There's no choice, Abbie," he said. "What else can I do?"

"Go away, start over again," she said.

"Did it work?"

They were silent. I reached out my hand and faded away.

"Why don't you come lie down up here?" my father said. "We have a little time before the enforcers come on duty and kick you out."

She didn't move.

"They've been nice to me," she said. "Nurse Eliot helped me put all the flowers in water while you slept."

He looked around him and made out their shapes. "Daffodils," he said.

"It's Susie's flower."

My father smiled beautifully. "See," he said, "that's how. You live in the face of it, by giving her a flower."

"That's so sad," my mother said.

"Yes," he said, "it is."

My mother had to balance somewhat precariously on one hip near the edge of his hospital bed, but they managed. They managed to stretch out together beside each other so they could stare into each other's eyes.

"How was it seeing Buckley and Lindsey?"

"Incredibly hard," she said.

They were silent for a moment and he squeezed her hand.

"You look so different," he said.

"You mean older."

I watched him reach up and take a strand of my mother's hair and loop it around her ear. "I fell in love with you again while you were away," he said.

I realized how much I wished I could be where my mother was. His love for my mother wasn't about looking back and loving something that would never change. It was about loving my mother for everything—for her brokenness and her fleeing, for her being there right then in that moment before the sun rose and the hospital staff came in. It was about touching that hair with the side of his fingertip, and knowing yet plumbing fearlessly the depths of her ocean eyes.

My mother could not bring herself to say "I love you."

"Will you stay?" he asked.

"For a while."

This was something.

"Good," he said. "So what did you say when people asked you about family in California?"

"Out loud I said I had two children. Silently I said three. I always felt like apologizing to her for that."

"Did you mention a husband?" he asked.

And she looked at him. "No."

"Man," he said.

"I didn't come back to pretend, Jack," she said.

"Why did you come back?"

"My mother called me. She said it was a heart attack and I thought about your father."

"Because I might die?"

"Yes."

"You were sleeping," he said. "You didn't see her."

"Who?"

"Someone came in the room and then left. I think it was Susie."

"Jack?" my mother asked, but her alarm was only at half-mast.

"Don't tell me you don't see her."

She let go.

"I see her everywhere," she said, breathing out her relief. "Even in California she was everywhere. Boarding buses or on the streets outside schools when I drove by. I'd see her hair but it didn't match the face or I'd see her body or the way she moved. I'd see older sisters and their little brothers, or two girls that looked like sisters and I imagined what Lindsey wouldn't have in her life — the whole relationship gone for her and for Buckley, and then that would just hit me, because I had left too. It would just spin onto you and even to my mother."

"She's been great," he said, "a rock. A spongelike rock, but a rock."

"So I gather."

"So if I tell you that Susie was in the room ten minutes ago, what would you say?"

"I'd say you were insane and you were probably right."

My father reached up and traced the line of my mother's nose and brought his finger over her two lips. As he did, the lips parted ever so slightly.

"You have to lean down," he said, "I'm still a sick man."

And I watched as my parents kissed. They kept their eyes open as they did, and my mother was the one to cry first, the tears dropping down onto my father's cheeks until he wept too.

## TWENTY-ONE

After I left my parents in the hospital, I went to watch Ray Singh. We had been fourteen together, he and I. Now I saw his head on his pillow, dark hair on yellow sheets, dark skin on yellow sheets. I had always been in love with him. I counted the lashes of each closed eye. He had been my almost, my might-have-been, and I did not want to leave him any more than I did my family.

On the listing scaffold behind the stage, with Ruth below us, Ray Singh had gotten close enough to me so that his breath was near mine. I could smell the mixture of cloves and cinnamon that I imagined he topped his cereal with each morning, and a dark smell too, the human smell of the body coming at me where deep inside there were organs suspended by a chemistry separate from mine.

From the time I knew it would happen until the time it did, I had made sure not to be alone with Ray Singh inside or outside school. I was afraid of what I wanted most—his kiss. That it would not be good enough to match the stories everyone told or those I read in *Seventeen* and *Glamour* and *Vogue*. I feared that I would not be good enough—that my first kiss would equal rejection, not love. Still, I collected kiss stories.

"Your first kiss is destiny knocking," Grandma Lynn said over the phone one day. I was holding the phone while my father went to get my mother. I heard him in the kitchen say "three sheets to the wind."

"If I had it to do over again I would have worn something stupendous—like Fire and Ice, but Revlon didn't make that lipstick back then. I would have left my mark on the man."

"Mother?" my mother said into the bedroom extension.

"We're talking kiss business, Abigail."

"How much have you had?"

"See, Susie," Grandma Lynn said, "if you kiss like a lemon, you make lemonade."

"What was it like?"

"Ah, the kiss question," my mother said. "I'll leave you to it." I had been making my father and her tell it over and over again to hear their different takes. What I came away with was an image of my parents behind a cloud of cigarette smoke—the lips only vaguely touching inside the cloud.

A moment later Grandma Lynn whispered, "Susie, are you still there?"

"Yes, Grandma."

She was quiet for a while longer. "I was your age, and my first kiss came from a grown man. A father of a friend."

"Grandma!" I said, honestly shocked.

"You're not going to tell on me, are you?"

"No."

"It was wonderful," Grandma Lynn said. "He knew how to kiss. The boys who kissed me I couldn't even tolerate. I'd put my hand flat against their chests and push them away. Mr. McGahern knew how to use his lips."

"So what happened?"

"Bliss," she said. "I knew it wasn't right, but it was wonderful — at least for me. I never asked him how he felt about it, but then I never saw him alone after that."

"But did you want to do it again?"

"Yes, I was always searching for that first kiss."

"How about Grandaddy?"

"Not much of a kisser," she said. I could hear the clink of ice cubes on the other end of the phone. "I've never forgotten Mr. McGahern, even though it was just for a moment. Is there a boy who wants to kiss you?"

Neither of my parents had asked me this. I now know that they knew this already, could tell, smiled at each other when they compared notes.

I swallowed hard on my end. "Yes."

"What's his name?"

"Ray Singh."

"Do you like him?"

"Yes."

"Then what's the holdup?"

"I'm afraid I won't be good at it."

"Susie?"

"Yes?"

"Just have fun, kid."

But when I stood by my locker that afternoon and I heard Ray's voice say my name — this time behind me and not above me — it felt like anything but fun. It didn't feel not fun either. The easy states of black and white that I had known before did not apply.

I felt, if I were to say any word, churned. Not as a verb but as an adjective. Happy + Frightened = Churned.

"Ray," I said, but before the name had left my mouth, he leaned into me and caught my open mouth in his. It was so unexpected, even though I had waited weeks for it, that I wanted more. I wanted so badly to kiss Ray Singh again.

The following morning Mr. Connors cut out an article from the paper and saved it for Ruth. It was a detailed drawing of the Flanagan sinkhole and how it was going to be filled in. While Ruth dressed, he penned a note to her. "This is a crock of shit," it said. "Someday some poor sap's car is going to fall into it all over again."

"Dad says this is the death knell for him," Ruth said to Ray, waving the clipping at him as she got into Ray's ice blue Chevy at the end of her driveway. "Our place is going to be swallowed up in subdivision land. Get this. In this article they have four blocks like the cubes you draw in beginning art class, and it's supposed to show how they're going to patch the sinkhole up."

"Nice to see you too, Ruth," Ray said, reversing out of the driveway while making eyes at Ruth's unbuckled seat belt.

"Sorry," Ruth said. "Hello."

"What does the article say?" Ray asked.

"Nice day today, beautiful weather."

"Okay, okay. Tell me about the article."

Every time he saw Ruth after a few months had passed, he was reminded of her impatience and her curiosity—two traits that had both made and kept them friends.

"The first three are the same drawing only with different arrows pointing to different places and saying 'topsoil,' 'cracked limestone,' and 'dissolving rock.' The last one has a big headline that says, 'Patching it' and underneath it says, 'Concrete fills the throat and grout fills the cracks.'"

"Throat?" Ray said.

"I know," said Ruth. "Then there's this other arrow on the other side as if this was such a huge project that they had to pause a second so readers could understand the concept, and this one says, 'Then the hole is filled with dirt.' "

Ray started laughing.

"Like a medical procedure," Ruth said. "Intricate surgery is needed to patch up the planet."

"I think holes in the earth draw on some pretty primal fears."

"I'll say," Ruth said. "They have throats, for God's sake! Hey, let's check this out."

A mile or so down the road there were signs of new construction. Ray took a left and drove into the circles of freshly paved roads where the trees had been cleared and small red and yellow flags waved at intervals from the tops of waist-high wire markers.

Just as they had lulled themselves into thinking that they were alone, exploring the roads laid out for a territory as yet uninhabited, they saw Joe Ellis walking up ahead.

Ruth didn't wave and neither did Ray, nor did Joe make a move to acknowledge them.

"My mom says he still lives at home and can't get a job."

"What does he do all day?" Ray asked.

"Look creepy, I guess."

"He never got over it," Ray said, and Ruth stared out into the rows and rows of vacant lots until Ray connected with the main road again and they crossed back over the railroad tracks moving toward Route 30, which would take them in the direction of the sinkhole.

Ruth floated her arm out the window to feel the moist air of the morning after rain. Although Ray had been accused of being involved in my disappearance, he had understood why, knew that the police were doing their job. But Joe Ellis had never recovered from being accused of killing the cats and dogs Mr. Harvey had killed. He wandered around, keeping a good distance from his neighbors and wanting so much to take solace in the love of cats and dogs. For me the saddest thing was that these animals smelled the brokenness in him — the human defect — and kept away.

Down Route 30 near Eels Rod Pike, at a spot that Ray and Ruth were about to pass, I saw Len coming out of an apartment over Joe's barbershop. He carried a lightly stuffed student knapsack out to his car. The knapsack had been the gift of the young woman who owned the apartment. She had asked him out for coffee one day after they met down at the station as part of a criminology course at West Chester College. Inside the knapsack he had a combination of things — some of which he would show my father and some that no child's parent needed to see. The latter included the photos of the graves of the recovered bodies — both elbows there in each case.

When he had called the hospital, the nurse had told him Mr. Salmon was with his wife and family. Now his guilt thickened as he pulled his car into the hospital parking lot and sat for a moment with the hot sun coming through the windshield, baking in the heat.

I could see Len working on how to state what he had to say. He could work with only one assumption in his head — after almost seven years of ever more dwindling contact since late 1975, what my parents would hope for most was a body or the news that Mr. Harvey had been found. What he had to give them was a charm.

He grabbed his knapsack and locked up the car, passing by the girl outside with her replenished buckets of daffodils. He knew the number of my father's room, so he did not bother announcing himself to the fifth-floor nurses' station but merely tapped lightly on my father's open door before walking in.

My mother was standing with her back toward him. When she turned, I could see the force of her presence hit him. She was holding my father's hand. I suddenly felt terribly lonely.

My mother wobbled a bit when she met Len's eyes, and then she led with what came easiest.

"Is it *ever* wonderful to see you?" she tried to joke.

"Len," my father managed. "Abbie, will you tilt me up?"

"How are you feeling, Mr. Salmon?" Len asked as my mother pressed the up arrow button on the bed.

"Jack, please," my father insisted.

"Before you get your hopes up," Len said, "we haven't caught him."

My father visibly deflated.

My mother readjusted the foam pillows behind my father's back and neck. "Then why are you here?" she asked.

"We found an item of Susie's," Len said.

He had used almost the same sentence when he'd come to the house with the jingle-bell hat. It was a distant echo in her head.

The night before, as first my mother watched my father sleeping and then my father woke to see her head beside his on his pillow, they had both been staving off the memory of that first night of snow and hail and rain and how they had clung to each other, neither of them voicing aloud their greatest hope. Last night it had been my father who'd finally said it: "She's never coming home." A clear and easy piece of truth that everyone who had ever known me had accepted. But he needed to say it, and she needed to hear him say it.

"It's a charm off her bracelet," Len said. "A Pennsylvania keystone with her initials on it."

"I bought that for her," my father said. "At Thirtieth Street Station when I went into the city one day. They had a booth, and a man wearing safety glasses etched in initials for free. I brought Lindsey one too. Remember, Abigail?"

"I remember," my mother said.

"We found it near a grave in Connecticut."

My parents were suddenly still for a moment—like animals trapped in ice—their eyes frozen open and beseeching whoever walked above them to release them now, please.

"It wasn't Susie," Len said, rushing to fill the space. "What it means is that Harvey has been linked to other murders in Delaware and Connecticut. It was at the grave site outside Hartford where we found Susie's charm."

My father and mother watched as Len fumbled to open the slightly jammed zipper of his knapsack. My mother smoothed my father's hair back and tried to catch his eye. But my father was focused on the prospect Len presented—my murder case reopening. And my mother, just when she was beginning to feel on more solid ground, had to hide the fact that she'd never wanted it to begin again. The name George Harvey silenced her. She had never known what to say about him. For my mother, connecting her life to his capture and punishment spoke more about choosing to live with the enemy than about having to learn to live in the world without me.

Len pulled out a large Ziploc bag. At the bottom corner of the bag my parents could see the glint of gold. Len handed it to my mother, and she held it in front of her, slightly away from her body.

"Don't you need this, Len?" my father asked.

"We did all the tests on it," he said. "We've documented where it was found and taken the required photographs. The time may come when I would have to ask for it back, but until then, it's yours to keep."

"Open it, Abbie," my father said.

I watched my mother hold open the bag and lean over the bed. "It's for you, Jack," she said. "It was a gift from you."

As my father reached in, his hand shook, and it took him a

second to feel the small, sharp edges of the keystone against the flesh of his fingers. The way he drew it out of the bag reminded me of playing the game Operation with Lindsey when we were little. If he touched the sides of the Ziploc bag an alarm would go off and he would have to forfeit.

"How can you be sure he killed these other girls?" my mother asked. She stared at the tiny ember of gold in my father's palm.

"Nothing is ever certain," Len said.

And the echo rang in her ears again. Len had a fixed set of phrases. It was this same phrase that my father had borrowed to soothe his family. It was a cruel phrase that preyed on hope.

"I think I want you to leave now," she said.

"Abigail?" my father queried.

"I can't hear any more."

"I'm very glad to have the charm, Len," my father said.

Len doffed an imaginary cap to my father before turning to go. He had made a certain kind of love to my mother before she went away. Sex as an act of willful forgetting. It was the kind he made more and more in the rooms above the barbershop.


I headed south toward Ruth and Ray, but I saw Mr. Harvey instead. He was driving an orange patchwork car that had been pieced together from so many different versions of the same make and model that it looked like Frankenstein's monster on wheels. A bungee cord held the front hood, which fluttered up and down as it caught the oncoming air.

The engine had resisted anything but a shimmer above the speed limit no matter how hard he pressed the gas pedal. He had slept next to an empty grave, and while he'd been sleeping he had dreamed of the 5! 5! 5!, waking near dawn to make the drive to Pennsylvania.

The edges of Mr. Harvey seemed oddly blurred. For years he

had kept at bay the memories of the women he killed, but now, one by one, they were coming back.

The first girl he'd hurt was by accident. He got mad and couldn't stop himself, or that was how he began to weave it into sense. She stopped going to the high school that they were both enrolled in, but this didn't seem strange to him. By that time he had moved so many times that he assumed that was what the girl had done. He had regretted it, this quiet, muffled rape of a school friend, but he didn't see it as something that would stay with either one of them. It was as if something outside him had resulted in the collision of their two bodies one afternoon. For a second afterward, she'd stared. It was bottomless. Then she put on her torn underpants, tucking them into her skirt's waistband to keep them in place. They didn't speak, and she left. He cut himself with his penknife along the back of his hand. When his father asked about the blood, there would be a plausible explanation. "See," he could say, and point to the place on his hand. "It was an accident."

But his father didn't ask, and no one came around looking for him. No father or brother or policeman.

Then what I saw was what Mr. Harvey felt beside him. This girl, who had died only a few years later when her brother fell asleep smoking a cigarette. She was sitting in the front seat. I wondered how long it would take before he began to remember me.


The only signs of change since the day Mr. Harvey had delivered me up to the Flanagans' were the orange pylons set around the lot. That and the evidence that the sinkhole had expanded. The house's southeast corner sloped downward, and the front porch was quietly sinking into the earth.

As a precaution, Ray parked on the other side of Flat Road,

under a section of overgrown shrubbery. Even so, the passenger side skimmed the edge of the pavement. "What happened to the Flanagans?" Ray asked as they got out of his car.

"My father said the corporation that bought the property gave them a settlement and they took off."

"It's spooky around here, Ruth," Ray said.

They crossed the empty road. Above them the sky was a light blue, a few smoky clouds dotting the air. From where they stood they could just make out the back of Hal's bike shop on the other side of the railroad tracks.

"I wonder if Hal Heckler still owns that?" Ruth said. "I had a crush on him when we were growing up."

Then she turned toward the lot. They were quiet. Ruth moved in ever-diminishing circles, with the hole and its vague edge as their goal. Ray trailed just behind Ruth as she led the way. If you saw it from a distance, the sinkhole seemed innocuous—like an overgrown mud puddle just starting to dry out. There were spots of grass and weeds surrounding it and then, if you looked close enough, it was as if the earth stopped and a light cocoa-colored flesh began. It was soft and convex, and it drew in items placed on top of it.

"How do you know it won't swallow us?" Ray asked.

"We're not heavy enough," Ruth said.

"Stop if you feel yourself sinking."

Watching them I remembered holding on to Buckley's hand the day we went to bury the refrigerator. While my father was talking to Mr. Flanagan, Buckley and I walked up to the point where the earth sloped down and softened, and I swore I felt it give ever so slightly beneath my feet. It had been the same sensation as walking in the graveyard of our church and suddenly sinking into the hollow tunnels that the moles had dug among the headstones.

Ultimately it was the memory of those very moles—and the

pictures of their blind, nosy, toothsome selves that I sought out in books — that had made me accept more readily being sunk inside the earth in a heavy metal safe. I was mole-proof, anyway.

Ruth tiptoed up to what she took to be the edge, while I thought of the sound of my father's laughter on that long-ago day. I made up a story for my brother on the way home. How underneath the sinkhole there was a whole village inside the earth that no one knew about and the people who lived there greeted these appliances like gifts from an Earthly heaven. "When our refrigerator reaches them," I said, "they will praise us, because they are a race of tiny repairmen who love to put things back together again." My father's laughter filled the car.

"Ruthie," Ray said, "that's close enough."

Ruth's toes were on the soft part, her heels were on the hard, and there was a sense as I watched her that she might point her fingers and raise her arms and dive right in to be beside me. But Ray came up behind her.

"Apparently," he said, "the earth's throat burps."

All three of us watched the corner of something metal as it rose.

"The great Maytag of 'sixty-nine," Ray said.

But it was not a washer or a safe. It was an old red gas stove, moving slow.

"Do you ever think about where Susie Salmon's body ended up?" asked Ruth.

I wanted to walk out from underneath the overgrown shrubs that half-hid their ice blue car and cross the road and walk down into the hole and back up and tap her gently on the shoulder and say, "It's me! You've done it! Bingo! Score!"

"No," Ray said. "I leave that to you."

"Everything is changing here now. Every time I come back something is gone that made it not just every other place in the country," she said.

"Do you want to go inside the house?" Ray asked, but he was thinking of me. How his crush had come when he was thirteen. He had seen me walking home from school ahead of him, and it was a series of simple things: my awkward plaid skirt, my peacoat covered in Holiday's fur, the way what I thought of as my mousy brown hair caught the afternoon sun so that the light moved fluidly from spot to spot as we walked home, one behind the other. And then, a few days later, when he had stood in social science class and accidentally read from his paper on *Jane Eyre* instead of the War of 1812—I had looked at him in a way he thought was nice.

Ray walked toward the house that would soon be demolished, and that had already been stripped of any valuable doorknobs and faucets late one night by Mr. Connors, but Ruth stayed by the sinkhole. Ray was already inside the house when it happened. As clear as day, she saw me standing there beside her, looking at the spot Mr. Harvey had dumped me.

"Susie," Ruth said, feeling my presence even more solidly when she said my name.

But I said nothing.

"I've written poems for you," Ruth said, trying to get me to stay with her. What she had wished for her whole life happening, finally. "Don't you want anything, Susie?" she asked.

Then I vanished.

Ruth stood there reeling, waiting in the gray light of the Pennsylvania sun. And her question rang in my ears: "Don't you want anything?"

On the other side of the railroad tracks, Hal's shop was deserted. He had taken the day off and brought Samuel and Buckley to a bike show in Radnor. I could see Buckley's hands move over the curved front-wheel casing of a red minibike. It would be his birthday soon, and Hal and Samuel watched him. Hal had wanted to give Samuel's old alto sax to my brother, but my Grandma Lynn had intervened. "He needs to bang on things, honey," she said. "Save the subtle stuff." So Hal and Samuel had chipped in together and bought my brother a secondhand set of drums.

Grandma Lynn was at the mall trying to find simple yet elegant clothes that she might convince my mother to wear. With fingers made dexterous from years of practice, she pulled a near-navy dress from a rack of black. I could see the woman near her alight on the dress in greenish envy.

At the hospital, my mother was reading aloud to my father from a day-old *Evening Bulletin,* and he was watching her lips move and not really listening. Wanting to kiss her instead.

And Lindsey.

I could see Mr. Harvey take the turn into my old neighborhood in broad daylight, past caring who spotted him, even depending on his standard invisibility — here, in the neighborhood where so many had said they would never forget him, had always thought of him as strange, had come easily to suspect that the dead wife he spoke of by alternate names had been one of his victims.

Lindsey was at home alone.

Mr. Harvey drove by Nate's house inside the anchor area of the development. Nate's mother was picking the wilted blossoms from her front kidney-shaped flower bed. She looked up when the car passed. She saw the unfamiliar, patched-together car and imagined it was a college friend of one of the older children home for the summer. She had not seen Mr. Harvey in the driver's seat. He turned left onto the lower road, which circled around to his old street. Holiday whined at my feet, the same kind of sick, low moan he would let out when we drove him to the vet.

Ruana Singh had her back to him. I saw her through the dining room window, alphabetizing stacks of new books and placing them in carefully kept bookshelves. There were children out in their yards on swings and pogo sticks and chasing one another with water pistols. A neighborhood full of potential victims.

He rounded the curve at the bottom of our road and passed the small municipal park across from where the Gilberts lived. They were both inside, Mr. Gilbert now infirm. Then he saw his old house, no longer green, though to my family and me it would always be "the green house." The new owners had painted it a lavendery mauve and installed a pool and, just off to the side, near the basement window, a gazebo made out of redwood, which overflowed with hanging ivy and children's toys. The front flower beds had been paved over when they expanded their front walk, and they had screened in the front porch with frost-resistant glass, behind which he saw an office of some sort. He heard the sound of girls laughing out in the backyard, and a woman came out of the front door carrying a pair of pruning shears and wearing a sun hat. She stared at the man sitting in his orange car and felt something kick inside her — the queasy kick of an empty womb. She turned abruptly and went back inside, peering at him from behind her window. Waiting.

He drove down the road a few houses further.

There she was, my precious sister. He could see her in the upstairs window of our house. She had cut all her hair off and grown thinner in the intervening years, but it was her, sitting at the drafting board she used as a desk and reading a psychology book.

It was then that I began to see them coming down the road.

While he scanned the windows of my old house and wondered where the other members of my family were — whether my father's leg still made him hobble — I saw the final vestiges of the animals and the women taking leave of Mr. Harvey's house. They straggled forward together. He watched my sister and thought of the sheets he had draped on the poles of the bridal tent. He had stared right in my father's eyes that day as he said my name. And the dog — the one that barked outside his house — the dog was surely dead by now.

Lindsey moved in the window, and I watched him watching her. She stood up and turned around, going farther into the room to a floor-to-ceiling bookshelf. She reached up and brought another book down. As she came back to the desk and he lingered on her face, his rearview mirror suddenly filled with a black-and-white cruising slowly up the street behind him.

He knew he could not outrace them. He sat in his car and prepared the last vestiges of the face he had been giving authorities for decades — the face of a bland man they might pity or despise but never blame. As the officer pulled alongside him, the women slipped in the windows and the cats curled around his ankles.

"Are you lost?" the young policeman asked when he was flush with the orange car.

"I used to live here," Mr. Harvey said. I shook with it. He had chosen to tell the truth.

"We got a call, suspicious vehicle."

"I see they're building something in the old cornfield," Mr. Harvey said. And I knew that part of me could join the others then, swoop down in pieces, each body part he had claimed raining down inside his car.

"They're expanding the school."

"I thought the neighborhood looked more prosperous," he said wistfully.

"Perhaps you should move along," the officer said. He was embarrassed for Mr. Harvey in his patched-up car, but I saw him jot the license plate down.

"I didn't mean to scare anyone."

Mr. Harvey was a pro, but in that moment I didn't care. With each section of road he covered, I focused on Lindsey inside reading her textbooks, on the facts jumping up from the pages and into her brain, on how smart she was and how whole. At Temple she had decided to be a therapist. And I thought of the mix of air that was our front yard, which was daylight, a queasy mother and a cop — it was a convergence of luck that had kept my sister safe so far. Every day a question mark.


Ruth did not tell Ray what had happened. She promised herself she would write it in her journal first. When they crossed the road back to the car, Ray saw something violet in the scrub halfway up a high dirt berm that had been dumped there by a construction crew.

"That's periwinkle," he said to Ruth. "I'm going to clip some for my mom."

"Cool, take your time," Ruth said.

Ray ducked into the underbrush by the driver's side and climbed up to the periwinkle while Ruth stood by the car. Ray wasn't thinking of me anymore. He was thinking of his mother's smiles. The surest way to get them was to find her wildflowers like this, to bring them home to her and watch her as she pressed them, first opening their petals flat against the black and white of dictionaries or reference books. Ray walked to the top of the berm and disappeared over the side in hopes of finding more.

It was only then that I felt a prickle along my spine, when I saw his body suddenly vanish on the other side. I heard Holiday, his fear lodged low and deep in his throat, and realized it could not have been Lindsey for whom he had whined. Mr. Harvey crested the top of Eels Rod Pike and saw the sinkhole and the orange pylons that matched his car. He had dumped a body there. He remembered his mother's amber pendant, and how when she had handed it to him it was still warm.

Ruth saw the women stuffed in the car in blood-colored gowns. She began walking toward them. On that same road where I had been buried, Mr. Harvey passed by Ruth. All she could see were the women. Then: blackout.

That was the moment I fell to Earth.

## TWENTY-TWO

R uth collapsing into the road. Of this I was aware. Mr.
Harvey sailing away unwatched, unloved, unbidden — this I lost.

Helplessly I tipped, my balance gone. I fell through the open
doorway of the gazebo, across the lawn and out past the farthest
boundary of the heaven I had lived in all these years.

I heard Ray screaming in the air above me, his voice shouting
in an arc of sound. "Ruth, are you okay?" And then he reached
her and grabbed on.

"Ruth, Ruth," he yelled. "What happened?"

And I was in Ruth's eyes and I was looking up. I could feel the
arch of her back against the pavement, and scrapes inside her
clothes where flesh had been torn away by the gravel's sharp
edges. I felt every sensation — the warmth of the sun, the smell of
the asphalt — but I could not see Ruth.

I heard Ruth's lungs bubbling, a giddiness there in her stomach, but air still filling her lungs. Then tension stretching out the
body. Her body. Ray above, his eyes — gray, pulsing, looking up

and down the road hopelessly for help that was not coming. He had not seen the car but had come through the scrub delighted, carrying a bouquet of wildflowers for his mother, and there was Ruth, lying in the road.

Ruth pushed up against her skin, wanting out. She was fighting to leave and I was inside now, struggling with her. I willed her back, willed that divine impossible, but she wanted out. There was nothing and no one that could keep her down. Flying. I watched as I had so many times from heaven, but this time it was a blur beside me. It was lust and rage yearning upward.

"Ruth," Ray said. "Can you hear me, Ruth?"

Right before she closed her eyes and all the lights went out and the world was frantic, I looked into Ray Singh's gray eyes, at his dark skin, at his lips I had once kissed. Then, like a hand unclasping from a tight lock, Ruth passed by him.

Ray's eyes bid me forward while the watching streamed out of me and gave way to a pitiful desire. To be alive again on this Earth. Not to watch from above but to be — the sweetest thing — beside.

Somewhere in the blue blue Inbetween I had seen her — Ruth streaking by me as I fell to Earth. But she was no shadow of a human form, no ghost. She was a smart girl breaking all the rules.

And I was in her body.

I heard a voice calling me from heaven. It was Franny's. She ran toward the gazebo, calling my name. Holiday was barking so loud that his voice would catch and round in the base of his throat with no break. Then, suddenly, Franny and Holiday were gone and all was silent. I felt something holding me down, and I felt a hand in mine. My ears were like oceans in which what I had known, voices, faces, facts, began to drown. I opened my eyes for the first time since I had died and saw gray eyes looking back at me. I was still as I came to realize that the marvelous weight weighing me down was the weight of the human body.

I tried to speak.

"Don't," Ray said. "What happened?"

I died, I wanted to tell him. How do you say, "I died and now I'm back among the living"?

Ray had kneeled down. Scattered around him and on top of me were the flowers he'd been gathering for Ruana. I could pick out their bright elliptical shapes against Ruth's dark clothes. And then Ray leaned his ear to my chest to listen to me breathing. He placed a finger on the inside of my wrist to check my pulse.

"Did you faint?" he asked when these checked out.

I nodded. I knew I would not be granted this grace on Earth forever, that Ruth's wish was only temporary.

"I think I'm fine," I tried, but my voice was too faint, too far away, and Ray did not hear me. My eyes locked on to his then, opening as wide as I could make them. Something urged me to lift up. I thought I was floating back to heaven, returning, but I was trying to stand up.

"Ruth," Ray said. "Don't move if you feel weak. I can carry you to the car."

I smiled at him, one-thousand-watted. "I'm okay," I said.

Tentatively, watching me carefully, he released my arm but continued to hold on to my other hand. He went with me as I stood, and the wildflowers fell to the pavement. In heaven, women were throwing rose petals as they saw Ruth Connors.

I watched his beautiful face break into a stunned smile. "So you're all right," he said. Cautious, he came close enough to kiss me, but he told me he was checking my pupils to see if they were equal in size.

I was feeling the weight of Ruth's body, both the luscious bounce of breasts and thighs but also an awesome responsibility. I was a soul back on Earth. AWOL a little while from heaven, I had been given a gift. By force of will I stood as straight as I could.

"Ruth?"

I tried to get used to the name. "Yes," I said.

"You've changed," he said. "Something's changed."

We stood near the center of the road, but this was my moment. I wanted so much to tell him, but what could I say then? "I'm Susie, I have only a little time." I was too afraid.

"Kiss me," I said instead.

"What?"

"Don't you want to?" I reached my hands up to his face and felt the light stubble of a beard that had not been there eight years ago.

"What's happened to you?" he said, bewildered.

"Sometimes cats fall ten flights out of the windows of highrises and land on their feet. You only believe it because you've seen it in print."

Ray stared at me, mystified. He leaned his head down and our lips touched, tender. At the roots I felt his cool lips deep down inside me. Another kiss, precious package, stolen gift. His eyes were so close to me I saw the green flecks in the gray.

I took his hand, and we walked back to the car in silence. I was aware that he dragged behind, stretching my arm out behind me as we held hands and scanning Ruth's body to make sure she was walking fine.

He opened the door of the passenger side, and I slid into the seat and placed my feet on the carpeted floor. When he came around to his side and ducked inside he looked hard at me once more.

"What's wrong?" I asked.

He kissed me lightly again, on the lips. What I had wanted for so long. The moment slowed down, and I drank it in. The brush of his lips, the slight stubble of his beard as it grazed me, and the sound of the kiss—the small smack of suction as our lips parted after the pushing together and then the more brutal breaking away. It reverberated, this sound, down the long tunnel of loneliness and making do with watching the touch and caress of others on Earth. I had never been touched like this. I had only been hurt by hands past all tenderness. But spreading out into my heaven after death had been a moonbeam that swirled and blinked on and off — Ray Singh's kiss. Somehow Ruth knew this.

My head throbbed then, with the thought of it, with me hiding inside Ruth in every way but this — that when Ray kissed me or as our hands met it was my desire, not Ruth's, it was *me* pushing out at the edges of her skin. I could see Holly. She was laughing, her head tilted back, and then I heard Holiday howling plaintively, for I was back where we had both once lived.

"Where do you want to go?" Ray asked.

And it was such a wide question, the answer so vast. I knew I did not want to chase after Mr. Harvey. I looked at Ray and knew why I was there. To take back a piece of heaven I had never known.

"Hal Heckler's bike shop," I stated firmly.

"What?"

"You asked," I said.

"Ruth?"

"Yes?"

"Can I kiss you again?"

"Yes," I said, my face flushing.

He leaned over as the engine warmed and our lips met once more and there she was, Ruth, lecturing a group of old men in berets and black turtlenecks while they held glowing lighters in the air and called her name in a rhythmic chant.

Ray sat back and looked at me. "What is it?" he asked.

"When you kiss me I see heaven," I said.

"What does it look like?"

"It's different for everyone."

"I want details," he said, smiling. "Facts."

"Make love to me," I said, "and I'll tell you."

"Who are you?" he asked, but I could tell he didn't know what he was asking yet.

"The car is warmed up," I said.

His hand grabbed the shiny chrome stick on the side of the steering wheel and then we drove — normal as day — a boy and a girl together. The sun caught the broken mica in the old patched pavement as he made the U-turn.

We drove down to the bottom of Flat Road, and I pointed to the dirt path on the other side of Eels Rod Pike, which led up to a place where we could cross the railroad tracks.

"They'll have to change this soon," Ray said as he shot across the gravel and up onto the dirt path. The railroad stretched to Harrisburg in one direction and Philadelphia in the other, and all along it buildings were being razed and old families were moving out and industrial tenants in.

"Will you stay here," I asked, "after you're done with school?"

"No one does," Ray said. "You know that."

I was almost blinded by it, this choice; the idea that if I'd remained on Earth I could have left this place to claim another, that I could go anywhere I wanted to. And I wondered then, was it the same in heaven as on Earth? What I'd been missing was a wanderlust that came from letting go?

We drove onto the slim patch of cleared earth that ran along either side of Hal's bike shop. Ray stopped and braked the car.

"Why here?" Ray asked.

"Remember," I said, "we're exploring."

I led him around to the back of the shop and reached up over the doorjamb until I felt the hidden key.

"How do you know about that?"

"I've watched hundreds of people hide keys," I said. "It doesn't take a genius to guess."

Inside it was as I remembered it, the smell of bike grease heavy in the air.

I said, "I think I need to shower. Why not make yourself at home?"

I walked past the bed and turned on the light switch on the cord—all the tiny white lights above Hal's bed glittered then, the only light save the dusty light coming from the small back window.

"Where are you going?" Ray asked. "How do you know about this place?" His voice had a frantic sound it hadn't just a moment before.

"Give me just a little time, Ray," I said. "Then I'll explain."

I walked into the small bathroom but kept the door slightly ajar. As I took Ruth's clothes off and waited for the hot water to heat up, I hoped that Ruth could see me, could see her body as I saw it, its perfect living beauty.

It was damp and musty in the bathroom, and the tub was stained from years of having anything but water poured down its drain. I stepped up into the old claw-foot tub and stood under the water. Even at the hottest I could make it, I still felt cold. I called Ray's name. I begged him to step inside the room.

"I can see you through the curtain," he said, averting his eyes.

"It's okay," I said. "I like it. Take your clothes off and join me."

"Susie," he said, "you know I'm not like that."

My heart seized up. "What did you say?" I asked. I focused my eyes on his through the white translucent liner Hal kept for a curtain—he was a dark shape with a hundred small pinpoints of light surrounding him.

"I said I'm not that kind."

"You called me Susie."

There was silence, and then a moment later he drew back the curtain, being careful to look only at my face.

"Susie?"

"Join me," I said, my eyes welling up. "Please, join me."

I closed my eyes and waited. I put my head under the water

and felt the heat of it prickling my cheeks and neck, my breasts and stomach and groin. Then I heard him fumbling, heard his belt buckle hit the cold cement floor and his pockets lose their change.

I had the same sense of anticipation then as I sometimes had as a child when I lay down in the back seat and closed my eyes while my parents drove, sure we would be home when the car stopped, that they would lift me up and carry me inside. It was an anticipation born of trust.

Ray drew back the curtain. I turned to face him and opened my eyes. I felt a marvelous draft on the inside of my thighs.

"It's okay," I said.

He stepped slowly into the tub. At first he did not touch me, but then, tentatively, he traced a small scar along my side. We watched together as his finger moved down the ribbony wound.

"Ruth's volleyball incident, nineteen seventy-five," I said. I shivered again.

"You're not Ruth," he said, his face full of wonder.

I took the hand that had reached the end of the cut and placed it under my left breast.

"I've watched you both for years," I said. "I want you to make love to me."

His lips parted to speak, but what was on his lips now was too strange to say out loud. He brushed my nipple with his thumb, and I pulled his head toward me. We kissed. The water came down between our bodies and wet the sparse hair along his chest and stomach. I kissed him because I wanted to see Ruth and I wanted to see Holly and I wanted to know if they could see me. In the shower I could cry and Ray could kiss my tears, never knowing exactly why I shed them.

I touched every part of him and held it in my hands. I cupped his elbow in my palm. I dragged his pubic hair out straight between my fingers. I held that part of him that Mr. Harvey had forced inside me. Inside my head I said the word *gentle,* and then I said the word *man.*

"Ray?"

"I don't know what to call you."

"Susie."

I put my fingers up to his lips to stop his questioning. "Remember the note you wrote me? Remember how you called yourself the Moor?"

For a moment we both stood there, and I watched the water bead along his shoulders, then slip and fall.

Without saying anything further, he lifted me up and I wrapped my legs around him. He turned out of the path of the water to use the edge of the tub for support. When he was inside of me, I grabbed his face in my hands and kissed him as hard as I could.

After a full minute, he pulled away. "Tell me what it looks like."

"Sometimes it looks like the high school did," I said, breathless. "I never got to go there, but in my heaven I can make a bonfire in the classrooms or run up and down the halls yelling as loud as I want. But it doesn't always look like that. It can look like Nova Scotia, or Tangiers, or Tibet. It looks like anything you've ever dreamed."

"Is Ruth there?"

"Ruth is doing spoken word, but she'll come back."

"Can you see yourself there?"

"I'm here right now," I said.

"But you'll be gone soon."

I would not lie. I bowed my head. "I think so, Ray. Yes."

We made love then. We made love in the shower and in the bedroom and under the lights and fake glow-in-the-dark stars. While he rested, I kissed him across the line of his backbone and blessed each knot of muscle, each mole and blemish.

"Don't go," he said, and his eyes, those shining gems, shut and I could feel the shallow breath of sleep from him.

"My name is Susie," I whispered, "last name Salmon, like the fish." I leaned my head down to rest on his chest and sleep beside him.

When I opened my eyes, the window across from us was dark red and I could feel that there was not much time left. Outside, the world I had watched for so long was living and breathing on the same earth I now was. But I knew I would not go out. I had taken this time to fall in love instead—in love with the sort of helplessness I had not felt in death—the helplessness of being alive, the dark bright pity of being human—feeling as you went, groping in corners and opening your arms to light—all of it part of navigating the unknown.

Ruth's body was weakening. I leaned on one arm and watched Ray sleeping. I knew that I was going soon.

When his eyes opened a short while later, I looked at him and traced the edge of his face with my fingers.

"Do you ever think about the dead, Ray?"

He blinked his eyes and looked at me.

"I'm in med school."

"I don't mean cadavers, or diseases, or collapsed organs, I mean what Ruth talks about. I mean us."

"Sometimes I do," he said. "I've always wondered."

"We're here, you know," I said. "All the time. You can talk to us and think about us. It doesn't have to be sad or scary."

"Can I touch you again?" He shook the sheets from his legs to sit up.

It was then that I saw something at the end of Hal's bed. It was cloudy and still. I tried to convince myself that it was an odd trick of light, a mass of dust motes trapped in the setting sun. But when Ray reached out to touch me, I didn't feel anything.

Ray leaned close to me and kissed me lightly on the shoulder. I didn't feel it. I pinched myself under the blanket. Nothing.

The cloudy mass at the end of the bed began to take shape now. As Ray slipped out of the bed and stood, I saw men and women filling the room.

"Ray," I said, just before he reached the bathroom. I wanted to say "I'll miss you," or "don't go," or "thank you."

"Yes."

"You have to read Ruth's journals."

"You couldn't pay me not to," he said.

I looked through the shadowy figures of the spirits forming a mass at the end of the bed and saw him smile at me. Saw his lovely fragile body turn and walk through the doorway. A tenuous and sudden memory.

As the steam began to billow out from the bathroom, I made my way, slowly, to the small child's desk where Hal stacked bills and records. I began to think of Ruth again, how I hadn't seen any of it coming — the marvelous possibility that Ruth had dreamed of since our meeting in the parking lot. Instead, I saw how hope was what I had traded on in heaven and on Earth. Dreams of being a wildlife photographer, dreams of winning an Oscar in junior year, dreams of kissing Ray Singh once more. Look what happens when you dream.

In front of me I saw a phone and picked it up. Without thinking, I punched in the number to my house, like a lock whose combination you know only when you spin the dial in your hand.

On the third ring, someone picked up.

"Hello?"

"Hello, Buckley," I said.

"Who is this?"

"It's me, Susie."

"Who's there?"

"Susie, honey, your big sister."

"I can't hear you," he said.

I stared at the phone for a minute, and then I felt them. The room was full now of these silent spirits. Among them were children as well as adults. "Who are you? Where did you all come from?" I asked, but what had been my voice made no noise in the room. It was then that I noticed it. I was sitting up and watching the others, but Ruth was lying sprawled across the desk.

"Can you throw me a towel?" Ray yelled after shutting off the water. When I did not answer he pulled back the curtain. I heard him get out of the tub and come to the doorway. He saw Ruth and ran toward her. He touched her shoulder and, sleepily, she roused. They looked at each other. She did not have to say anything. He knew that I was gone.

I remembered once, with my parents and Lindsey and Buckley, riding backward on a train into a dark tunnel. That was how it felt to leave Earth the second time. The destination somehow inevitable, the sights seen in passing so many times. But this time I was accompanied, not ripped away, and I knew we were taking a long trip to a place very far away.

Leaving Earth again was easier than coming back had been. I got to see two old friends silently holding each other in the back of Hal's bike shop, neither of them ready to say aloud what had happened to them. Ruth was both more tired and more happy than she had ever been. For Ray, what he had been through and the possibilities this opened up for him were just starting to sink in.

## TWENTY-THREE

The next morning the smell of his mother's baking had sneaked up the stairs and into Ray's room where he and Ruth lay together. Overnight, their world had changed. It was that simple.

After leaving Hal's bike shop, being careful to cover any trace that they had ever been there, Ray and Ruth drove in silence back to Ray's house. Later that night, when Ruana found the two of them curled up together asleep and fully clothed, she was glad that Ray had at least this one weird friend.

Around three A.M., Ray had stirred. He sat up and looked at Ruth, at her long gangly limbs, at the beautiful body to which he had made love, and felt a sudden warmth infuse him. He reached out to touch her, and just then a bit of moonlight fell across the floor from the window where I had watched him sit and study for so many years. He followed it. There on the floor was Ruth's bag.

Careful not to wake her, he slid off the bed and walked over to it. Inside was her journal. He lifted it out and began to read:

"At the tips of feathers there is air and at their base: blood. I hold up bones; I wish like broken glass they could court light . . . still I try to place these pieces back together, to set them firm, to make murdered girls live again."

He skipped ahead:

"Penn Station, bathroom stall, struggle which led to the sink. Older woman.
"Domestic. Ave. C. Husband and wife.
"Roof on Mott Street, a teenage girl, gunshot.
"Time? Little girl in C.P. strays toward bushes. White lace collar, fancy."

He grew incredibly cold in the room but kept reading, looking up only when he heard Ruth stir.
"I have so much to tell you," she said.

Nurse Eliot helped my father lower himself into the wheelchair while my mother and sister fussed about the room, collecting the daffodils to take home.
"Nurse Eliot," he said, "I'll remember your kindness but I hope it will be a long time before I see you again."
"I hope so too," she said. She looked at my family gathered in the room, standing awkwardly about. "Buckley, your mother's and sister's hands are full. It's up to you."
"Steer her easy, Buck," my father said.
I watched the four of them begin to trail down the hall to the elevator, Buckley and my father first while Lindsey and my mother followed behind, their arms full of dripping daffodils.
In the elevator going down, Lindsey stared into the throats of the bright yellow flowers. She remembered that Samuel and Hal had

found yellow daffodils lying in the cornfield on the afternoon of the first memorial. They had never known who placed them there. My sister looked at the flowers and then my mother. She could feel my brother's body touching hers, and our father, sitting in the shiny hospital chair, looking tired but happy to be going home. When they reached the lobby and the doors opened I knew they were meant to be there, the four of them together, alone.

While Ruana's hands grew wet and swollen paring apple after apple, she began to say the word in her mind, the one she had avoided for years: *divorce.* It had been something about the crumpled, clinging postures of her son and Ruth that finally freed her. She could not remember the last time she had gone to bed at the same time as her husband. He walked in the room like a ghost and like a ghost slipped in between the sheets, barely creasing them. He was not unkind in the ways that the television and newspapers were full of. His cruelty was in his absence. Even when he came and sat at her dinner table and ate her food, he was not there.

She heard the sound of water running in the bathroom above her and waited what she thought was a considerate interval before calling up to them. My mother had called that morning to thank her for having talked to her when she called from California, and Ruana had decided to drop off a pie.

After handing a mug of coffee each to Ruth and Ray, Ruana announced that it was already late and she wanted Ray to accompany her to the Salmons', where she intended to run quietly to the door and place a pie on their doorstep.

"Whoa, pony," Ruth managed.

Ruana stared at her.

"Sorry, Mom," Ray said. "We had a pretty intense day yesterday." But he wondered, might his mother ever believe him?

Ruana turned toward the counter and brought one of two pies she had baked to the table, where the scent of it rose in a steamy mist from the holes cut into the crust. "Breakfast?" she said.

"You're a goddess!" said Ruth.

Ruana smiled.

"Eat your fill and then get dressed and both of you can come with me."

Ruth looked at Ray while she said, "Actually, I have somewhere to go, but I'll drop by later."

Hal brought the drum set over for my brother. Hal and my grandmother had agreed. Though it was still weeks before Buckley turned thirteen, he needed them. Samuel had let Lindsey and Buckley meet my parents at the hospital without him. It would be a double homecoming for them. My mother had stayed with my father for forty-eight hours straight, during which the world had changed for them and for others and would, I saw now, change again and again and again. There was no way to stop it.

"I know we shouldn't start too early," Grandma Lynn said, "but what's your poison, boys?"

"I thought we were set up for champagne," Samuel said.

"We are later," she said. "I'm offering an apéritif."

"I think I'm passing," Samuel said. "I'll have something when Lindsey does."

"Hal?"

"I'm teaching Buck the drums."

Grandma Lynn held her tongue about the questionable sobriety of known jazz greats. "Well, how about three scintillating tumblers of water?"

My grandmother stepped back into the kitchen to get their drinks. I had come to love her more after death than I ever had on Earth. I wish I could say that in that moment in the kitchen she decided to quit drinking, but I now saw that drinking was part of what made her who she was. If the worst of what she left on Earth was a legacy of inebriated support, it was a good legacy in my book.

She brought the ice over to the sink from the freezer and splurged on cubes. Seven in each tall glass. She ran the tap to make the water as cold as it would come. Her Abigail was coming home again. Her strange Abigail, whom she loved.

But when she looked up and through the window, she swore she saw a young girl wearing the clothes of her youth sitting outside Buckley's garden-shed fort and staring back at her. The next moment the girl was gone. She shook it off. The day was busy. She would not tell anyone.

When my father's car pulled into the drive, I was beginning to wonder if this had been what I'd been waiting for, for my family to come home, not to me anymore but to one another with me gone.

In the afternoon light my father looked smaller somehow, thinner, but his eyes looked grateful in a way they had not in years.

My mother, for her part, was thinking moment by moment that she might be able to survive being home again.

All four of them got out at once. Buckley came forward from the rear passenger seat to assist my father perhaps more than he needed assistance, perhaps protecting him from my mother. Lindsey looked over the hood of the car at our brother—her habitual check-in mode still operating. She felt responsible, just as my brother did, just as my father did. And then she turned back and saw my mother looking at her, her face lit by the yellowy light of the daffodils.

"What?"

"You are the spitting image of your father's mother," my mother said.

"Help me with the bags," my sister said.

They walked to the trunk together as Buckley led my father up the front path.

Lindsey stared into the dark space of the trunk. She wanted to know only one thing.

"Are you going to hurt him again?"

"I'm going to do everything I can not to," my mother said, "but no promises this time." She waited until Lindsey glanced up and looked at her, her eyes a challenge now as much as the eyes of a child who had grown up fast, run fast since the day the police had said too much blood in the earth, your daughter/sister/child is dead.

"I know what you did."

"I stand warned."

My sister hefted the bag.

They heard shouting. Buckley ran out onto the front porch. "Lindsey!" he said, forgetting his serious self, his heavy body buoyant. "Come see what Hal got me!"

He banged. And he banged and he banged and he banged. And Hal was the only one still smiling after five minutes of it. Everyone else had glimpsed the future and it was loud.

"I think now would be a good time to introduce him to the brush," Grandma Lynn said. Hal obliged.

My mother had handed the daffodils to Grandma Lynn and gone upstairs almost immediately, using the bathroom as an excuse. Everyone knew where she was going: my old room.

She stood at the edge of it, alone, as if she were standing at the edge of the Pacific. It was still lavender. The furniture, save for a reclining chair of my grandmother's, was unchanged.

"I love you, Susie," she said.

I had heard these words so many times from my father that it shocked me now; I had been waiting, unknowingly, to hear it from my mother. She had needed the time to know that this love would not destroy her, and I had, I now knew, given her that time, could give it, for it was what I had in great supply.

She noticed a photograph on my old dresser, which Grandma Lynn had put in a gold frame. It was the very first photograph I'd ever taken of her — my secret portrait of Abigail before her family woke and she put on her lipstick. Susie Salmon, wildlife photographer, had captured a woman staring out across her misty suburban lawn.

She used the bathroom, running the tap noisily and disturbing the towels. She knew immediately that her mother had bought these towels — cream, a ridiculous color for towels — and monogrammed — also ridiculous, my mother thought. But then, just as quickly, she laughed at herself. She was beginning to wonder how useful her scorched-earth policy had been to her all these years. Her mother was loving if she was drunk, solid if she was vain. When was it all right to let go not only of the dead but of the living — to learn to accept?

I was not in the bathroom, in the tub, or in the spigot; I did not hold court in the mirror above her head or stand in miniature at the tip of every bristle on Lindsey's or Buckley's toothbrush. In some way I could not account for — had they reached a state of bliss? were my parents back together forever? had Buckley begun to tell someone his troubles? would my father's heart truly heal? — I was done yearning for them, needing them to yearn for me. Though I still would. Though they still would. Always.

Downstairs Hal was holding Buckley's wrist as it held the brush stick. "Just pass it over the snare lightly." And Buckley did and looked up at Lindsey sitting across from him on the couch.

"Pretty cool, Buck," my sister said.

"Like a rattlesnake."

Hal liked that. "Exactly," he said, visions of his ultimate jazz combo dancing in his head.

My mother arrived back downstairs. When she entered the room she saw my father first. Silently she tried to let him know she was okay, that she was still breathing the air in, coping with the altitude.

"Okay, everyone!" my grandmother shouted from the kitchen, "Samuel has an announcement to make, so sit down!"

Everyone laughed and before they realigned into their more closed selves — this being together so hard for them even if it was what they all had wanted — Samuel came into the room along with Grandma Lynn. She held a tray of champagne flutes ready to be filled. He glanced at Lindsey briefly.

"Lynn is going to assist me by pouring," he said.

"Something she's quite good at," my mother said.

"Abigail?" Grandma Lynn said.

"Yes?"

"It's nice to see you too."

"Go ahead, Samuel," my father said.

"I wanted to say that I'm happy to be here with you all."

But Hal knew his brother. "You're not done, wordsmith. Buck, give him some brush." This time Hal let Buckley do it without assistance, and my brother backed Samuel up.

"I wanted to say that I'm glad that Mrs. Salmon is home, and that Mr. Salmon is home too, and that I'm honored to be marrying their beautiful daughter."

"Hear! Hear!" my father said.

My mother stood to hold the tray for Grandma Lynn, and together they distributed the glasses across the room.

As I watched my family sip champagne, I thought about how their lives trailed backward and forward from my death and then, I saw, as Samuel took the daring step of kissing Lindsey in a room full of family, became borne aloft away from it.

These were the lovely bones that had grown around my absence: the connections — sometimes tenuous, sometimes made at great cost, but often magnificent — that happened after I was gone. And I began to see things in a way that let me hold the world without me in it. The events that my death wrought were merely the bones of a body that would become whole at some unpredictable time in the future. The price of what I came to see as this miraculous body had been my life.

My father looked at the daughter who was standing there in front of him. The shadow daughter was gone.

With the promise that Hal would teach him to do drum rolls after dinner, Buckley put up his brush and drumsticks, and the seven of them began to trail through the kitchen into the dining room, where Samuel and Grandma Lynn had used the good plates to serve her trademark Stouffer's frozen ziti and Sara Lee frozen cheesecake.

"Someone's outside," Hal said, spotting a man through the window. "It's Ray Singh!"

"Let him in," my mother said.

"He's leaving."

All of them save my father and grandmother, who stayed together in the dining room, began to go after him.

"Hey, Ray!" Hal said, opening the door and nearly stepping directly in the pie. "Wait up!"

Ray turned. His mother was in the car with the engine running.

"We didn't mean to interrupt," Ray said now to Hal. Lindsey and Samuel and Buckley and a woman he recognized as Mrs. Salmon were all crowded together on the porch.

"Is that Ruana?" my mother called. "Please ask her in."

"Really, that's fine," Ray said and made no move to come closer. He wondered, *Is Susie watching this?*

Lindsey and Samuel broke away from the group and came toward him.

By that time my mother had walked down the front path to the driveway and was leaning in the car window talking to Ruana.

Ray glanced at his mother as she opened the car door to go inside the house. "Anything but pie for the two of us," she said to my mother as they walked up the path.

"Is Dr. Singh working?" my mother asked.

"As usual," Ruana said. She watched to see Ray walking, with Lindsey and Samuel, through the door of the house. "Will you come smoke stinky cigarettes with me again?"

"It's a date," my mother said.

"Ray, welcome, sit," my father said when he saw him coming through the living room. He had a special place in his heart for the boy who had loved his daughter, but Buckley swooped into the chair next to my father before anyone else could get to him.

Lindsey and Samuel found two straight chairs from the living room and brought them in to sit by the sideboard. Ruana sat between Grandma Lynn and my mother and Hal sat alone on one end.

I realized then that they would not know when I was gone, just as they could not know sometimes how heavily I had hovered in a particular room. Buckley had talked to me and I had talked back. Even if I hadn't thought I'd been talking to him, I had. I became manifest in whatever way they wanted me to be.

And there she was again, alone and walking out in the cornfield while everyone else I cared for sat together in one room. She would always feel me and think of me. I could see that, but there was no longer anything I could do. Ruth had been a girl haunted and now she would be a woman haunted. First by accident and now by choice. All of it, the story of my life and death, was hers if she chose to tell it, even to one person at a time.

\*    \*    \*

It was late in Ruana and Ray's visit when Samuel started talking about the gothic revival house that Lindsey and he had found along an overgrown section of Route 30. As he told Abigail about it in detail, describing how he had realized he wanted to propose to Lindsey and live there with her, Ray found himself asking, "Does it have a big hole in the ceiling of the back room and cool windows above the front door?"

"Yes," Samuel said, as my father grew alarmed. "But it can be fixed, Mr. Salmon. I'm sure of it."

"Ruth's dad owns that," Ray said.

Everyone was quiet for a moment and then Ray continued.

"He took out a loan on his business to buy up old places that aren't already slated for destruction. He wants to restore them," Ray said.

"My God," Samuel said.

And I was gone.

# BONES

Y ou don't notice the dead leaving when they really choose to leave you. You're not meant to. At most you feel them as a whisper or the wave of a whisper undulating down. I would compare it to a woman in the back of a lecture hall or theater whom no one notices until she slips out. Then only those near the door themselves, like Grandma Lynn, notice; to the rest it is like an unexplained breeze in a closed room.

Grandma Lynn died several years later, but I have yet to see her here. I imagine her tying it on in her heaven, drinking mint juleps with Tennessee Williams and Dean Martin. She'll be here in her own sweet time, I'm sure.

If I'm to be honest with you, I still sneak away to watch my family sometimes. I can't help it, and sometimes they still think of me. They can't help it.

After Lindsey and Samuel got married they sat in the empty house on Route 30 and drank champagne. The branches of the overgrown trees had grown into the upstairs windows, and they huddled beneath them, knowing the branches would have to be cut. Ruth's father had promised he would sell the house to them only if Samuel paid him in labor as his first employee in a restoration business. By the end of that summer, Mr. Connors had cleared the lot with the help of Samuel and Buckley and set up a trailer, which during the day would be his work quarters and at night could be Lindsey's study room.

In the beginning it was uncomfortable, the lack of plumbing and electricity, and having to go home to either one of their parents' houses to take showers, but Lindsey buried herself in school work and Samuel buried himself in tracking down the right era doorknobs and light pulls. It was a surprise to everyone when Lindsey found out she was pregnant.

"I thought you looked fatter," Buck said, smiling.

"You're one to talk," Lindsey said.

My father dreamed that one day he might teach another child to love ships in bottles. He knew there would be both sadness and joy in it; that it would always hold an echo of me.

I would like to tell you that it is beautiful here, that I am, and you will one day be, forever safe. But this heaven is not about safety just as, in its graciousness, it isn't about gritty reality. We have fun.

We do things that leave humans stumped and grateful, like Buckley's garden coming up one year, all of its crazy jumble of plants blooming all at once. I did that for my mother who, having stayed, found herself facing the yard again. Marvel was what she did at all the flowers and herbs and budding weeds. Marveling was what she mostly did after she came back — at the twists life took.

And my parents gave my leftover possessions to the Goodwill, along with Grandma Lynn's things.

They kept sharing when they felt me. Being together, thinking and talking about the dead, became a perfectly normal part of their life. And I listened to my brother, Buckley, as he beat the drums.

Ray became Dr. Singh, "the real doctor in the family," as Ruana liked to say. And he had more and more moments that he chose not to disbelieve. Even if surrounding him were the serious surgeons and scientists who ruled over a world of black and white, he maintained this possibility: that the ushering strangers that sometimes appeared to the dying were not the results of strokes, that he had called Ruth by my name, and that he had, indeed, made love to me.

If he ever doubted, he called Ruth. Ruth, who had graduated from a closet to a closet-sized studio on the Lower East Side. Ruth, who was still trying to find a way to write down whom she saw and what she had experienced. Ruth, who wanted everyone to believe what she knew: that the dead truly talk to us, that in the air between the living, spirits bob and weave and laugh with us. They are the oxygen we breathe.

Now I am in the place I call this wide wide Heaven because it includes all my simplest desires but also the most humble and grand. The word my grandfather uses is *comfort*.

So there are cakes and pillows and colors galore, but underneath this more obvious patchwork quilt are places like a quiet room where you can go and hold someone's hand and not have to say anything. Give no story. Make no claim. Where you can live at the edge of your skin for as long as you wish. This wide wide Heaven is about flathead nails and the soft down of new leaves, wild roller coaster rides and escaped marbles that fall then hang then take you somewhere you could never have imagined in your small-heaven dreams.

*   *   *

One afternoon I was scanning Earth with my grandfather. We were watching birds skip from top to top of the very tallest pines in Maine and feeling the bird's sensations as they landed then took flight then landed again. We ended up in Manchester, visiting a diner my grandfather remembered from his days traveling up and down the East Coast on business. It had gotten seedier in the fifty intervening years and after taking stock we left. But in the instant I turned away, I saw him: Mr. Harvey coming out of the doors of a Greyhound bus.

He went into the diner and ordered a cup of coffee at the counter. To the uninitiated, he still looked every bit as ordinary as he could, except around the eyes, but he no longer wore his contacts and no one took the time to look past his thick lenses anymore.

As an older waitress passed him a Styrofoam cup full of boiling coffee, he heard a bell over the door behind him tinkle and felt a cold blast of air.

It was a teenage girl who had sat a few rows ahead of him for the last few hours, playing her Walkman and humming along with the songs. He sat at the counter until she was done using the bathroom, and then he followed her out.

I watched him trail her in the dirty snow along the side of the diner and out to the back of the bus station, where she would be out of the wind for a smoke. While she stood there, he joined her. She wasn't even startled. He was another boring old man in bad clothes.

He calculated his business in his mind. The snow and cold. The pitched ravine that dropped off immediately in front of them. The blind woods on the other side. And he engaged her in conversation.

"Long ride," he said.

She looked at him at first as if she couldn't believe he was talking to her.

"Um hmmm," she said.

"Are you traveling alone?"

It was then that I noticed them, hanging above their heads in a long and plentiful row. Icicles.

The girl put out her cigarette on the heel of her shoe and turned to go.

"Creep," she said, and walked fast.

A moment later, the icicle fell. The heavy coldness of it threw him off balance just enough for him to stumble and pitch forward. It would be weeks before the snow in the ravine melted enough to uncover him.

But now let me tell you about someone special:

Out in her yard, Lindsey made a garden. I watched her weed the long thick flower bed. Her fingers twisted inside the gloves as she thought about the clients she saw in her practice each day—how to help them make sense of the cards life had dealt them, how to ease their pain. I remembered that the simplest things were the ones that often eluded what I thought of as her big brain. It took her forever to figure out that I always volunteered to clip the grass inside the fence so I could play with Holiday while we did yard work. She remembered Holiday then, and I followed her thoughts. How in a few years it would be time to get her child a dog, once the house was settled and fenced-in. Then she thought about how there were now machines with whipcords that could trim a fence post to post in minutes—what it had taken us hours of grumbling to achieve.

Samuel walked out to Lindsey then, and there she was in his arms, my sweet butterball babe, born ten years after my fourteen years on Earth: Abigail Suzanne. Little Susie to me. Samuel placed Susie on a blanket near the flowers. And my sister, my Lindsey, left me in her memories, where I was meant to be.

\* \* \*

And in a small house five miles away was a man who held my mud-encrusted charm bracelet out to his wife.

"Look what I found at the old industrial park," he said. "A construction guy said they were bulldozing the whole lot. They're afraid of more sinkholes like that one that swallowed the cars."

His wife poured him some water from the sink as he fingered the tiny bike and the ballet shoe, the flower basket and the thimble. He held out the muddy bracelet as she set down his glass.

"This little girl's grown up by now," she said.

Almost.

Not quite.

I wish you all a long and happy life.

## ACKNOWLEDGMENTS

I owe a debt to my passionate early readers: Judith Grossman, Wilton Barnhardt, Geoffrey Wolff, Margot Livesey, Phil Hay, and Michelle Latiolais. As well as the workshop at the University of California, Irvine.

To those who joined the party late but brought the most awesome refreshments: Teal Minton, Joy Johannessen, and Karen Joy Fowler.

To the pros: Henry Dunow, Jennifer Carlson, Bill Contardi, Ursula Doyle, Michael Pietsch, Asya Muchnick, Ryan Harbage, Laura Quinn, and Heather Fain.

Abiding thanks to: Sarah Burnes, Sarah Crichton, and the glorious MacDowell Colony.

A smarty-pants badge of honor to my informants: Dee Williams, Orren Perlman, Dr. Carl Brighton, and the essential facts-on-file team of Bud and Jane.

And to my continuing troika, whose sustaining friendship and rigorous reading and rereading are, next to tapioca and coffee, what keep me going on a day-to-day basis: Aimee Bender, Kathryn Chetkovich, Glen David Gold.

And a *woof!* to Lilly.

# THE
# LOVELY
# BONES

*a novel by*
*Alice Sebold*

## A READING GROUP GUIDE

# THE ODDITY OF SUBURBIA

## An essay by Alice Sebold

My family was watching television when a couple—the mother and father to a woman who lived one street over with her family—were hit by a car and landed on our front lawn. The man who hit them leapt out of his car and shouted to two boys playing basketball in the driveway of the house across from ours. He yelled: "These people need an ambulance." He then proceeded to jump back in his car and drive three houses down, where he calmly parked in his own driveway and went inside his house. The daughter of the couple who had been hit had been walking behind her parents and, having lapped them once, now came upon the scene. We heard the screaming and ran out. Both of her parents were killed. One died on our lawn, the other died later, in a hospital. And the man who struck them? He was both one of our neighbors and, by profession, a paramedic.

As I grew up and left home, living in Manhattan and just outside L.A., I began to realize more and more that within the suburban world of my upbringing there were as many strange stories as there were in the more romanticized parts of the world. Ultimately, the East Village had nothing on Nowhere U.S.A., and I returned, after several failed attempts at "the urban novel," to the material I knew best. Of course, I found the elements for *The Lovely Bones* in a combination of things, but a major element in its pages is the oddness of what we often condescendingly refer to as the suburbs.

In those places—like the place where I grew up—where all

the houses of a particular development share the same floor plan or, in upper-end versions of recent years, vary among three or four, live people with lives much more complex than the architecture containing them would suggest. But it took me years to go home again in my mind and imagination. To see the incidents that occurred all around me as a child and as a teenager as worthy of narrative. But growing up in one of many supposed Nowhere U.S.A.'s has created for me a bottomless well of narrative ideas.

Who would have thought that the place I most despised growing up — where I felt like the weirdest freak and the biggest loser — would turn out to be a gift to me? But what I have finally, to my joy, been made aware of is that while I grew up hearing that there were "a thousand stories in the naked city and none of them the same," this was as true of the look-alike houses all around me as it was of the places I lived as an adult. The difference perhaps is that you have to look harder in the suburbs, past the floor plans and into the human heart.

# WORDS TO LIVE BY

### The author of *The Lovely Bones* talks with
### David Mehegan of the *Boston Globe*

Nothing about Alice Sebold would suggest that she has been the most popular novelist in America for the last seven months — not her casual clothes nor the Spanish-style bungalow that she shares with her husband, the novelist Glen David Gold. Sebold, forty, is reflective, relaxed, often quite funny, and determined that her quiet writing life will go on, despite all that has happened since July 2002.

That's when her first novel, *The Lovely Bones,* was published. It's about Susie Salmon, a fourteen-year-old girl who has been raped and murdered. Susie narrates from heaven the murder and the later histories of her family, friends, and the killer. Sebold and her publisher, Little, Brown and Company, had hoped for a good first-novel sale for the unorthodox narrative — a few thousand copies would be considered a success. What they got was the biggest-selling novel of 2002. Nielsen BookScan, the book-tracking service, places *The Lovely Bones* at the top for last year, with 1.5 million copies sold, ahead of such power authors as J. K. Rowling, Tom Clancy, and John Grisham. After thirty-four weeks on the *New York Times* hardcover fiction bestseller list, *The Lovely Bones* is in its twentieth printing, with at least 2.37 million copies in print. In addition, *Lucky,* Sebold's 1999 memoir of her rape, has spent twenty-two weeks on the *Times* paperback list.

On the surface, the phenomenon is another example of the unpredictability of readers' tastes and needs, and of how word-of-mouth praise, smart marketing, and lucky breaks can come together to put a book into orbit. On a personal level, though, Sebold's own story illustrates how writing, and the writer's life, rescued her from a sinkhole of trauma, isolation, and despair.

One night during her freshman year at Syracuse University in 1981, Sebold was jumped from behind, punched, and dragged at knifepoint into a tunnel entrance to an amphitheater. The man forced her to strip in the cold darkness, then raped her. Police later told her she was lucky; a previous rape victim had been killed.

Seventeen years later, after wrestling with drugs and despair, she wrote about her experience in *Lucky:* the rape, the 1982 trial in which the rapist was convicted and sent to prison, and especially the lingering, bitter aftermath. The psychological trauma, Sebold wrote, isolated her from friends, lovers, other rape victims, and family. Even her father, shocked and confused, wanted to know: "How could he have raped you unless you let him?"

The damage, she says, can fester under layers of time and change, and an ignorant, thoughtless remark can easily reopen the wound. "There is no way you can tell someone in that moment what you are experiencing," she says, "that their behavior does nothing but alienate you, makes you experience your own alienation."

Sebold returned to college in the fall of 1981 and took a poetry workshop with poet Tess Gallagher, who urged her to write about her experience. Sebold did, beginning with the line "If they caught you . . ." Not long after, she spotted the rapist on the street and went to the police, who arrested him. Gallagher helped her a second time by going with her to the preliminary hearing, where she had to come face to face with the defendant.

Sebold graduated but still struggled to put the rape behind her. In *Lucky,* she wrote, "I had changed. . . . In my world, I saw violence everywhere." She entered a master's program in poetry at the University of Houston but soon washed out. She went to New York, rented a room on the Lower East Side, worked as a hostess in a midtown club, and began "dabbling" in heroin, snorting the drug with her boyfriend. (She says she never became addicted.) Sebold was writing, too; her first novel, *Tripping,* in 1986 was nominated in manuscript for a Pushcart Prize, but it was never published.

She could have been ruined by drugs but in 1989 was offered an interview for a job at New York's Hunter College. They were desperate for an adjunct instructor; she had teaching experience from graduate school and had studied with Gallagher and Tobias Wolff at Syracuse. It was a part-time job—teaching freshman composition—but Sebold discovered she liked teaching young writers and was good at it. And it helped stabilize her life. In *Lucky,* she writes, "My students became the people who kept me alive." Eventually she dumped the boyfriend, moved uptown, gave up heroin.

She wrote short stories and a second novel—none published—but mostly she worked with student writers, at Hunter, New York University, Bucknell University, and other colleges. She taught at Hunter for almost ten years until 1995, when she decided to try another master's program, in creative writing, at the University of California at Irvine. She met Glen David Gold on her first day of class. In time they became a couple, but he vowed he wouldn't propose to her until his own first novel was accepted. His *Carter Beats the Devil* was published in 2001, and they were married that year.

At Irvine, Susie Salmon, the main character of *The Lovely Bones,* was born.

Sebold says she had been working on another book, but "I was not compelled by it. I went and read some poems and came back to the desk and wrote that first chapter in one sitting. So Susie came upon me more than me deciding, 'I'm going to write about a teenager, she'll be dead and speaking from heaven.' That idea of a shadow that travels with you, that has another destiny than you might have imagined, has always fascinated me. For me, that shadow has always been a teenage girl who died."

In the book, Susie gazes down from "my heaven," which seems to be a combination of park and playground. She wants to help her loved ones, or lead them to the man who killed her. But like Sebold in the aftermath of her rape, Susie can't break through a frustrating, invisible barrier between herself and others.

Sebold worked on the book in her Irvine fiction workshop, which was led at one point by novelist Margot Livesey of Cambridge, Massachusetts. "She struck me as immensely determined as a writer," Livesey recalls. "She had a strong sense of the novel. Though she acknowledged that the premise was far-fetched, there was a real ambition, a desire to make the book as good as possible."

Still, it was hard going, and Sebold realized that before she could finish Susie's story, there was another book about a young rape victim that she had to write.

She went back to Syracuse and researched everything that had happened to her in 1981, scouring police, medical, and court records. She interviewed the investigator and prosecutor. The result was *Lucky,* an unflinching account that she says was cathartic and healing, for her parents as much as herself.

Back at work on Susie's story, she finally showed 150 pages to her agent, Henry Dunow of New York. "I thought it was brilliant," Dunow says, "as startling and moving a batch of pages as I had seen in years." He sent it to Scribner, the publisher of *Lucky,* which had an option to make a first offer on Sebold's second book.

"There was a polite but modest offer," Dunow says. "They were nervous about the subject in two dimensions: the violence toward a child and the heavenly narrator."

He declined the offer. Several other publishers turned the book down, but Little, Brown snapped it up with an offer Dunow describes as "a good level for a first novel but not a spectacular deal by any means." Sebold buckled down and finished the book.

From there, *The Lovely Bones* built momentum like a runaway train. An excerpt appeared in *Seventeen* magazine, and the reader response was electric. At Book Expo America, the big spring trade show, booksellers were so excited that Little, Brown had to print more advance reader copies, which is almost unheard of. It instantly became a Book-of-the-Month Club selection. Then, just weeks before the book hit the shelves, a huge break: The novelist Anna Quindlen told *Today* show viewers, "If you only have time to read one book this summer, it's *The Lovely Bones*."

The book exploded out of the gate, pushed in part by Michiko Kakutani's rave review in the *New York Times*. On July 14, *The Lovely Bones* hit the *Times* bestseller list and hasn't dropped off since.

Sebold says she doesn't know why *The Lovely Bones* resonates with so many people. "I don't feel particularly connected to what is going on in society. This book was not calculated in any way," she says. "If I were a savvy calculator, I would have published my first novel before I was thirty-nine."

Without intending to, Sebold touched a nerve in America, having to do with the horror of lost children and the healing from unimaginable loss. Some say the reader response had to do with still-raw emotions after September 11, others relate it to the several infamous child murders in the last year.

"When a book is both good and well published," Livesey says, "success may seem self-evident. But other books are good and well published and not on the bestseller list. I do think there is something radiant and heartfelt about the early chapters. It is haunting and persuasive and memorable."

"From a parent's point of view," says Dunow, "that first chapter is almost unbearable, but Alice pulls you through with a message of healing that speaks to people."

Some critics dismissed *The Lovely Bones* as a crude anodyne. In a scathing review in the *New York Review of Books,* Daniel Mendelsohn called its success "symptomatic of a larger cultural dysfunction" and sneered at the novel's "proleptic yearning for relief . . . its emphasis on the bathetic appeal of victimhood, its pseudo-therapeutic lingo of healing."

Sebold shrugs at that view. "I have my own beliefs, and that's certainly reflected in my characters," she says. "I have a tendency to feel that it's possible to keep hope alive and that sometimes in the darkest circumstances that's all you've got going for you. If that makes me disgusting, I embrace my disgust."

The least-expected difficulty of her fantastic success — her fans' desire for a more personal connection — occurs most often at book signings. "There are people who are hoping that you can give them something," she says. "They come up and tell me of a person they had lost, sometimes a child or a parent. I want to be able to acknowledge people, but if there are 200 in line, you have thirty seconds to do it."

Sebold seems well insulated from hype, criticism, celebrity, or the commercial publishing marketplace. She likes a quiet life, has few close friends, and makes new ones slowly.

Money and fame are OK, she makes clear, but the most important effect of her success is the unfettered freedom to do the thing she loves best: write.

"I want to work on my next book," she says, "and try to be here to garden a little in the fall, and read. I'm married to the man I want to be married to, live in a certain way that I like living. It's very weird to succeed at thirty-nine years old and realize that in the midst of your failure, you were slowly building the life that you wanted anyway."

*The complete text of David Mehegan's article on Alice Sebold and* The Lovely Bones *originally appeared in the* Boston Globe *on February 25, 2003. Reprinted with permission.*

# Reading Group Questions and Topics for Discussion

1. Although many readers remember the first lines of *The Lovely Bones* as "My name was Salmon, like the fish . . . ," the novel's opening is actually a brief passage about a snow globe that Susie observed as a child. What is the significance of this beginning? In a "perfect world," it would seem, one is both imprisoned and protected. Is Susie's heaven a blessing or a curse?

2. In Susie's heaven, the dead enjoy a number of comforts and simple pleasures. Yet it is far from a perfect place — not all wishes can be granted, and many of the inhabitants are victims of tragic crimes. Why do the heavens of different characters — e.g., Franny, Holly, Flora Hernandez — take such different forms? Is Sebold offering a rosy view of death and its aftermath? Or do you think she is saying something more profound about the individual experiences of loss and grief?

3. Rape is one of the most alienating experiences imaginable. Susie's rape ends in murder and changes her family and friends forever. Alienation is transferred, in a sense, to Susie's parents and siblings. How does each member of Susie's family experience loneliness and isolation after her death?

4. Ruth Connors inadvertently becomes Susie's main connection to Earth. How does this in turn change Ruth? Does it seem

strange that someone who wasn't close to Susie during her life is so deeply affected by her death? Is Ruth's obsession with murdered girls exploitive of Susie's fate, or is it healing in some way?

5. *The Lovely Bones* takes place in an American suburb in the 1970s. In what ways is this setting important to how the story unfolds? What is the significance of specific elements of Susie's landscape: the similar houses in her neighborhood, the remaining vestiges of old farmland, the sinkhole where Mr. Harvey hides her body? Why do you think the author chose this particular time period? How might the story be different if it were happening today?

6. Susie's closest sibling, Lindsey, carries a unique burden as a result of her sister's death. What was the sisters' relationship like before the tragedy? What are the particular expectations and pressures Lindsey must cope with? How does Susie's death change Lindsey?

7. How does Susie's view of sex change in the course of the novel? During her own life, she exchanges an almost chaste kiss with Ray. After her rape, she has the opportunity to observe her parents, Lindsey and Samuel, as well as her mother and Detective Fenerman. Is Susie's impression of sexuality altered by what she observes? How does her own experience with Ray and Ruth fit in?

8. How does Abigail cope with Susie's death? What does she seek in her interaction with Len Fenerman? What do you think of her decision to leave her family? Why does she return? Do you believe this is the right choice for her?

9. Why does the author include scenes from Mr. Harvey's perspective, including details about his childhood? Do these details

help to humanize him, or are they immaterial in view of the horrible nature of his crimes? What does Sebold's depiction of Mr. Harvey say about the nature of evil?

10. Buckley claims to see Susie, though she never mentions consciously revealing herself to him. Do you believe he really sees her, or does he make up these encounters in an attempt to cope with her death? How do you explain tragedy to a child? Do Jack and Abigail do a good job of helping Buckley understand the loss of his sister?

11. In *The Lovely Bones,* adult relationships (Abigail and Jack, Ray's parents, Len and Abigail) are dysfunctional and troubled, while the relationships of younger people (Lindsey and Samuel, Ray and Susie, Ray and Ruth) seem to have depth, maturity, and potential. Is this a naïve view of young love? Or do the younger characters in the book have an advantage over the adults?

12. Does Jack Salmon allow himself to be swallowed up by his grief? Is there a point where he should let go? Susie observes that "The living deserve attention, too." Does Jack's grief increase his family's suffering, or is there something admirable about his holding on so tightly to Susie's memory and not denying his profound sadness?

13. One of the most talked-about scenes in the book is Ray and Susie's lovemaking (via Ruth's body). What is the significance of this experience for Susie? For Ruth? For Ray? Is it difficult to make this leap of faith with Susie? What do you think the importance of this episode is in the book?

14. Mr. Harvey dies in a way that seems to indicate a larger justice at work. Certainly his victims rejoice from heaven at his demise.

But does his death really bring justice to those he has hurt? Can it compensate them for what they have lost? Why do you think the author chose not to have Mr. Harvey apprehended by the police? Why is Susie's body never found?

15. Even in heaven, Susie must move through different stages of dealing with her death and its aftermath. What forms does her progress take? Why is she not allowed to meet Mr. Harvey's other victims right away? How does Susie's journey mirror that of the people she has left behind on Earth?

16. What is the significance of the novel's title? What does Susie mean when she refers to the "lovely bones" (page 320)?

# LUCKY

## A memoir by Alice Sebold

"A rueful, razor-sharp memoir . . . funnier than you'd think was possible. . . . Sebold's commanding skill as a narrator (at her best, describing the awful crime itself, she brings to mind a fierce young Joan Didion) forces you to relive her terror. . . . She tells what it's like to go through a particular kind of nightmare in order to tell what it's like — slowly, bumpily, triumphantly — to heal."
— Sarah Kerr, *Vogue*

"A literary memoir that shines with personality. There is such openness in Sebold's brash, vibrant style that the book feels like the long version of a friend's breathless account of an ordeal."
— Carmen Scheidel, *Time Out New York*

"Gruesome and strangely enchanting. . . . The quiet achievement of Sebold's memoir is that she handles her subject with the integrity of a journalist and the care of a survivor."
— Casey Greenfield, *Newsday*

"*Lucky* is exhilarating to read . . . sharp-eyed and unsentimental. . . . The ironic, nervy Sebold refused to let the experience diminish her . . . or her sense of humor."    — Francine Prose, *Elle*

"*Lucky* — which reads like a John Grisham page-turner — can't help but haunt you. . . . Sebold's is a story about having the courage to speak about the unspeakable."
— Sheryl Altman, *Biography*

BACK BAY BOOKS
Available wherever books are sold